D0088104

FOURTH

Telling the Story

THE CONVERGENCE OF PRINT, BROADCAST AND ONLINE MEDIA

THE MISSOURI GROUP

BRIAN S. BROOKS

GEORGE KENNEDY

DARYL R. MOEN

DON RANLY

School of Journalism
University of Missouri–Columbia

Bedford/St. Martin's
Boston • New York

For Bedford/St. Martin's

Executive Editor for Communication: Erika Gutierrez
Editor: Stephanie Ricotta
Developmental Editor: Linda Stern
Senior Production Supervisor: Nancy J. Myers
Marketing Manager: Adrienne Petsick
Project Management: Books By Design, Inc.
Cover Design: Billy Boardman
Cover Photo: Journalists Judith Miller and Andrew Cooper Face Jail Time. Getty Images.
Composition: Books By Design, Inc.
Printing and Binding: RR Donnelley & Sons Company

President: Joan E. Feinberg
Editorial Director: Denise B. Wydra
Director of Development: Erica T. Appel
Director of Marketing: Karen R. Soeltz
Director of Editing, Design, and Production: Marcia Cohen
Assistant Director of Editing, Design, and Production: Elise S. Kaiser
Manager, Publishing Services: Emily Berleth

Library of Congress Control Number: 2009921706

Copyright © 2010 by Bedford/St. Martin's

All rights reserved. No part of this book may be reproduced, stored in a retrieval system, or transmitted in any form or by any means, electronic, mechanical, photocopying, recording, or otherwise, except as may be expressly permitted by the applicable copyright statutes or in writing by the Publisher.

Manufactured in the United States of America.

4 3 2 1 0 9
f e d c b a

For information, write: Bedford/St. Martin's, 75 Arlington Street, Boston, MA 02116 (617-399-4000)

ISBN-10: 0-312-55430-3
ISBN-13: 978-0-312-55430-9

Acknowledgments
Acknowledgments and copyrights appear at the back of the book on pages 383–84, which constitute an extension of the copyright page.

Preface

We wrote *Telling the Story* to provide students with a concise introduction to reporting and writing the news that slights neither the craft nor the theory of journalism. The text guides students with clear explanations of key principles as well as vivid real-world examples from the best work of journalists writing today. In addition, in keeping with the accelerating convergence of media that future journalists will encounter in the news room, *Telling the Story* continues to offer students more emphasis on technology and writing for multiple media than any other newswriting and reporting book.

Students graduating today can no longer expect to write only for print or television. Emerging technologies are changing the way the news is produced and consumed, and that means newswriters need to be prepared to write for a wide range of electronic media, as well as traditional print, television and radio outlets. *Telling the Story*, Fourth Edition, meets the challenge of preparing students with up-to-date information and important new guidelines on how to deal with the ongoing changes in journalism.

Despite this dramatic transformation in the media, though, the fundamentals of journalism have not changed. The Fourth Edition of *Telling the Story*, like the first three editions, continues to discuss the bedrocks of journalism, whether stressing the unchanging goals of fairness and accuracy, applying long-standing principles of ethics and law to the challenges of new media or recognizing the importance of strong writing. We illustrate key ideas with actual examples of newswriting—many now annotated in detail as visual models. Our emphasis on good writing, accompanied by thousands of online practice exercises (on bedfordstmartins.com/newscentral), means even more help for students desiring to improve their journalistic skills.

FEATURES OF THE TEXT

Telling the Story has been widely praised for its fresh, no-nonsense style and clear, concise writing. As in previous editions, *Telling the Story*, Fourth Edition, provides the following features:

- **Concise yet comprehensive instruction on all aspects of reporting and writing the news.** From the basics of interviewing and story writing to beat reporting and writing for different media, *Telling the Story* teaches students the essentials through a streamlined, practical approach.
- **A focus on storytelling.** From life stories to world-news reports, local meetings to national press conferences, good journalism means good writing. Using real-life examples, analyzing numerous news excerpts and providing a consistent focus on writing essentials, The Missouri Group demonstrates how to create rich and well-crafted stories.
- **The most and best coverage of media convergence and online journalism.** *Telling the Story* ensures that students learn how to prepare stories for multiple forms of media simultaneously and use new technologies effectively. Reflecting current trends, the book's coverage includes the rising role of technology and the emergence of integrated news rooms, the future of converging media and the growing influence of online journalism.
- **Coverage of legal and ethical issues.** Two chapters give in-depth analysis and advice on key issues dealing with conflicts of interest, invasion of privacy and avoiding deceit and plagiarism.
- **Chapter on math for journalists.** *Telling the Story* includes the unique chapter "Reporting with Numbers," which stresses the importance of using and understanding data—a vital skill as business news stories come to the forefront.
- **Coverage of proofreading symbols, AP style and common grammar issues.** Appendixes 1, 2 and 3 provide helpful information students need to turn in polished, professionally edited copy.
- **Crisis Coverage journalism simulation.** Appendix 4 serves as a handbook to the free, interactive CD-ROM available with this text.

NEW TO THIS EDITION

We've made substantial changes in the Fourth Edition to meet the needs of students facing rapid transformations in the field of journalism:

- *Expanded* coverage of technological reporting and delivery tools throughout the book, but especially in Chapters 1, 2 and 4. In this edition we have added new treatment of blogging, podcasting and syndicated news feeds to help students understand the key developments that are shaping the news today. We also provide concrete guidance in using these new tools in reporting the news, with advice geared toward gathering and verifying information for multiple delivery formats.
- *Updated* focus on storytelling across media platforms. While the essential principles of newswriting have not changed, *Telling the Story*'s Chapters 6, 7 and 13 have been reworked to show specific journalistic writing conventions in online and broadcast media as well as traditional print media—from structuring a lead to organizing a story.

- *New* annotated model stories. Five annotated news stories help students identify good writing skills and well-structured techniques—from the classic inverted-pyramid structure to the news narrative.
- *Ten new* "On the Job" boxes. Always a highly praised feature, new "On the Job" boxes present profiles of working journalists—from professionals who write and report locally, nationally and internationally across the media. These invaluable boxes provide students with a real-life picture of 21st-century journalism.
- *More* help online for issues in grammar and style. *Exercise Central for AP Style* (bedfordstmartins.com/newscentral) is the largest online resource for practice in journalistic writing, with thousands of exercises. With the new edition of *Telling the Story*, this powerful and free electronic tool is now better than ever; along with the traditional coverage of the Twenty Common Errors students make in journalistic writing, new coverage now extends to five key areas of journalistic style—from abbreviations and capitalization to numbers, attribution and copy editing symbols.
- *New* up-to-the-moment RSS feeds on the News Central Web site. RSS feeds from a variety of media outlets have been added to the book's newly designed Web site (bedfordstmartins.com/newscentral) in order to bring students breaking news all the time, making it easier than ever for them to stay on top of issues of the day across a number of beats.

RESOURCES FOR STUDENTS AND INSTRUCTORS

A number of ancillary materials enable students and instructors to get the most benefit from using *Telling the Story*, Fourth Edition:

- *Workbook for TELLING THE STORY*, Fourth Edition. Supplementing the activities at the end of each chapter in the text, the substantially revised workbook provides students with the extra practice they need to develop and master the principles of journalism, the skills of reporting and the craft of newswriting. More than 300 class-tested assignments reinforce the essential skills students need to learn, from basic interviewing and computer-assisted reporting to writing a lead and organizing a complex story. Special attention is paid to reporting with numbers and statistics and to accessing information from electronic sources. Challenge exercises in each chapter offer more complex assignments for students to tackle.
- *Instructor's Manual to Accompany TELLING THE STORY*, Fourth Edition. This electronic manual (available at bedfordstmartins.com/tellingthestory/catalog) includes sample syllabi and chapter overviews, as well as answers to the end-of-chapter questions from the main text and answers to all the questions in the workbook.
- *News Central Web site* (bedfordstmartins.com/newscentral). Here students can find links to research tools and online exercises, as well as

up-to-the-moment RSS feeds providing students with breaking news all the time.

- *Exercise Central for AP Style* (bedfordstmartins.com/newscentral). Revised for this new edition and available on News Central, this free database offers more than 2,500 questions targeting the 20 grammar and usage errors most commonly made by journalism students. In addition, it provides a new set of exercises that focus on mastering five key elements of the Associated Press style of writing.

- *Crisis Coverage CD-ROM.* Created by Bob Bergland, Jeanette Browning and students at Missouri Western State College, this interactive journalism simulation CD-ROM presents a crime scenario in real time, using text as well as audio and video clips. This CD-ROM is available free to users of *Telling the Story*, Fourth Edition.

ACKNOWLEDGMENTS

We would like to thank our colleagues and students at the University of Missouri–Columbia who have used and critiqued the material in this book. In addition, we are grateful to the instructors who thoughtfully reviewed the text and contributed ideas to the previous editions, and in particular we thank those who reviewed the Fourth Edition: Mary Carmen Cupito, Northern Kentucky University; Deneen Gilmour, North Dakota State University; Neil Goldstein, Montgomery County Community College; Terry Heifetz, Ball State University; Michelle Johnson, Emerson College; Roberta Kelly, Washington State University; Elliot King, Loyola College in Maryland; Richard L. Krupnow, University of Wisconsin Colleges, Fox Valley; Kevin M. Lerner, Seton Hall University; John S. Lusk, St. Clair County Community College; Marie Masters, Macomb Community College; James D. McJunkins Sr., Clark Atlanta University; Michael L. Mercer, University of the Incarnate Word; Michael A. Mullins, Glendale Community College; Ray Murray, Oklahoma State University; Carol Smith Passariello, Westchester Community College; Bob R. Qualls, Lyon College; Suzy Smith, Ball State University; and Barbara Feinman Todd, Georgetown University.

We would also like to thank our editors at Bedford/St. Martin's who have guided, and sometimes prodded, us along the way. In particular, thanks are due to executive editor Erika Gutierrez, editor Stephanie Ricotta and developmental editor Linda Stern, whose suggestions and enthusiasm helped shape the book. A thank-you to Mae Klinger, editorial assistant, for her help with all of the many details. In addition, we wish to thank project manager Emily Berleth and production supervisor Nancy Myers. We would also like to acknowledge and thank marketing manager Adrienne Petsick for her creative efforts in launching this edition. And as always, we thank our wives, Anne, Robin and Eva Joan, who have been helping us with this publishing project now for nearly 25 years.

We value your comments. You can reach any of us by e-mail at:

Brian S. Brooks: brooksbs@missouri.edu
George Kennedy: kennedyg@missouri.edu
Daryl R. Moen: moend@missouri.edu
Don Ranly: ranlyd@missouri.edu

Contents in Brief

Contents

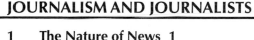

PART IV   **COVERING AND WRITING NEWS**

PART V   **MEDIA WRITING**

1 The Nature of News

Journalism, like the world it seeks to describe, is in turmoil. New technology is expanding both the tools journalists have for reporting the news and the options consumers have for receiving it. At the same time, however, audiences for traditional media are shrinking, and the business model that has supported journalism for a century is broken—or at least badly bent.

The annual *State of the News Media* report by the Project for Excellence in Journalism sums up the situation this way: "The journalism of the future increasingly appears to be a hybrid that takes advantage of the technology rather than fights it. But the questions of who will pay and how they will do it seem more pressing than ever."

While economic pressures force cutbacks and layoffs in television and newspaper news rooms, young—and not so young—entrepreneurs are coming up with new models for doing and delivering journalism. Take a look, for example, at MediaStorm.com, where you'll find fascinating pieces of in-depth reporting using print, still photography and video. (Brian Storm, its creator, even includes a section offering advice for others who want to follow the path he is discovering.) Or visit Newsy.com, where another journalism school graduate collects video reports from news sources around the world and packages them to provide a variety of perspectives on important issues.

MinnPost.com and stlbeacon.com are two of the many local news sites that are trying to adapt to the Internet the nonprofit model that National Public Radio and its local affiliates use with success. Most of these new sources are staffed by journalists with experience in the traditional media.

It's turmoil—but exciting and promising turmoil.

Still, journalists in the 21st century are doing what journalists have always done. They are telling the world its stories. The difference is that today they're telling those stories on Web sites and cell phones as well as in newspapers, magazines and broadcast programs.

Of course, how they tell those stories has changed dramatically. Communication from the most remote locations is instant. The Internet gives news consumers the ability to read, watch or listen whenever they wish—and to respond. Traditional print and broadcast media are joining forces and sharing resources in the latest trend, something called *convergence*.

CONVERGENCE IN JOURNALISM

Convergence is the term that describes efforts to use the different strengths of different media to reach broader audiences and tell the world's stories in new ways. Convergence demands of journalists new skills and new flexibility. Print reporters find themselves summarizing their stories into a television camera. Videographers find themselves selecting images to be published in the partner newspaper. Both print and broadcast journalists look for Web links to connect their stories to the worldwide audience and nearly infinite capacity of the Internet. Cell phones and MP3 players provide new outlets and require new storytelling techniques.

The technological revolution also has exploded traditional definitions of just who is a journalist. Millions of people across the world have launched **blogs**—online journals. Although one estimate is that only 5 percent of those sites include original reporting, and although most have tiny audiences, many have become influential voices in the public conversation. In an effort to add personality and encourage interactivity with audience members, traditional news organizations are encouraging and sometimes requiring staff members to write blogs.

Increasingly, members of the public are being invited to respond to stories that are published or broadcast. Citizens are even enlisted as amateur reporters. To take one example, *The News-Press* in Fort Myers, Fla., asked its readers for help in an investigation of whether a local sewer district was overcharging customers. Not only did readers provide their own examples, but some who were professional engineers volunteered to study documents and share their expertise with the newspaper and the entire community. The result: a communitywide conversation that led to reductions in sewer rates. The Gannett Co., owner of *The News-Press*, calls this "crowdsourcing." A better label might be "citizen sourcing."

Despite the changes brought by technology and convergence, the fundamentals of journalism haven't changed—the definition of news, the vital role of journalism in a democratic society, and the importance of accuracy and fairness. Moreover, the basic skills required of every journalist haven't changed, either. Whatever the medium, news-gathering and storytelling skills are essential to good journalism.

WHAT NEWS IS

The criteria that professional reporters and editors use to decide what news is can be summarized in three words:

- Relevance.
- Usefulness.
- Interest.

Relevance, usefulness and *interest* are the broad guidelines for judging the news value of any event, issue or personality. Those criteria apply generally, but each journalist and each news organization uses them in a specific context that gives them particular meaning. That context is supplied by the *audience*—the people that the organization is trying to reach.

Within those broad standards, journalists look for more specific elements in each potential story. The most important are these:

- *Impact.* The potential impact of a story is another way of measuring its relevance and usefulness. How many people are affected by an event or idea? How seriously does it affect them? The greater the impact, the better the story. Sometimes, of course, impact isn't immediately obvious. Sometimes it isn't very exciting. The challenge for good journalism is making such dull but important stories lively and interesting. That may require relying on the next three elements.
- *Conflict.* Conflict is a recurring theme in all storytelling, whether the stories told are journalism, literature or drama. Struggles between people, among nations or with natural forces make fascinating reading. Conflict is such a basic element of life that journalists must resist the temptation to overdramatize or oversimplify it.
- *Novelty.* Novelty is another element common to journalism and other kinds of stories. People or events may be interesting and therefore newsworthy just because they are unusual or bizarre.
- *Prominence.* Names make news. The bigger the name, the bigger the news. Ordinary people have always been intrigued by the doings of the rich and famous. Both prominence and novelty also can be, and often are, exaggerated to produce "news" that lacks real relevance and usefulness.
- *Proximity.* Generally, people are more interested in and concerned about what happens close to home. When they read or listen to national or international news, they often want to know how it relates to their own community. Many newspapers are experimenting with **hyperlocal** coverage—reporting that's intensely local in emphasis—as they seek to reconnect with readers by reporting at the neighborhood level, sometimes by soliciting contributions from residents, or citizen journalists. Independent Web sites devoted to this kind of extremely local coverage are springing up across the country. Increasingly, however, journalists and scholars are recognizing that communities of interest—in a sport, a hobby or an issue—are at least as important as geographical communities.
- *Timeliness.* News is supposed to be new. With the Internet and cable and satellite television, "new" means instantaneous. Events are reported as they happen. The challenge for journalists is clear. Speed conflicts with thoughtfulness and thoroughness. Opportunities for error multiply. Perspective and context are needed more than ever but are more difficult to supply with little time for thinking. Despite the drawbacks of 24/7 coverage, it's clear that for news to be relevant and useful, it must be timely. For example, it is more useful to write about an issue facing the city council before it is decided than afterward. Timely reporting gives people a chance to be participants in public affairs rather than mere spectators.

The online age, with its often-confusing multitude of sources, splintering of audiences and growing complaints about negative news, has inspired most journalists to add some new criteria for assessing the value of stories:

- *Engagement.* When news was only broadcast or printed on paper, the flow of information was one-way—from journalists to audiences. No more. Today, a news report is often just the beginning of the conversation. Audience members online respond, correct and criticize the journalism. Many reporters and commentators maintain blogs to encourage such involvement. Some news organizations create extensive electronic Listserv mailing lists to involve audience members as active participants in news gathering itself. Increasingly, a goal of both individual journalists and news organizations is this engagement of the public with the news and with the news provider.
- *Solutions.* Scholars and audiences alike complain that journalists too often report problems and controversies without offering solutions to the problems or ways of resolving the controversies. The author Richard Saul Wurman and the journalist Al Neuharth have both advocated a "journalism of hope." More and more journalists are seeking out expert sources not only to explain complex problems but to suggest solutions.

Notice that this list suggests two important things about news. First, not all news is serious, life-and-death stuff. Journalism has been described as "a culture's conversation with itself." The conversation that holds a culture together includes talk of crime, politics and world affairs, of course, but it also includes talk of everyday life. It includes humor and gossip. All of that can be news. Second, news is more than collections of facts. Telling the news usually means telling stories. The narrative, the humanity, the drama of storytelling—these are the art of journalism. To gather the facts for their stories, journalists use many of the same techniques used by sociologists, political scientists and historians. But to tell their stories so that those facts can be understood, journalists often use the techniques of other storytellers, such as novelists and screenwriters.

News Emphasis in Different Media

Differences among the news media give different weights to those criteria and require different approaches to telling stories. For example, newspapers and magazines are better than television or radio for explaining the impact of an issue or the causes of a conflict. Scholars have learned that, although most people say they get most of their news from television, few can remember very much of what they've seen or heard on a newscast. But print can't compete with television in terms of speed or emotional power. The differing strengths and limitations of each medium make it more likely that you'll find a lengthy explanatory story in a newspaper or magazine, while you're more likely to learn of an event from television, radio or the Internet. The newspaper lets you read the details of a budget or a box score, and television shows you the worker whose job was cut or the player scoring the winning basket. The unique power of online journalism is that it brings together the immediacy of television and the comprehensive authority of print, with endless opportunities to pursue your interests through the Web. And you can join the public conversation by posting comments to an existing blog or launching your own.

Citizen Journalism

The most exciting—and, to some traditional journalists, most worrying—development is **citizen journalism**: news coverage, usually online, by people who don't work for commercial companies. Some citizen journalists are producing regular reporting for growing audiences. Their focus may be on local communities, as is the case with Backfence.com and YourHub.com. Or it may be broader, as with the activist indymedia.org, an international collective that publishes online editions in a number of major cities, with a strongly anti-establishment slant.

The Project for Excellence in Journalism has identified at least 1,500 Web sites operated by citizen journalists. Most of them offer written stories, blogs and video. Few of these citizen journalism outlets are profitable, and many are deliberately nonprofit. Their goal, whether local or international, is to cover communities and issues that even local newspapers and broadcast stations don't reach. Their audiences are people who don't feel adequately served by the traditional media. Some observers have likened citizen journalists to the pamphleteers who were the pioneers of American journalism two centuries ago.

THE ROLE OF JOURNALISM AND THE CHALLENGES IT FACES

The First Amendment to the U.S. Constitution protects the five freedoms that the nation's founders considered essential to a democracy — the freedom of speech, religion, press, petition and assembly. In the 1830s, the French aristocrat Alexis de Tocqueville came to study the U.S. and wrote his classic *Democracy in America*. He was struck by the central role played by the only journalism available then: the newspapers. "We should underrate their importance if we thought they just guaranteed liberty; they maintain civilization," he wrote.

More than 200 years after they were guaranteed, the First Amendment freedoms are still essential and still under threat. After the terrorist attacks of Sept. 11, 2001, a new emphasis on national and personal security tempted government officials and citizens alike to question just how much freedom is compatible with safety. The role of journalism in guaranteeing liberty and maintaining civilization is challenged by those who make news and those who need it.

The Public's View of the News Media

American journalism is also under threat from growing public skepticism about how well today's journalists are fulfilling their historic roles.

In a national survey conducted by researchers at the Missouri School of Journalism, 85 percent of respondents said they see bias in news coverage. Half said journalism is too sensational. Seventy percent said the news media are often influenced by powerful people and organizations. Nearly two-thirds said journalists often invade people's privacy. (Still, 56 percent said they trust the information provided by their local newspaper, and 58 percent said the same for local television and radio.)

In that same survey, 93 percent said freedom of the press is important to our system of government, 75 percent said journalism helps them understand what is going on in America, and 75 percent said journalism helps them be more thoughtful about public issues. More than 80 percent said investigative reporting is important, and two-thirds said journalists are good watchdogs over public officials. Even though both daily newspaper circulation and television news viewing have declined in recent years, 76 percent in the survey said they watch local TV news at least three days a week, and 66 percent said they read a local newspaper at least three days a week. (For regular samplings of public opinion about journalism, visit **http://people-press.org**, the Web site of the Pew Research Center for the People and the Press.)

Principles of Journalism Today

What these citizens seem to be saying is that the work journalists do is important, but journalists aren't doing it well enough. The past decade has seen the emergence of several major efforts to improve the performance of American journalism.

One of those efforts has been driven by an informal association called the Committee of Concerned Journalists and the related Project for Excellence in Journalism. The project conducts regular research on journalism and issues reports, which can be accessed on its Web site, **www.journalism.org**. Among the project's reports are the annual *State of the News Media* assessments. Another product of these reformers is a book every student and practitioner of journalism should read. *The Elements of Journalism* was written by two leaders of the committee, Bill Kovach and Tom Rosenstiel.

The book argues that "the purpose of journalism is to provide people with the information they need to be free and self-governing." It proposes 10 principles to achieve this purpose:

1. Journalism's first obligation is to the truth.
2. Its first loyalty is to citizens.
3. Its essence is a discipline of verification.

Audiences of the 21st century

- By 2010, married couples will no longer make up a majority of households.
- By 2025, Americans over 64 will outnumber teenagers 2–1.
- By 2050, one-fifth of the U.S. population will be Hispanic.

—Undercovered: The New USA *(New Directions for News)*

4. Its practitioners must maintain an independence from those they cover.
5. It must serve as an independent monitor of power.
6. It must provide a forum for public criticism and compromise.
7. It must strive to make the significant interesting and relevant.
8. It must keep the news comprehensive and proportional.
9. Its practitioners must be allowed to exercise their personal conscience.
10. Citizens, too, have rights and responsibilities when it comes to the news.

"The computer is an icon for our age, but reason and imagination, which yield understanding, are yet to be programmable."
— *Richard Saul Wurman*

In these principles, you can hear echoes of the Journalist's Creed, written nearly a century before by Walter Williams, founding dean of the world's first journalism school, at the University of Missouri. Williams wrote that "the public journal is a public trust . . . (and) that acceptance of a lesser interest than the public interest is a violation of that trust."

These efforts to reform, or restore, journalism recognize the vital functions of journalists in a free society:

- *Journalists report the news.* This first and most obvious function is the foundation of the rest. Reporters cover Congress and council meetings, describe accidents and disasters, show the horrors of war and the highlights of football games. This reporting takes many forms—live television, online bulletins, next-day newspaper analyses, long-form magazine narratives and, increasingly, blogs and video posts from nonjournalists who happen to witness subway crashes or tsunamis. No wonder journalism has been called the first rough draft of history.
- *Journalists monitor power.* Americans are usually concerned about the power of government. Lately, private power has become more of a worry and more a source of news. Monitoring is required even if power is used legitimately—when governments raise taxes or take us to war, for example, or businesses close plants or cut health-care benefits for employees. When the power is used illegally or immorally, another important function of journalism comes into play.
- *Journalists uncover injustice.* Reporters reveal that wounded war veterans are being mistreated at the nation's leading military hospital, Walter Reed. Others uncover the corrupt relationship between a local police department and a towing service that improperly keeps cars it seizes and sells some to the police chief's family. In those cases and thousands more, journalists bring to light dangerous or illegal abuses that might otherwise go unchecked.
- *Journalists tell compelling stories, some that delight us and some that dismay us.* The *(New Orleans) Times-Picayune*'s coverage of Hurricane Katrina and its aftermath, in print and online, did both. Barton Gellman examined the unique role of Vice President Dick Cheney in a *Washington Post* series and then in a book, *Angler*. Television's *60 Minutes* and *Frontline* present true-life dramas. Bloggers bring firsthand experiences and, often, great passion to their posts.
- *Journalists sustain communities.* These may be small towns, cities or even virtual communities of people connected only by the Internet and shared interests. By their reporting, monitoring, revealing and storytelling, jour-

nalists serve as the nervous system of the community. They convey information and argument. Their work is, in the words of the late journalism scholar James Carey, the community's "conversation with itself."

Other scholars use other terms for this combination of functions. One is "agenda setting," the placing of issues on the public agenda for discussion and decision. Another is "gate keeping," the process by which some events and ideas become news and others do not. Now that the Internet has flooded the world with information, another role is emerging—that of navigation, guiding readers and viewers through oceans of fact, rumor and fantasy in search of solid meaning. Bloggers such as Matt Drudge sometimes serve as agenda setters for mainstream journalists. Entertainers such as Jon Stewart serve as sources not only of laughs but of information. Even in the Internet age, however, the news you read on Google or some other Web site probably was first reported in one of the traditional news rooms.

ACCURACY, FAIRNESS AND THE PROBLEM OF OBJECTIVITY

The goal toward which most journalists strive has seldom been expressed any better than in a phrase used by Bob Woodward, a reporter, author and editor at *The Washington Post*. Woodward was defending in court an investigative story published by the *Post*. The story, he said, was "the best obtainable version of the truth."

A grander-sounding goal would be "the truth," unmodified. But Woodward's phrase, while paying homage to the ideal, recognizes the realities of life and the limitations of journalism. Despite centuries of argument, philosophers and theologians are still unable to agree on what truth is. Even if there were agreement on that basic question, how likely is it that the Roman Catholic Church and the Planned Parenthood organization would agree on the "truth" about abortion, for example, or that candidates for president would agree on the "truth" about their opponent's record?

"Just the Facts"

In American daily journalism, that kind of dispute is left to be argued among the partisans on all sides, on the editorial pages and in commentaries. The reporter's usual role is simply to find and write the facts. The trouble is, this task often turns out to be not so simple.

Sometimes it's hard to get the facts. The committee searching for a new university president announces that the field of candidates has been narrowed to five, but the names of the five are not released, and committee members are sworn to secrecy. What can you do to get the names? Should you try?

Sometimes it's hard to tell what the facts mean. The state supreme court refuses to hear a case in which legislators are questioning the constitutionality of a state spending limit. The court says only that there is no "justiciable controversy." What does that mean? Who won? Is the ruling good news or bad news, and for whom?

Sometimes it's even hard to tell what *is* fact. A presidential commission, after a yearlong study, says there is no widespread hunger in America. Is that conclusion a fact? Or is it simply the commission's statement that is the fact? And how can you determine whether the commission is correct?

Daily journalism presents still more complications. As a reporter, you usually have only a few hours—at most a few days—to try to learn as many facts as possible. Then, even in such a limited time, you may accumulate information enough for a story of 2,000 words, only to be told that there is space or time enough for 1,000 or fewer. The new media offer more space but often even less time for reporting. When you take into account all these realities and limitations, you can see that reaching the best obtainable version of the truth is challenge enough for any journalist.

On the Job

A Career Crosses Media Lines

Scott Norvell's career has covered the full spectrum of journalism. He graduated from journalism school as a news editorial major and began work on a daily paper in Texas. Before long, though, he switched to an alternative weekly. Then came a three-year stint freelancing in Central America. A newspaper job for his wife, Shelley, brought the couple back to the States, where Scott was hired to help launch the Web site for CNN. Shelley was transferred to Miami, and Scott—despite a total lack of television experience—was hired as bureau chief by the new Fox News network.

Networking of a different sort helped him land this job, he recalls; he had met his new boss years earlier in Guatemala. What also helped was Scott's command of Spanish and his experience in the Caribbean.

After three years in Miami, the couple moved to London, where Scott became Fox bureau chief and Shelley continued to work for Cox newspapers. A year later they moved again, this time to New York, where Scott took over the Fox Web site and later became New York bureau chief. In 2003, they returned to London, where he now supervises Fox's coverage of Europe as bureau chief and vice president.

Along the way, Scott has learned the importance of knowing at least one additional language, the desirability of technical skills with computers and video, and—above all—the continued centrality of writing. "Arguably, mastery of the written word is even more critical as the amount of information proliferates and competition increases," he says.

Like the economy, news has become globalized. Finding stories that are compelling and original is the key to a correspondent's success today.

How can you tell when the goal has been reached? Seldom, if ever, is there a definitive answer. But there are two questions every responsible journalist should ask about every story before being satisfied: Is it accurate? Is it fair?

Accuracy

Accuracy is the most important characteristic of any story, great or small, long or short. Accuracy is essential in every detail. Every name must be spelled or pronounced correctly; every quote must be just what was said; every set of numbers must add up. And that still isn't good enough. You can get the details right and still mislead unless you are accurate with context, too. The same statement may have widely different meanings depending on the circumstances in which it was uttered and the tone in which it was spoken. Circumstances and intent affect the meaning of actions as well. You will never have the best obtainable version of the truth unless your version is built on accurate reporting of detail and context.

Fairness

Nor can you approach the truth without being fair. Accuracy and fairness are related, but they are not the same. The relationship and the difference show clearly in this analogy from the world of sports:

The referee in a basketball game is similar, in some ways, to a reporter. Each is supposed to be an impartial observer, calling developments as he or she sees them. (Of course, the referee's job is to make judgments on those developments, while the reporter's job is just to describe them. Rendering judgment is the role of columnists, bloggers and other opinion writers.) Television has brought to sports the instant replay, in which a key play—for example, whether a player was fouled while taking a shot—can be examined again and again, often from an angle different from the referee's view. Sometimes the replay shows an apparent outcome different from the one the official called. The difference may be due to human error on the official's part, or it may be due to the differences in angle and in viewpoint. Referees recognize this problem. Still, every official knows that an occasional mistake will be made. That is unavoidable. What can, and must, be avoided is unfairness. Referees must be fair, and both players and fans must believe they are fair. Otherwise, their judgments will not be accepted; they will not be trusted.

With news, too, there are different viewpoints from which every event or issue can be observed. Each viewpoint may yield a different interpretation of what is occurring and of what it means. There is also, in journalism as in sports, the possibility of human error, even by the most careful reporters.

Fairness requires that you as a reporter try to find every viewpoint on a story. Hardly ever will there be only one; often there are more than two. Fairness requires that you allow ample opportunity for response to anyone who is being attacked or whose integrity is being questioned in a story. Fairness requires, above all, that you make every effort to avoid following your own biases in your reporting and your writing.

Bias

National surveys show that citizens don't think journalists do enough to keep bias out of the news. More than eight out of 10 in the University of Missouri study summarized earlier said they see bias at least sometimes. Of those, about twice as many said the bias seemed to be liberal as thought it conservative. A chorus of critics claims that journalists lean to the left. A smaller chorus complains of a rightward tilt. Books and cable television talk shows add heat, if not light, to the criticism. How valid is it?

One answer is that American journalism has many biases built into it. For example, journalists are biased toward conflict. War is a better story than peace. Journalists are biased toward novelty. Airplanes that don't crash are seldom reported. Journalists are biased toward celebrity. Millions of babies are adopted every year, but Angelina Jolie and Brad Pitt's adoption of a baby makes news.

There's a less obvious but even more important bias, too. This one probably accounts for much of the criticism. It is hidden in the job description of journalism. What do journalists say they do? What are they proudest of? What do they honor?

Journalists describe themselves as the outside agitators, the afflicters of the comfortable and the comforters of the afflicted. Journalists see their job as being the watchdog of the powerful, the voice of the voiceless, the surrogate for the ordinary citizen, the protector of the abused and downtrodden. Journalists expect themselves to be forever skeptical, consistently open-minded, respectful of differences and sensitive to what sociologists call "the other." Neither patriotism nor religion is exempt from their critical examination.

Does that job description seem more "liberal" or more "conservative"?

Consider that conservatives generally are respectful of authority and supportive of the status quo. Is it any surprise, then, that the overwhelming majority of conservatives and many liberals see a liberal bias in journalism? Notice that this bias has little or nothing to do with partisan politics.

Now suppose we had a journalism that wasn't questioning, disrespectful of authority, open to new ideas, dogging the powerful or speaking for the weak. Who would benefit, and who would suffer? Would society and democracy be better or worse off?

While it may seem superficially to be liberal, though, at a deeper level American journalism is profoundly conservative. Think of the foundation stones on which the American way of life is based. Among them are capitalism, the two-party system, the myths of the ethnic melting pot and of social mobility. When was the last time you saw any of those questioned seriously in the mainstream press? And do you remember Hurricane Katrina and its aftermath, when issues of race and class were thrust into the news? Journalists don't often talk about those, either.

One conclusion suggested by this analysis is that, in societies that aren't free—such as 18th-century America—a free press is a revolutionary instrument. In a society like 21st-century America that considers itself free and is, overall, self-satisfied, the free press becomes, at a fundamental level, conservative.

Objectivity

The rules that mainstream journalists follow in attempting to screen out personal bias and arrive at the best obtainable version of the truth are commonly summarized as *objectivity*. Objectivity has been and still is accepted as a working credo by most American journalists, students and teachers of journalism. It has been exalted by leaders of the profession as an essential, if unattainable, ideal. Its critics, by contrast, have attacked objectivity as, in the phrase of sociologist Gaye Tuchman, a "strategic ritual" that conceals a multitude of professional sins while producing superficial and often misleading coverage.

In his classic *Discovering the News*, Michael Schudson traces the rise of objectivity to the post–World War I period, when scholars and journalists alike turned to the methods and the language of science in an attempt to make sense of a world that was being turned upside down by the influence of Sigmund Freud and Karl Marx, the emergence of new economic forces and the erosion of traditional values. Objectivity was a reliance on observable facts, but it was also a methodology for freeing factual reporting from the biases and values of source, writer or reader. It was itself a value, an ideal.

Schudson wrote, "Journalists came to believe in objectivity, to the extent that they did, because they wanted to, needed to, were forced by ordinary human aspiration to seek escape from their own deep convictions of doubt and drift."

Objectivity, then, was a way of applying to the art of journalism the methods of science. Those methods emphasized reliance on observable fact. They also included the use of a variety of transparent techniques for pursuing truth and verifying facts. In science, transparency means that researchers explain their objectives, their methods, their findings and their limitations. In journalism, only part of that methodology is usually followed.

In *The Elements of Journalism*, Bill Kovach and Tom Rosenstiel worry that a kind of phony objectivity has replaced the original concept. The objectivity of science does not require neutrality or an artificial balance of two sides in a dispute. Scientists are free to, and expected to, state their conclusions, as long as they report how they reached those conclusions. However, as usually practiced today, objectivity in journalism employs both neutrality and balance, sometimes instead of the kind of openness that is essential in science. This misunderstanding, or misapplication, of the real principles of objectivity has opened the way for critics to call for its abandonment. Journalists would be more honest, these critics argue, if they were open about their biases. In much of Europe, for example, journalists practice and audiences expect openly biased reporting.

The problem with that approach is easy to see in European journalism or, closer to home, in the opinionated journalism of partisan publications, cable television or many blogs. One-sided reports appeal to audiences that share the reporter's bias, but they repel those who don't. Fairness and accuracy too often are casualties in this journalism of assertion rather than of verification.

Properly understood, objectivity provides the journalistic method most likely to yield the best obtainable version of the truth. True objectivity adds scientific rigor to journalistic art. Without that combination, journalists and audiences alike can be misled.

In 1947 the Hutchins Commission on freedom of the press concluded that what a free society needs from journalists is "a truthful, comprehensive and intelligent account of the day's events in a context which gives them meaning." The goal of this chapter is to show you how the journalists of today and tomorrow understand that need, how they are trying to meet it, and the complexity of the task. The rest of the book will help you develop the skills you'll need to take up the challenge. There are few challenges as important or as rewarding.

Suggested Readings

Journalism reviews: Any issue of *Columbia Journalism Review*, *American Journalism Review*, *Quill* or *The American Editor*, bulletin of the American Society of Newspaper Editors, offers reports and analyses of the most important issues in contemporary journalism.

Kovach, Bill, and Tom Rosenstiel. *The Elements of Journalism: What Newspeople Should Know and the Public Should Expect.* Rev. ed. New York: Three Rivers Press, 2007. This little book is packed with practical advice and inspiration, a kind of applied ethics for journalists in any medium.

Schudson, Michael. *Discovering the News: A Social History of American Newspapers.* New York: Basic Books, 1978. This well-written study traces the development of objectivity in American journalism.

Wurman, Richard Saul. *Information Anxiety.* New York: Doubleday, 1990. This guide for consumers of information can also serve as a guide for journalists as they seek to provide understanding.

Suggested Web Sites

www.cjr.org   *Columbia Journalism Review* is the oldest of the magazines devoted to the critical analysis of journalists' performance. You'll find critiques of major stories and essays on ethics, along with book reviews and trade news. *American Journalism Review* (**www.ajr.org**) offers similar content.

www.journalism.org   This site, for the Project for Excellence in Journalism, contains relevant research and articles on the current state of journalism. See especially the *State of the News Media* reports for the most comprehensive look at the current performance of all the major news media.

www.people-press.org   The Web site of the Pew Research Center for the People and the Press offers frequent reports of relevant studies and a useful online archive.

www.poynter.org   This site is an excellent starting point. The Poynter Institute is the leading center of continuing professional education for journalists. On this site you'll find not only a guide to the services and resources of the institute itself, but also links to the sites of every major professional organization and a variety of other useful resources.

Exercises

1. The Project for Excellence in Journalism monitors the news flow through dozens of different channels. Visit **www.journalism.org** and examine that flow. What do you find? Which reports seem most thorough? Which reveal the writer's biases? Which are you most inclined to believe?

2. Spend some time with the citizen journalists at **www.backfence.com** and **www.Indymedia.org**. Compare their reports with the stories in the mainstream media from the same geographic areas. Where does the coverage overlap, and what stories are different in each medium? Which sources seem to serve the citizens best?

3. Most Americans say they get most of their news from television. Watch an evening newscast on one of the major networks. Then read *The New York Times* or *USA Today* for the same day. Compare the number of stories, the topics and the depth of coverage. How well informed are those television-dependent Americans?

4. Get copies or visit the Web sites of today's issue of your local newspaper, a paper from a city at least 50 miles away and a paper of national circulation, such as *USA Today* or *The Wall Street Journal*. Analyze the front or home page of each according to the criteria discussed in this chapter.

What can you tell about the editors' understanding of each paper's audience by looking at the selection of stories?

If you find stories on the same topic on two or more front pages, determine if they are written differently for different audiences. Are there any attempts to localize national stories? Suggest any possibilities for local angles you can think of.

On the basis of what you've learned in this chapter, do you agree or disagree with the editors' news judgments? Why?

5. As a class project, visit or invite to your class the editor of your local paper and the news director of a local television or radio station. Study their products before the visit. Then interview them about how they decide the value of news stories, how they assess the reliability of sources and how they try to ensure accuracy.

6. Take a cruise on the information superhighway. Sample some of the sources you find. Describe briefly at least five sources of information you can use as a journalist and at least five sources of news you can use as a consumer.

2 Redefining News: Citizen Journalism and Convergence

Whe terrorists planted bombs on a London subway, the first images of the disaster came from survivors who used their mobile phones to take photos and transmit them to the outside world from below ground. When a tsunami hammered Indonesia and when Hurricane Katrina ravaged the U.S. Gulf Coast, some of the first photos came from citizens. Even video footage shot with cell phones has become part of the news report. A Japanese truck driver shot footage of a 12-car pileup on an expressway, and the video quickly made its way onto television at NHK, the nation's public broadcast network.

Citizen journalism—nonjournalists' gathering and writing the news—is cropping up on Web sites around the world, much of it on established sites of the mainstream media. The British Broadcasting Corporation asked users around the world to snap photos of scheduled anti-war protests and send them in. Hundreds of photos were submitted from around the world. A citizen in Virginia shot photos of an F-15 military aircraft crash that she sent to a local television station. The photo taken immediately following the impact was used in the newscast along with video footage taken later.

In this chapter you will learn:
1. How citizen journalism is changing the news industry.
2. Why many media companies are embracing citizen journalism.
3. Why convergence is the latest craze in news rooms.
4. Why preparing for a multimedia future is important.

THE CHANGING FACE OF JOURNALISM

Much of the video and still footage taken by people who happen to be on the scene of a news event finds its way to **moblogs**, a form of Internet blogging in which the user publishes blog entries directly to the Web from a mobile phone or other mobile device. But when footage finds its way onto the sites of mainstream media, as the examples above show, citizen journalists effectively serve as an extension of the media outlet's traditional reporting staff.

Sometimes citizen journalism works; sometimes it goes awry. A citizen journalist on iReport.com posted a false story that Apple's Steve Jobs had suffered a heart attack. The erroneous story, which rattled Wall Street, could have had a major impact on Apple's stock had it not been quickly corrected. CNN's iReport is almost completely open and permits users to post "news"—unedited and unvetted—after a minimal registration process. Observed Scott Karp of Publishing 2.0, a Web site that reports on the evolution of media, "The problem is—and this is something that advocates of citizen journalism typically overlook—that if a platform is open, and anyone can participate, that means not only can well-intentioned citizens participate but so can bad actors, spammers, liars, cheats and thieves."

That's why most mainstream media outlets are allowing citizens to participate, but they are moderating what goes onto their sites. As a result, back in the news room, journalists often find that their roles have changed. Not only do they perform their traditional roles, but they also edit stories, photos and videos shot by readers and viewers; moderate Internet discussion forums and write blogs. As a result, today's news rooms look different from those of the past, and the Internet sites of traditional media companies are getting more and more attention. Many media outlets update news on their Web sites 24 hours a day, seven days a week. That means more and more journal-ists—even in newspaper news rooms—are being trained in digital audio and video editing. Some find themselves in front of television cameras to create mini-newscasts for the Web site.

Journalists call this phenomenon—the coordinating of print, broadcast and online reporting in a news operation—convergence. It's the transformation of traditional media into something entirely new—a 24/7 news operation in which the Web, not the traditional product, comes first. The concept is that customers should be able to get news on their terms, however and whenever they want it. Radio and televi-sion stations put their recorded newscasts online, and some customers tune in on the Web. Sometimes these Web-based newscasts even con-tain material that didn't make it into the traditional newscast, includ-ing full-length video of the mayor's press conference. Sometimes that happens even on a newspaper Web site.

Perhaps even more surprising, many news operations—even newspapers—think "Web first." Wrote an editor of *The Philadelphia Inquirer*, "Let's break as much news as we can online, particularly if it's a story, column or review that readers might get from another source, or that benefits from the strengths of the Web."

As we learned in Chapter 1, these two phenomena—citizen journalism and convergence—are driving fundamental change in the media industry. In this chapter, we look at how they are altering the face of the media industry and perhaps changing even the very defini-tion of news.

CITIZEN JOURNALISM

If citizens were once passive consumers of the news, that's certainly no longer true. Some older members of the public may still be passive consumers, but younger readers and viewers want to be part of the dia-logue. That's the driving force behind citizen journalism.

The Public Drives Change

Many journalists would define news as information that comes from trained professionals. Many citizens, on the other hand, could care less about the source; if it's interesting or informative, it's news. And whether information comes from a neighbor or from a blogger in California or China or Chile, it can have importance and credibility in the mind of the consumer regardless of its source.

One of the first to understand the significance of this change was Dan Gillmor, a veteran newspaperman and former columnist for the *San Jose Mercury News* who has become a leading advocate for citizen journalism. In *We the Media: Grassroots Journalism by the People, for the People*, Gillmor writes of the terrorist attacks of Sept. 11, 2001:

> We watched — again and again — the awful events. Consumers of news learned the *what* about the attacks, thanks to the television networks that showed the horror so graphically. Then we learned some of the *how* and *why* as print publications and thoughtful broadcasters worked to bring depth to events that defied mere words. Journalists did some of their finest work and made me proud to be one of them.
>
> But something else, something profound, was happening this time around: News was being produced by regular people who had something to say and show, and not solely by the "official" news organizations that had traditionally decided how the first draft of history would look. This time, the first draft of history was being written, in part, by the former audience. It was possible — it was inevitable — because of new publishing tools available on the Internet.
>
> Another kind of reporting emerged during those appalling hours and days. Via emails, mailing lists, chat groups, personal Web journals — all nonstandard news sources — we received valuable context that the major American media couldn't, or wouldn't, provide. We were witnessing — and in many cases were part of — the future of news.

Make no mistake about it: Technology has brought us to this point. Today, anyone can be a publisher, thanks to technological improvements that permit inexpensive printing, the ability to create digital audio and video with ease, and the simplicity of distributing text, photos, audio and video over the Internet. In South Korea, a citizen journalism Web site called OhmyNews.com adopted the slogan, "Every citizen is a reporter." At the OhmyNews site, that's true, and the model is rapidly spreading worldwide.

So what does all this mean for those who would become professional journalists? It means you won't have a one-way channel of communication through which to talk to your audience. The audience will want to talk back and participate in the process of gathering and distributing news. It also means you're likely to be working with citizens who aren't trained journalists and therefore have little or no sense of the concept of verification — checking information that goes into the news report to make sure it is as correct as humanly possible. Already, mainstream news organizations are starting to feel the change.

MSNBC.com, a joint venture of Microsoft and *NBC News* and the companion site of the MSNBC cable news channel, is a mainstream media outlet that has embraced the concept (see Figure 2.1). On the MSNBC site, readers are advised, "MSNBC is looking for your help. If

Figure 2.1
Budding journalists can participate in the news dialogue at MSNBC.com, where they are asked to submit photos, videos and stories of events they witness.

you are a witness to a big news event send us your video and photos at CJ@MSNBC.com." Readers are even given assignments:

- *Assignment 1: The war in Iraq.* When reporting, you might want to ask, "How does the fighting in Fallujah affect, if at all, my hometown?" Are former neighbors of yours now fighting in Iraq? How has their deployment affected their families/my family? What have you seen? How have you and others been responding to the Iraq war?
- *Assignment 2: Travel safety and security.* While on your travels for the upcoming holidays, what have you observed about our nation's roads and ports? Did you feel safe when you walked through your airport? Many states are still on high terror alert levels, and security is always a concern.
- *Assignment 3: Your Thanksgiving visit home.* We've been reading a lot of e-mails from viewers about how many impromptu political discussions have bubbled up in dinner conversations amongst friends and family. This holiday may be no different. Are you living in a blue state traveling home to a red one? Was there a difference in culture or atmosphere between the place you live now, and the place you once called home? Are your previously apathetic parents/siblings/cousins now actively involved in the political process?

How Important Is Verification?

Public participation is quite a departure from what was once the norm in journalism. Historically, journalism in the U.S. and around the world has been a form of one-way communication. In its infancy, early journalists like Tom Paine used it as a soapbox through which to influence public opinion. Later, as the craft was professionalized, the partisan press of early America yielded, in large part, to a more balanced approach founded on the elusive concept of objectivity. But journalism remained a one-way channel: Reporters wrote about or broadcasted information to the masses.

In that environment, the concept of journalist as **gatekeeper** prevailed. Editors decided what stories would go into the paper or the newscast. They were the powerful gatekeepers who decided what the public got to read and see.

Today, it's clear that the concept of editor as gatekeeper has at least partially evaporated. In a world in which anyone can be a reporter, and anyone can be a publisher, the media have been democratized. For those who truly believe that multiple voices give rise to a better-educated electorate, on its face that's a good thing.

But what of the quality of information produced by untrained journalists? As noted by Bill Kovach and Tom Rosenstiel in their seminal work, *The Elements of Journalism*, one of the great virtues of mainstream journalism is the process of verification. In other words, the journalistic process of checking and rechecking information and using multiple sources provides some assurance that a report is reasonably accurate. Such rigor is often missing in citizen journalism reports, which sometimes are little more than opinion pieces.

That doesn't diminish the fact that in the eyes of the public, citizen-generated content has great value. Indeed, some of it is good, and some of it is excellent. Many mainstream journalists now recognize the value of citizen-produced content, and more and more are embracing citizens as partners in the news-gathering process. After all, a citizen-provided exclusive photograph that otherwise would be unavailable is a real plus for the medium that publishes it. A citizen expert can add depth and explanation to a story that a nonexpert reporter would be hard-pressed to produce.

Even if journalists don't accept the change—and some are resistant—it's happening. The public, you see, is demanding it. The evidence of that may be found in the reality that more and more newspapers, magazines and online sites are allowing readers to comment on articles, talk back or contribute. Clearly, readers and viewers seek a dialogue with those who run and work for their newspapers, magazines, radio and television stations, and Web sites. They want to be part of the discussion. So whether imperfect or not, citizen journalism is here to stay.

Citizen Journalism: Here to Stay

When citizen journalism first appeared, most mainstream media rejected it as amateurish and unprofessional. Many journalists felt threatened by it. But many in the public found it liberating and saw citizen journalism as a way of bashing the established media, which they distrusted or viewed as biased. A rather nasty dialogue resulted on several blogs as journalists reacted.

Today, however, many media companies have taken Gillmor's advice to embrace citizen journalism as a complement to the traditional news report and a way to reconnect with readers and viewers. There's no doubt that those who are allowed to contribute to the news feel a sense of satisfaction with the fruit of their labors and a real connection to the media outlets that publish their work. And, of course, there's the reality that citizen journalism brings a fresh perspective to the news.

As a result, the mainstream media are not only allowing but also encouraging increased dialogue with the audience—in effect, giving readers and viewers the chance to talk back, air their opinions and contribute new information. The growth of such media is phenomenal:

- Across the country, newspaper and television station Web sites contain blogs by reporters and editors that attempt to make the news-gathering process more transparent and that provide a chance for the audience to comment or react. Blogs also allow traditional media to get the news out more rapidly, give the news more personality and create a space for more informal approaches to writing.
- In some communities, newspapers have popped up that are written and photographed by readers with the help of professional editors. Two examples are *The Northwest Voice* in Bakersfield, Calif., and *My Missourian* in Columbia, Mo. Both are published by traditional newspaper operations and have companion Web sites full of citizen-generated content.
- Community Web sites packed with citizen-generated blogs abound. A notable example is BlufftonToday.com, an effort of the *Bluffton Today* newspaper in Bluffton, S.C. (see Figure 2.2). It's a dramatic departure from the first efforts to create newspaper Web sites, which often did little more than regurgitate the contents of that day's newspaper. Bluffton Today.com contains community blogs, expert blogs and staff blogs. As a result, everyone is part of the dialogue. Add video and audio, as many newspapers are doing, and newspaper Web sites are more lively than ever.
- Social-networking sites such as Facebook, MySpace and YouTube also rate as news sources for some. On those sites, users create places to discuss the latest in politics or the state of global warming. To users, news is available at these sites. It may not be news in the traditional sense, but users still regard it as useful information.

Many editors and publishers now realize that readers and viewers want to talk back and participate in discussions, and Web sites of traditional media are allowing that to happen. In the process, they are

Figure 2.2
On BlufftonToday.com, regular citizens are able to post their own blogs, upload pictures or send in a news tip, which makes the site an interactive forum for information exchange.

connecting with the audience in ways that were never before possible. The media are creating positive discussions with audiences that quite recently felt talked to and alienated.

The trend, then, is toward Big Media using the phenomenon of citizen journalism to its advantage. Citizen journalism isn't going away, so it's time for the news media to embrace it. Citizen journalism is not, as some feared, a significant threat to mainstream journalism. It does, however, require journalists to welcome the public to the discussion.

The Coming of Web 2.0

Initially, the Web was merely a replica of traditional media forms. Publishers published, and consumers consumed. Call it Web 1.0. Although that's certainly the way most of the Web still works, Web 2.0 is here, and it differs from Web 1.0 in three fundamental ways:

- Members of the public become publishers.
- Members of the public help to decide what's news and how it's presented.
- Members of the public build communities to help process information.

Blogs have become a major means of receiving information and reacting to it. **Podcasts** and the ability to deliver them over the Internet have made it inexpensive for citizens to become broadcasters. **Wikis** (for example, Wikipedia.com) allow people to share information and edit that information as they see fit. People who were once only news consumers are now news editors and publishers. They publish with sites like Twitter.com, a **social-networking** and micro-blogging service that allows its users to send and read other users' updates (called *tweets*), text-based posts of up to 140 characters. Or they use Qik.com, a video-blogging service that allows users to stream video from their cell phones to the Web.

They also are their own news aggregators. Serious news consumers can use **RSS** feeds to automate the collection of news from various sites on the Internet. Combined with video-capture devices such as TiVo, such software allows consumers to read, listen to or watch the news on their own terms—when, where and how they want it. Further, news from traditional Web sites, such as that of *The New York Times* (**NYTimes.com**), is easily combined with news from nontraditional sites such as DrudgeReport.com or rocwiki.org, a city guide edited entirely by readers in Rochester, N.Y.

The world's largest newspaper-industry trade association, IFRA, compiled this list of exemplary Web 2.0 sites to demonstrate how the Web is evolving:

- *Basecamphq.com:* Group collaboration software.
- *Delicious.com:* A service that allows users to bookmark and tag content that interests them and get insight into the tagging of others.
- *Dropcash.com:* Fund-raising software.
- *Flickr.com:* A site that allows users to publish, share and collaborate on picture albums (now owned by Yahoo).
- *Flock.com:* A Mozilla-based browser that incorporates an RSS aggregator and blogging.
- *Meebo.com:* Instant-messaging software for all the major IM clients that doesn't require users to download or use those clients.
- *Rollyo.com:* A search engine that searches only the sites that the user selects.
- *Zimbra.com:* A Web 2.0 rival to Microsoft Outlook, a popular e-mail program.

Web 2.0 is all about collaboration and sharing, the very forces that are driving citizen journalism.

Forms of Citizen Journalism

In an article in *Online Journalism Review*, J.D. Lasica sorted the media forms used in citizen journalism into six types:

- *Audience-participation sites.* Some mainstream media outlets like MSNBC.com give readers the chance to contribute to the Web site through user comments attached to news stories, personal blogs, photos or video footage captured from mobile phone cameras, or local news written by members of the community.

- *Independent news or information Web sites.* These sites are published by individuals who are not normally associated with the traditional media. DrudgeReport.com is an example.
- *Participatory news sites.* On these sites, readers get to write, take photos and publish their work, perhaps even in newspaper format, with the assistance of professional editors. Most are tied to traditional media Web sites. MyMissourian.com and NorthwestVoice.com are examples.
- *Collaborative and contributory news sites.* These sites, often focusing on a specific subject matter, are based on reader comments and contributions. Slashdot.org and Kuro5hin.org are examples.
- *Thin media.* Targeted news content is directed to those with narrowly defined interests through mailing lists and e-mail newsletters.
- *Personal broadcasting sites.* On these sites, the operators provide news-based subject matter in a specific area of interest, such as technology. The result is downloadable audio or video in various formats, including Windows Media, QuickTime, podcasts and vodcasts. An example is KenRadio.com (see Figure 2.3).

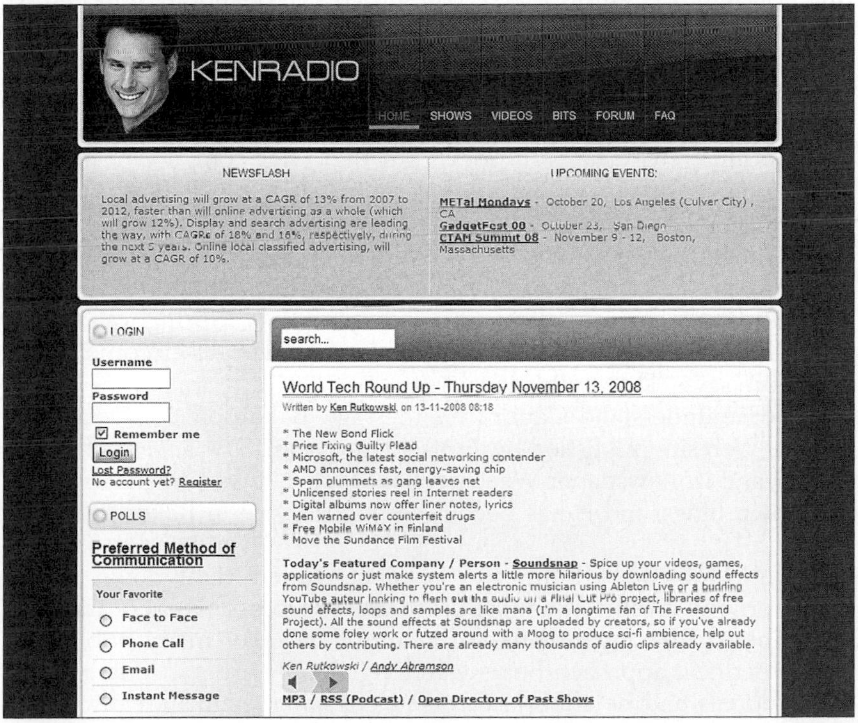

Figure 2.3
Listeners can tune in to KenRadio.com to hear a daily live talk-radio show on technology and media news from around the world.

Many consumers wouldn't stop there. Is *The Daily Show* a news program? It is to many young adults and others, even though the show is clearly intended to be entertainment, not a serious news report. Is the stuff found on social-networking sites such as Facebook and MySpace news? It is for many. The public, then, is using its new-found power in the news marketplace to shake the very definition of traditional news. If it's something someone wants or needs to know, no matter the source, it's news.

Managing the Change

If citizen journalism and its enabler, Web 2.0, are changing the way news is consumed, the question becomes this: How should journalists adapt to that change? Robert Cauthorn, chief executive officer of CityTools.net, urges journalists to forget news and concentrate on storytelling.

While no journalist would agree with Cauthorn's suggestion to "forget news," his point about storytelling is one that most editors now embrace. The narrative writing style has become more and more popular in magazines and newspapers, and arguably that's storytelling at its best. But storytelling, Cauthorn believes, should be collaborative in nature. "If you let people write on your Web sites," he told a group of world-wide publishers, "they are on your side. Let people comment on your stories. Don't seek to dominate the discussion, which is the usual media role. You cannot stop the trend toward distributed discussion."

"Paper won't disappear (in the future), but paper-less media will soak up more of our time. We will eventually become paper-less the way we once became horseless. Horses are still around, but they are ridden by hobbyists, not consumers."

—Paul Saffo, Institute for the Future

To illustrate, Cauthorn points out that Digg.com, a Web site devoted to covering technology, now has more daily traffic than *The New York Times* Web site, despite the newspaper's valuable brand. Digg got there by sharing the authority to cover technology news with its readers. Readers can write for the site, and all members can rate the articles. The rating system provides some assurance that the highest-ranked articles are also authoritative. "Allow your readers to become stars," Cauthorn says. "That builds loyalty."

Some understand Cauthorn's message. Bakotopia.com is a community Web site published by, but separate from, *The Bakersfield Californian* and its newspaper Web site. Bakotopia allows citizens to set up their own blogs, and it has become a popular site in Bakersfield (see Figure 2.4).

YourHub.com attempts to connect readers right down to the neighborhood level. The concept is to create discussion about issues of great concern in tiny portions of a community. For many publishers, this hyperlocal approach bears watching. People are passionate about their schools and neighborhoods, and engaging them in a discussion about those things has value.

That's exactly what Cauthorn is trying to do with CityTools. The idea is to connect people and categorize information at the neighborhood

Figure 2.4
Although affiliated with *The Bakersfield Californian*, Bakotopia is entirely community-run. Users can create a profile, share videos and photos, post events and connect with other users.

level. Readers are able to rate all content, creating an online community valuable to everyone in the area.

Well-tailored content, whether geographic in nature or designed to appeal to users with common interests regardless of location, offers great commercial opportunities for publishers. Such online communities make it possible to offer **contextual advertising**, advertising related to the content, which is exactly the kind of targeted advertising for which businesses are willing to pay a premium. It's also the kind of local advertising that newspapers and television stations have been unable to offer. The potential result is a new stream of revenue.

The concept of building online communities to which information and advertising can be marketed is merely an extension of an old staple, the intensely local news carried by weekly newspapers. In this case, however, the readers get to talk back.

But is this content news? Well, that depends on your definition. More important, it depends on the definition of your audience. If people crave the information, it probably qualifies as news.

Rob Curley, now an editor at the *Las Vegas Sun*, understands the value and appeal of hyperlocal content. Before joining the *Sun*, Curley

The convergent news room of the *Lawrence (Kan.) Journal-World*.

worked at newspapers in Kansas and Florida and at *The Washington Post* to build Web sites with database-driven coverage. Curley's formula: restaurant guides, guides of things to do today and guides tailored to the uniqueness of communities. In Lawrence, Kan., for example, he created the definitive Web site on all things related to the University of Kansas Jayhawks teams.

While working for the *Naples Daily News* in Florida, Curley designed a database that provided copious detail about the community's annual wine dinners to raise money for charity. Lavish dinners catered by some of the world's leading chefs were the province of Naples' high society, but everyone in the city — or around the world — could share in the experience by going to the Naples Web site. There you could find the menus for the dinners, held at the homes of Naples' leading citizens, and photos of the event. You also could find details of the wines offered at the related wine auction and the prices they brought. The wine dinner and auction constitute the big event in Naples each year, and Curley's tailored Web site produced high traffic on those pages.

In Washington, he created LoudonExtra.com, a hyperlocal site focused on the affluent Virginia suburbs, and onBeing (**http://specials .washingtonpost.com/onbeing**), a video-based site featuring personality profiles. All of those efforts were designed to give people what Curley believes they want: intense amounts of news about their local communities and the people who live there.

One of Curley's axioms is that content should be platform-independent. If the customer wants it in the newspaper, on television or on the Web site, fine. But if the reader would prefer an instant message or an e-mail reminder, that should be available, too. Like many others, Curley is now providing content on third-generation mobile phones; 3G technology makes it easy to deliver not only text but also video over telephones, an innovation that's already commonplace in Japan, Korea and parts of Europe. Many U.S. news organizations are gearing up to deliver content in this way.

CONVERGENCE

If citizen journalism is changing the way journalists and the public think about news, convergence is changing the very news rooms in which journalists operate. Indeed, news room managers are reorganizing, reinventing and repopulating their operations. They are altering copy flow patterns to put the Web first, changing their online sites dramatically and hiring new kinds of journalists to make it all happen.

Different News Rooms, Different Skills

It's clear that if mainstream journalists are to become players in the new media marketplace, they have to become multimedia journalists. They must understand not only the basics of writing and editing but also the fundamentals of audio and video production, blogging, mobile phone technology and more.

"What I'm looking for," a Florida newspaper editor said, "is someone who can cover the Super Bowl for my newspaper, then do a completely different story for our Web site that takes advantage of the strengths of that medium. Then I want that same person to be able to do a standup for the television station."

That quotation speaks volumes about the changing face of the media industry. Historically, journalists were trained for jobs as newspaper reporters, magazine designers, television reporters or producers, or photojournalists or for a host of other roles. But rarely was one reporter expected to be able to function across media boundaries—in print, in broadcast and in online media. Today, that's changing.

Increasingly, editors like the one in Florida are looking for journalists who can function in the world of cross-media collaboration. From coast to coast, newspapers are striking alliances with television stations, sometimes owned by the same company and sometimes not. Other newspapers are collaborating with radio stations and expect their reporters to produce not only written reports of a meeting but also audio reports. Almost all reporters must produce for the Web as well.

If citizen journalism is challenging the norms of traditional journalism, and perhaps even redefining news, convergence is changing the industry itself. *Convergence* is the hottest buzzword in the media industry these days, but defining it isn't easy. To some people, convergence occurs when a newspaper or television station starts publishing material on the Internet. According to others, convergence occurs when print reporters start carrying tape recorders and produce material for radio as well as the newspaper, or when advertising salespeople start selling ads for radio as well as newspapers.

While those may indeed be forms of convergence, in its most complete sense convergence involves alliances of four communication forms:

- Print (usually a newspaper or magazine).
- Broadcast or cable television and perhaps radio.
- The Internet.
- Mobile phones and other wireless devices.

Without question, those last two are essential to any serious definition of convergence. Why? Because the Internet and wireless devices such as mobile telephones and **personal digital assistants** allow consumers to search for and find information they want and need whenever and wherever they like, a possibility generally absent in traditional media. Sure, with the newspaper you can search through the stock listings for the closing share price of Merck, the pharmaceutical giant. But you cannot read about Merck's latest drugs and the company's chances of winning federal approval for them unless the newspaper's editors happen to provide that story for you. On the Internet, a simple search produces the story.

As a result, the best definition of *convergence* might read like this: Convergence is the practice of sharing and cross-promoting content from a variety of media, some interactive, through news room collaborations and partnerships. However one defines it, though, convergence is changing the face of the media landscape.

Enlightened editors and publishers of this new era—like Curley—believe the key to success is giving readers what they want, when they want it. That's precisely the attitude of those driving the most successful convergence experiments in the U.S. The *Tampa Tribune*-WFLA-TBO.com convergence effort of Media General in Tampa is the most celebrated of those experiments. It also is one of the oldest, having started in 2000 (see Figure 2.5).

Several years after convergence, the converged news room in Tampa has little trouble getting either breaking or routine news onto all three platforms, says Gil Thelen, former publisher of *The Tampa*

Figure 2.5
The *Tampa Tribune*-WFLA-TBO.com collaboration was one of the earliest and most successful media convergences. Readers can find video footage of breaking news provided by News Channel 8 right alongside *The Tribune*'s print story on TBO.com.

Tribune and the original leader of the effort. But it wasn't easy to get to that point. Some employees quit rather than learn new ways of doing things. Others stayed, complained and ultimately complied. Eventually, crossover reporting in Tampa became increasingly common, as these stories demonstrate:

- A *Tribune* story about a passenger who landed a plane after the pilot became ill carried the bylines of both a *Tribune* reporter and the WFLA anchor.
- A report on dog bites ran as a two-part WFLA series, a front-page *Tribune* story and a TBO.com package.
- A *Tribune* story on the removal of a statue from a shopping center included a picture by the photo editor, who also shot video for WFLA.

More recently, the company, like many other traditional media companies, announced yet another round of layoffs coupled with further melding of the newspaper, television and online staffs. Indeed, the problems of traditional media are forcing some changes once thought impossible; the *Miami Herald*, the *Sun-Sentinel* in Fort Lauderdale and the *Palm Beach Post* reached an experimental news-sharing agreement in an effort to cut costs. The three companies already were cooperating on a distribution deal. One blogger termed the news-sharing deal "mind-boggling," insisting it was unthinkable because *The Herald*, in his view, was a far superior newspaper.

But if the idea of sharing news is tough, even tougher is bridging the cultural differences in the way television and newspaper reporters have traditionally operated. That became evident in Dallas when *The Dallas Morning News* and WFAA, both owned by the Belo Corp., started cooperating. How was the television critic for *The Morning News* supposed to critique a show on the television station with which the newspaper partnered? Would everything he wrote be seen as biased? Not sure, the newspaper decided that for the time being it would not do any television criticism at all.

On other fronts, things were easier. When the television station and the newspaper decided to have their movie critics collaborate, both agreed that *The Morning News'* more stringent ethical standards, which called for refusing freebies from any source, would prevail. (See Chapter 15.) That agreement signaled a cultural shift for the television station — but arguably a positive one.

Without a doubt, more and more media companies are headed in this direction. Gannett, the nation's largest newspaper company, announced in late 2006 the creation of what it calls Gannett Information Centers. The concept, piloted at several Gannett newspapers, is simple, as described by Gannett Chief Executive Officer Craig Dubow in a letter to Gannett employees:

> The Information Center is a way to gather and disseminate news and information across all platforms, 24/7. The Information Center will let us gather the very local news and information that customers want, then distribute it when, where and how our customers seek it.

In Dubow's words, the result of the pilot projects was remarkable:

> Breaking news on the Web and updating for the newspaper draws more people to both those media. Asking the community for help gets it — and delivers the newspaper into the heart of community conversations once again. Rich and deep databases with local information gathered efficiently are central to the whole process. The changes impact all media, and the public has approved. Results include stronger newspapers, more popular Web sites and more opportunities to attract the customers advertisers want.

With testimonials like that, it's certain that the rest of the industry will follow.

The New York Times has changed its approach, too. It created a continuous news desk, which updates the work of reporters in the field

24 hours a day. David Stout, a domestic correspondent for the continuous desk, said of his assignment, "Part of my job is to synthesize the reporting of my colleagues. In return for their help, I try to repay them by keeping them apprised of news developments (I keep a constant eye on wire service reports) and, occasionally, going to news conferences." All that is designed to keep the *Times'* Web site fresh and current 24 hours a day.

A similar desk was established at the *San Antonio Express-News*. In announcing the creation of a digital news desk, the editor wrote, "We are excited to announce . . . a cross-departmental team of editors, reporters and videographers/photographers that will focus exclusively on gathering and producing content for the Web."

Cable news networks also are changing. CNN recently assigned journalists to 10 additional cities across the U.S. They are, in effect, one-person bureaus that use inexpensive cameras to report the news single-handedly in a medium that once sent multiple-person crews to almost all assignments.

Even National Public Radio finds itself immersed in convergence. Coupled with a traditional radio piece about a community organizer in South Chicago was an audio slide show for npr.org, the network's Web site. NPR reporters had become photojournalists, probably the last thing they expected to do when they signed on with a radio network.

Advertising and public relations practitioners also are taking note. They must learn to take advantage of new ways to disseminate their messages. Shel Holtz coaches corporate communicators and advertising and public relations professionals on how to reach audiences through Web 2.0. His book titles show how leaders in his field are taking note of changes in media. They include *Public Relations on the Net*, *Blogging for Business* and *How to Do Everything with Podcasting*. Good advertising and public relations people follow the audiences, and audience patterns are indeed changing.

Why Convergence?

Although converged news rooms may be the wave of the future, most news rooms today are decidedly traditional. For every Tampa-like convergence operation, there are hundreds of traditional newspaper or television news rooms. Those news rooms typically look much as they did 25 years ago except for their embedded online operations. Today, almost every television or radio station, magazine and newspaper has a Web site.

It's also true that most traditional news operations are still profitable. It's not at all unusual for a daily newspaper to earn a profit of 10 cents or more on every dollar it earns—less than 20 years ago but still significant. Many television stations earn even more. So why the interest in convergence? It's quite simple, really. Most media-industry financial trends are headed in the wrong direction. Audiences, and therefore profits, are shrinking, and media-industry managers are worried. Many see convergence as the long-term answer to their problems.

To understand today's media-industry climate, consider these facts about newspapers, published by the Newspaper Association of America, the industry's leading U.S. trade organization:

- *The daily newspaper industry is in decline.* There were 1,452 daily newspapers in the U.S. at the end of 2005, compared with 1,745 as recently as 1980.
- *The number of daily newspaper readers is falling.* In 1970, 78 percent of the nation's adults read a newspaper daily, but by 2008 that percentage had declined to 48. Worse, survey after survey has revealed that the biggest decline is among readers 34 and younger. That statistic sounds an ominous note for the future: As older readers die, there is no one to replace them. Research suggests that those who fail to develop the newspaper reading habit early will not acquire it later in life.
- *Newspaper circulation is plummeting.* According to the Audit Bureau of Circulation, newspaper readership is declining precipitously in major markets, and the trend is accelerating.

But if the newspaper industry is dying, as some argue, it is far from dead. Consider this:

- Newspapers remain one of the most profitable industries around, helped in large part by their near-monopoly situation in most cities.
- The number of *weekly* newspapers has increased slightly—from 6,580 in 1996 to 6,659 in 2005. And weekly circulation grew by almost 4 million copies during that time. Indeed, small newspapers are thriving even as the metros decline.
- Newspapers now trail both television and direct mail in the amount of advertising they attract, but they still capture a large share of the U.S. advertising dollar.

Newspapers' competitors have their own problems. Network and local television both have experienced audience declines and the resulting pressure on advertising revenue. The creation of new U.S. broadcast networks such as Fox and CW has fragmented television audiences, and the proliferation of cable channels has divided those audiences into even smaller segments.

Cable channels are worrisome indeed for network television; unlike the networks, they are ideally positioned to deliver targeted audiences to advertisers because of their focus on specific types of information (sports, health and fitness, children, and so on). Like newspapers, network television is best able to deliver mass audiences, not the cohesive audiences that many advertisers covet. Radio does a better job of targeting specific audiences, but its impact on the media

On the Job

Persistence Pays Off

April Eaton began her career by serving internships at *The Washington Post* and at the Atlanta bureau of CBS News. Then she served as a news room assistant at *USA Today.*

That was in 1986. "I then decided to deviate from what was slowly amounting to a newspaper career," she says.

"I wanted to work in television news—not print. A contact at CBS News in New York told me either to plug away and send résumé tapes to tiny TV markets that won't pay me much but will teach me a lot . . . or go back to school and get my master of arts degree."

She chose the latter strategy, and after graduation she worked as a general-assignment reporter and fill-in anchor for three and a half years at WLOS-TV in Asheville, N.C. Then she became an education reporter at NewsChannel 5 in Nashville, Tenn.

Eaton has a few words of advice for "reporters-in-the-making":

1. If you really want to be in the news business, keep at it. Don't let "there-are-no-jobs" comments slow you down.
2. Constantly work to improve your writing.
3. It's okay to know you do good work; just don't let your head get so huge you can't make it through the news room door.
4. Remember, someone helped you get to where you are, so reach back and help others.

Eaton has made yet another career move. She's now senior corporate relations manager at Allstate Insurance Co. in Nashville.

---

industry, as measured by its share of advertising dollars, is relatively small, and most stations don't even cover news these days.

Magazines, like radio and cable television, deliver target audiences to advertisers, but they do so at a rapidly increasing cost and together account for only about 5 percent of U.S. advertising dollars. In the long term, like newspapers, magazines are threatened by rising production costs, and their distribution relies heavily on ever-escalating postal rates.

The only reasonable conclusion is that the future lies with Internet-based media, perhaps in combination with the existing media. Users are able to interact with online material in ways that are not possible in traditional media, and any type of media—text, video, audio, still photographs and graphics—can be delivered there. Citizen journalists can and will play a role in the production of that content, which is a feat more difficult to accomplish with traditional media.

All this explains why convergence is so appealing to media managers, even if the very norms of journalism are being shaken.

Traditional Media: Where Are They Headed?

If the Internet is the news medium of the future, as many believe, where does that leave the existing media? Well, it leaves them in a position of change, to be sure, but most are jockeying for a good seat in the new arena.

Newspapers hold the franchise for local news coverage, and they are unlikely to let it slip away without a fight. No startup Web site can hope to duplicate the news-gathering apparatus already in place at the local newspaper (see Figure 2.6). Even with the much-publicized cuts in newspaper staffing that have occurred nationwide in recent years, most newspapers employ many more journalists than all the television stations in their markets combined. But they also are reorganizing their news rooms to tackle the new realities of the marketplace (see Figure 2.7), which means there are increased opportunities for tech-savvy graduates of journalism programs.

There may be fewer newspapers in the future, but the medium won't go away anytime soon. The reality is that newspapers are embracing the Web. Almost all of them have Web sites, and a few of them have even begun to figure out how to make the medium complement, rather than duplicate, their existing products.

Similarly, the Internet is not yet in a position to challenge television, but its real potential in the video realm is its ability to deliver news and entertainment programming on demand. Station and network executives are scrambling to figure out how to do that, and high-speed,

On the Job

Editing Online News

Sarah Rupp graduated with a degree in newspaper journalism but immediately found herself working at online sites.

Right out of school, she landed an internship at MSNBC.com in Redmond, Wash. She later worked at other online sites, including ABCNews.com, before landing at seattlepi.com, which operates 24/7.

"I usually work a day shift, which means that I have to keep the site fresh with new articles, story updates, breaking news and photos," Rupp says. "Throughout the day we add new wire stories, staff stories, photo galleries and other Web-only features. . . . Besides doing the daily stuff, I also get to work on special projects like producing video and putting together new content channels for the site."

She enjoys the work: "The great thing about working for a news Web site is you get the chance to do a little of everything — writing, editing, choosing stories, designing graphics, building Web pages, posting photos and editing audio clips.

"There are a lot of exciting things going on in online journalism. . . . No longer are reporters the only people who report the news. That means the very definition of what 'news' is has changed and will continue to change."

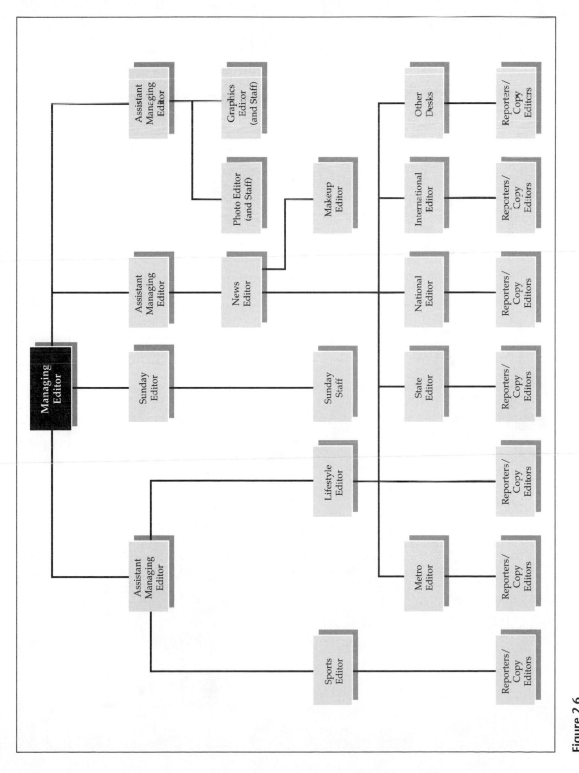

Figure 2.6
This news room organization format is typical for a metropolitan daily newspaper.

How decisions are made using the team concept

Managing Editor

Planning Editors
- Job descriptions
- Newspaper section mission statements

News Content Editor
Features Content Editor
Assistant Managing Editor for Administration
Teams Editor
Production Editor
Visual Content Editor
Teams Editor
Teams Editor

Teams
- Leader vision
- Team mission
- Job descriptions
- Beat structure
- Budgets

Section Coordinating Editors
- Coordinating editors' vision
- Section mission statements
- Budgets

T E A M S

Life Group	City Group	General Assignment Group	State Group	Business Group
Social Issues	Urban Issues	GA/Days	State	Business
Life	Suburbs	GA/Nights	Politics/	Innovation
Consumer	Public Safety	News	Government	Projects
Culture	Sports	Columnists	Health/	*Other Reporting*
		Nation/World	Science	*Activities:*
		Wash. Bureau	Education	Public Journal-
				ism, Computer-
				Assisted
				Reporting

A Section	B Section	Sports Section	Features Sections	Business Section
1A Editor	Section Editor	Section Editor	Section Editor	Section Editor
Night 1A Editor	Night Section Editor	Night Section Editor	Assistant Section Editor	Night Section Editor
Weekend 1A Editor	Weekend Section Editor	Sunday Section Editor	Assistant Section Editor	

Figure 2.7

Some newspapers are organizing their staff members into teams rather than using traditional beat systems. The teams may be responsible for content in both the print and online editions. This chart is based on a model provided by the Minneapolis *Star Tribune*.

fiber-optic Internet connections into the home might be the answer. Today, television stations are following newspapers' lead and trying to determine how the Internet figures into their future.

Magazines, too, are embracing the Internet, and a few of them, *Slate* being a primary example, are Internet-only magazines. Newsletters, many of which have small circulations, are finding the Internet a more suitable and more cost-efficient place for their content than the printed page.

All of this means we're in a period of evolution. As more and more content moves to the Internet, traditional media outlets will begin to decline. Online distribution just makes sense. It's less expensive than carrier or mail delivery for newspapers and magazines, and it doesn't require a massive investment in printing presses and the environmentally unfriendly production of paper in massive quantities. Online delivery gives the media industry a means of providing audio and video on demand in place of traditional television, most of which the viewer must watch when the station chooses to transmit it, not necessarily when the viewer wants to consume it. TiVo alters that a bit, but users tend to record movies and TV shows, not news programs.

Still, it's important to remember that this is an evolutionary process. For the lifetimes of those entering the field of journalism today, there will still be newspapers, magazines and television stations. That means there will be jobs in those media — good jobs (see the box "Jobs in Journalism" and Figure 2.8). But those entering the field also should

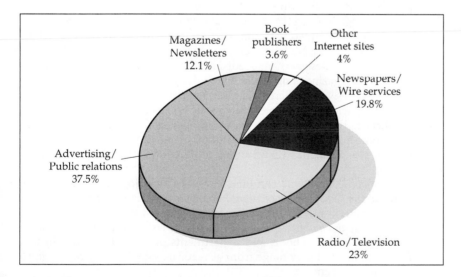

Figure 2.8
Journalism students seek work in a range of industries. (*Source:* Annual Survey of Journalism and Mass Communication Students, 2005, University of Georgia Grady School of Journalism.)

prepare for a multimedia world. A newspaper designer might also be asked to design the newspaper's Web site. Similarly, a television reporter might be asked to write a story for the station's Web site or even for a collaborating newspaper.

It's a multimedia world in which convergence will increasingly reign.

JOURNALISM JOBS

Training to become a journalist prepares you for many jobs. Some are obvious, some not. Most jobs, regardless of the medium, fall into one of these categories:

- *Writing and reporting.* At newspapers, most writing jobs are full-time staff positions, but many magazines rely much more heavily on freelance writers who are paid by the story. The skills of reporting and writing go together. No one in journalism can be a good writer without first being a good reporter.
- *Editing.* Great jobs abound for those who can edit well. Newspapers, magazines, radio and television stations, and some Web sites have copy editors, assignment editors and editorial assistants. At newspapers, the entry-level position of copy editor often pays more than the entry-level position of reporter because copy editors are in greater demand.
- *Photography and video.* Printed publications and Web sites use lots of photographs and therefore need photographers. At newspapers, most are staff photographers, but at many magazines freelance photography is more common. Video is becoming important for all media operations that run Web sites. No longer is video merely the province of television.
- *Art and design.* Designers are needed in all media. There are jobs for newspaper and magazine designers and Web designers. Even television stations need Web designers. There also is an increasing demand for information graphics specialists—people who produce maps, charts and graphs.
- *Production.* Television producers are in high demand. It's quite possible to become a news producer right out of journalism school. Web producers are also in demand, and more production jobs exist in the print media.
- *Tech support.* Those who combine a knowledge of journalism with computer literacy can find jobs anywhere. Media outlets around the world have a strong interest in computer-literate journalists.
- *Advertising and public relations.* Advertising and public relations often are taught within schools and departments of journalism. Jobs in this field abound, and they range from advertising sales to creative design to account management.
- *Management.* Many who enter journalism eventually will become assignment editors, managing editors or executive editors. Those jobs pay more and are a natural progression for reporters and copy editors.

Jobs in Journalism

Jobs abound for those who seek to enter the media industry. Here are a few of the possibilities for each medium. Entry-level Jobs that beginners are likely to land are marked with an asterisk.

Newspapers (Daily and Weekly)

Reporter*
Copy editor*
Page designer*
Information graphics specialist*
Photographer*
Assignment editor
News editor
Managing editor
Executive editor
Columnist

Magazines

Writer*
Fact checker*
Editorial assistant*
Copy editor*
Page designer*
Senior writer
Senior editor
Contributing writer
Managing editor
Editor
Columnist

Television

Reporter*
Producer*

Desk assistant*
Videographer*
Anchor
News director
Executive producer

Radio

Reporter*
Producer*
Anchor
News director

Online Media

Writer*
Producer*
Graphics specialist*
Executive producer (titles vary)

Other Jobs

Advertising salesperson*
Advertising copywriter*
Advertising account manager*
Public relations practitioner*
Account executive
Art director
Media critic
Foreign correspondent

Suggested Readings

Gillmor, Dan. *We the Media: Grassroots Journalism by the People, for the People.* Sebastopol, Calif.: O'Reilly Media, 2006. A treatise on the importance of citizen journalism by a longtime newspaper reporter and editor.

Hewitt, Hugh. *Blog: Understanding the Information Reformation That's Changing Your World.* Nashville: Thomas Nelson, 2005. A conservative attorney and commentator provides a view of the ubiquity of blogs.

Meyer, Philip. *The Vanishing Newspaper: Saving Journalism in the Information Age.* Columbia: University of Missouri Press, 2004. An excellent book on the role of newspapers in the news-gathering process.

Suggested Web Sites

http://journalists.org   The Online News Association was organized in 1999 to promote online news sites.

www.magazine.org   Magazine Publishers of America is the professional organization for magazine journalists.

www.naa.org   The Newspaper Association of America, based in Reston, Va., is the newspaper industry's leading trade association.

www.nab.org   The National Association of Broadcasters is the primary trade organization of the broadcast industry.

www.stateofthenewsmedia.org   Each year, the Project for Excellence in Journalism updates this site with the latest statistics on the media industry.

Exercises

1. Find two newspaper Web sites that carry staff-generated blogs. Compare and contrast them. Are the reporters or editors responsive to readers' comments? Is the discussion lively or slow?

2. Analyze a citizen journalism site in your community or in your area. How does the information in the top three stories compare with the top three stories on the Web site of your local newspaper?

3. Provide a revised definition of news using the new realities of citizen journalism. Define it for different audiences, including you and your friends, and your parents.

4. The Internet, in addition to being a place to publish, is a useful source of information for journalists. Using the Internet, locate information on the most recent U.S. census and report the following:

   The population of your state
   The population of your city
   The range of income levels within your city, and the percentage of the population that falls within each income level
   The demographic breakdown of your city by race

5. Make a list of at least 10 sources of information available on the Internet that would be good resources for journalists. Explain why you chose each, and describe how you would assess the reliability of information these sources provide.

6. Go to a blog or discussion board, and follow one thread of discussion. Describe how the information you found might be useful to a reporter. Also describe how you would verify the information you found there.

3 Interviewing

Information is the raw material of a journalist. Although some information is gathered from records and some from observation, most is gathered in person-to-person conversations — interviews. The skills that go into these conversations are the basic reporting tools of any reporter in any medium. If you're interviewing for television, broadcast or webcast, your goals and techniques may be different from those of a print reporter, but the basics are the same.

You met Scott Norvell, London bureau chief for Fox News, in Chapter 1's "On the Job" feature. Here's his take on the importance of interviewing:

> Don't fall into the very easy trap of doing all your research electronically or online. Nothing substitutes for face-to-face communication or even phone conversations. I recently was following up a story that had been done by a couple other outlets, one about the apparent rise in religious fervor among young Europeans. What I found out in the course of a conversation with someone, something that none of the other outlets had noted in their stories, was that the rise in church attendance and religious feelings as noted by pollsters was occurring primarily among young immigrants and not natives, and young Muslims at that.
>
> The entire story changed, and I would never have learned that tidbit had I merely followed the lead of the other outlets that reported the story. I coaxed it out of a pollster during a lengthy phone conversation.

This chapter will help you develop the skills you'll need to coax important information from your sources.

BUILDING TRUST

The first requirement of any successful interview is a reasonable degree of trust between reporter and source. Usually, as a reporter you will have to earn that trust. ESPN writer Wright Thompson had to earn the trust of a family in an especially sensitive situation. Here's how he did it:

> About a year ago, I wanted to do a story about a former college football player named Ernest Blackwell, who had gone on a rampage in his neighborhood, shooting a child and almost kicking another to death. He'd collapsed on a police gurney afterward and died en route to the hospital. No one could figure out what happened. Media outlet after media outlet approached the family. All got turned down.
>
> When I called, I had a line. I told them I was going to talk to the cops and was going to do a story about Ernest. The police, I told them, would give me more than enough detail about the last five minutes of Ernest's life. Then I said, "I think there's a lot more to his life than the last five minutes. I think he deserves to be remembered for how he lived and not just how he died."
>
> That did it; I was in. Have a plan. You must give someone a reason why it's better if they talk to you than if they don't.

Because Thompson earned the trust of the Blackwell family, he was able to develop the insights that allowed him to write this:

> Those who knew him wonder how Blackwell arrived on that day with so much rage in his heart, so much bad intent. Truth is, none of them could peer into the man's soul and see the hate that grew until it reached the breaking point.
>
> On Aug. 11, 2004, Blackwell could take no more.
>
> "Lord, why didn't I see the signs?" says his aunt Joyce Strong, who mostly raised Blackwell. "Why didn't I see he was reaching out for help? He must have been a ticking time bomb waiting to go off."

That's the payoff on the investment in building trust.

You probably won't have many assignments that difficult. It always helps, though, to have a plan. It also helps to have the honesty and empathy that lead strangers to be honest with you. The key to a successful interview, Thompson has learned, is simple: "Act like a human being."

PREPARING FOR THE INTERVIEW

How you prepare for the interview depends in part on what kind of story you intend to write. You may be doing a news story, a personality profile or an investigative piece. In each case, you check the newspaper library and search online databases, talk to other reporters, and, if there's enough time, read magazine articles and books.

To prepare for a news story, you pay more attention to the subject of the story than to the personality of the individual to be interviewed. To prepare for a profile, you look for personality quirks and the subject's interests, family, friends, travels and habits. To prepare for an investigative piece, you want to know both your subject matter and the person you are interviewing. In all these stories, do not overlook other reporters and editors who know something about the person or subject. Let's look at each of these three types of stories more closely.

The News Story

Usually, there isn't much time to prepare for a news story interview. You'll be lucky if you have a few minutes to dig into your news room's files on the event or the issue. With a few more minutes, you can go online to see what other reporters have written on similar topics. Those hurried searches will provide a bit of background and perhaps some context. Then you're out the door. Still, there are some important mental steps you can take while you chase the news.

First, review in your head what you've turned up in your quick background research. If you're off to meet a political candidate, a public official or a celebrity, when was she last in the news? For what? What is your audience (or your boss) most likely to want to know now? If you're headed for a crime scene or a disaster, what do you know about the neighborhood? Has anything like this happened lately? What was the outcome?

Second, plan your approach. Who will you seek out at the scene? Who's likely to be in charge? What do you know about that person and her or his attitude toward reporters? Are you alone on this assignment and expected to capture audio or video? If so, double-check your equipment. Will you be reporting live on camera? If so, double-check your appearance.

Finally, plan out your first few questions. Sometimes those are obvious. If the news is a crime or disaster, you'll want to know what happened. Is anybody hurt? What's the damage? If the story is focused on an issue or a person, you'll have some choices to make. Ideally, your

On the Job

Getting the Interview

Sophia Maines works for the combined newspaper/Web site/cable television news room in Lawrence, Kan. She describes her job:

"Whether my interview is for television or the Web or for print, I approach the interviewee with the same sense of curiosity and desire to get the full story. The colorful quotes that are good for television are good for the Web and for print as well. Whether capturing a scene for video or print, I always want to be as close to the action as possible, and I want to be on the scene of breaking news as early as possible."

She explains, "I am no longer a newspaper staff writer. My title recently changed simply to reporter. While seemingly small, the change reflects a significant shift at our media company in the way reporters capture and deliver the news. We are no longer writers, but reporters capable of utilizing a variety of media to present the news to our customers.

"Today, my toolbox no longer contains simply a pencil and pad of paper. Now, when I rush out to cover a breaking news story, I may bring an MP3 recorder, a video camera, and a point-and-shoot camera.

"When I return with all the makings of a story, my first thought no longer is about how to prepare the story for print. Typically my first objective is to prepare something for our Web site. . . . All our content is available online as soon as possible. This content rarely is text alone. Today's news often is delivered with video, audio, photography and text.

"As a reporter in a new era for journalism, I am called upon to be flexible and adept in a wide variety of media. It is a more interesting role, I believe, than staff writer."

backgrounding has gotten you past the most basic "Who are you?" and "Why are you here?" questions. So you may want to start with something like "What are you hoping to accomplish here?" or "Why do you think this issue is so important?"

From there, follow your instinct and your training to locate the story.

The Profile

A reporter who decided to write a profile of Joan Gilbert, a local freelance writer, prepared differently. Because the reporter had used the writer as a source in an earlier story, she knew something about her. But she needed to know more. So she looked in *Contemporary Authors* and found biographical information. She also asked Gilbert to send her copies of some of the articles she had written. Before the reporter went to see the writer, she read several of the articles. She also interviewed the editor at one of the magazines that bought the writer's material.

The reporter was prepared. Or so she thought. She had to pass one more test. The freelance writer was an animal lover, and when the reporter arrived, she first had to make friends with a handful of dogs. Fortunately, she loved dogs. That immediately established rapport with the freelancer. The resulting story was full of lively detail:

> Joan Gilbert stretches lazily to soft sunbeams and chirping birds. She dresses casually in blue denim shorts and a plaid, short-sleeved blouse. She and her favorite work companions, five playful dogs, file out the door of her little white house to begin their day with a lazy walk in the surrounding woods. When she returns, she'll contentedly sit down at her typewriter. Such is work.
>
> Joan Gilbert is a freelance writer.

Walt Harrington specialized in in-depth profiles when he worked for *The Washington Post Magazine*. In his book, he talked about the time they take:

> Each took between one and three months to complete. All included many hours of conversation with the subjects. Most include days of tagging along as they did whatever they usually did. . . . With actress Kelly McGillis, I spent a hot August month traipsing to daily rehearsals and then back to Kelly's apartment, where she would analyze her day on stage. Most of these profiles also included numerous interviews with the subjects' family, friends, and enemies. For the George Bush and Carl Bernstein profiles, I did about eighty interviews each. Always there are also newspaper and magazine clippings, books, and documents to read.

Few journalists are afforded the luxury of three months to work on a profile, but whether you do eight or 80 interviews, the lessons are still the same: Be prepared. Be there.

The Investigative Piece

The casual atmosphere of the Joan Gilbert and Kelly McGillis interviews is not always possible for the investigative reporter. Here, the adversarial relationship determines both the preparation required and the atmosphere of the interview itself. An investigative reporter is like an attorney in a courtroom. Wise attorneys know what the answers to their questions will be. So do investigative reporters. Preparation is essential.

Gathering Information

In the early stages of the investigation, you conduct some fishing-expedition interviews: Because you don't know how much the source knows, you cast around. Start with people on the fringes. Gather as much as you can from them. Study the records. Only after you have most of the evidence do you confront your central character. You start with a large circle and gradually draw it smaller.

Requesting an Interview

Getting the interview is sometimes as big a challenge as the interview itself. Sources who believe you are working on a story that will be critical of them or their friends often try to avoid you. Steve Weinberg, author of an unauthorized biography of industrialist Armand Hammer, had to overcome the suspicion of many former Hammer associates. Their former boss had told all of them not to talk to Weinberg. Instead of calling, Weinberg approached them by mail.

"I sent letters, examples of my previous work, explained what I wanted to cover and why I was doing it without Hammer's blessing," Weinberg says.

He recommends that you use a letter or an e-mail to share some of what you know about the story that might surprise or impress the source. For instance, a remark such as "And last week, when I was checking all the land records . . . " indicates the depth of your research.

In his letter to former Hammer assistants, Weinberg talked about how Hammer was one of the most important people in the history of business. The letter opened doors to seven of Hammer's former executive assistants.

Weinberg, former director of Investigative Reporters and Editors, also offered to show the sources relevant portions of his manuscript as an accuracy check. He made it clear in writing that he would maintain control of the content.

Requesting an interview in writing can allow you to make your best case for getting it. And an offer to allow your sources to review the story assures them that you are serious about accuracy. E-mail makes both the request and the offer simpler and faster for both parties.

BROADCAST INTERVIEWS

When you're interviewing someone in front of a camera, the basic rules of interviewing for print don't change. Some of your objectives and techniques, however, do. You may find yourself interviewing a print reporter about a story he or she is working on—or you may be that print reporter. Also, the growing importance of streaming video online pushes more print journalists to use video cameras themselves for webcast versions of their stories.

The first thing to remember is that broadcast journalism is a performance. Television journalists, at least those who appear on camera, are performers. Sure, they have to report and write; but they also have to be able to convey their stories with both words and body language to people who are watching and listening—not reading. An important part of the television reporter's performance is the interview.

Interviews for print are often conducted to develop information that can be used in further reporting. Interviews on camera usually have a different goal. That goal is the sound bite, the few seconds of words with accompanying video that convey not information so much as emotion. Print is a medium of information; television is a medium of emotion. The best interviews for television are those that reveal how a situation feels to the participants or witnesses.

Al Tompkins, the Poynter Institute's group leader for broadcast and online journalism, offers what he calls "a new set of interviewing tools" intended to produce better storytelling for television. You can find these and other tools at **www.poynter.org**. Here are some that show both differences and similarities in print and television interviewing:

- *Ask objective and subjective questions.* To gather facts, ask objective questions: "When?" "Where?" "How much?" Subjective questions, however, usually produce the best sound bites: "Why?" "Tell me more." "Can you explain?"
- *Focus on one issue at a time.* Vague, complicated questions produce vague, complicated, hard-to-follow answers. Remember that readers can reread until they understand, but viewers can't rewind an interview. Help them follow the story by taking your interviewee through it one step at a time.
- *Ask open-ended questions.* For print, you often want a simple yes or no. That kind of answer stops a television interview. Open-ended questions encourage conversation, and conversation makes a good interview.
- *Keep questions short.* Make the interviewee do the talking. Tompkins points out that short questions are more likely to produce focused

responses. They also keep the viewer's attention on the person being interviewed and what she or he has to say.

- *Build to the point.* The best interviews are like the best stories. They don't give away the punch line in the first few words. Soft, easy questions encourage relaxation and trust. Then move to the heart of the issue.
- *Be honest.* As true for television as for print and online, the importance of honesty is too often overlooked by rookie reporters. You do neither your source nor yourself a favor if you lead the source to expect an interview about softball when you have an indictment in mind. Tell the source ahead of time that you'll want to ask some tough questions. Say, and mean, that you want to get the whole story, to be fair. Then politely but firmly dig in.

As Tompkins notes, honesty has the added benefit of helping you defend yourself against any later accusations of malice.

TELEPHONE AND E-MAIL INTERVIEWS

In general, the best interviews are done in person, but time, distance and other limitations often force you to use the telephone instead. The same principles of preparation and trying to establish rapport apply. Taking notes can be easier, because you're at your own desk and the person on the other end of the call won't be distracted by what he or she can't see.

One common telephone technique, however, can raise questions of both legality and ethics: recording the conversation. Recording is the only way to ensure total accuracy in quotes, but not every source is eager or even willing to be recorded. Ask first. "You don't mind if I record this to make sure I'm completely accurate, do you?" If the answer is "I don't mind," go ahead. You're being both ethical and legal.

In some states, recording a phone conversation is legal as long as one party to the conversation gives consent. If yours is one of those states—and make sure you find out—you can record your calls even without the source's knowledge or approval. Such secret recording should only be done when you have good reason to expect a challenge to your work and only after you consult with your editor.

Don't do e-mail interviews unless you absolutely have to. Even then, if at all possible, establish contact with your source first in person or by phone. That's important for building trust, establishing rapport and—even more basic—making sure you're really dealing with the person you want to interview. The classic *New Yorker* cartoon explains the risk. Two dogs are talking to each other in front of a computer. One says, "On the Internet, nobody knows you're a dog." Nobody can be absolutely sure who's on the other end of an e-mail interview, either.

Sometimes you have no other choice. An e-mail interview, once you've made contact and established identity, can be useful and even surprisingly revealing. Some people will say things at a keyboard they wouldn't say face to face. Some get carried away by the power of their own prose. Some, of course, are cryptic and not forthcoming.

In any case, follow-up questions are at least as important as in face-to-face or phone interviews. Don't forget that e-mail is permanent. Don't ask anything you wouldn't want to see forwarded to others. Do make your questions clear and grammatically correct.

A virtue of an e-mail interview, of course, is that the answers are equally permanent. They can't be taken back or denied later. And it's hard to misquote an e-mail answer.

Approach e-mail interviews with caution, and avoid them when you can; but they're better than no interview at all.

SETTING UP THE INTERVIEW

Something as trifling as your appearance may determine whether you have a successful interview. You would hardly wear cutoff shorts into a university president's suite, and you wouldn't wear a three-piece suit to talk to underground revolutionaries. Although it is your right to style your hair however you wish and to wear whatever clothes you want, it is the source's prerogative to refuse to talk to you.

The award-winning writer Rick Bragg told the editors of *Best Newspaper Writing* that his choice of clothing was important in establishing rapport with a man whose mother had died of injuries suffered 17 years earlier. Police were investigating the death as a homicide. "I think he (the son) was more than just a little put off with how brusque some of the other reporters had been," Bragg said, "and I showed up in a pair of jeans and a T-shirt because I knew where I was going, and I didn't see much point in hiding behind a Brooks Brothers suit."

Bragg chose to fit in with the environment. That environment, too, is important. You've already heard Harrington talk about spending hours with actress Kelly McGillis at work and at her apartment. Most interviews are conducted in the source's office. However, especially if the story is a profile or a feature, it usually is better to get the source away from his or her work. If you are doing a story about a rabbi's hobby of collecting butterflies, seek a setting appropriate to the topic. Suggest meeting where the rabbi keeps his collection.

In some interviews, it is to your advantage to get the source on neutral territory. If you have some questions for the university provost or a public official, suggest meeting in a coffee shop at a quiet time. A person feels more powerful in his or her official surroundings.

It is important, too, to let the source know how much time you need and whether you expect to return for further information. And if you don't already know how the source might react to a digital recorder, ask when you are making the appointment.

This reporter dresses to fit in with the marchers he is interviewing; he gains their confidence by being friendly and attentive.

PREPARING QUESTIONS

You have now done the appropriate homework. You have made an appointment and told the source how much time you need. You are properly attired. Before you leave for the interview, write down a list of questions you want to ask. The best way to encourage a spontaneous conversation is to have your questions prepared. Barbara Walters once told a reporter that she writes as many as 500 questions on index cards and then selects the best ones for use during the interview.

Having questions prepared relieves you of the need to be mentally searching for the next question as the source is answering the last one. If you are trying to think of the next question, you will not be paying close attention to what is being said, and you might miss the most important part of the interview.

Researching Questions

Preparing the questions for an interview is hard work, even for veterans. If you are writing for your campus newspaper, Web site or television station, seek suggestions from other staff members. You will find ideas in previous stories and your newspaper's or station's electronic database. If you anticipate a troublesome interview with the chancellor, you might want to seek advice from faculty members, too. What questions would they ask if they were you? Often, they have more background knowledge, or they might have heard some of the faculty talk around campus. Staff members are also valuable sources of information.

Although you may ask all of your prepared questions in some interviews, in most you probably will use only some of them. Still, you will have benefited from preparing the questions in two important ways. First, even when you don't use many, the work you did thinking of the questions helped prepare you for the interview. Second, sources who see that you have a prepared list often are impressed with your seriousness.

On the basis of the information you have gathered already, you know what you want to ask. Now you must be careful about how you ask the questions.

Phrasing Questions

A young monk who asked his superior if he could smoke while he prayed was rebuked sharply. A friend advised him to rephrase the question. "Ask him if you can pray while you smoke," he said. The young monk was discovering that how questions are structured often determines the answer. Journalists face the same challenge. Reporters have missed many stories because they didn't know how to ask questions. Quantitative researchers have shown how just a slight wording change can affect the results of a survey. If you want to know whether citizens favor a city plan to beautify the downtown area, you can ask the question in several ways:

- Do you favor the city council's plan to beautify the downtown area?
- The city council plans to spend $3 million beautifying the downtown area. Are you in favor of this?
- Do you think the downtown area needs physical changes?
- Which of the following actions do you favor?
  — Building a traffic loop around the downtown area.
  — Prohibiting all automobile traffic in an area bounded by Providence Road, Ash Street, College Avenue and Elm Street.
  — Having all the downtown storefronts remodeled to carry out a single theme and putting in brick streets, shrubbery and benches.
  — None of the above.

How you structure the question may affect the survey results by several percentage points. Similarly, how you ask questions in an interview may affect the response.

By the phrasing of the question, many reporters signal the response they expect or the prejudices they hold. For instance, a reporter who says, "Don't you think that the city council should allocate more money to the parks and recreation department?" is not only asking a question but also influencing the source or betraying a bias. A neutral phrasing would be, "Do you think the city council should allocate more money to the parks and recreation department?" Another common way of asking a leading question is this: "Are you going to vote against this amendment like the other legislators I've talked to?"

If you have watched journalists interviewing people live on television, you have seen many examples of badly phrased questions. Many times they are not questions at all. The interviewers make statements and then put the microphone in front of the source: "You had a great game, Bill"; "Winning the election must be a great feeling." The source is expected to say something. What, precisely, do you want to know?

Sometimes a reporter unwittingly blocks a response by the phrasing of the question. A reporter who was investigating possible job discrimination against women conducted several interviews before she told her city editor she didn't think the women with whom she talked were being frank with her. "When I ask them if they have ever been discriminated against, they always tell me no. But three times now during the course of the interviews, they have said things that indicate they have been. How do I get them to tell me about it?" she asks.

"Perhaps it's the way you are asking the question," the city editor replied. "When you ask someone whether they have ever been discriminated against, you are forcing them to answer yes or no. Don't be so blunt. Ask them if others with the same qualifications at work have advanced faster than they have. Ask if they are paid the same amount as men for the same work. Ask them what they think they would be doing today if they were male. Ask them if they know of any qualified women who were denied jobs."

The city editor was giving the reporter examples of both closed- and open-ended questions. Each has its specific strengths.

Open-Ended Questions

Open-ended questions allow the respondent some flexibility. Women may not respond frankly when asked whether they have ever been discriminated against. The question calls for a yes-no response. But an open-ended question such as "What would you be doing today if you were a man?" is not as personal. It does not sound as threatening to the respondent. In response to an open-ended question, the source often reveals more than he or she realizes or intends to.

A sportswriter who was interviewing a pro scout at a college football game wanted to know whom the scout was there to see. When the scout declined diplomatically to be specific, the reporter tried another approach. He asked a series of questions:

- "What kind of qualities does a pro scout look for in an athlete?"
- "Do you think any of the players here today have those talents?"
- "Who would you put into that category?"

The reporter worked from the general to the specific until he had the information he wanted. Open-ended questions are less direct and less threatening than questions calling for yes-no or other specific responses. They are more exploratory and more flexible. However, if you want to know a person's biographical data, don't ask "Can you tell me about yourself?" Of course he or she can. Ask what you specifically want to know: "Where did you grow up and go to school?" "When did you get married?" "How did you start your career?"

Closed-Ended Questions

Eventually the reporter needs to close in on a subject, to pin down details, to get the respondent to be specific. **Closed-ended questions** are designed to elicit specific responses.

Instead of asking the mayor, "What did you think of the conference in Washington, D.C.?" you ask, "What did you learn in the session 'Funds You May Not Know Are Available'?" Instead of asking a previous employee to appraise the chancellor-designate's managerial abilities, you ask, "How well does she listen to the people who work for her?" "Do the people who work for her have specific job duties?" "Does she explain her decisions?"

A vague question invites a vague answer. By asking a specific question, you are more likely to get a specific answer. You are also communicating to your source that you have done your homework and that you are looking for precise details.

Knowing exactly when to ask a closed-ended question or when to be less specific is not something you can plan ahead of time. The type of information you are seeking and the chemistry between the interviewer and the source are the determining factors. You must make on-the-spot decisions. The important thing is to keep rephrasing the question until the source answers it adequately. Gary Smith wrote in *Intimate Journalism*, "A lot of my reporting comes from asking a question three different ways. Sometimes the third go at it is what produces

"I try never to go to an interview as a hostile antagonist. I am merely a reporter asking questions, with no ax to grind. I am a person with a family, a home, an unbalanced checkbook, a weight problem and a car that goes 'thonka-thonka-thonka' when it's cold. Unless my interview subject is Ivana Trump or Meryl Streep or Richard Nixon, my life is probably, at least in one way or two ways, similar to the person of whom I'm asking the questions."

—Tad Bartimus, former AP regional reporter

the nugget, but even if the answers aren't wonderful or the quotes usable, they can still confirm or correct my impressions."

Here are a few questions that illustrate the differences between open- and closed-ended questions.

Closed-Ended Questions	Open-Ended Questions
Do you like the proposal?	What are the strengths of the proposal? What are its weaknesses?
Did you have trouble coping when your child was in the car accident?	How did you cope after your child was in the car accident? Why did you attend counseling sessions?
Did you keep your promise to diet today?	What did you eat today?
Did you give the theater teacher permission to stage that play?	What did you tell the theater teacher when she asked if her group could perform the play?
Do you use iChat in your work?	How do you use iChat in your work?

INTERVIEW APPROACHES

For most news stories and personality profiles, you benefit if your subject is at ease. Often that can be accomplished by starting off with small talk. Ask about a trophy, the plants or an engraved pen. Bring up something humorous you found during your research. Ask about something you know the source will want to talk about. If you think the subject might be skeptical about your knowledge of the field, open with a question that demonstrates your knowledge.

Reporters who can show sources what they have in common usually have success getting information. Remember Wright Thompson's advice: "Act like a human being." Here's how he does that: "I've cried on the phone before. I've yelled at someone. I've told incredibly personal details about myself, because it's not fair for me to expect something I'm not willing to give."

When he was assigned to write about a high school athlete who had been killed in a car wreck, he recalls, "I didn't try to be impartial. A young girl dying was an awful thing, and I didn't try to be a noninvolved outsider. That would have made reporting the story impossible. So I let myself feel the same things as the others around me. I wept at her funeral. I helped her friends make a mix tape of her favorite songs. I was intimately involved, and I think that made me uniquely qualified to channel their pain."

CNN talk-show host Larry King interviews journalist Bob Woodward of *The Washington Post.*

Rapport also depends on where you conduct the interview. Many people, especially those unaccustomed to being interviewed, feel more comfortable in their workplace. Go to them. Talk to the businessperson in the office, to the athlete in the locker room, to the conductor in the concert hall. In some cases, though, you may get a better interview elsewhere if the source cannot relax at the workplace or is frequently interrupted. Reporters have talked to politicians during car rides between campaign appearances. They've gone sailing with businesspeople and hunting with athletes. One student reporter doing a feature on a police chief spent a weekend with the chief, who was painting his home. To do a profile, which requires more than one interview, vary the location. New surroundings can make a difference.

Scott Kraft of the Associated Press once did a story on a couple who for more than two years drove the streets of Los Angeles looking for the man who had raped their 12-year-old daughter. The search was successful.

"When I knocked on their door in May, I wanted them to know that I would be careful and honest, and I wanted them to tell me everything, even though it would probably be difficult," he wrote in *Editor & Publisher.*

Kraft conducted interviews in three locations. The first was in the family's living room. The second was in a car as they revisited the places where the family had searched. The third was by phone. Kraft said the mother talked more candidly on the phone after her children had gone to school.

There are times when you would rather have the source edgy, nervous or even scared. When you are doing an investigation, you may want the key characters to feel uneasy. You may pretend you know more than you actually do. You want them to know that the material you have is substantive and serious. Seymour Hersh, a Pulitzer Prize–winning investigative reporter, uses this tactic. *Time* magazine once quoted a government official commenting on Hersh: "He wheedles, cajoles, pleads, threatens, asks a leading question, uses little tidbits as if he knew the whole story. When he finishes you feel like a wet rag."

In some cases, however, it is better even in an investigation to take a low-key approach. Let the source relax. Talk around the subject, but gradually bring the discussion to the key issues. The surprise element may work to your advantage.

So may the sympathetic approach. When the source is speaking, you may nod or punctuate the source's responses with comments such as "That's interesting." Sources who think you are sympathetic are more likely to volunteer information. Researchers have found, for instance, that a simple "mm-hmmm" affects the length of the answer interviewers get.

Where you sit in relation to the person you are interviewing can be important. Unless you deliberately are trying to make interviewees feel uncomfortable, do not sit directly in front of them. Permit your sources to establish eye contact if and when they wish.

Some people are even more disturbed by the way a reporter takes notes. A digital recorder ensures accuracy of quotes, but it makes many speakers self-conscious or nervous. If you have permission to use a recording device, place it in an inconspicuous spot and ignore it except to make sure it is working properly. Taking notes, whether by pad and pen or electronically, may interfere with your ability to digest what is being said. But not taking any notes at all is risky. Only a few reporters can leave an interview and accurately write down what was said. Certainly no one can do it and reproduce direct quotes verbatim. You should learn shorthand or develop a note-taking system of your own.

ENSURING ACCURACY

Accuracy is a major problem in all interviews. Both the question and the answer may be ambiguous. You may not understand what is said. You may record it incorrectly. You may not know the context of the remarks. Your biases may interfere with the message.

Taking Notes

Knowing the background of your sources, having a comfortable relationship with them and keeping good notes are important elements of accuracy. All those were missing when a journalism student, two weeks into an internship at a major daily, interviewed the public information officer for a sheriff's department about criminal activity in and around a shelter for battered women. The reporter had never met the source, whom she interviewed by phone. She took notes on her interview with the deputy and others in whatever notebook happened to be nearby. She didn't record the time, date or even the source. There were no notes showing context, just fragments of quotes, scrawled in nearly illegible handwriting.

After the story was published, the developer of the shelter sued. Questioned by attorneys, the deputy swore that the reporter misunderstood him and used some of his comments out of context. In several cases, he contended, she completed her fragmentary notes by putting her own words in his mouth. He testified that most reporters come to see him to get acquainted. Many call back to check his quotes on sensitive or complex stories. She did neither.

When the court ordered the reporter to produce and explain her notes, she had trouble reconstructing them. She had to admit on several occasions that she wasn't sure what the fragments meant.

The accuracy of your story is only as good as your notes. David Finkel, whose story on a family's TV-watching habits became a Pulitzer Prize finalist, took extra steps to be certain his material was accurate. Observing what his subject was watching, he obtained transcripts of the shows so he could quote accurately from them. If he knew transcripts would not be available, he set his recorder near the television to record the program.

Here are some helpful guidelines for taking notes during an interview:

- Develop a consistent shorthand. For example, always use "w/" to mean "with."
- Use a spiral-bound notebook with pages that are easy to turn and that lie flat.
- Make sure to have several working pens or sharpened pencils.
- Leave a wide margin so that you can annotate notes later on.
- Look up frequently as you write.
- Ask for the spellings of names.
- Always take notes, even if you are using a digital recorder.

Some possibilities for making errors or introducing bias are unavoidable, but others are not. To ensure the most accurate and complete reporting possible, you should use all the techniques available to

> *"Today one has the impression that the interviewer is not listening to what you say, nor does he think it important, because he believes that the tape recorder hears everything. But he's wrong; it doesn't hear the beating of the heart, which is the most important part of the interview."*
>
> — *Gabriel García Márquez,*
> *Colombian writer*
> *and Nobel laureate*

obtain a good interview, including observing, understanding what you hear, asking follow-up questions and pacing the interview.

Observing

Wright Thompson says, "It's all about the scenes. Don't just ask questions. Be an observer." Like any good writer, he offers an example to show what he means:

> I was doing a story about former Heisman Trophy winner Eric Crouch. It was almost exactly one year since he'd won the trophy, and that year had been tough for him. He'd quit pro football and had been forced to ask some hard questions about his life. As we sat in an Omaha bar, a clip of him running the football came on the television. One of the women at the table said, "You're on TV, Eric." I remember he looked up at the screen and spat, "That's not me, man." Then he took a shot of liquor. No amount of interviewing could breathe life into the idea that he had changed like that scene.

Understanding What You Hear

Understanding what you see and hear is crucial to the news-gathering process. Don't be embarrassed to admit you haven't grasped something. It is better to admit to one person that you don't understand than to advertise your ignorance in newsprint or on the Internet.

Asking Follow-Up Questions

If you understand what the source is saying, you can ask meaningful follow-up questions. There is nothing worse than briefing your city editor or executive producer on the interview and having him or her ask you, "Well, did you ask . . . ?" Having to say no is embarrassing.

Even if you go into an interview armed with a list of questions, the most important probably will be the ones you ask in response to an answer. A reporter who was doing a story on bidding procedures was interviewing the mayor. The reporter asked how bid specifications were written. In the course of his reply, the mayor mentioned that the president of a construction firm had assured him the last bid specifications were adequate. The alert reporter picked up on the statement:

> "When did you talk to him?"
> "About three weeks ago," the mayor said.
> "That's before the specifications were published, wasn't it?"
> "Yes, we asked him to look them over for us."
> "Did he find anything wrong with the way they were written?"
> "Oh, he changed a few minor things. Nothing important."
> "Did officials of any other construction firms see the bid specifications before they were advertised?"
> "No, he was the only one."

Gradually, on the basis of one offhand comment by the mayor, the reporter was able to piece together a solid story on the questionable relationship between the city and the construction firm.

Pacing the Interview

Although most questions are designed to get information, some are asked as a delaying tactic. A reporter who is taking notes may fall behind. Emily Yoffe, a senior editor of *Texas Monthly*, will say, "Hold on a second—let me get that" or "Say that again." Other questions are intended to encourage a longer response. "Go on with that" or "Tell me more about that" encourages the speaker to add more detail.

Another technique for making the source talk on is not a question at all; it is a pause. You are signaling the source that you expect more. But the lack of a response from you is much more ambiguous than "Tell me more about that." It may indicate that you were skeptical of what was just said, that you didn't understand, that the answer was inadequate or several other possibilities. The source will be forced to react. The only problem with this, says AP special correspondent Saul Pett, "is that it invites the dull to be dull at greater length."

Reporters should do research after an interview to ascertain specific figures when a source provides an estimate. For example, if a shop owner says he runs one of 20 pizza parlors in town, check with the city business-license office to get the exact number.

ENDING THE INTERVIEW

Many dull interviews become interesting after they end. There are two things you should always do when you finish your questions: Check key facts, figures and quotes with the interviewee and then put away your pen but keep your ears open. You are not breaching any ethical rule if you continue to ask questions after you have put away your pen or turned off the digital recorder. That's when some sources loosen up.

Before you leave, ask if there's anything you forgot to ask. Put the burden on the source. You are also doing your subject a favor by giving the person a chance to contribute to the direction of the interview. You may have missed some important signals during the conversation, and now the source can be more explicit about what he or she wanted to say. Sometimes this technique leads to entirely new subjects.

Quickly review your notes and check facts, especially dates, numbers, quotes, spellings and titles. Besides helping you get it right, this shows the source you are careful. If necessary, arrange a time when you can call to check other parts of the story or clear up questions you may have as you are writing. Researchers have found that more than half of direct quotations are inaccurate, even when the interview is recorded. That reflects a sloppiness that is unacceptable. Make sure you are the exception.

Interviewing Checklist

I. Before the interview
   A. Know the topic
      1. Seek specific information
      2. Research the topic
      3. List the questions
   B. Know the person
      1. Know salient biographical information
      2. Know the person's expertise regarding the topic
   C. Set up the interview
      1. Set the time
         a. At the interviewee's convenience—but suggest a time
         b. Length of time needed
         c. Possible return visits
      2. Set the place
         a. Interviewee's turf, or
         b. Neutral turf
   D. Discuss arrangements
      1. Will you bring a recording device?
      2. Will you bring a photographer?
      3. Will you let the interviewee check the accuracy of quotes?
II. During the interview
   A. When you arrive
      1. Control the seating arrangement
      2. Place the digital recorder at an optimum spot
      3. Warm up the interviewee briefly with small talk
      4. Set the ground rules
         a. Put everything on the record
         b. Make everything attributable
   B. The interview itself
      1. Use good interviewing techniques
         a. Ask open-ended questions
         b. Allow the person to think and to speak; pause
         c. Don't be threatening in voice or manner
         d. Control the flow but be flexible
      2. Take good notes
         a. Be unobtrusive
         b. Be thorough
      3. Use the digital recorder
         a. Assume it's not working
         b. Note digital counter at important parts
   C. Before you leave
      1. Ask if there's anything else the interviewee wants to say
      2. Check the facts—spellings, dates, statistics, quotes
      3. Set a time for rechecking facts, quotes
      4. Discuss when and where the interview might appear
      5. Ask if the interviewee wants a copy after publication or broadcast
III. After the interview
   A. Organize your notes—immediately
   B. Craft a proper lead
   C. Write a coherent story
   D. Check accuracy with the interviewee

As a matter of courtesy, tell the source when the story might appear. You may even offer to send along a copy of the article or broadcast when it's completed.

Remember that although the interview may be over, your relationship with the source is not. When you have the story written, call the source and confirm the information. Better to discover your inaccuracies before they are published than after.

WHAT TO QUOTE DIRECTLY

Crisp, succinct, meaningful quotes spice up any story. But you can overdo a good thing. You need direct quotes in your stories, but you also need to develop skill in recognizing what is worth quoting.

Unique Material

When you can say, "Ah, I never heard that before," you can be quite sure your readers also would like to know exactly what the speaker said. Instead of quoting someone at length, look for the kernel. Sometimes it is something surprising, something neither you nor your readers would expect that person to say. For example, when Pat Williams, then general manager of the Orlando Magic, spoke about the team's bad record, he said: "We can't win at home. We can't win on the road. As general manager, I just can't figure out where else to play." When singer Dolly Parton was asked how she felt about dumb-blonde jokes, she replied: "I'm not offended at all because I know I'm not a dumb blonde. I also know I'm not a blonde." Striking statements like these should be quoted, but there is no reason to place simple, factual material inside quotation marks.

A direct quotation should say something significant. Also, a direct quotation should not simply repeat what has been said indirectly. It should move the story forward. Here's a passage from a *USA Today* story about a proposed law that would bar health-insurance companies, employers and managed-care plans from discriminating against people because of their genetic makeup:

> Fear of insurance discrimination based on the results of genetic tests has been on the rise for years. "It stops many people cold from getting tested," says Karen Clarke, a genetic counselor at Johns Hopkins University in Baltimore.

The quotation is useful, it is informative, and it moves the story forward.

Sometimes spoken material is unique not because of individual remarks that are surprising or new, but because of extended dialogue

---

Use direct quotes when

- Someone says something unique.
- Someone says something memorable.
- Someone important says something important.

that can tell the story more effectively than writers can in their own words. The writer of the following story made excellent use of dialogue:

> Lou Provancha pushed his wire-rimmed glasses up on his nose and leaned toward the man in the wheelchair.
>
> "What is today, Jake?" he asked.
>
> Jake twisted slightly and stared at the floor.
>
> "Jake," Provancha said, "Jake, look up here."
>
> A long silence filled the tiny, cluttered room on the sixth floor of the University Medical Center.
>
> Provancha, a licensed practical nurse at the hospital, glanced at the reporter. "Jake was in a coma a week ago," he explained. "He couldn't talk."
>
> Provancha pointed to a wooden board propped up on the table beside him.
>
> "Jake, what is today? What does it say here? What is this word? I've got my finger pointed right at it."
>
> Jake squinted at the word. With a sudden effort, like a man heaving a bag of cement mix onto a truck bed, he said, "Tuesday."
>
> Provancha grinned. It was a small victory for them both.

The Memorable Expression

When looking for quotable expressions, be on the lookout for the clever, the colorful, the colloquial. For example, an elderly man talking about his organic garden said, "It's hard to tell people to watch what they eat. You eat health, you know."

A professor lecturing on graphic design said, "When you think it looks like a mistake, it is." The same professor once was explaining that elements in a design should not call attention to themselves: "You don't walk up to a beautiful painting in someone's home and say, 'That's a beautiful frame.'"

A computer trainer said to a reporter: "Teaching kids computers is like leading ducks to water. But teaching adults computers is like trying to teach chickens to swim."

Sometimes something said uniquely is a colloquialism. Colloquialisms can add color and life to your copy. For example, a person from Louisiana may say: "I was just fixing to leave when the phone rang." A person from certain parts of Pennsylvania "makes the light out" when turning off the lights. And people in and around Fort Wayne, Ind., "redd up" the dishes after a meal, meaning that they wash them and put them where they belong.

Important Quotes by Important People

If citizen Joe Smith says, "Something must be done about this teachers' strike," you may or may not consider it worth quoting. But if the mayor says, "Something must be done about this teachers' strike," many papers

---

He Said, She Said:
Punctuating Direct Quotations

"Always put the comma inside quotation marks," she said. Then she added, "The same goes for the period."

"Does the same rule apply for the question mark?" he asked.

"Only if the entire statement is a question," she replied, "and never add a comma after a question mark. Also, be sure to lowercase the first word of a continuing quote that follows an attribution and a comma.

"However, you must capitalize the first word of a new sentence after an attribution," she continued. "Do not forget to open and close the sentence with quotation marks."

"Why are there no quotation marks after the word 'comma' at the end of the third paragraph?" he asked.

"Because the same person is speaking at the beginning of the next paragraph," she said. "Notice that the new paragraph does open with quotation marks. Note, too, that a quote inside of a quotation needs a single quotation mark, as around the word 'comma' above."

---

would print the quote. Generally reporters quote public officials or known personalities in their news stories (though not everything the famous say is worth quoting). Remember, prominence is an important property of news.

Quoting sources that readers are likely to know lends authority, credibility and interest to your story. Presumably, a meteorologist knows something about the weather, a doctor about health, a chemistry professor about chemicals. However, it is unlikely that a television star is an expert on cameras, even if he or she makes commercials about cameras.

QUOTING ACCURATELY

The first obligation of any reporter is to be accurate. Before there can be any discussion of whether or how to use direct quotations, you must learn to get the exact words of the source.

It's not easy.

Scribbled notes from interviews, press conferences and meetings are often difficult to decipher and interpret. A study by Adrienne Leher, a professor of linguistics at the University of Arizona, found that only 13 of 98 quotations taken from Arizona newspapers proved to be verbatim when compared to recordings. Only twice, however, were the nonverbatim quotes considered "incompatible with what was intended."

The first priority of any reporter is accuracy.

Verification

When someone important says something important but perhaps false, just putting the material in quotes does not relieve you of responsibility for the inaccuracies. Citizens, officials and candidates for office often say things that may be partially true or altogether untrue and perhaps even libelous. Quotations, like any other information you gather, need verification.

During Sen. Joseph McCarthy's investigations into communism and espionage in the 1950s, many newspapers, in the interest of strict objectivity, day after day quoted the Wisconsin senator's charges and countercharges. Some publishers did this because they agreed with his stance and because his remarks sold newspapers. Few papers thought it was their responsibility to quote others who were pointing out the obvious errors and inconsistencies in the demagogue's remarks. Today, however, in the interest of balance, fairness and objectivity, many media sources leave out, correct or point out the errors in some quotations. This may be done in the piece itself or in an accompanying story.

If candidate Billy Joe Harkness says that his opponent Jimbo McGown is a member of the Ku Klux Klan, you should check before you print the charge. Good reporters don't stop looking and checking just because someone gives them some information. Look for yourself. Prisoners may have an altogether different account of a riot from the one the prison officials give you. Your story will not be complete unless you talk to all sides.

"When you see yourself quoted in print and you're sorry you said it, it suddenly becomes a misquotation."

— *Dr. Laurence J. Peter,*
author of Peter's Quotations
and The Peter Principle

Correcting Grammar in Quotations

When do you, or should you, correct grammatical errors in a direct quotation appearing in print or online? Should you expect people in news conferences or during informal interviews to speak perfect English? Journalists of an earlier generation routinely corrected the garbled syntax used in news conferences by President Dwight Eisenhower. In the 21st century, changed standards and live television made President George W. Bush's adventures with the language common knowledge.

Although quotation marks mean you are capturing the exact language of a speaker, it is accepted practice in many news rooms to correct mistakes in grammar and to convey a person's remarks in complete sentences. None of us speaks regularly in perfect, grammatical sentences. But if we were writing down our remarks instead, presumably we would write in grammatically correct English.

Most papers have no written policy on correcting grammatical errors in direct quotations. Because so many variables are involved, these matters are handled on a case-by-case basis. Some argue you should sacrifice a bit of accuracy in the interest of promoting proper English. However, some would let public figures be embarrassed by quoting them using incorrect grammar.

The Associated Press Stylebook takes a purist stance:

> Never alter quotations even to correct minor grammatical errors or word usage. Casual minor tongue slips may be removed by using ellipses but even that should be done with extreme caution. If there is a question about a quote, either don't use it or ask the speaker to clarify.

The Washington Post's rules on quotes serve as an excellent guide for any beginning reporter:

> When we put a source's words inside quotation marks, those exact words should have been uttered in precisely that form. Sometimes we

will want to avoid humiliating a speaker by paraphrasing in grammatical form an ungrammatical statement, or by presenting in a form acceptable for publication a statement that includes profanities. When we do so, however, we should not use quotation marks. A paraphrase should not be treated as a quotation. At the same time, we should not deprive our readers of the statements of legitimate news sources who characteristically speak so ungrammatically, or use such profane language, that we cannot quote them verbatim. This may mean stretching our rules occasionally to publish profane language we would normally avoid. When in doubt about how to quote a source, consult an editor.

When quoting people for whom English is not their first language, special care should be taken. If such quotations make the speaker look stupid or foolish, we should consider paraphrasing them (outside of quotation marks, of course). When appropriate, a story should note that a source was struggling with English.

Correcting quotations is even more difficult for radio and television reporters. That's why they don't worry about it as much. Online and print writers and editors might remember that the quotation they use may have been heard by millions of people on radio or television. Changing the quote even slightly might make viewers and listeners question the credibility of print and online reports.

A letter in *The Washington Post* criticized the newspaper for quoting exactly a mother of 14 children who was annoyed at then Mayor Marion Barry's advice to stop having babies. The quote read: "And your job is to open up all those houses that's boarded up." The writer then accused the *Post* of regularly stringing together quotes of the president to make him appear articulate. The writer concluded: "I don't care whether the *Post* polishes quotes or not. I simply think that everyone — black or white, rich or poor, president or welfare mother — deserves equal treatment."

That's good advice.

Suggested Readings

Boynton, Robert. *The New New Journalism: Conversations with America's Best Nonfiction Writers on Their Craft*. New York: Vintage Books, 2005. For this book, Boynton interviewed such giants of the trade as Richard Ben Cramer, Leon Dash and Michael Lewis.

Forde, Kathy Roberts. *Literary Journalism on Trial: Masson v. New Yorker and the First Amendment*. Amherst: University of Massachusetts Press, 2008. This is a scholarly examination of a libel trial that tested the limits of accuracy and the meaning of "truth."

Grobel, Lawrence. *The Art of the Interview: Lessons from a Master of the Craft*. New York: Three Rivers Press, 2004. The lessons here cover all the important steps, from landing the interview to establishing rapport with hostile subjects.

Harrington, Walt. *American Profiles*. Columbia: University of Missouri Press, 1992. Fifteen excellent profiles and the author's explanation of how and why he does what he does.

Weinberg, Steve. "Thou Shalt Not Concoct Thy Quote." *Fineline* (July/August 1991): 3–4. Presents reasons for allowing sources to review quotations before publication.

Suggested Web Sites

www.ajr.org   At the Web site of the *American Journalism Review*, search for "conducting an interview" to access a variety of useful articles.

www.cjr.org   This is the site of the *Columbia Journalism Review*. Follow the same procedure as with AJR, above.

www.newslab.org   This site is an excellent source of tips on television. NewsLab works with television news rooms to find better ways of telling complex stories.

www.poynter.org   This is an extremely useful site. Go to the "Resource Center" section, which you'll find at the bottom of the home page under "About Poynter," and check out the bibliography of articles, both scholarly and professional, and books on interviewing. Print, television and online media are all included.

Exercises

1. You've just learned that Sarah Palin, the Alaska governor and 2008 Republican vice presidential candidate, is coming to speak to the local Republican club. Prepare just in case you get the chance to interview her. Go beyond Google and beware of Wikipedia. Write a background memo explaining what you want to cover in your interview and why.

2. List five open-ended questions you would ask Governor Palin in the interview you prepared for in exercise 1.

3. List five closed-ended questions you would ask Governor Palin in the interview you prepared for in exercise 1.

4. Interview a student also enrolled in this reporting class. Write a two- to three-page story. Be sure to focus on one aspect of the student's life. Ask your classmate to read the story and to mark errors of fact and perception. The instructor will read your story and the critique.

5. Using the resources suggested above and any others you can find, do a database search for articles about journalists' use of anonymous sources. Write a short report on your findings.

6. Attend a meeting, a press conference or a speech, and record it. While there, write down the quotes you would use if you were writing the story for your local news source. Then listen to the recording, and check the accuracy of the quotes. What do you learn?

4 Gathering and Verifying Information

Italian astronomer Galileo Galilei wrote in the 17th century, "All truths are easy to understand once they are discovered; the point is to discover them." Discovering the truth is also the point of journalistic reporting.

Truth is the primary defense against libel, as we will learn in Chapter 14. But it's also at the heart of credibility, a quality that readers feel is too often lacking in today's journalism. Survey after survey shows that the public views the news media as biased and inaccurate. Reporters rank alongside used-car salespeople in prestige and trustworthiness.

That's an appalling state of affairs for a craft about which Bill Kovach and Tom Rosenstiel, authors of *The Elements of Journalism*, assert, "The essence of journalism is a discipline of verification."

The problem, as Kovach and Rosenstiel note, is that getting it right isn't easy. It's been that way at least since the fifth century B.C., when Thucydides wrote in the introduction to his account of the Peloponnesian War:

> With regard to my factual reporting of events . . . I have made it a principle not to write down the first story that came my way, and not even to be guided by my own general impressions; either I was present myself at the events which I have described or else heard of them from eye witnesses whose reports I have checked with as much thoroughness as possible. Not that even so the truth was easy to discover: different eye witnesses gave different accounts of the same events, speaking out of partiality for one side or the other, or else from imperfect memories.

Any reporter who has ever covered a breaking news event like a war, a fire, an accident or a disaster has encountered the same situation — conflicting accounts of what happened and a near inability to sort it all out. But sort it out we must. That's the job of journalists, and gathering facts is at the heart of what journalists do.

In this chapter, we'll explore the discipline of getting information — and getting it right.

In this chapter you will learn:
1. How to use computerized sources of information to check facts.
2. Where to find information on the Web.
3. How to evaluate information found on the Web.
4. How to use traditional sources of information to check facts.

ACCURATE INFORMATION: THE BASIS OF A GOOD STORY

Ask any editor whether a reporter can be a good writer without being good at gathering information, and you're likely to hear a resounding "No!"

The Discipline of Multiple Sources

Sure, good writing is important, as we'll explore in later chapters, but the quality of writing depends in large part on good fact gathering, which we call good reporting. It's almost impossible to write a great story without first doing a great job of reporting. Gathering that information requires skilled interviewing, as we discussed in Chapter 3. It also requires knowing how to use the many other sources of information readily available. Make no mistake about it: There are hundreds of places to find information.

Good reporters know that the worst kind of news story is one with a single source. Rarely is such a story worth publishing. Even a personality profile should be based on more than just an interview with the source. To get a fuller perspective, it's important to talk with individuals who know the subject. Gathering information from multiple sources is one of the keys to good writing and good communication. It's also the best way to ensure accuracy by verifying information. When more and more sources are checked and cross-checked, the chances of a story being accurate greatly improve.

Imagine how many sources Steve Fainaru of *The Washington Post* checked in his Pulitzer Prize–winning, 10-part series on how private security contractors in Iraq operate outside many of the laws and rules governing the presence of U.S. forces there. Here's an excerpt:

By Steve Fainaru
Washington Post Foreign Service

BAGHDAD—The convoy was ambushed in broad daylight last Nov. 16, dozens of armed men swarming over 37 tractor-trailers stretching for more than a mile on southern Iraq's main highway. The attackers seized four Americans and an Austrian employed by Crescent Security Group, a small private security firm. Then they fled.

None of the hostages has been found, eight months after one of the largest and most brazen kidnappings of Americans since the March 2003 invasion.

Crescent is shuttered, like dozens of other companies that have come and gone in Iraq's booming market for private security services. The firm leaves behind a trail of broken lives and a record of alleged misconduct. In March, the U.S. military barred Crescent from U.S. bases after it was found with weapons pro-hibited for private security companies, including rocket launchers and grenades, according to documents and interviews with former Crescent employees and U.S. officials.

An investigation by *The Washington Post* found that Crescent violated U.S. military regulations while being paid millions of dollars to support the U.S.-led mission in Iraq. The company routinely sacrificed safety to cut costs. On the day of the kidnappings, just seven Crescent guards protected the immense convoy as it drove through southern Iraq, a force that security experts described as inadequate to fend off a major attack.

Former senior managers with Crescent denied any wrongdoing and said the guards who were seized had been well equipped and simply failed to thwart the kidnappers.

"We pretty much catered to them. We spoiled them," said Scott Schneider, the company's former director of security. "You know, basically the operators screwed up," he added. "I mean, you hate to speak ill of people, but the way the situation transpired, they just made mistake after mistake" as the convoy came under attack.

Schneider oversaw Crescent's security operations for more than two years, despite having pleaded guilty, according to court records, to misdemeanor charges of breaking and entering and domestic violence in Michigan in the mid-1990s. Under U.S. law, it is a felony for domestic violence offenders to carry firearms, a prohibition that was adopted by the Defense Department for military and civilian personnel.

Crescent's managing partner, Franco Picco, said he fired Schneider, who earned $10,000 a month, after becoming aware of his criminal background shortly after the kidnappings.

Based in Kuwait City, about an hour from Iraq's southern border, Crescent was formed in 2003, part of a security industry that mushroomed overnight in Iraq in response to troop shortages and mounting insurgent attacks. By this year, the Private Security Company Association of Iraq, a trade group based in Baghdad's Green Zone, listed 177 active foreign and Iraqi security companies. The Pentagon has said that some 20,000 security contractors support the U.S.-led coalition, although some estimates are considerably higher.

The industry is largely unregulated by the U.S. and Iraqi governments, leaving companies to establish their own standards for operating on the battlefield.

This article is based on two eyewitness accounts of the ambush, company documents and interviews with former Crescent employees, including the four missing Americans. Two weeks before they were taken, the men expressed growing concern for their personal safety to a reporter traveling with them in Iraq.

"We're not the badasses we used to think we were," said one of them, Paul Reuben, now 40, a former Marine from Buffalo, Minn., sitting in his Kuwait City dormitory on the eve of a convoy mission. "I realize I'm vulnerable."

The guards have not been seen since the Jan. 3 airing of a video made by their captors. Picco said he is convinced that the men are still alive. He said he has spent more than $300,000 seeking information about their fate and blamed U.S. and British authorities for failing to follow up leads that he believes would have led to their release.

"Alive or dead, I will bring them back," Picco said during an interview this month in Kuwait City, where he continues to run logistics and catering businesses. "Whether it takes me 10 years or a month. That's just the moral thing to do. . . . These guys are part of me."

To successfully produce a series of this magnitude, Fainaru had to talk with hundreds of sources and find whatever documents were available. It was a daunting task that took the better part of a year. But the meticulous way in which he documented what occurred and reconstructed events was indeed worthy of a Pulitzer. Clearly, multiple sources helped Fainaru convince himself and his editors that he had the story right.

The Discipline of Verification

Journalists, when operating as they should, follow much the same investigative system used by scientists. They develop a hypothesis and then seek facts to support or reject it. In the 20th century, journalists developed the concept of objectivity—an elusive idea that was often interpreted the wrong way.

As Philip Meyer of the University of North Carolina suggests to Kovach and Rosenstiel in *The Elements of Journalism*, "I think [the] connection between journalism and science ought to emphasize objectivity of method. That's what scientific method is—our humanity, our subjective impulses . . . directed toward deciding what to investigate by objective means."

What objectivity isn't, Kovach and Rosenstiel argue, is blind loyalty to the concepts of fairness and balance. Fairness, they argue, can be misunderstood if it is seen as a goal unto itself. Fairness should mean that a journalist is fair to the facts and to the public's understanding of them. It should not mean, "Am I being fair to my sources, so that none of them will be unhappy?" or "Does my story seem fair?" Those are subjective judgments that lead the journalist away from the task of independent verification.

Similarly, balance should not mean that it's necessary to get an equal number of scientists speaking on each side of the global-warming debate if an overwhelming number of scientists in fact believe that global warming is a reality.

Kovach and Rosenstiel argue that sharpening the meaning of verification and resisting the temptation to simplify it are essential to improving the credibility of what journalists write.

So, too, is the journalistic process of layered editing. At a good newspaper or magazine, once the reporter writes a story, it is subject to extensive review by several editors. Each may find facts to correct or language to clarify in the quest for a story that is as compelling—and accurate—as possible. Thus, as a story flows through the editorial process, the goal is to make it as nearly perfect as possible.

Editors talk about the need to look at a story on both the micro and macro levels. Micro editing is the process of paying attention to detail:

- Are the facts correct?
- Are the names spelled correctly?
- Is the grammar sound?

Macro editing, on the other hand, looks at the big picture:

- Will readers understand this?
- Are there unanswered questions or inconsistencies in the story?
- Does this agree with what I know about previous stories on the subject?

All of this, and much more, goes into the editorial process of verification. In the end, the idea is to get it right.

As they strive to get it right, journalists use all types of sources: interviews, source documents and a variety of other sources. Those range from the obvious, such as a Google search, to online sites and computer databases and to traditional sources such as printed almanacs and encyclopedias. In this chapter, we explore the many possible sources of information. Good reporters make frequent use of them all.

COMPUTERIZED SOURCES OF INFORMATION

Reporters and editors today have a wealth of information available at their fingertips. In addition to making raw data available, computers help reporters organize and analyze information.

From the news library in your local office to national databases of published newspaper, magazine and broadcast stories, the amount of online information is staggering. Primary sources of computerized information include:

- *The news library, or morgue,* maintained by your own publication or broadcast station.
- *Search engines* (Google, Yahoo, Live Search).
- *News sites, portals and content aggregators* (USATODAY.com, NYTimes .com, MSNBC.com, CNN.com, Yahoo News, Google News).
- *Other sites on the World Wide Web.* Millions of organizations maintain Web sites with useful information.
- *Commercial database services* (Dialog, LexisNexis and others).
- *Government databases* (city, county, state and federal).
- *Special-interest databases* (those created by organizations with a cause).
- *CD-ROMs and DVDs.* Not all are entertainment-oriented. Some contain useful factual information.
- *Self-constructed databases and spreadsheets.*

Ten sources of story ideas

- Other people.
- Other publications.
- News releases.
- A social services directory.
- Government reports.
- Stories in your own newspaper.
- Advertisements.
- Wire copy.
- Local news briefs.
- You.

Your News Library: The Place to Start

Computer databases are a marvel that good reporters and editors have learned to cherish. Before they were available, doing research for a story was a laborious process that involved a trip to the newspaper, magazine or television station library, or morgue, to sift through hundreds or even thousands of tattered, yellowed clippings. Too often, clippings had disappeared, were misfiled or had been misplaced, which made such research a hit-and-miss proposition. Despite those shortcomings, the library was considered a valuable asset. Reporters were routinely admonished to check there first.

You will still hear that advice in news rooms today, but many of today's news libraries are computerized, which almost ensures that an item will not disappear and will be easy to locate. Typically, you can do a check of the computerized library from your own computer. That makes it easier than ever to do good background work on a story. Your ability to search the library is limited only by your skill with search techniques and your access to the databases you need.

News libraries are what computer experts call **full-text databases**, which means that all words in the database have been indexed and are searchable. Such capability gives you great flexibility in structuring searches using **Boolean search commands**. Boolean operators such as AND, OR and NOT allow you to structure the search to find material most closely related to the subject being researched. For example, if you are interested in finding articles on former South African President Nelson Mandela's visits to the U.S., you might issue this command on the search line:

Mandela AND United ADJ States

The computer would then search for all articles that contain the name "Mandela" and also contain the words "United" and "States" adjacent to each other. In this example, AND and ADJ (for "adjacent") are the Boolean operators. This search would produce all articles on Mandela and the United States but would exclude articles involving Mandela and, for example, the United Arab Emirates, despite the presence of the word "United" (it's not adjacent to the word "States"). The result of such a search in most cases would be a report from the computer telling you how many articles match your search criteria:

Search found 27 articles. Would you like to see them or further narrow
your search?

At that point, you would have the option of further limiting the search (by date, for example) or reading all 27 articles.

Remember that computers don't really think. In our sample search, an article on Mandela's visit to Miami that did not contain the words "United States" would not have been found. Therefore, you need to understand the limitations as well as the power of computer-assisted database searching. Good reporters quickly learn to take into account such possibilities and learn to recast their searches in other ways.

There are other limitations. Many library databases do not allow you to see photos, nor can you see articles as they appeared in the newspaper or magazine. Nor do most current systems permit you to hear how a broadcast story was used on the air. Instead, you have access only to a text-based version of what appeared. That limits your ability to learn how the story was presented. If necessary, however, you can

On the Job

News Is Information

Three years after graduation, Charles Hammer worked for Delphi, an online service provider and portal. Earlier, he was a deputy producer at Access Atlanta, the online service of *The Atlanta Journal-Constitution*. There, he was responsible for developing content, designing quizzes and surveys, and creating new sections of the service. He's also worked at Condé Nast and elsewhere. Now he's manager of Web product development at John Wiley and Sons, a publishing company.

Hammer is one of the many journalism graduates who are discovering that the so-called new media offer an increasing number of job opportunities. He describes what attracted him to a nontraditional news job upon leaving college:

"The line between journalist and reader will blur as technology evolves. The amount of information available will be staggering. Traditional news sources will be challenged by anyone who has access to a computer, a television or even a telephone.

"To be a journalist in the new media, you must think of news as information. You must be able to present information over different media, whether it be a computer, a television, a telephone or a newspaper. But most importantly, you must not forget what you learned in your journalism classes: Present reliable, well-written information in an easy-to-read format—or the reader will go elsewhere."

always resort to looking up the original in bound volumes or on microfilm. Most newspapers save old editions in one or both of those forms. Many radio and television stations maintain tape libraries of old newscasts. While these older forms of storage may be less convenient to use, taking the time to search them is often worth the effort.

Some newer library computer systems overcome the traditional disadvantages of computerization by allowing you to view graphical reproductions of the printed page on the screen. You can view photographs, charts and maps in the same way. In broadcast applications, more and more libraries permit storage of digital video and sound clips. As such systems proliferate, the shortcomings of present computer libraries will disappear. Despite current limitations, few veteran reporters would be willing to return to the days of tattered yellow clippings. They know that computerization has made the library a more reliable source of background information.

Thus, the best reporters of today do what good reporters have always done: Check the morgue first. They simply do it with computers.

Search Engines

For many journalists, the first stop after the morgue is Google. Google or one of the other search engines (Yahoo, Live Search, Dogpile or Ask) can indeed be helpful to a journalist. The key to using them successfully is the ability to recognize whether the information contained on the Web site to which the search takes you is accurate and therefore usable.

Information from well-known sites may be reliable; information from Web sites advocating a cause may not be. Be wary of Wikipedia, a user-written and user-edited encyclopedia. While much of the information on Wikipedia is excellent, anyone can enter erroneous information into it. Errors or misrepresentations are usually corrected quickly by others, but beware of depending on information from only that source. We discuss how to evaluate such information in the "Evaluating Links" box in this chapter.

News Sites, Portals, Public Forums and Content Aggregators

Some might consider it strange to think of news Web sites, portals and content aggregators as useful sources of information for reporters. Don't tell that to the reporters who use them.

Such sites are accessible to anyone with a computer and an Internet connection. News sites are those published by established media outlets such as *The New York Times* (**http://nytimes.com**) and CBS (**www.cbsnews.com**), while portals are designed as entry points to the Web, such as America Online (**www.aol.com**). Most portals now have news and other information as well as forums (or electronic bulletin boards) for discussions on topics ranging from genealogy to stamp collecting to sports. Forum participants exchange messages on every conceivable topic. Some even write computer software that facilitates the pursuit of their passion, and they frequently make that software available to others interested in the topic.

Online forums provide fertile information to reporters attempting to research a story. If you are assigned to do a story on genealogy and know nothing about the subject, what better way to gauge the pulse of those passionate about the subject than by tapping into their discussions? By logging on to one of the public genealogy forums, you can do just that.

Or, if you want to interview those who participated in World War II's Battle of the Bulge, try posting a request for names on one of these services. Chances are you will be inundated with contact information for individuals and veterans' groups that would be delighted to help.

The popularity of public forums is almost impossible to overstate. What people like about online public forums is that they do what radio talk shows do—give people a place where they can exchange ideas with those who share similar interests. Writing in *Editor & Publisher*, Barry Hollander, a journalism professor at the University of Georgia,

Evaluating Links

The Web is a great resource for reporters, but determining the credibility of online information can be problematic. If the source is a respected media organization such as *The New York Times* or *The Washington Post*, chances are the information is solid. But if it was published by an organization promoting a cause, there is ample reason to be wary.

Stan Ketterer, a journalist and journalism professor, tells reporters to evaluate information on the Web by following the same standard journalistic practices that they would use for assessing the credibility and accuracy of any other type of information:

- *Before using information from a Web site in a story, verify it with a source.* There are exceptions to this rule, including taking information from a highly credible government site like the Census Bureau. Sometimes you can't contact the source on a breaking story because of time constraints. An editor must clear all exceptions.
- *In most cases, information taken directly from the Web and used in a story must be attributed.* If you have verified the information on a home page with a source, you can use the organization in the attribution, for example, "according to the EPA" or "EPA figures show." If you cannot verify the information after trying repeatedly, attribute unverified information to the Web page—for example, "according to the Voice of America's site on the World Wide Web." Consult your editor before using unverified information.
- *If you have doubts about the accuracy of the information and you cannot reach the source, get it from another source, such as a book or another person.* When in doubt, omit the information.
- *Check the extension on the site's Internet address to get clues as to the nature of the organization and the likely slant of the information.* The most common extensions used in the U.S. are *.gov* (government), *.edu* (education), *.com* (commercial), *.mil* (military), *.org* (not-for-profit organization) and *.net* (Internet administration). Most of the government and military sites have credible and accurate information. In many cases, you can take the information directly from the site and attribute it to the organization. But consult your editor until you get to know these sites.
- *Treat the sites of colleges and universities as you would other sites.* If college and university sites have source documents, such as the Constitution, attribute the information to the source document. But beware. Personal home pages can have .edu extensions, and the information on them is not always credible.
- *In almost all cases, do not take information directly from the home pages of commercial and not-for-profit organizations and use it without verification.*
- *Check the date when the page was last updated.* The date generally appears at the top or bottom of the first page of the site. Although a recent date does not ensure that the information is current, it does indicate that the organization is paying close attention to the site. If no date appears, if the site has not been updated for a while, or if it was created some time ago, do not use the information unless you verify it with a source.

contrasts the skyrocketing popularity of talk radio with the continuing decline of newspaper circulation:

> Newspapers used to be an important part of what bound communities together, a common forum for ideas and discussion. But as communities fragmented along racial and demographic lines, newspapers have done a better job of chronicling the decline than offering ways to offset the trend.
>
> A sense of connection is needed. Newspapers, and [their] electronic editions in particular, offer one opportunity to bring people together in ways similar to talk radio.

Over the years, newspapers, magazines, and radio and television stations have attempted to connect with their readers and listeners by doing people-on-the-street interviews. Interviewing people at random seldom produces good results because interviewees often know nothing about the topic or don't care. By tapping into the forums on various online sites, you are assured of finding knowledgeable people to interview.

These services give reporters a way to reconnect with the public and even find expert sources for stories. With their huge amounts of easily accessible material, they also are useful sources of information for reporters and editors.

Then there are the news aggregators — sites such as Yahoo News (**http://news.yahoo.com**) and Google News (**http://news.google.com**) — which link to news stories from a plethora of news sites. News aggregators have become, in effect, a good place for one-stop news shopping.

Other Sites on the World Wide Web

When a little-known, California-based cult called Heaven's Gate staged a mass suicide, newspapers and radio and television stations had no trouble finding background data on the group. The Heaven's Gate site on the Internet gave reporters a mother lode of information about the sect and its leader.

That incident illustrates what a powerful source of information the Internet — and particularly its user-friendly interface, the World Wide Web — has become.

The Internet is not a single computer network but rather a series of interconnected networks throughout the world. That arguably makes it the world's first truly international news medium.

For the journalist, the Internet serves two primary purposes:

- *It is an increasingly robust source of online information, including federal, state and local government data, and information published by companies on almost any imaginable topic.* Need information on a new drug? Chances are you can find it on the Internet, complete with more detail than you ever wanted to know. Need to know about Estonia? Plenty of

Web sites are available to tell you what you need to know or to give you the latest news from Tallinn, its capital. Further, most North American newspapers, magazines, and radio and television stations have a substantial Internet presence, sometimes complete with archives of previously published stories. Some experts, in fact, now refer to the Internet as the world's largest library. That's good stuff for a reporter who needs to do a quick bit of research to provide background material or context for a news story.

- *It is a publishing medium that offers new opportunities for media companies and journalists and new jobs for journalism and mass communications graduates.* In recent years, media companies large and small alike have established a presence on the Web in the belief that this is an exciting new medium of increasing interest to the public and one with enormous commercial potential (see Figure 4.1). Media companies also use the Internet to attract readers and viewers to their more profitable traditional products. Today, however, as the Web becomes more and more important, traditional media are moving to Web-first models that operate 24 hours a day, seven days a week. Often, a story is published first on the Web and later in the newspaper or on the newscast.

Figure 4.1
Established by the *San Jose Mercury News*, MercuryNews.com is a substantial Internet resource for both national news and regional coverage of Northern California.

Commercial databases make it easy to see what has been written about a subject in other newspapers. But there are potential problems with using excerpts from those stories:

- *Copyright laws must be obeyed.* Take care not to use too much material without obtaining permission.
- *Not all articles that appeared in a newspaper can be found in a database.* Wire service and market reports, death notices, box scores, social announcements and items written by freelancers often are excluded.
- *Publication doesn't ensure accuracy.* History is littered with incidents of newspapers quoting each other's inaccuracies.
- *The reporter who wrote the story may not have any real knowledge of the subject matter.* Using information from that reporter may introduce an inaccuracy into your story.
- *Databases aren't infallible.* The information is entered by humans, who are susceptible to mistakes. Also, databases are occasionally doctored in an attempt to prove a position or promote a cause.

The Internet also serves as an excellent medium for transmitting photos and even audio and video clips. It's possible to tap into the Louvre Museum's Web site and see paintings from that famous collection in full color. YouTube is a hot site for posting videos—and some of them are quite good and have news value.

Many observers of the media industry believe that the Internet, with its ability to give the consumer a choice of full-text, full-motion video and audio, will become the preferred news medium of the future. Indeed, surveys show that it already is the top choice with people under 30. As the World Wide Web improves and evolves, it is increasingly possible to read on your computer the text of a presidential address or to watch video of the address being delivered. On that same computer, you might watch a movie, do holiday shopping or order groceries.

Just a few years ago, slow connections into people's homes made it impossible to play audio or watch video on the Web. Now, however, most telephone companies offer high-speed digital subscriber line service, and cable television companies offer high-speed broadband services. Many are rolling out ever-more-capable services based on fast, high-bandwidth, fiber-optics technology. As the speed of the pipeline into the home accelerates, so does the popularity and capability of the Web.

As the capability of the Web grows, we begin to see the power and possibilities of the "information superhighway" envisioned by so many just a few years ago. Now, it is becoming reality.

Commercial Database Services

When newspapers and magazines entered the computer era in the early 1970s, publishers were quick to realize the potential value of saving and reselling previously published information. Newspapers and magazines quickly began selling access to their archives by establishing alliances with companies founded for that purpose.

On many topics, searching your own news library will not be sufficient. If U.S. Rep. Barney Frank is making his first appearance in your community and you have been assigned to cover him, your morgue probably won't help; little will have been written about him in your city. It probably will be much more useful to read recent articles published in Massachusetts, Frank's home state. By doing so, you will be armed with questions to ask about recent events of interest to him. In such situations, the national commercial databases are invaluable.

One of the leading commercial database services is LexisNexis, which provides full-text access to hundreds of newspaper and magazine libraries. It is a rich source of background information for a reporter who wants to see what has already been written on a given subject.

Government Databases

For years, government agencies have maintained large databases of information as a means of managing the public's business. They cover almost every conceivable service that government offers, from airplane registration and maintenance records to census data to local court records. They are maintained not only by the federal and state governments but also by even the smallest of city and county agencies.

Because most of these databases were begun many years ago, they often reside on large mainframe computers. Data are stored in various file formats, and it often is difficult to access the information. Independent analyses of the data once were impossible because the data were controlled by government agencies. Further, few newspapers had the resources or the computers on which to do independent analyses. After the introduction of personal computers in the early 1980s, however, reporters began finding ways to interpret mainframe data.

A breakthrough technology involved the purchase of nine-track mainframe data tapes from government agencies and subsequent analysis on personal computers equipped with nine-track drives. Newspapers started to win Pulitzer Prizes using this technique, and soon the National Institute for Computer-Assisted Reporting was established at the University of Missouri to spread the word about the technique. Suddenly, reporters had at their disposal the technology to make better use of existing open-records laws, at both state and federal levels.

Among the reporters taking advantage of the technology is Penny Loeb of *U.S. News & World Report*. When she worked for *New York Newsday*, she used a computer analysis of tax and property records to reveal an astounding story: The City of New York owed $275 million to taxpayers as a result of overpayments on real estate, water and sewer taxes. To get that story, Loeb had to analyze millions of computer records. Doing that by hand would have consumed a lifetime, but with the assistance of a computer, she accomplished the task in a matter of weeks.

Still, Loeb cautions against expecting instant stories:

> Don't just go get a computer tape and expect a great story. You need a tip that there is a problem that computerized data can confirm. Or you may have seen a problem occur repeatedly, such as sentencing discrimination. The computer can quantify the scope.

Analyses of this type usually are done with **relational database programs**. Relational database programs, unlike simpler **flat-file databases**, permit you to compare one set of data to another. A classic example would be to compare a database of a state's licensed school-bus drivers to another database of the state's drunken-driving convictions. The result would be a list of school-bus drivers guilty of such offenses.

After the introduction of this technology, investigative reporters were among the first to use it. But once such databases are available in easily accessible computer form, you can use them in your day-to-day work just as easily. For example, you might want to analyze federal records on airplane maintenance to produce a story on the safety record of a particular airline. If the records are maintained in an easily accessible format, the next time an airplane crashes it will be possible to call up the complete maintenance record of the aircraft merely by entering the plane's registration number. Such information can be extremely useful, even in a deadline situation.

Another common use of computers has been to compare bank records on home mortgages to census data. By tracking how many mortgages are issued to homeowners in predominantly black or Hispanic areas, reporters have been able to document the practice of redlining, through which banks make it difficult or impossible for minorities to obtain loans.

Again, such records are useful even after the investigation is complete. Access to driver's license records, census data, bank records and other forms of data can be used daily to produce news stories, charts, maps and other graphic devices. Numbers can be useful in helping to tell a story. They can be particularly effective as the basis for charts that illustrate the impact of the numbers.

Special-Interest Databases

Numerous special-interest groups have discovered the usefulness of placing information in computerized databases, and they are eager to make journalists aware of the existence of that information. Some of that material may be quite useful; indeed, it may be unobtainable from other sources. But just as journalists must be wary of news releases issued by organizations promoting a cause, they must be equally wary of information in such databases. It is important to remember that organizations of this type will promote their perspective on a topic, often without any concern for balancing the information with opposing views.

CD-ROMs and DVDs

During the past few years, the massive amount of information stored on compact discs and digital video discs has become a terrific new source of reference. Encyclopedias, dictionaries, telephone directories, census data and thousands of other titles are available on CD-ROMs and DVDs, which are an efficient and inexpensive way to store vast amounts of information. Topics range from garden plants to armaments. CD-ROM and DVD titles can be quick and effective references for the journalist on deadline.

Self-Constructed Databases

When Elliot Grossman of *The Morning Call* in Allentown, Pa., tried to document abuses of parking privileges by local police officers, he sifted through thousands of paper records to prepare his story. Grossman discovered that over the years a scam had allowed hundreds of police officers to park their private cars almost anywhere: They simply signed the backs of parking tickets and sent them to the Allentown Parking Authority. Any excuse, it seemed, would suffice for one of Allentown's finest.

Some data on parking tickets were available electronically, but the Parking Authority refused to release the computer tapes necessary for a quick analysis. So Grossman, with the help of a news clerk and reporting interns, decided to do the research the hard way. He set out to build his own database to document the extent of the problem.

For two weeks, Grossman and his helpers sat at laptop computers in the offices of the Parking Authority and entered data on the type of violation, the location of the vehicle, the date and time of the violation, and the license plate number. In many cases, other notations were made on the officer's badge number or the reason the officer was parked at the location. The result was a body of information that allowed Grossman to confirm his suspicions that many of the tickets were dismissed without good reason. What had begun as a rule allowing the cancellation of tickets for officers on official business had grown into a local scandal, and Grossman was able to expose it.

TRADITIONAL SOURCES OF INFORMATION

Accessing information through computerized sources is quick and easy, but more traditional reference sources also are valuable. In some cases, the sources listed below cannot be found on computers.

The Newspaper Library

Every working reporter gets this advice from an editor early in his or her career: Check the morgue. The morgue, or newspaper library, is usually the first stop for a reporter on any kind of assignment. Occasionally, there may be no time for such a check. When a fire or accident occurs, for example, the reporter rushes directly to the scene; there's no time for background preparation. But on any kind of story other than a breaking news event, the reporter's first stop should be the morgue.

Covering a speech? Look up background information on the speaker. Covering a sports event? What are the teams' records? Who are the coaches? What's the history of the rivalry? Reporters answer questions like these, and many others, by checking the newspaper library.

Today, most newspaper libraries are computerized, but this is still true: The morgue is almost always your first stop in reporting a story.

One other note on the print or broadcast morgue: Here you can find photos of a speaker or coach you haven't met. They will help you recognize that person for a possible one-on-one interview before the speech or game begins.

Other Traditional Sources

Traditional sources of information—such as reference books, dictionaries and encyclopedias—still play an important role in the production of the daily news product. Good reporters and editors make a habit of checking every verifiable fact. Here is a list of 20 commonly used references. Many of these are now also available online.

- *City directories*. You can find these directories, not to be confused with telephone books, in most cities. They provide the same information as the telephone directory but also may provide information on the occupations of citizens and the owners or managers of businesses. Useful street indexes provide information on the names of next-door neighbors.
- *Local and area telephone directories*. Use telephone books for verifying the spelling of names and addresses. They usually are reliable, but they are not infallible. Remember that people move and have similar names. Almost all telephone numbers in North America are now listed on various Internet-based services, including Switchboard (**www.switchboard.com**).
- *Maps of the city, county, state, nation and world*. Local maps usually are posted in the news room. Look for others in atlases.
- *State manuals*. Each state government publishes a directory that provides useful information on various government agencies. These directories sometimes list the salaries of all state employees.
- *Bartlett's Familiar Quotations* (Little, Brown).
- *Congressional Directory* (Government Printing Office). Provides profiles of members of Congress.
- *Congressional Record* (Government Printing Office). Contains complete proceedings of the U.S. House and Senate.
- *Current Biography* (Wilson). Profiles of prominent persons, published monthly.
- *Dictionary of American Biography* (Scribner's).
- *Facts on File* (Facts on File Inc.). A weekly compilation of news from metropolitan newspapers.
- *Guinness Book of World Records* (Guinness Superlatives). World records listed in countless categories.
- *National Trade and Professional Associations of the United States* (Columbia Books, Washington, D.C.).
- *Readers' Guide to Periodical Literature* (Wilson). An index to magazine articles on a host of subjects.

- *Statistical Abstract of the United States* (Government Printing Office). A digest of data collected and published by all federal agencies.
- *Webster's Biographical Dictionary* (Merriam-Webster).
- *Webster's New World College Dictionary*, Fourth Edition (Wiley). The primary reference dictionary recommended by both the Associated Press and United Press International.
- *Webster's Third New International Dictionary* (Merriam-Webster). The unabridged dictionary recommended by AP and UPI.
- *Who's Who* (St. Martin's). World listings.
- *Who's Who in America* (Marquis). A biennial publication.
- *World Almanac and Book of Facts* (Newspaper Enterprise Association). Published annually.

Those useful publications, and many others like them, enable reporters to verify data and to avoid the embarrassment caused by errors in print. Traditional sources of information other than interviews are printed government records, documents from businesses, pamphlets published by government and nongovernment agencies, books, newspapers, magazines and a host of others.

Be careful, though, when using material from a source with which you are not familiar. Some publications come from biased sources promoting a cause. It's the reporter's job to determine whether the information is biased or reliable. A good way to do that is to balance information from one source with information from another source with an opposing viewpoint. It may not always be possible for you to determine who's correct. Ensuring balance between two viewpoints is the next best thing.

Suggested Readings

Brooks, Brian S., James L. Pinson, and Jean Gaddy Wilson. *Working with Words: A Handbook for Media Writers and Editors*. New York: Bedford/St. Martin's, 2006. A definitive work on the correct use of language in journalistic writing and editing.

Callahan, Christopher, and Leslie-Jean Thornton. *A Journalist's Guide to the Internet: The Net as a Reporting Tool*. Boston: Allyn and Bacon, 2007. A useful guide to using the Internet as a reporting resource.

Goldstein, Norm, ed. *Associated Press Stylebook and Briefing on Media Law*. New York: Associated Press, 2008. The definitive work on stylistic matters in journalistic writing.

Houston, Brant. *Computer-Assisted Reporting: A Practical Guide*. New York: Bedford/St. Martin's, 2003. An excellent introduction to computer-assisted reporting by the executive director of Investigative Reporters and Editors.

IRE Journal. This monthly magazine is available from Investigative Reporters and Editors, Columbia, Mo. It offers regular articles on the use of computers in the news-gathering process.

Schlein, Alan M. *Find It Online: The Complete Guide to Online Research*. Edited by Peter Weber and J.J. Newby. Tempe, Ariz.: BRB Publications, 2004. Basic information on the use of Web resources.

Suggested Web Sites

www.ire.org   Investigative Reporters and Editors maintains an excellent Web site for anyone interested in investigative reporting.

www.nicar.org   The National Institute for Computer-Assisted Reporting conducts seminars for reporters in data analysis with computers.

www.reporter.org   At this site you'll find useful links to a variety of news support organizations.

Exercises

1. Choose any story in your local newspaper, and explain how that story could have been improved with a database search. List the databases you would have searched for the story.

2. If you were interested in determining where Apple Inc. is located and the name of its chief financial officer, where would you look? What other sources of information might be available?

3. Write a one-page biographical sketch of your congressional representative based on information you retrieve from your library or a database.

4. Using the Internet, find the following information:

   The census of Rhode Island in 2000.
   The size of Rwanda in land area.
   The latest grant awards by the U.S. Department of Education.
   The names of universities in Norway that provide outside access via the Internet.
   The name of a Web site that contains the complete works of Shakespeare.
   The name of a Web site that contains federal campaign contribution data.

5   Reporting with Numbers

Brooks Egerton, a *Dallas Morning News* reporter, had reported on a wealthy man who had shot an unarmed prostitute in the back and had gotten probation for the killing. The sentence seemed so unusual that Egerton wondered how common it was for killers to get probation.

Egerton and his colleague Reese Dunklin started asking people in the law and court systems about the issue. They learned that probation for murder was rare, that normally probation would be considered for something like a mercy killing. The story may have been stillborn right there, but the reporters decided to see if they could put some numbers on it.

They obtained a database of all people on probation in Texas. Then they cross-referenced thousands of police and court records, many of which they obtained by filing about 100 requests under the Texas Public Information Act. Some of the information they gathered the old-fashioned way—they talked people into giving it to them.

What they found was stunning. From 2000 to 2006, Texas judges sentenced 120 convicted killers to probation. Forty-seven of them were in Dallas County, a disproportionate number based on population and number of cases handled. Armed with the numbers, they interviewed more than 200 people and showed their findings to a half dozen legal scholars. The data, Dunklin said, "can liberate you to write with authority."

The numbers were all there, but the reporters put a human face on the stories by talking about specific cases to show the inequities in the system. To illustrate the disparities in sentencing, they told the story of Eddie Mae Dudley, who killed another woman in a fight over a beer. She served seven years. Then she shot and killed one of her housemates, an elderly stroke victim, while he lay drunk in bed. For that murder, she received five years' probation in a plea bargain.

They also told the story of Jacqueline Fox, 17, who had no record. Her ex-boyfriend threatened her at gunpoint. He beat her so hard with a two-by-four that the board broke. Fox stabbed him with a knife and killed him. After waiting in jail four and a half months, she was offered a plea bargain: She would plead guilty and get 10 years' probation, twice that of Dudley, a two-time killer. Fox accepted.

The numbers don't lie. Supported by interviews with law and court officials, with victims' families and even with some of the murderers, the stories were convincing and readable. (Figure 5.1 shows how the series was presented on the Web.) The Dallas County District Attorney's office began reviewing the probation-for-murder plea bargains that its prosecutors had made to see if they should try to revoke probation in any of the cases.

Journalists have a responsibility to understand numbers so that they are able to report clearly and accurately on everything from courts

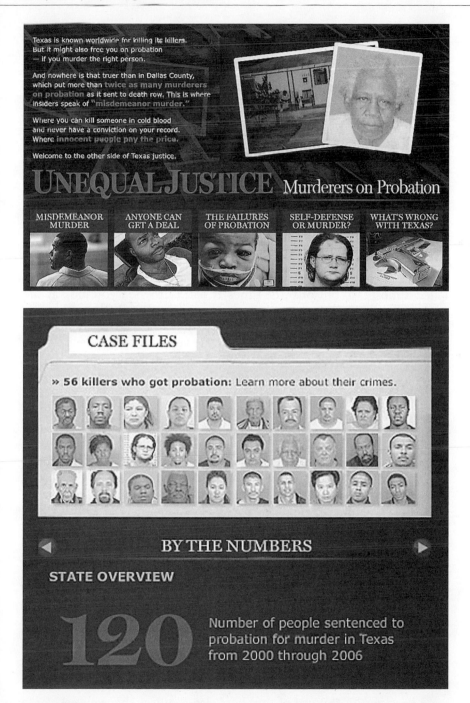

Figure 5.1
To write the "Unequal Justice" series, *Dallas Morning News* reporters Brooks
Egerton and Reese Dunklin relied on large amounts of statistical information.

to schools. This chapter will help you help readers sort through the numbers.

PROPORTION

One of the most important services journalists perform for their readers is to give **proportion** to numbers in the news—explaining things relative to the size or the magnitude of the whole. A municipal budget that is going up by $500,000 would be a windfall for a small town in New Hampshire but a minor adjustment for a metropolis such as New York, Chicago or Minneapolis.

Other figures might mean a lot or a little, depending on the context. If you know little or nothing about baseball, you might think that Babe Ruth's career batting average of .342—34.2 hits for every 100 times at bat—indicates that Ruth wasn't a good hitter. After all, he failed almost two out of three times at bat. But when you look at the context—other players' averages—you realize that Ruth was exceptional. For instance, in 2008, only two major league players had a higher average—and that was only for the year, not for a career.

Percentages and Percentage Change

Percentages are basic building blocks used to explain proportion. Batting averages explain the percentage of hits compared with the number of times at bat. The political strength of a public official is partly reflected in the percentage of the votes won at the polls. Stories about budgets, taxes, wages, retail sales, schools, health care and the environment all are explained with percentages.

To calculate a percentage, take the portion that you want to measure, divide it by the whole and then move the decimal two places to the right. For example, suppose you want to know what portion of the city's budget is allocated to police services. Divide the police budget by the city budget, move the decimal point two places to the right, and you get the percentage of the budget that pays for police services.

> *To compute a percentage*
>
> **Step 1**   Portion (police budget) ÷ whole (city budget) = .xxx
>
> $30,000,000 ÷ $120,000,000 = .25
>
> **Step 2**   Move the decimal point two places to the right: 25 percent

Precision in the use of numbers also requires that you ask some basic questions. Reporters need to be careful of percentages that might be used in misleading ways or percentages that tell only part of a story.

If someone is giving you percentages, you must ask what **population** the figures are based on. For instance, suppose a juvenile officer tells you that 70 percent of the juvenile offenders do not have to return to his program. Your first question should be, "What population was used to figure the percentage?" Was it all the juveniles in the program during the last calendar year? If so, perhaps the success rate is high because the period being measured isn't long enough. And how has your source counted juveniles who are old enough now to be certified as adults? How does he account for juveniles who may have committed a crime in another jurisdiction?

The officer's answer may be that the figure is based on a sample of the population in the program over 10 years. A **sample** is a small number of people picked at random so as to be representative of the population as a whole. Using common statistical tables, researchers draw a sample of the names of all juveniles who were in the program over 10 years and contact them. From those contacts, they can determine the success rate. If the figure is based on a scientific sampling like the one just described, there will also be a **margin of error**, which will be expressed as "plus or minus x points." Say that the margin of error for this sample is 4. That means that the success rate is between 66 and 74 percent.

The base on which a percentage is calculated is significant. Say a colleague is making $40,000, and you make $30,000. The salary is the base. Your employer decides to give your colleague a 4 percent increase and to give you a 5 percent increase. Before you begin feeling too good about the honor, consider that your colleague's raise is $1,600, and your raise is $1,500. Your colleague won a bigger raise, and the gap between the two of you grew. You spend dollars, not percentages.

Hence, if you have different bases on which to figure the percentages, the comparisons are invalid.

Here's another illustration. If you compare the amount of nuclear energy produced by countries on a percentage basis—that is, what percentage of the energy produced in a country is nuclear energy?—the U.S. would rank near the bottom. But if you compare the actual amount of energy produced by nuclear power, the U.S. produces more nuclear energy than any other country. The percentages aren't parallel with the amounts because the base—the total amount of energy produced—is different in each country. The base that you use for figuring percentages depends on the question you're asking and the comparison you want to make.

More confusion often occurs when people talk about the difference between two percentage figures. For example, say the mayor wins the election with 55 percent of the vote and has only one opponent, who receives 45 percent. The mayor won by a margin of 10 percentage points. The percentage points, in this case, equal the difference between

55 and 45. However, the mayor won 22 percent more votes (10 divided by 45 equals .22). Because the percentages are based on the same whole number — in this case, the total number of voters — the percentages can be compared. But if you compare the percentage of a city budget devoted to law enforcement in consecutive years, you will need to include the actual dollar amounts with the percentages because total spending probably changed from one year to the next.

Another important aspect of percentages is the concept of **percentage change**. This number explains how much something goes up or down. In the city budget summary shown in Figure 5.2, look under "Appropriations" and then under "Actual Fiscal Year 2009." Total spending was $18,654,563. The proposed budget for 2009 ("Adopted Fiscal Year 2010") is $19,570,518. What is the percentage increase? You find the percentage change by doing the following calculation: increase (or decrease) divided by the old budget.

To compute a percentage increase or decrease

Step 1   Find the increase (or decrease).

$19,570,518 – $18,654,563 = $915,955 (increase)

Step 2   Increase (or decrease) ÷ base amount = .xxx

$915,955 ÷ $18,654,563 = .049

Step 3   Move the decimal point two places to the right: 4.9 percent

Rounded off, this is a 5 percent increase in spending.

If the 2010 budget is increased 4.9 percent again, that will be a $958,955 increase, or $43,000 more, because of the bigger base.

When changes are large, sometimes it is better to translate the numbers into plain words rather than use a percentage figure. When Congress was debating whether to pass a $700 billion bailout of the financial system in late 2008, some journalists translated that figure to about $2,300 per person in the U.S., just to make the numbers more intelligible to most readers.

Averages and Medians

Averages and medians are numbers that can be used to describe a general trend. For any given set of numbers, the average and the median might be quite close, or they might be quite different. Depending on what you are trying to explain, it might be important to use one instead of the other or to use both.

The **average** — also called the *arithmetic mean* — is the number you obtain when you add a list of figures and then divide the total by the number of figures in the list. The **median** is the midpoint of the list — half the figures fall above it, and half the figures fall below it.

When Averages Distort

Take a set of scores from a final exam in a class of 15 students. The students scored 95, 94, 92, 86, 85, 84, 75, 75, 65, 64, 63, 62, 62, 62, 62. Both the average and the median are 75.

The picture can look quite different when the figures bunch at one end of the scale. Consider this example from professional baseball:

In 2008 the Chicago Cubs had a payroll of $118.3 million. With a range of salaries from $392,500 to $16 million, the median income was $3.18 million. However, the average was only $473,383 ($118,345,833 ÷ 25 players).

To compute an average

Step 1   Add the figures.

Step 2   Divide the total by the number of figures:

Total ÷ number of figures

The result is the average.

To find the median

Step 1   Arrange the figures in rank order.

Step 2   Identify the figure midway between the highest and lowest numbers. That figure is the median.
Note: When you have an even number of figures, the median is the average of the two middle figures.

As a general rule, you are safe using averages when there are no large gaps among the numbers. If you took an average of 1, 4, 12, 22, 31, 89 and 104, you would get 37.6. The average distorts the numbers because the average is higher than five of the seven numbers. The mean, or midpoint, is 22. On the other hand, if you had numbers ranging from 1 to 104 and the numbers were distributed evenly within that range, the average would be an accurate reading.

Rates

A rate is used to make fair comparisons between different populations. One example of a rate comparison is per capita, or per person, spending, such as for school funding. Even though a big-city school budget looks incredibly large to someone in a small community, the money has to stretch over more students than it would in a smaller district. As a result, spending per capita provides a better comparison between districts with different enrollments. Suppose your school district (district A) has 1,000 students and spends $2 million. You want to compare spending in your district with spending in district B, which has 1,500 students and a budget of $3 million. You would use the following formula to calculate per capita spending.

To compute a per capita rate

Budget in dollars ÷ number of people = dollar amount per capita

District A: $2,000,000 ÷ 1,000 = $2,000 per capita
District B: $3,000,000 ÷ 1,500 = $2,000 per capita

School district B spends $1 million more a year than district A, but both districts spend the same amount per pupil.

To compare crime incidents or spending amounts among municipalities with varying populations, reporters should use per capita figures.

Remember the "Unequal Justice" series mentioned at the beginning of this chapter? After the series appeared, an attorney in the Dallas County District Attorney's office suggested that the reason Dallas County's numbers were higher was that Dallas County handled more murder and homicide cases than other jurisdictions. Dunklin was able to counter that he and his colleagues had gone beyond the raw numbers and had calculated the rates of homicides. That satisfied the attorney, and he dropped that suggestion. In other words, the reporters used the numbers correctly to reveal facts that even the district attorney's office didn't know.

INTEREST AND COMPOUNDING

Interest is a financial factor in just about everyone's life. Most people have to pay it when they borrow money, and many people earn it when they deposit money at a bank. Consumers pay interest on home mortgages, car loans and credit card balances. Individuals and businesses earn interest when they deposit money in a financial institution or make a loan. Federal regulations require the interest rates charged by or paid by most institutions to be expressed as an **annual percentage rate (APR)**, so that interest rates are comparable from one institution to another.

There are two types of interest: simple and compound. **Simple interest** is interest to be paid on the **principal**, the amount borrowed. It is calculated by multiplying the amount of the loan by the annual percentage rate.

Suppose a student borrows $1,000 from her grandfather at a 5 percent annual rate to help cover college expenses. She needs only a one-year loan, so the cost is figured as simple interest. To calculate simple interest, multiply the principal by the interest rate: $1,000 × .05 = $50. To find the amount the student will repay her grandfather at the end of a year, add the principal to the interest. The student will owe $1,050.

If the loan is made over a period longer than a year, the borrower pays **compound interest**. Compound interest is interest paid on the total of the principal and the interest that already has accrued.

Suppose the student borrows $1,000 at an annual percentage rate of 5 percent and pays her grandfather back four years later, after graduation. She owes 5 percent annual interest for each year of the loan. But because she has the loan for four years, each year she owes not only simple interest on the principal but also interest on the interest that accrues each year.

At the end of year 1, she owes $1,050. To see how much she will owe at the end of year 2, she has to calculate 5 percent interest on $1,050: $1,050 × .05 = $52.50.

Here is how to calculate the interest for all four years. (Note that 1.05 is used instead of .05 to produce a running total. If you multiply 1,000 by 1.05, you get 1,050; if you multiply 1,000 by .05, you get 50, which you then have to add to 1,000 to get the principal and interest.)

$1,000 × 1.05 × 1.05 × 1.05 × 1.05 = $1,215.51

Because most consumers pay off student loans, car loans, mortgages and credit card debt over a period of time, and because interest is compounded more often than once a year, calculations usually are far more complicated than those in the example. Many financial Web sites and computer programs offer calculators for computing interest. For instance, you can select from a variety of calculators on *USA Today's* Web site (**www.usatoday.com**) in the Money section.

Student loans taken out through federal programs administered by banks, credit unions and universities are a prime example of more complicated transactions. Suppose a student has a $5,000 guaranteed student loan with an interest rate of 8 percent per year. After finishing school, the student has 10 years to repay, and each year she pays 8 percent interest on the amount of the original principal that is left unpaid. If the student makes the minimum payment of $65 on time each month for the 10-year life of the loan, she will pay the bank a total of $7,800. She pays $2,800 in interest on top of the original principal of $5,000. Had she not paid the balance down each month, the interest she owed would have been higher.

Consumers get the benefits of compounding when they put money in interest-bearing accounts, because their interest compounds. The same effect takes place when people make good investments in the stock market, where earnings are compounded when they are reinvested.

INFLATION

Inflation is an increase in the cost of living over time. Because prices rise over time, wages and budgets, too, have to increase to keep up with inflation. A worker who received a 2 percent pay increase each year would have the same buying power each year if inflation rose at 2 percent. Because of inflation, reporters must use a few simple computations to make fair comparisons between dollar amounts from different years.

Let's say the teachers in your local school district are negotiating for a new contract. They claim that their pay is not keeping pace with inflation. You know that the starting salary for a teacher in 1997 was $30,000 and that the starting salary in 2007 was $35,000. To determine whether the teachers' claim is true, you convert 1997 dollars to 2007 dollars, and you find that the starting salary in 2007 would have been $38,750 if the district had been keeping up with inflation. In other words, in constant dollars, first-year teachers earned $3,750 less in 2007 than they earned in 1997. (Numbers that are adjusted for inflation are called *constant*, or *real, dollars*. Numbers that are not adjusted for inflation are called *nominal*, or *current, dollars*.)

The most common tool used to adjust for inflation is the Consumer Price Index, which is reported each month by the U.S. Bureau of Labor Statistics of the U.S. Department of Labor. You can get current CPI numbers on the Web at **www.bls.gov/cpi**.

TAXES

Reporters not only pay taxes, but also have to report on them. Governments collect taxes in a variety of ways, but the three major categories are sales taxes, income taxes and property taxes.

Sales Taxes

State, county and municipal governments can levy sales taxes on various goods and services. Sales taxes — also known as *excise taxes* — are the simplest to figure out.

To figure a sales tax, multiply the price of an item by the sales tax rate. Add the result to the original price to obtain the total cost.

Take the example of a student buying an $1,800 computer before beginning school at the University of Florida. If he shops in his home state of Iowa, where the sales tax is 5 percent, he will pay a tax of $90, and the computer will cost him $1,890. If he buys the computer after arriving in Florida, where the sales tax is 6 percent, he will pay a tax of $108, and the computer will cost him $1,908.

Sales taxes are an excellent way for you to track sales in your city, county or state. The appropriate government unit—a finance or comptroller's office, for instance—will have sales tax revenues, which are a direct reflection of sales and, therefore, an excellent way to use numbers to report on the economy in your area.

Income Taxes

The government taxes a percentage of your income to support such services as building roads, running schools, registering people to vote and encouraging businesses to grow. Income taxes are paid to the federal government, to most state governments, and to some municipalities.

Calculating income taxes can be tricky because many factors affect the amount of income that is subject to the tax. For that reason, the only way to figure a person's income tax is to consult the actual numbers and follow tables published by the Internal Revenue Service (**www.irs.gov**) or the state department of taxation.

Governments use tax incentives to encourage people to undertake certain types of economic activities, such as buying a home, saving for retirement, and investing in business ventures. By giving people and businesses tax deductions, the government reduces the amount of income that is taxable.

A tax deduction is worth the tax rate times the amount of the tax deduction. The most common tax deduction is for the interest people pay on their home loans. Tax deductions are worth more to people with higher incomes. Take the example of two families who own homes. Both pay $2,500 in interest on their home mortgage in a year, the cost of which is deductible for people who itemize. The lower-income family is in the lowest federal income tax bracket, in which the tax rate is 10 percent, so that family saves $250 on its tax bill ($2,500 × .10 = $250). The higher-income family who is in the federal income tax bracket of 33 percent, saves $825 on its tax bill ($2,500 × .33 = $825). In fact, the family in the 33 percent tax bracket probably owns a more expensive home and probably pays much more than $2,500 in mortgage interest a year. The impact is that the family saves even more on its income tax.

Income tax rates are based on your *adjusted gross income*. If you make $8,025 or less after deductions, you will pay a tax of 10 percent ($802.50). If you make between $8,025 and $32,550 after deductions—enough to move you into the 15 percent bracket—you will pay $802.50 plus 15 percent of the amount over $8,025.

Property Taxes

City and county governments collect property taxes. When people talk about property taxes, they usually mean taxes on the value of houses, buildings and land. In some places, people also are taxed each year on the value of their cars, boats and other personal property.

The two key factors in property taxes are the assessed value and the millage rate. The **assessed value** is the amount that a government appraiser determines a piece of property is worth. The **millage rate**— the rate per thousand dollars—is the tax rate determined by the government. You figure the property taxes by multiplying the assessed value by the millage rate. For example, owners of a house valued at $140,000 taxed at a millage rate of 2.25 would pay $315 in taxes ($140,000 ÷ 1,000 × 2.25).

Counties and cities hire professional appraisers to assess the values of land and buildings in their jurisdiction, and typically their assessments have been far lower than the actual market value of the property. Because of abuses and public confusion, most states in recent years have ordered revaluations to bring assessments into line with market values, and they have adjusted millage rates accordingly, though assessments can vary widely from appraiser to appraiser.

Appraisals are based on complicated formulas that take into account the size, location and condition of the property. Still, the government may say your house is worth $160,000, even if you know you could sell it for $180,000.

When you are reporting tax rate changes, you should find out how they affect houses in different value brackets to help explain the impact. By talking to the assessor or tax collector, you should be able to report, for instance, that the taxes for a house valued at $140,000 would cost $315 and that taxes for a house valued at $250,000 would be $562.50.

BUDGETS

Budget stories usually deal with

- Changes.
- Trends.
- Comparisons.

The budget is the blueprint that guides the operation of any organization, and a reporter must learn to read a budget just as a carpenter must learn to read a set of blueprints. It's not as difficult as it appears at first glance.

In many cases today, you'll be able to get the budget (and other financial information as well) for your city or school district on computer disk or tape. You can probably also view it on a local Web site, but you probably cannot download that file into a spreadsheet database. However, once you have the budget on a disk, you can create your own spreadsheet and perform analyses that not long ago were only in the power of the institution's budget director. This is one of many ways the computer has become an essential news room tool. However, with the computer or without, first you need to know the basics of budgeting.

On the Job

Working with Numbers

From city budgets to election results to the economic meltdown, today's important stories frequently involve numbers. Too often, unfortunately, reporters avoid them or leave their interpretation to officials.

But understanding how to interpret and present numbers in a news story can make a big difference. As the computer-assisted reporting editor for three newspapers and as training director for Investigative Reporters and Editors, Jennifer LaFleur saw that reporters who had these skills were able to break important stories. For instance, at *The Dallas Morning News*, math skills led education reporters to uncover millions of dollars in misspending in the Dallas Independent School District.

LaFleur has noticed these common problems over the years:

- The love for the superlative inspires some reporters to use phrases such as "Texas has the most hunting accidents" or "California has the most cars" without putting them in perspective. Big states have lots of everything, so adjust the numbers for the population.
- Things cost more today than in the past, but too often reporters fail to adjust the figures for inflation. A 1950 dollar was not what it is today.
- In striving for precision, some reporters give readers a false message. A poll of 400 people just can't be that precise, so we shouldn't report that 43.23 percent of respondents said something.

"In a time when every reporter is asked to do more, no reporter should be without the basic skills to interpret the numbers they run across every day," says LaFleur. "They should know how to compute a percent change, percent of total and per capita and know what all those things mean."

She now works for a nonprofit investigative news room—ProPublica—where many of her first stories involved the nation's economic crisis and the 2008 presidential election. Both topics centered around important numbers that reporters had to understand and interpret.

Budget Basics

Every budget, whether it's your personal budget or the budget of the U.S. government, has two basic parts—*revenues* (income) and *expenditures* (outgo). Commercial enterprises earn their income primarily from sales; not-for-profit organizations depend heavily on contributions from public funding and private donors. Government revenues come from sources such as taxes, fees and service charges, and payments from other agencies (such as state aid to schools). The budget usually shows, in dollar amounts and percentages, the sources of the organization's money. Expenditures go for such items as staff salaries, supplies, utility bills, construction and maintenance of facilities, and insurance. Expenditures usually are listed either by line or by program. The difference is this: A **line-item budget** shows a separate line for each expenditure, such as "Salary of police chief—$150,000." A **program budget** provides less detail but shows more clearly what each activity of the agency costs—for example, "Burglary prevention program—$250,000."

Finding Stories in Budget Changes, Trends and Comparisons

Guidelines for reporting numbers

- Cite sources for all statistics.
- Use numbers judiciously for maximum impact.
- Long lists of figures are difficult to read in paragraph form. Put them in charts and graphs when appropriate.
- Graphs sometimes include estimates. If you use figures from a graph, make sure they are precise.
- Round off large numbers in most cases. For example, use $1.5 million rather than $1,489,789.
- Always double-check your math and verify any statistics a source gives you.
- Be especially careful with handwritten numbers. It is easy to drop or transpose figures in your notes. Write neatly; when you read your notes, you'll want to be able to tell a 1 from a 7.
- If you don't understand the figures, get an explanation.

Now let's see what kinds of stories budgets might yield and where to look for those stories. Take a minute to scan Figure 5.2, a summary page from the annual budget of a small city. You can apply the skills of reading a city's annual budget to similar accounting documents on other beats—for example, annual reports of businesses and not-for-profit organizations.

General Fund—Summary

Purpose

The General Fund is used to finance and account for a large portion of the current operation expenditures and capital outlays of city government. The General Fund is one of the largest and most important of the city's funds because most governmental programs (Police, Fire, Public Works, Parks and Recreation, and so on) are generally financed wholly or partially from it. The General Fund has a greater number and variety of revenue sources than any other fund, and its resources normally finance a wider range of activities.

Appropriations

	Actual Fiscal Year 2007	Actual Fiscal Year 2008	Actual Fiscal Year 2009	Adopted Fiscal Year 2010
Personnel services	$9,500,353	$11,306,619	$11,245,394	$12,212,336
Materials and supplies	1,490,573	1,787,220	1,794,362	1,986,551
Training and schools	93,942	150,517	170,475	219,455
Utilities	606,125	649,606	652,094	722,785
Services	1,618,525	1,865,283	1,933,300	2,254,983
Insurance and miscellaneous	1,792,366	1,556,911	1,783,700	1,614,265
Total operating	15,101,884	17,316,156	17,579,325	19,010,375
Capital additions	561,145	1,123,543	875,238	460,143
Total operating and capital	15,663,029	18,439,699	18,454,563	19,470,518
Contingency	——	200,000	200,000	100,000
Total	$15,663,029	$18,639,699	$18,654,563	$19,570,518

Figure 5.2
Summary page of a typical city budget.

The most important budget stories usually deal with changes, trends and comparisons. Budget figures change every year. As costs increase, so do budgets. But look under "Department Expenditures" in our sample budget at the line for the Parks and Recreation Department. There's a decrease between Actual Fiscal Year 2009 and Adopted Fiscal Year 2010. Why? The summary page doesn't tell you, so you'll have to look further. Sometimes that information will be in the detail pages; other times, you'll have to ask the department director. You might discover, as we did, that the drop resulted from a proposal by the

General Fund — Summary (continued)

Department Expenditures

	Actual Fiscal Year 2007	Actual Fiscal Year 2008	Actual Fiscal Year 2009	Adopted Fiscal Year 2010
City Council	$75,144	$105,207	$90,457	$84,235
City Clerk	61,281	70,778	74,444	91,867
City Manager	155,992	181,219	179,125	192,900
Municipal Court	164,631	196,389	175,019	181,462
Personnel	143,366	197,844	186,247	203,020
Law Department	198,296	266,819	248,170	288,550
Planning & Community Development	295,509	377,126	360,272	405,870
Finance Department	893,344	940,450	983,342	1,212,234
Fire Department	2,837,744	3,421,112	3,257,356	3,694,333
Police Department	3,300,472	4,007,593	4,139,085	4,375,336
Health	1,033,188	1,179,243	1,157,607	1,293,362
Community Services	50,882	74,952	74,758	78,673
Energy Management	——	——	54,925	66,191
Public Works	2,838,605	3,374,152	3,381,044	3,509,979
Parks and Recreation	1,218,221	1,367,143	1,400,334	1,337,682
Communications & Info. Services	532,153	730,129	742,835	715,324
City General	1,864,200	1,949,543	1,949,543	1,739,500
Total Department Expenditures	15,663,028	18,439,699	18,454,563	19,470,518
Contingency	——	200,000	200,000	100,000
Total	$15,663,028	$18,639,699	$18,654,563	$19,570,518

city staff to halt funding of a summer employment program for teenagers. That's a story.

Another change that may be newsworthy is the increase in the Police Department budget. In 2008 the budget was $4,007,593, and the budget adopted for 2010 is $4,375,336. In this case, we found that most of the increase was going to pay for an administrative reorganization that would add new positions at the top of the department. The patrol division was actually being reduced. Another story.

Look again at that Police Department line. Follow it back to Actual Fiscal Year 2007, and you'll see that the increase the year before was even bigger. In two years, the expenditures for police increased by nearly one-third, from $3.3 million actually spent in 2007 to nearly $4.4 million budgeted for 2010. That's an interesting trend. The same pattern holds true for the Fire Department. More checking is in order. With copies of previous budgets, you can see how far back the growth trend runs. You can also get statistics on crimes and fires from the individual departments. Are the budget makers responding to a demonstrated need for more protection, or is something else at work behind the scenes?

More generally, you can trace patterns in the growth of city services and city taxes, and you can compare those with changes in population. Are the rates of change comparable? Is population growth outstripping growth in services? Are residents paying more per capita for city services than they paid five or 10 years ago? More good story possibilities.

Another kind of comparison can be useful to your readers, too. How does your city government compare in cost and services with the governments of comparable cities? Some professional organizations have recommended levels of service—such as the number of police officers or firefighters per 1,000 inhabitants—that can help you help your readers assess how well they're being governed.

The same guidelines can be applied to the analysis of any budget. The numbers will be different, as will the department names, but the structures will be much the same. Whether you're covering the school board or the statehouse, look for changes, trends and comparisons.

FINANCIAL REPORTS

Another document that is vital to understanding the finances of local government or of any organization is the annual financial report. The report explains the organization's financial status at the end of a fiscal year, which often is not the same as the end of the calendar year. (For example, a fiscal year might end on June 30.) In the report you will find an accounting of all the income the organization received during the year from taxes, fees, state and federal grants, and other sources. You'll also find status reports on all the organization's operating funds, such as its capital improvement fund, its debt-service fund and its general fund.

Making sense of a financial report, like understanding a budget, isn't as hard as it may look. For one thing, the financial officer usually includes a narrative that highlights the most important points, at least from his or her viewpoint. But you should dig beyond the narrative and examine the numbers for yourself. The single most important section of the report is the statement of revenues, expenditures and changes, which provides important measures of the organization's financial health. Depending on the comprehensiveness of the statement, you may have to refer to the budget document as well. You can check:

- Revenues actually received compared with budgeted revenues.
- Actual spending compared with budgeted spending.
- Actual spending compared with actual revenue.
- Changes in balances available for spending in years to come.

The guidelines offered here should help you shape your questions and understand the answers. With financial statements, as with budgets, look for changes, trends and comparisons, and ask for explanations.

MAKING SENSE OF NUMBERS FROM POLLS

Every day, new poll results illustrate what people think about various topics in the news. And just about every day, journalists confuse readers when they try to interpret the results.

The most important thing to keep in mind about polls and surveys is that they are based on samples of a population. Because a survey reflects the responses of a small number of people within a population, every survey has a margin of error. The results must be presented with the understanding that scientific sampling is not a perfect predictor for the entire population.

Suppose your news organization buys polling services that show that Candidate Hernandez has support from 58 percent of the people surveyed, Candidate Jones has support from 32 percent, and 10 percent are undecided. The polling service indicates that the margin of error of the poll is plus or minus five percentage points. The margins separating the candidates—53 to 63 percent for Hernandez, 27 to 37 percent for Jones and 5 to 15 percent undecided—are well above the margin of error, so you can write that Hernandez is leading in the poll.

Now suppose Hernandez has 50 percent support and Jones has 45 percent. The difference between them is within the margin of error, less than plus or minus five percentage points. Thus you should report that the race is too close to call, and only that one candidate "appears to be leading."

Information about a poll to share with your audience

- The identity of the survey's sponsor.
- The exact wording of the questions asked.
- A definition of the population sampled.
- The sample size and response rate.
- The margin of error.
- Which results are based on only part of the sample (for example, probable voters).
- When the interviews were conducted.
- How the interviews were conducted—in person, by mail, and so on.

—AP Managing Editors Association

Cautions about using poll data

- The people interviewed must be selected in a truly random fashion if you want to generalize from their responses to the whole population.
- The closer the results, the harder it is to say anything definitive.
- Beware of polls that claim to measure opinion on sensitive, complicated issues.

Journalists faced exactly that problem in the presidential elections in 2008. For weeks, the difference in the polls between Barack Obama and John McCain often fell within the margin of error, yet many in the media inaccurately reported each little change as an advantage for one candidate or the other. Most of the media reported on the Minnesota Senate race, which eventually was decided only after a recount, more carefully. One of them that did was *The Washington Post*:

> **Obama Widens Lead in Four Key States**
> By Chris Cillizza
> washingtonpost.com
> Tuesday, October 14, 2008; 6:32 AM
>
> In Minnesota, Sen. Norm Coleman (R) has slipped into a dead heat with his Democratic opponent Al Franken; Franken stands at 38 percent to 36 percent for Coleman and 18 percent for independent candidate Dean Barkley.

Note that while Franken had a two-point lead, the writer said the contest was a dead heat because it was within the margin of error of three points. The poll turned out to be accurate; the race was so close that there was a recount.

Lesson number one is not to write that one candidate is ahead of another unless the difference between them is larger than the margin of error for both candidates combined. Lesson two is that if you look at smaller groups within your polling group, the margin of error will be even larger. Subgroups within a sample are subject to a larger margin of error because fewer people are in the subgroup. Fewer respondents means less accuracy. If you wanted to write about how many women supported Obama or McCain in 2008 according to the survey quoted by the *Post*, you would have to use the margin of error based on the smaller number of women surveyed. Suppose you wanted to know how women in the survey were going to vote. If women were half the sample, the margin of error would approximately double. Being honest about figures that are so unreliable can be difficult, but doing so is the only way to keep your reporting accurate and fair.

MIXING NUMBERS AND WORDS

Whatever the story and whatever the subject, you probably can use numbers to clarify issues for readers and viewers. All too often, however, numbers are used in ways that muddy the water. Many journalists have some trepidation about working with numbers, and they create confusion unwittingly when they work with the volatile mixture of numbers and words.

Jennifer LaFleur (see the "On the Job" feature in this chapter) says she has seen numerous reports from government agencies with math errors that a quick double check by a reporter would find. "Reporters background-check sources. They verify anecdotes with documents. But seldom do we double-check numbers," she reminds us.

In *Mathsemantics: Making Numbers Talk Sense*, Edward MacNeal asserts that reporters and editors need to be far more careful in applying numbers in the news by questioning the accuracy and meaning of the numbers they gather and report.

For example, consider the following lead: "Each year 65,000 bicyclists go to the emergency room with injuries. Of those, 70–80 percent die because they weren't wearing helmets."

That means that more than 45,000 bicyclists, and perhaps as many as 52,000, are dying each year, or between about 125 and 140 each day. It's much more likely that the figures meant something else entirely—that 70 to 80 percent of the bicyclists who died of their injuries would have been spared had they been wearing helmets. With the figures given, we still don't know how many bicyclists died.

Journalists can also encourage misunderstandings by describing large increases in percentage terms. For example, when gasoline prices increased from about \$2 to nearly \$4 a gallon in 2007–2008, some in the media reported, accurately, that the price had doubled. Others, however, incorrectly called it a 200 percent increase instead of a 100 percent increase: $\$2 + (100\% \times \$2) = \$4$.

Another trouble spot for mixing numbers and words occurs when reporters calculate how much larger or more expensive something is. For example, a class that grew from 20 students to 100 students is five times bigger than it was ($5 \times 20 = 100$), but it has four times as many students as it had before: $(4 \times 20) + 20 = 100$.

The lesson to be learned from these examples is not to avoid numbers, but rather to use great care to ensure accuracy. Picking the right numbers to use and using them wisely will help your news stories have the biggest impact.

CURRENCY EXCHANGE

If you're writing about travel or international business, you need to understand currency exchange. Currency rates change frequently, though not by much unless there is some significant event that makes a currency more or less valuable. The most popular vacation destination for American travelers overseas is mainland Europe, most of which uses the euro. In late 2008, \$1 would buy .69 of one euro (69 eurocents). Because you get less than one, you know that euros are more expensive than dollars.

Another popular location to visit and study is England, which, unlike most of its European neighbors, uses the pound. In late 2008, you could exchange $1 for .55 British pound (55 pence), which means London is even more expensive than mainland Europe. You can find dozens of calculators on the Web that will convert currency for you, and you should use them if you are doing stories. If you are traveling, it may be enough to know that it takes approximately $1.40 to equal one pound.

Suggested Readings

Cohen, Sarah. *Numbers in the Newsroom: Using Math and Statistics in the News*. Columbia, Mo.: Investigative Reporters and Editors, 2001. Great, readable information on how to do basic math, graphs and polls.

Crossen, Cynthia. *Tainted Truth: The Manipulation of Fact in America*. New York: Simon and Schuster, 1994. An illuminating account of several instances in which public relations executives manipulated press coverage by twisting the numbers.

Cuzzort, R.P., and James S. Vrettos. *The Elementary Forms of Statistical Reason*. New York: St. Martin's Press, 1996. A basic guide for nonmathematicians in the humanities and social sciences who must work with statistics.

Meyer, Philip. *Precision Journalism*. 4th ed. Lanham, Md.: Rowman and Littlefield Publishers, 2002. A step-by-step guide to using social science research methods in news reporting.

Paulos, John Allen. *A Mathematician Reads the Newspaper*. New York: Anchor Books, 1997. The book, structured like the morning paper, investigates the mathematical angles of stories in the news and offers novel perspectives, questions and ideas.

Seltzer, Richard A. *Mistakes That Social Scientists Make*. New York: St. Martin's Press, 1996. A useful book about the kinds of errors social scientists often make during their research.

Suggested Web Sites

www.bls.gov/data/inflation_calculator.htm The Bureau of Labor Statistics has a calculator that enables you to adjust dollar amounts for inflation. In addition, the Web site provides Consumer Price Index information for the entire nation, broken down by region and type of spending.

www.dallasnews.com/sharedcontent/dws/spe/ 2007/unequal/index2.html Here you can read the *Dallas Morning News* series "Unequal Justice" for yourself. Of particular interest is the interactive graphic that presents the data to support the series.

www.math.temple.edu/~paulos John Allen Paulos, a professor at Temple University, is the author of *Innumeracy: Mathematical Illiteracy and Its Consequences*. At this site you can read more from the master of numbers.

www.minneapolisfed.org The Federal Reserve Bank of Minneapolis maintains a great Web site that helps you calculate inflation. It also has clear and simple explanations of how inflation is calculated and how to use the Consumer Price Index.

www.people-press.org The Pew Research Center for the People and the Press offers its own credible polls on politics and public issues. It offers all the data you need to accurately assess the polls.

www.usatoday.com/money *USA Today*'s site offers calculators to figure everything from interest rates to currency conversions.

Exercises

1. The federal minimum wage began in 1938 at 25 cents. In 1968, it was $1.60. Calculate how much 25 cents in 1938 is worth today and what $1.60 in 1968 is worth today. Compare those numbers with the present minimum wage. Suggest a story idea based on the result. (Consult **www.dol.gov/esa/minwage/america.htm** for the current federal and state minimum wages.)

2. Find out from your campus financial aid office how much the graduating class has borrowed in Stafford Loans, the largest category of student loans. Calculate how much debt the average graduate will have in Stafford Loans. Then calculate how much debt the average indebted graduate will have. (The results will probably be quite different.) Find out what the total amount of payments owed will be for the average graduate with loans.

3. Find out how much your college charged for tuition in 1990, 2000 and today. Adjust those numbers for inflation so they can be compared. (Use an inflation calculator like the one at **www.minneapolisfed.org**.) Write a story about the cost of going to college, and use figures adjusted for inflation.

4. The Clery Act requires colleges and universities to publicly report crimes that occur on campus. Many post the data on their Web site. Get the numbers for your campus; then do a Web search to find statistics for comparable campuses. Write a story about crime on your campus after comparing rates of crime on different campuses. If the campuses have different student populations, convert the crimes to per capita numbers for comparison.

5. Get a copy of your city or university budget, and come up with five questions that a reporter should ask about the changes, patterns and trends that the budget suggests. The budget may be available on the Internet.

6. If a city budgets $186,247 for personnel in 2008 and $203,020 in 2009, what is the percentage increase?

7. A city of 219,000 had 103 murders last year. Another city of 88,812 in the same state had 48 murders. How many murders were there per 1,000 residents in each city?

6 The Inverted Pyramid

The **inverted pyramid**—a news story structure that places all the important information in the first paragraph—has written the first draft of history in the United States for generations. Here is the Associated Press lead on the first use of the atomic bomb in 1945:

> An atomic bomb, hailed as the most destructive force in history and as the greatest achievement of organized science, has been loosed upon Japan.

And here is how the AP started its story of the first moon landing in 1969:

> Man came to the moon and walked its dead surface Sunday.

When terrorists attacked the World Trade Center in 2001, the AP informed the world this way:

> In an unprecedented show of terrorist horror, the 110-story World Trade Center towers collapsed in a shower of rubble and dust Tuesday morning after two hijacked airliners carrying scores of passengers slammed into the side of the twin symbols of American capitalism.

As these examples show, journalists have been using the inverted pyramid for generations to record the daily history of world events. Whether reading or listening, consumers have learned about news, from hurricanes to election results to financial system meltdowns, largely through the inverted pyramid. Specialized financial news services such as Bloomberg News rely on the inverted pyramid. So do newspapers, despite many editors' emphasis on encouraging new writing forms. So do radio, television and newsletters. Businesspeople often use the inverted pyramid in company memos so their bosses don't have to read to the end to find the main point. Public relations professionals use it in news releases to get the attention of news editors.

In this chapter you will learn:
1. How to translate news values into leads.
2. How to organize a story using the inverted pyramid.
3. How to improve your accuracy.

THE IMPORTANCE OF THE INVERTED-PYRAMID STORY

Frequently misdiagnosed as dying, the inverted pyramid has more lives than a cat—perhaps because the more people try to speed up the dissemination of information, the more valuable the inverted pyramid becomes. In the inverted pyramid, information is arranged from most important to least important. The king in *Alice in Wonderland* would never succeed in the electronic news service business. When asked where to start a story, he replied, "Begin at the beginning and go on till you come to the end; then stop." Reporters, however, often begin a story at its end. Subscribers to financial news services want the news quickly and clearly. This is a typical Bloomberg lead:

"Because a story is important, it doesn't follow that it must be long."
— *Stanley Walker, city editor*

(Bloomberg) — The global financial crisis is turning into a bigger drain on the U.S. federal budget than experts estimated two weeks ago, ballooning the deficit toward $2 trillion.

Organizing facts from most important to least important plays to many newspaper readers, who, on average, spend 15 to 20 minutes a day reading the paper, and online readers, who move around Internet sites as if they were walking on hot coals. Their reading is measured in seconds, not minutes. If a reporter were to write an account of a car accident by starting when the driver left the house, many readers would never read far enough to learn that the driver had been killed. Instead, such a story starts with its climax:

> Two people died Thursday when a backhoe fell off a truck's flatbed and sliced the top off an oncoming vehicle near Fairchild Air Force Base.

Some journalism history books attribute the introduction of the inverted pyramid to the use of the telegraph during the Civil War. Forced to pay by the word, newspapers supposedly instructed their correspondents to put the most important information at the top. Researchers at the University of Southern California have found that the inverted pyramid was used even earlier. Whatever its origins, the inverted-pyramid lead, the first paragraph or two, is presented as simply and clearly as possible. It sets the tone. It advertises what is coming in the rest of the story, and it conveys the most important information.

The inverted pyramid

- Requires the writer to rank the importance of information.
- Puts the most important information first.
- Arranges the paragraphs in descending order of importance.

The lead sits atop other paragraphs arranged in descending order of importance. These paragraphs explain and provide evidence to support the lead. The need to produce multiple newspaper editions with the same story running different lengths in each one makes it important that stories can be shortened quickly. The inverted pyramid serves that need well. On the Internet, space is not a consideration, but readers' time is. That's why the same inverted pyramid that is used in newspapers is the most common story structure found on such Web news sites as CNN.com, MSNBC.com, CBSNews.com and ABCNews.com.

In Chapter 13, you will learn details about writing news for the Web. However, you will find that most Web news sites rely on the inverted pyramid to present information quickly. For example, when a bus accident killed three students, CNN.com used the inverted pyramid as it followed the story the second day:

> HUNTSVILLE, Alabama (CNN) — National Transportation Safety Board investigators were in Huntsville on Tuesday, trying to determine what caused a school bus to plunge off a highway overpass the day before.
>
> The bus, carrying 43 students from Huntsville's Lee High School, fell 30 feet to the street below the overpass and landed on its front end before flipping over.

The inverted pyramid does have some shortcomings. Although it delivers the most important news first, it does not encourage people to read the entire story. Stories stop; they don't end. There is no suspense. In a Poynter Media Institute study (**www.poynter.org**), researchers found that half of the 25 percent of readers who started a story dropped out midway through. Interest in an inverted-pyramid story diminishes as the story progresses. But the way people use it attests to its value as a quick form of information delivery. Readers can leave whenever their needs are met, not when a writer finishes a story. In an age when time is golden, the inverted pyramid still offers value.

The day when the inverted pyramid is relegated to journalism history is not yet here and probably never will be. A majority of the news stories in today's newspapers and on Internet sites are written in the inverted-pyramid form. The trend is changing—as it should be—but it's changing slowly. Some of the new media will require other forms. For instance, tailored stories for news-on-demand services that will reach a general audience need not use the inverted pyramid. Nor will those sites devoted to literary journalism (**www.vanityfair.com**) and the newsmagazines *Time* and *Newsweek*, which depend on different angles and plenty of writer's voice. Still, as long as print, digital and television journalists continue to emphasize the quick, direct, simple approach to communications, the inverted pyramid and modifications of it will have a role.

There are many other ways to structure a story. You will learn about some of the options in Chapter 7. Before you get to the alternatives, however, you should master the inverted pyramid. Those who do will have mastered the art of making news judgments. The inverted pyramid requires you to identify and rank the most newsworthy elements in each story. That is important work. No matter what kinds of stories you write—whether obituaries, accidents, speeches, press conferences, fires or meetings—you will be required to use the skills you learn here.

FINDING THE LEAD

To determine a **lead**—a simple, clear statement consisting of the first paragraph or two of an inverted-pyramid story—you must first recognize what goes into one. As you read in Chapter 1, you begin by determining the story's *relevance, usefulness* and *interest* among readers. One way to measure those standards is to ask "So what?" or "Who cares?" So what if there's been a car accident downtown? If it's one of hundreds a month, it may not be news. Any holdup in a community of 5,000 may be news because the "so what" is that holdups are uncommon. Residents probably know the person working at the store. Neither

The six basic questions

1. Who?
2. What?
3. When?
4. Where?
5. Why?
6. How?

More questions

1. So what?
2. What's next?

newspapers nor radio and television stations may report a holdup in a metropolitan area, though, because holdups are common in cities. But if the holdup appears to be part of a pattern or if someone is killed, the story becomes more significant. One holdup may not be news, but a holdup that authorities believe is one of many committed by the same person may be news. The "so what" is that if the police catch this robber, they stop a crime spree. To determine the "so what," you have to answer six basic questions: who, what, when, where, why and how.

The information from every event you witness and every story you hear can be reduced to answers to who, what, when, where, why and how. If the answers add up to a significant "so what," you have a story. Consider this example of an incoming call at fire department headquarters:

> "Fire Department," the dispatcher answers.
> "Hello. At about 10 o'clock, I was lying on my bed watching TV and smoking," the voice says. "I must have fallen asleep about 10:30 because that's when the football game was over. Anyway, I woke up just now, and my bedroom is on fire. . . ."

That dialogue isn't informative or convincing. More likely, our sleepy television viewer awoke in a smoke-filled room, grabbed his cell phone and punched 9-1-1. The conversation at headquarters would more likely have gone like this:

> "Fire Department."
> "FIRE!" a voice at the other end yells.
> "Where?" the dispatcher asks.
> "1705 West Haven Street."

"Writing is easy; all you do is sit staring at a blank sheet of paper until the drops of blood form on your forehead."

— Gene Fowler, author

When fire is licking at their heels, even nonjournalists know the lead. How the fire started is not important to the dispatcher; that a house is burning—and where that house is located—is.

The journalist must go through essentially the same process to determine the lead. Whereas the caller served himself and the fire department, reporters must serve their readers. What is most important to them?

After the fire is over, there is much information a reporter must gather. Among the questions a reporter would routinely ask are these:

- When did it start?
- When was it reported?
- Who reported it?
- How was it reported?
- How long did it take the fire department to respond?
- How long did it take to extinguish the fire?
- How many fires have been attributed to careless smokers this year?
- How does that compare with figures in previous years?
- Were there any injuries or deaths?
- What was the damage?

- Who owned the house?
- Did the occupant or owner have insurance on the house?
- Will charges be filed against the smoker?
- Was there anything unusual about this case?
- Who cares?

With this information in hand, you can begin to write the story.

Writing the Inverted-Pyramid Lead

Start by looking over your notes.

Who? The owner, a smoker, Henry Smith, 29. The age is important. Along with other personal information, such as address and occupation, it differentiates him from other Henry Smiths in the readership area.

What? Fire caused damage estimated by the fire chief at $2,500.

Where? 1705 W. Haven St.

When? The call was received at 10:55 p.m., Tuesday. Firefighters from Station 19 arrived at the scene at 11:04. The fire was extinguished at 11:30. Those times are important to gather even if you don't use them. They show if the fire department responded quickly.

Why? The fire was started by carelessness on the part of Smith, according to Fire Chief Bill Malone.

How? Smith told fire officials that he fell asleep in bed while he was smoking a cigarette.

If you had asked other questions, you might have learned more from the fire department:

- This was the eighth fire this year caused by smoking in bed.
- All last year there were four such fires.
- Smith said he had insurance.
- The fire chief said no charges will be filed against Smith.
- It was the first fire at this house.
- Smith was not injured.

Have you figured out the "so what"?

Assume your city editor has suggested you hold the story to about four paragraphs. Your first step is to rank the information in descending order of importance. There are lots of fires in this town, but eight this year have been caused by smoking in bed. Perhaps that's the most important thing about this story. You begin to type:

> A fire started by a careless smoker caused an estimated $2,500 in damage to a home.

Only 16 words. You should try to hold every lead to fewer than 25 words unless you use more than one sentence. Maybe it's too brief, though. Have you left anything out? Maybe you should include the time element — to give the story a sense of immediacy. You rewrite:

> A Tuesday night fire started by a careless smoker caused an estimated
> $2,500 in damage to a home at 1705 W. Haven St.

The reader would also want to know "Where?" Is it near my house? Is it someone I know? Besides, you still have only 23 words.

Just then the city editor walks by and glances over your shoulder. "Who said it was a careless smoker?" the editor asks. "Stay out of the story."

You realize you have committed a basic error in newswriting: You have allowed an unattributed opinion to slip into the story. You have two choices. You can attribute the "careless smoker" information to the fire chief in the lead, or you can rewrite. You choose to rewrite by using the chief's exact words. You also realize that your sentence emphasizes the damage instead of the cause. You write:

> Fire that caused an estimated $2,500 in damage to a home at 1705 W. Haven
> St. Tuesday was caused by smoking in bed, Fire Chief Bill Malone said.

Now 28 words have answered the questions "What?" (a fire), "Where?" (1705 W. Haven St.), "When?" (Tuesday) and "How?" (smoking in bed). And the opinion is attributed. But you have not answered "Who?" and "Why?" You continue, still ranking the information in descending order of importance.

> The owner of the home, Henry Smith, 29, said he fell asleep in bed while
> smoking a cigarette. When he awoke about 30 minutes later, smoke filled
> the room.
>
> Firefighters arrived nine minutes after receiving the call. It took them
> about 26 minutes to extinguish the fire, which was confined to the bed-
> room of the one-story house.
>
> According to Chief Malone, careless smokers have caused eight fires this
> year.
>
> Smith, who was not injured, said the house was insured.

You take the story to the city editor, who reads through the copy quickly. Then she checks the telephone book and the city directory. As you watch, she changes the lead to emphasize the "so what." The lead now reads:

> A smoker who fell asleep in bed ignited a fire that caused minor damage to
> his home on W. Haven Street Tuesday, Fire Chief Bill Malone said. It was the
> city's eighth fire caused by smokers this year, twice as many as occurred all
> last year.

Too many numbers bog down a lead. Focus on the impact of the figures in the lead, and provide details later in the story.

The lead is 46 words, but it is broken into two sentences, which makes it more readable. The importance of the "so what" changed the direction of the story. The fire was minor; there were no injuries. However, the increase in the number of fires caused by smokers may force the fire department to start a public-safety campaign against careless smoking.

The city editor continues:

> The owner of the home, Henry Smith, 29, of 1705 W. Haven St., said he fell
> asleep in bed while smoking a cigarette. When he awoke about 30 minutes
> later, smoke filled the room.

Now, though, you have an even more serious problem. Both the telephone book and the city directory list the man who lives at 1705 W. Haven St. as Henry Smyth: S-m-y-t-h. City directories, like telephone books or any other sources, can be wrong. But at least they can alert you to possible errors. Confirm by going to original sources, in this case, Mr. Smyth.

Never put a name in a story without checking the spelling, even when the source tells you his name is Smith. Look at Figure 6.1 to see the completed fire story.

The Inverted-Pyramid Story

The identification of "who" is delayed until the next paragraph because the person is not someone readers would recognize and because his name would make the lead unnecessarily long. Also in the lead are the "what," "when," "how" and, most significantly here, the "so what."

The performance of the fire department is monitored.

Least important: If someone else had been hurt and charges had been filed, this information would move higher in the story.

A smoker who fell asleep in bed ignited a fire that caused minor damage to his home on W. Haven Street Tuesday, Fire Chief Bill Malone said. It was the city's eighth fire caused by smokers this year, twice as many as occurred all last year.

The owner of the home, Henry Smyth, 29, of 1705 W. Haven St., said he fell asleep in bed while smoking a cigarette. When he awoke about 30 minutes later, smoke filled the room.

The fire department, which received the call at 10:55 p.m., had the fire out by 11:30.

Malone said the damage, estimated at $2,500, was confined to the bedroom. The house was insured.

Careless smokers caused only four fires last year in the city. Malone said that he is considering a public awareness campaign to try to alert smokers to the hazards. Those four fires caused total damage of $43,000. This year, fires started by careless smoking have caused total damages of $102,500, Malone said.

No charges will be filed against Smyth because no one other than the smoker was endangered, Malone said.

The "who" is identified. More details on the "how" are given.

Details on the "so what" are given. The impact question is answered with the possible campaign.

Figure 6.1
The inverted-pyramid structure dictates that the most important information go in the lead paragraphs. It's the job of the writer and the editor to decide what that information is.

There are several lessons you can learn from this example:

- *Always* check names.
- Keep the lead short, usually fewer than 25 words, unless you use two sentences.
- Attribute opinion. (Smoking in bed is a fact. That it was careless is an opinion.)
- Find out the who, what, where, when, why and how. However, any of these elements that have no bearing on the story might not have to be included.
- Write a sentence or paragraph telling readers what the news means to them.
- Report information basic to the story, even if it is routine. Not everything you learn is important enough to be reported, but you'll never know unless you gather the information.

Emphasizing Different News Values

In the lead reporting the house fire, the "what" (fire) is of secondary importance to the "how" (how the fire started). A slightly different set of facts would affect the news value of the elements and, consequently, the lead. For instance, if Smyth turned out to have been a convicted arsonist, you probably would have emphasized that bizarre twist to the story:

> A convicted arsonist awoke Tuesday to find that his bedroom was filled with
> smoke. He escaped and later said that he had fallen asleep while smoking.
>> Henry Smyth, 29, who served a three-year term for . . .

That lead emphasizes the news value of novelty. If Smyth were the mayor, you would emphasize prominence:

> Mayor Henry Smyth escaped injury Tuesday when he awoke to find his
> bedroom filled with smoke. Smyth said he had fallen asleep while smoking
> in bed.

These differing news judgments play out daily in the media. In July 2008, the U.S. Department of Transportation said that over the preceding seven months, Americans had driven 40 billion miles fewer than a year earlier because of higher gasoline prices. The *Boston Herald* focused on the impact of lower gasoline tax revenues on the Massachusetts Department of Transportation. The ABC News Web site focused on how the declining tax revenues would affect the country's ability to repair roads and bridges. Then, using the interactivity of the Web, the site asked readers to describe how they were dealing with higher gasoline prices.

"What?" "So What?" and "What's Next?"

You know that the answer to "What?" often is the lead. The preceding examples also illustrate the "so what" factor in news. A $2,500 fire is not news to many people in large communities where there are dozens of fires daily. Even if you crafted a tightly written story about it, your editor probably would not want to print or broadcast it.

In small communities the story would have more impact because a larger proportion of the community is likely to know the victim and because there are fewer fires.

The "so what" factor grows more important as you add other information. If the fire occurred during a fire-safety campaign, the "so what" would be the need for fire safety even in a community where awareness of the problem had already been heightened. If the fire involved a convicted arsonist or the mayor, the "so what" would be stronger. Oddity or the involvement of well-known people increases the value of a story. If someone had been injured or the damage had been $250,000 instead of $2,500, the "so what" factor might even push the story into the metropolitan press. As you've seen above, once you have answered all six of the basic questions, it's important to ask yourself what the answers mean to the reader. That answer is your "so what" factor.

In many stories, it is also important to answer the question "What's next?" The City Council had its first reading of its budget bill. What's next? *Members will vote on it next month.* Jones was arrested Monday on a charge of passing bad checks. What's next? *The prosecuting attorney will decide whether there is enough evidence to file charges.*

A reader in a focus group once told researchers that she just wants the answers to "What?" "So what?" and "What's next?" That's a good guideline for all journalists to remember.

> *"Selecting the quotes isn't so hard; it's presenting them that causes the trouble. And the worst place to present them is at the beginning. Quote leads deserve their terrible reputation. Yet they still appear regularly in both print and broadcast journalism.*
>
> *"We can make three generalizations about quote leads. They're easy, lazy, and lousy. They have no context. The readers don't know who's speaking, why, or why it matters. Without context, even the best quotations are wasted."*
>
> **Paula LaRocque,** *former assistant managing editor,* The Dallas Morning News

VARIATIONS ON THE INVERTED-PYRAMID LEAD

No journalist relies on formulas to write inverted-pyramid leads, but you may find it useful, especially in the beginning, to learn some typical types of leads. The labels in the following sections are arbitrary, but the approaches are not.

The "You" Lead

Regardless of which of these leads journalists use, they are trying to emphasize the relevance of the news to the reader. One good way to highlight the relevance is to speak directly to the reader by using "you." This informal, second-person lead—the **"you" lead**—allows the writer to tell readers why they should care. For instance:

> You will make more money buying Savings Bonds starting tomorrow.
>
> The Treasury boosted the semiannual interest rate on Series EE Savings
>
> Bonds to 5.92 percent from 4.7 percent effective Tuesday.

Readers want to know what's in it for them. The traditional approach is less direct:

> The Treasury boosted interest on Savings Bonds Tuesday to the highest rate
>
> in three years.

As with any kind of lead, you can overdo the "you" lead. You don't need to write "You have another choice in the student president's race." Just tell readers who filed their candidacy. However, you may use those words in writing for radio or television news as a setup for the story to come.

The Immediate-Identification Lead

"Language is a very difficult thing to put into words."

— Voltaire, philosopher

In the **immediate-identification lead**, one of the most important facts is "who," or the prominence of the key actor. Reporters often use this approach when someone important or someone whose name is widely recognized is making news. Consider the following example:

> FORT WORTH, Texas (AP)—Dallas Cowboys cornerback Adam "Pacman" Jones was suspended for at least four games by the NFL on Tuesday for violating the league's personal conduct policy.

Names make news. When writing for your campus newspaper or your local newspaper, you would use names in the lead that are known, not necessarily nationally but locally. The name of your student body president, the chancellor, the city's mayor or an entertainer who has a local following would logically appear in the lead. None of them would be used in a newspaper 50 miles away.

In any accident, the "who" may be important because it is someone well known by name or position. If so, the name should be in the lead.

In small communities the "who" in an accident may always be in the lead. In larger communities names are not as recognizable. As a rule, if the name is well-known, it should appear in the lead.

The Delayed-Identification Lead

Usually a reporter uses a **delayed-identification lead** because the person, people or organization involved has little name recognition among

On the Job

Inverted Pyramid — A Basic Tool

As an education reporter at *The Daily Advertiser* in Lafayette, La., Tina Macias' time is split between writing human-interest stories and breaking news. She has covered bus wrecks, mold outbreaks and hurricanes.

Despite all the changes in the industry, she believes the inverted-pyramid format still is an essential tool, especially in this 24-hour news age.

Macias says the easiest and most efficient way to organize breaking news on the Web is with the inverted pyramid. Only months out of school, she found herself covering hurricanes Gustav and Ike. Her job was to get information fast and put it online and then follow with print stories. Most of the information about school closings, food stamps, curfews and power appeared on the Web in the inverted-pyramid format. This story was put online the Friday before Labor Day when Hurricane Gustav made landfall:

> With Hurricane Gustav edging toward the Gulf, and projections showing Acadiana in its path, public and private schools are preparing for the worst.

One day before she arrived at work, a colleague had reported the bare details of a school bus accident that morning. Macias' job was to update the story.

"As I started to make my phone calls, I thought about the vital information and how I could easily organize it," she says. She produced this inverted-pyramid lead:

> Nine people, including eight children, were transported to a local hospital Monday morning after a black Impala plowed into the side of a Lafayette Parish school bus.
> All were transported for minor or moderate injuries and complaints.

Though a rookie reporter, Macias was able to be productive immediately, in part because of two internships she held while attending journalism school.

---

the readers. Thus, in fairly large cities an accident is usually reported like this:

> MADISON, Wis. — A 39-year-old carpenter was killed today in a two-car collision two blocks from his home.
> Dead is William Domonske of 205 W. Oak St. Injured in the accident and taken to Mercy Hospital were Mary Craig, 21, of 204 Maple Ave., and Rebecca Roets, 12, of 207 Maple Ave.

However, in a smaller community, names almost always make news. If Domonske had lived in a smaller city — of 10,000, say — his name probably would be in the lead.

There are two other occasions when the reporter may choose to delay identification of the person involved in the story until the second paragraph. One occurs when the person is not well-known but the person's position, occupation, title or achievements are important or interesting. The other occurs when the lead is becoming too wordy.

When AP newsman Terry Anderson was released in Lebanon in 1992, his was a household name. Eight years later, during his court case, not many readers would have recognized his name.

A name that would appear in the lead in one city would appear in the second paragraph in another. The mayor of Birmingham, Ala., would be identified by title and name in Birmingham and by title only in Bridgewater, Conn.

When the title is better known than the name, writers usually use the title and delay the name until the second paragraph. Some titles are bulky: "Chairman of the Federal Communications Commission" assures clutter even before you add the name. "United Nations ambassador" deprives the writer of many options. When dealing with these types of positions, writers often choose to use the title alone and delay introducing the name until the second or third paragraph.

The Summary Lead

Reporters dealing with several important elements may choose to sum up what happened in a **summary lead** rather than highlighting a specific action. This is one of the few times that a general statement is preferable to specific action.

When Congress passed a bill providing employees with a family emergency the right to an unpaid leave from work, the writer had to make a choice: to focus on the main provision or to write a summary lead. The writer chose the latter:

> A bill requiring employers to give workers up to three months unpaid leave in family emergencies won Senate approval Thursday evening.

Several other provisions in the bill are explained later in the story: The unpaid leave can be for medical reasons or to care for a new child, and employers would have to continue health insurance benefits and restore employees to their previous jobs or equivalent positions.

You can also show the readers the "so what" with the "you" lead:

> The Senate voted Thursday to allow you to take up to three months unpaid leave in family emergencies without losing your health benefits.

Likewise, if a city council rewrites city ordinances, unless one of the changes is of overriding importance, most reporters will use a summary lead:

> MOLINE, Ill.—The City Council replaced the city's 75-year-old municipal code with a revised version Tuesday night.

Summary leads do not appear only in reports of board meetings. A Spokane, Wash., reporter used a summary lead to report a neighborhood dispute:

> An Idaho farmer's fence apparently was cut last week. It set off a chain of events Friday night that landed three people in the hospital, killed a cow and totaled a vehicle in the eastern Spokane Valley.

The basic question you must answer is whether the whole of the action is more important than any of its parts. If the answer is yes, a summary lead is in order.

The Multiple-Element Lead

Sometimes choosing one theme for the lead is too restrictive. In such cases the reporter can choose a **multiple-element lead** to work more information into the first paragraph. But you should write the lead within the confines of a clear, simple sentence or sentences. Consider this example:

Breaking stories into small segments increases readers' comprehension and retention.

> PORTLAND, Ore.—The City Council Tuesday ordered three department heads fired, established an administrative review board and said it would begin to monitor the work habits of administrators.

Notice that not only the actions but also the construction of the verb phrases within the sentence is parallel.

Some multiple-element leads consist of two paragraphs. This occurs when the reporter decides that several elements need prominent display. For example:

> The Board of Education voted Tuesday night to lower the tax rate 12 cents per $100 valuation. Members then approved a budget $150,000 less than last year's and instructed the superintendent to decrease the staff by 25 people.
>
> The board also approved a set of student-conduct rules, which include a provision that students with three or more unexcused absences a year will be suspended for a week.

This story, too, could emphasize the "so what" while retaining the multiple elements:

> The Board of Education lowered your real estate taxes Tuesday. Members also approved a budget $150,000 less than last year's and instructed the superintendent to decrease the staff by 25 people.

Simpler leads are preferable. But a multiple-element lead is one of your options. Use it sparingly.

Many newspapers are using graphic devices to take the place of multiple-element leads. They use summary boxes to list other actions. Because the box appears under the headline in type larger than the text, it serves as a graphic summary for the reader who is scanning the page. The box frees the writer from trying to jam too many details into the first few paragraphs (see Figure 6.2).

Another approach is to break the coverage of a single event into a main story and a shorter story or stories, called **sidebars**. This approach offers the advantage of presenting the information in short, palatable bites. It also allows the writer to elevate more actions into lead positions. Researchers have found that breaking stories into small segments increases readers' comprehension and retention. For instance,

---

Other Council Action
In other action, the council:
✓**Voted to repave Broadway Ave.**
✓**Rejected a new sign ordinance.**
✓**Hired four school crossing guards.**
✓**Expanded bus hours.**

Figure 6.2
A summary box can take the place of a multiple-element lead.

in the example above, the angle about the board of education superintendent having to decrease staff could be spun off into a short sidebar. On the Web, breaking the story into multiple stories or a main story and sidebars is standard practice. In print, it is more restricted because of space problems. On the Web, you can also link to related stories. You can run a summary box. You can add audio or video. The writing style remains the same, however.

Leads with Flair

Although the inverted pyramid tells readers the news first and fast, not all stories begin with the most important statement. When the news value you want to emphasize is novelty, often the lead is unusual.

"The lead should be a promise of great things to come, and the promise should be fulfilled."

— **Stanley Walker**, *city editor*

When a group of suspected drug dealers was arrested at a wedding, the Associated Press focused on the novelty:

> NARRAGANSETT, R.I. (AP)—The wedding guests included drug suspects, the social coordinator was a narcotics agent, the justice of the peace was a police chief, and 52 officers were party crashers.
>
> For the unsuspecting bride and groom, the ceremony Friday night was truly unforgettable—a sting operation set up by state and local police that led to 30 arrests.

Not exactly your traditional wedding or your traditional lead. Yet the essential information is contained within the first two paragraphs. A less imaginative writer would have written something like this:

> Thirty suspected drug dealers, including a couple about to be married, were arrested at a wedding Friday night.

That approach is like slapping a generic label on a Mercedes-Benz. The inverted pyramid approach is not so rigid that it doesn't permit fun and flair.

What is the difference between the two-paragraph, multiple-element lead on the board of education mentioned earlier and the two-step lead on the wedding story? In the first, the reporter was dealing with several significant actions. In the second, the reporter was dealing with only one, so she used the first paragraph to set up the surprise in the second.

STORY ORGANIZATION

Like the theater marquee, the lead is an attention getter. Sometimes the movie doesn't fulfill the promises of the marquee; sometimes the story doesn't fulfill the promises of the lead. In either case, the customer is dissatisfied.

The inverted pyramid helps you put information in logical order. It forces you to rank, in order of importance, the information you will present.

The One-Subject Story

As we have seen in this chapter, constructing an inverted-pyramid news story involves a series of judgments based on classic news values and the specific news outlet. A fire or an accident in one community is bigger news than a fire or accident in another, larger area. What has happened before will influence how a story is written.

Figure 6.3 shows a story about the arrest of a suspect in an assault case. Police say drugs were involved. If there had been a string of assaults or a pattern of drug-related violence, the writer probably would have emphasized different aspects. For instance, the writer could have emphasized the suspect's criminal record with this lead:

> A Columbia man who has been convicted of assault three times was
> arrested again Thursday night for an attack on his girlfriend.

There is almost always more than one way to write a story. The version that is published or broadcast is the result of the judgments of the writer and the editor. If the story in Figure 6.3 had already appeared on the Web or had been on television or radio, the newspaper probably would choose another angle, such as the one above, to make the story different.

Checklist for assembling the rest of the inverted pyramid

- Introduce additional important information you were not able to include in the lead.
- If possible, indicate the significance or "so what" factor.
- Elaborate on the information presented in the lead.
- Continue introducing new information in order of importance.
- Develop the ideas in the same order in which you have introduced them.
- Generally, use only one new idea in each paragraph.

The Multiple-Element Story

Multiple-element leads are most common when you are reporting on the proceedings of councils, boards, commissions, legislatures and courts. These bodies act on numerous subjects in one sitting. Frequently, their actions are unrelated, and more than one action is often important enough to merit attention in the lead. If you are writing for a newspaper, you have four options:

1. *You can write more than one story.* This, of course, requires permission from your editor. There may not be enough space for more than one story.
2. *You can write a summary box.* It would be displayed along with the printed story. In it you would list the major actions taken by the council or the decisions issued by the court.
3. *You can write a multiple-element lead and story.* Your lead would list all the major actions at the board meeting.
4. *You can write a single-element lead and cover the other elements further on in the story.* Your lead would focus on the element you found most interesting, relevant and useful.

Anatomy of a Single-Subject Inverted-Pyramid Story

Man Arrested in Attack, Charged with Child Endangerment

By Elizabeth Phillips
Columbia Missourian

The arrest, not the assault, is the latest development, so it is emphasized.

Police arrested a Columbia man in connection with an attack on his girlfriend Thursday night.

The lead gives "who," "what" and "when."

Details of the charges are in the second paragraph because the list is too long to put in the lead.

Darrell Vanness Johnson, 37, was arrested on suspicion of second-degree domestic assault, unlawful use of a weapon, felony possession of a controlled substance, misdemeanor possession of a controlled substance and endangering the welfare of a child at about 9 p.m. Thursday in the 1500 block of Greensboro Drive.

The name is not in the lead because most readers would not recognize it.

The writer adds details, attributed to the police, on how the assault occurred. This information includes the "why."

Johnson and his girlfriend began arguing over drugs Thursday evening, Columbia Police Sgt. Ken Hammond said. Johnson choked her and held a revolver to her head before she was able to escape and call 911 from a neighbor's house, Hammond said. Three children, two 9-year-olds and a 4-year-old, were in the home during the attack, Hammond said.

"Where" is identified. "When" is made more specific than in the lead.

This paragraph continues the chronology of the assault and capture.

When Columbia police arrived, Johnson was driving away from the Greensboro Drive home with the three children in the car, Hammond said. When police arrested Johnson, they found marijuana and cocaine, Hammond said.

Information about the children is pertinent because it adds to the "so what" — the children were also endangered.

The victim was taken to an area hospital by ambulance for treatment of bruises and scratches to the hands, neck and back, Hammond said. Her injuries were not life threatening.

The writer offers evidence of the injuries and attributes this information.

Now that the basic facts are established, the writer adds background on the suspect, attributed to a public safety Web site.

According to Missouri Case.net, Johnson has pleaded guilty to third-degree domestic assault three times in the past four years in Boone County Circuit Court, serving close to seven months in jail for those charges. He has also pleaded guilty to theft, first-degree trespass and second-degree property damage in Boone County Circuit Court, serving 75 days in Boone County Jail for the theft charge and receiving two years of unsupervised probation for the trespass and property damage charges.

Johnson violated his probation on the trespass and property damage charges and was scheduled to appear in Boone County Circuit Court for a probation violation hearing in December. He was charged with theft last October in Boone County Circuit Court.

The writer gives the "what's next."

He faces up to 40 years in prison and up to a year in jail in connection with the attack.

Copyright © 2006 *Columbia Missourian*

Figure 6.3
This typical one-subject story, written in the inverted-pyramid format, features a delayed-identification lead.

Let's go back to a multiple-element lead we saw earlier:

> The Board of Education voted Tuesday night to lower the tax rate 12 cents per $100 valuation. Members then approved a budget $150,000 less than last year's and instructed the superintendent to decrease the staff by 25 people.
>
> The board also approved a set of student-conduct rules, which include a provision that students with three or more unexcused absences a year will be suspended for a week.

Four newsworthy actions are mentioned in those two paragraphs: (1) changing the tax rate, (2) approving a budget, (3) cutting staff and (4) adopting conduct rules. In this and all stories that deal with several important elements, the writer highlights the most important elements. Sometimes several are equally important, as in the school board example. Most of the time, one action stands above the rest. When that is the case, it is important to summarize the other, lesser actions after the lead.

If you and your editor judge that changing the tax rate is more important than anything else that happened at the school board meeting, you would approach the story like this:

Lead	The Board of Education voted Tuesday night to lower the tax rate 12 cents per $100 valuation.
Support for lead	The new rate is $1.18 per $100 valuation. That means that if your property is assessed at $100,000, your school tax will be $1,180 next year.
Summary of other action	The board also approved a budget that is $150,000 less than last year's, instructed the superintendent to cut the staff by 25 and approved a set of rules governing student conduct.

Notice that the lead is followed by a paragraph that supports and enlarges upon the information in it before the summary paragraph appears. Whether you need a support paragraph before summarizing other action depends on how complete you are able to make the lead.

In every multiple-element story, the first two or three paragraphs determine the order of the rest of the story. To ensure the coherence of your story, you must describe the actions in the order in which you introduced them.

In Figure 6.4 you see a more detailed example of a multiple-element story. Notice the order in which the writer tells us the "who," "what," "when," "where," "why" and "how." Do you agree that the lead contains the most important elements? Could the story be cut from the bottom up, if necessary?

Anatomy of a Multiple-Element Inverted-Pyramid Story

U Earns C Average in Student-Access Report

By Norman Draper
Star Tribune

The University of Minnesota does better than most of the nation's major public universities in admitting minority students. But it fares poorly both in graduating them within six years and in admitting low-income students.

Those are among the findings of a report issued Monday by the national Education Trust. The report measured how well the nation's 50 flagship state universities are serving the nation's racial minority and poor students.

Overall, the report's findings described the nation's top state universities as looking "less and less like America—and more and more like gated communities of higher education." Too many, the report stated, aren't pushing hard enough to enroll more minority and poor kids.

The U of M generally fared relatively well in the report, though it earned only a C average based on six criteria. That's better than many state universities, which got Ds and Fs. Other universities in the survey included the University of Wisconsin-Madison, the University of North Carolina-Chapel Hill, the University of California-Berkeley and the University of Texas-Austin.

The U of M got an A in minority student access because the percentage of black, Hispanic and American Indian students in its fall 2004 freshman class—7.7 percent—was identical to the percentage of those students in the state's spring 2004 high school graduating class. Asian students were not counted as minority students in the report because they are not considered underrepresented.

The U got a D in minority student success because of the gap in graduation rates between white students (63.7 percent) and minority students (41.4 percent).

It also got a D in access for low-income students. That's because the number of such students at the U is lower than at all other Minnesota colleges and universities, as measured by the percentage of students who get federal grants.

(continued)

Left margin annotations:

The writer chooses two elements to put in the lead along with "who" and "what."

In order to tell the "what," the writer had to delay revealing the source of the report and the answer to "when."

Having established the most important elements, the writer summarizes the rest of the report.

Now the writer summarizes the local details.

Any of these details could have been in the lead. The writer and editor had to make judgments about the most important details.

Right margin annotations:

Are there any elements in the fifth paragraph that you think should be in the lead?

This is the context against which readers can measure the local university's performance.

Note that the writer offers not only the findings but also the reasons for the findings in this and succeeding paragraphs.

Notice that the letter grades used in the report give the reader a way to understand the results.

The terms *black, Hispanic, American Indian* and *Asian* are preferred by the *AP Stylebook*.

Figure 6.4
The writer for the Minneapolis *Star Tribune* took a national study and localized it for readers. The study produced multiple findings, so the writer and editor had to rank them from most to least important.

Figure 6.4
(continued)

Here and in the next
two paragraphs is
the university's
response to the
report.

Note how the
writer handles the
e-mail from the
spokesman.

"The University of Minnesota has long been concerned with issues of access for students from all walks of life," U spokesman Daniel Wolter said in an e-mailed response. "The issue of access for underrepresented minorities has been an important one for the U . . . and our A grade underscores that we're doing a good job on that front."

Wolter also cited the creation of a new administrative position—vice president for access and diversity—and the U's raising of $150 million in private gifts to support student scholarships as evidence that the U is committed to academic and racial diversity.

In regard to the two Ds, Wolter said, "We recognize those as areas for improvement," but he added that overall U graduation rates have doubled over the past decade.

The background helps readers understand who issued the report.

The Education Trust is a Washington, D.C., nonprofit organization dedicated to improving student achievement, with a special emphasis on low-income and racial minority students.

CHECKING ACCURACY AND ATTRIBUTIONS

All of us can improve our accuracy. Some improvement comes with experience, but most of the errors journalists make involve routine facts. In Chapter 3, you learned the importance of accurately capturing the words for quotes. Here are additional procedures you should use to produce more accurate stories.

Ensuring Accuracy

This correction is from *The Detroit News*: "Three million Americans are eligible for a low-income subsidy through Medicare Part D. A front-page story on Friday erroneously said 3 million Michigan residents were eligible." Corrections such as these routinely run in newspapers and on Web sites. The errors shouldn't be routine. In *An Essay on Criticism*, Alexander Pope wrote, "To err is human, to forgive is divine." However, readers are not apt to forgive. We all make errors, but our job as professional journalists is to be as accurate as humanly possible. There are three habits you should develop to be more accurate.

1. Go over your notes at the end of every interview. Read back the quotes and the facts as you have written them down. Don't assume anything. As you read earlier in the chapter, if someone tells you his name is Smith, ask how to spell it.

2. Carefully check your story against your notes and the documents you have collected to be certain you didn't introduce any errors while writing. We all make typing errors. We make errors because of background noise and commotion. If you recognize that you are not infallible, you will be a more accurate journalist.

3. When sources give you facts, if possible, check them. During an interview, the mayor may tell you that the city has 50 police officers. Check with the police department. The mayor may have the number wrong.

Another way to increase accuracy is to do a prepublication check of some sort with your sources. Some journalists object to such an accuracy check because they believe that it gives sources too much opportunity to object to what you will print. In some competitive situations, you might be afraid sources may approach other media to get their version of the story out even before you publish. But those situations are rare.

In a study published in the *Newspaper Research Journal*, researcher Duane Stoltzfus found that more newspapers than formerly believed were willing to permit their reporters to check stories or portions of stories with sources before publication. In all cases, sources are told that they are being asked to check the accuracy of the information. No journalist should cede authority for decisions about what goes in and what does not. But no journalist should be afraid to take every step possible to ensure accuracy. Some read back quotes; some read back facts gathered from that source. Some even describe information obtained from other sources.

The New York Times has a Credibility Group that recommends that the paper encourage "the practice of reporters' interim and final checks with sources to verify specific points." However, the group also says, "We do not advocate having sources look over entire articles." Stoltzfus also reported that *USA Today*, among many other newspapers, permits its reporters to decide whether to check with sources before publication.

If you are at a publication that permits prepublication checks, you do yourself and your profession a favor by performing them. Verify everything you intend to publish or broadcast. In the online world, where speed is king, verification sometimes is sacrificed in the rush to be first. Being first and wrong is never right. The bloggers will tell you that. In an effort to be transparent, some news Internet sites put a note on stories that have been corrected.

How and When to Attribute

Attribution is our way of telling readers that we aren't making this stuff up.

Primary Sources

Your first obligation is to go to primary sources whenever possible. The mayor is an official source, but he isn't the primary source for how many police officers the city employs. The police chief or someone authorized to speak for the department would be a primary, and more accurate, source. So would someone in the city personnel department. So would city records. However, not all facts need to be attributed. If you are reporting that there was a fire in a five-story building, you do not need to attribute that fact because it is verifiable to anyone who sees the burnt structure. However, if you are gathering information about a fire in another community, you should attribute it if you are unable to confirm it.

Witnesses

Witnesses are good sources for firsthand accounts, but they are not always accurate. One witness may say that the Toyota hit the Ford. Another may say the Ford hit the Toyota. Your primary source is the police officer. If the police officer can't sort it out, you may need to report the conflicting versions with attribution to all the parties. When you are reporting on deadline, you often have to deal with uncertainty. An Associated Press reporter dealt with one such instance this way: "The bus driver was either ejected or escaped from the vehicle before it fell, NTSB investigator Debbie Hersman said Tuesday."

Opinions

Always attribute opinions. "Augusta is the most livable city in the U.S." is an opinion regardless of who says it. If *Money* magazine publishes a list of the most livable cities in the United States, attribute that opinion to the magazine.

Transparency

Tell readers how you obtained the information. If you are using information from an e-mail sent to you by your source, tell readers that the source gave the information in an e-mail. If you are using instant messaging, tell readers. If someone is revealing something to you from a document that he or she will not let you see because it is confidential, say the source obtained the information from the document. Be transparent about your sources.

Suggested Readings

Brooks, Brian S., James L. Pinson and Jean Gaddy Wilson. *Working with Words*. 6th ed. New York: Bedford/St. Martin's, 2006. A must for any journalist. Provides excellent coverage of grammar and word usage and a strong chapter on "isms."

Gillman, Timothy. "The Problem of Long Leads in News and Sports Stories." *Newspaper Research Journal* (Fall 1994): 29–39. The researcher found that sentences in leads were longer than sentences in the rest of the story.

Kennedy, George. "Newspaper Accuracy: A New Approach." *Newspaper Research Journal* (Winter 1994): 55–61. The author suggests that journalists do accuracy checks before publication, with proper safeguards.

Stoltzfus, Duane. "Partial Pre-publication Review Gaining Favor at Newspapers." *Newspaper Research Journal* (Fall 2006): 23–37. The researcher surveyed the 50 largest newspapers to determine their policies toward prepublication review. He found that the trend is to permit it.

Suggested Web Sites

www.regrettheerror.com Regret the Error is a Web site that chronicles errors made in all media. It is valuable in that it shows how fallible even professional reporters are.

www.stateofthenewsmedia.com The Project for Excellence in Journalism produces an annual *State of the News Media* report that examines journalistic and economic trends.

www.wsu.edu:8080/~brians/errors/index.html
Paul Brians, a professor of English at Washington State University, will answer your questions about the English language.

Exercises

1. Identify the who, what, where, when, why and how, if they are present, in the following:

   The United Jewish Appeal is sponsoring its first-ever walk-a-thon this morning in Springfield to raise money for The Soup Kitchen, a place where the hungry can eat free.

2. Here are four versions of the same lead. Which version answers more of the six questions basic to all stories? Which questions does it answer?

   a. What began 12 years ago with a federal staff investigation and led to hearings and a court fight culminates today with a Federal Trade Commission rule to prevent funeral home rip-offs.

   b. The nation's funeral home directors are required to offer detailed cost statements starting today, a service they say they are now ready to provide despite nearly a dozen years of debate over the idea.

   c. A new disclosure law going into effect today will make it easier for us to determine the cost of a funeral.

   d. Twelve years after first being proposed, a federal regulation goes into effect today to require funeral homes to provide an itemized list of services and materials they offer, along with the cost of each item, before a person agrees to any arrangements.

3. Rewrite two of the leads in exercise 2 as "you" leads. Which are better, the third-person or second-person leads? Why are they better?

4. From the following facts, write a lead.

   Who: A nuclear weapon with a yield equivalent to 150,000 tons of TNT.

   What: Detonated.

   Where: 40 miles from a meeting of pacifists and 2,000 feet beneath the surface of Pahute Mesa in the Nevada desert.

When: Tuesday.
Why: To test the weapon.
How: Not applicable.

Other information: Department of Energy officials are the source; 450 physicians and peace activists were gathered to protest continued nuclear testing by the United States.

5. From the following facts, write the first two paragraphs of a news article.

   Who: A 7-year-old boy missing for three years.
   What: Found.
   Where: In Brick Township, N.J.
   When: Monday night.
   Why: Not applicable.
   How: A neighbor recognized the child's picture when it was shown after the movie *Adam: The Song Continues* and called police.

   Other information: Police arrested the boy's mother, Ellen Lynn Conner, 27; she faces Alabama charges of kidnapping and interference with a custody warrant.

6. From the following facts, write the first two paragraphs of a news article.

   Who: 40 passengers.
   What: Evacuated from a Northwest Airlines jet, Flight 428.
   Where: At the La Crosse, Wis., Municipal Airport.
   When: Monday following a flight from Minneapolis to La Crosse.
   Why: A landing tower employee spotted smoke near the wheels.
   How: Not applicable.

   Other information: There was no fire or injuries; the smoke was caused by hydraulic fluids leaking onto hot landing brakes, according to Bob Gibbons, a Northwest spokesman.

7. Describe picture and information-graphic possibilities for the story in exercise 6.

8. Collect six leads from newspapers or Internet news sites. For each, identify what questions are answered and what are not answered. Identify the kind of lead (summary, etc.).

7 Beyond the Inverted Pyramid

Newspapers, magazines and Web sites sometimes publish stories that are not suited for the inverted-pyramid structure. Here's the opening to a story written as if it were a novel, except that it is all true.

By Helen O'Neill
The Associated Press

LITTLE PRAIRIE, Wis. — It was cold the night Grandma Braun was taken, that bitter dead-of-winter cold when the country-side is sheathed in ice and the stillness is broken only by great gusts of snow that swirl across the fields and back roads, erasing footprints and car tracks and all traces of life.

Eighty-eight-year-old Hedwig Braun was in bed reading when the lights went out but she didn't pay much heed. In her tiny farmhouse on Bluff Road, miles from the nearest town, power outages are not uncommon. Pulling on her dressing gown and slippers, she lit a candle and padded into the kitchen. She poured a glass of milk, settled at the table and continued her book about angels.

The clock was stopped at 12:50 a.m.

A sudden blast of wind. A shadowy figure in the doorway.

"Eddie!" she screamed as the intruder lurched toward her, throwing something over her head. "Eddie come quick."

But her 88-year-old husband, asleep in the other room, didn't stir.

At 5-foot-2, weighing 80 pounds, Braun is a slip of a woman whose toughness is all inside. She had no strength to fight off her abductor. She didn't even try. She just prayed as she was flung into the trunk of her 1992 white Cadillac, kept praying as they tore down the country road, screeching to a halt beside a ditch, prayed even harder as she was tossed into the trunk of another car and they sped away again.

In the darkness, wedged against the spare tire, she wondered, "Why me? I'm just a no-body. What does he want with me?"

Want to read on? You are introduced to Grandma Braun, who was snatched out of her isolated home. What will become of her? Why was she taken? Using the inverted pyramid, we get to the point as quickly as possible. That approach saves readers' and listeners' time, but it's not the way to tell stories. If we want to engage our readers intellectually and emotionally, if we want to inform and entertain, we must use writing techniques that promise great things to come and then fulfill that promise. To that end, like Helen O'Neill, we should use the techniques of narration: scene re-creation, dialogue, foreshadowing and anecdotes. If we use these techniques and build the story around characters dealing with tension and follow the story through to a resolution, we reward readers.

Of course, when the kidnapping occurred, the news was disseminated through the inverted pyramid. During the investigation, there was no resolution. Only after it was all over could O'Neill or any other journalist go back and retell the entire story in chronological order. Even though readers already knew the broad outlines of the story, they didn't know many of the details that O'Neill was able to add by interviewing the victim, members of her family and law enforcement officials and by reading investigative and court records.

Although narrative techniques can and should be used in all kinds of writing, narration thrives in structures other than the inverted pyramid. Some story structures are hybrids of the inverted pyramid and chronology structures. Others are adaptations of chronology. These structures are even suitable for breaking news stories if you are able to gather enough information to write in scenes jammed with pertinent detail, if you are able to confirm the chronology and if you are able to capture the dialogue. These structures also support investigative reports, profiles, oddities and issue stories — all genres that allow you more time to gather the facts and write.

If time, detail and space are available, use the techniques of narration and structures other than the inverted pyramid. Whether you are writing about a car accident or profiling a community leader, whether you are writing for a newspaper, a magazine or the Web, writing the story will be easier if you know how to use some of the alternative techniques and story forms.

THE TECHNIQUES OF NARRATION

Exposition is the ordering of facts. Narration is the telling of a story. When we arrange facts from most to least important, we call the resulting structure the *inverted pyramid*. When we use characters, scenes, anecdotes and dialogue in chronology to build to a climax, we call the structure *narrative*.

Storytellers don't speak in monotone. They add inflection to maintain listeners' interest. To avoid telling stories in monotone, narrative writers capture scenes with detail and dialogue, foreshadow the good stuff to come, and tempt readers to continue reading by offering them treats in the form of anecdotes. They also use the complications in stories — Will the dance studio instructor be able to get her class ready for the recital in time? — to keep readers interested.

In exposition, the writer clearly stands between the reader and the information; the people in the story whisper to the writer, who turns and speaks to the reader. In narration, the storyteller moves aside and allows the reader to watch the action unfold. When you watch a movie or a live stage performance, you are watching narration unfold.

Vivid Scenes

Gene Roberts, former managing editor of *The New York Times*, tells about his first job at a daily newspaper. His publisher, who was blind,

Move your story along by

- Reconstructing vivid scenes.
- Letting the characters speak to each other through dialogue.
- Foreshadowing important events.
- Relating memorable anecdotes.

had the newspaper read to him each morning. One day, the publisher called Roberts into his office and complained, "Roberts, I can't see your stories. Make me see."

We should all try to make readers see, smell, feel, taste and hear. One way to do that is to use scenes. First, you have to be there. You need to capture the sights, sounds and smells that are pertinent.

A student reporter at South Dakota State University was there to capture this opening:

> Don Sheber's leathery, cracked hands have been sculpted by decades of wresting a living from the earth.
>
> But this year, despite work that often stretches late into the evening, the moisture-starved soil has yielded little for Sheber and his family.
>
> Sheber's hands tugged at the control levers on his John Deere combine last week as rotating blades harvested the thin stands of wheat that have grown to less than a foot high. . . .

The writer stepped aside and allowed the reader to visit Sheber on the farm. We can see and feel his hands. We can touch the John Deere, the small stands of wheat.

O'Neill's story about Grandma Braun's kidnapping is full of scenes such as this:

> Shackled in the darkness, praying for warmth — and for strength — Heddie Braun lost all sense of time.
>
> At one point, she thought she heard helicopters and wondered if she was in a flight path or near an airport. Try to remember everything, she told herself, so when they find you, you can be of some help.
>
> Briefly, she had glimpsed her masked abductor that first night as he carried her across a moonlit field and flung her inside a small, white utility trailer — the kind used for snowmobiles. But she had no idea where she was or how long she had been there.
>
> Her legs were pinned to the floor, the chains cutting into her ankles. At first, he had tied her wrists too, but she had cried in such pain that he eventually released them.
>
> In one corner a sputtering kerosene tank cast an eerie orange glow on the dirty mattress on which she was lying. A few blankets were thrown over her.
>
> She prayed and dozed fitfully and tried not to think of the pain. Every now and then he came with food — orange juice and a hamburger.

To write such scenes, you must use all your senses to gather information, and your notebook should reflect that reporting. Along with the results of interviews, your notebook should bulge with details of sight and smell, sound and touch. Gather details indiscriminately. Later, you can discard those that are not germane.

Good writing doesn't tell; it shows

1. Gather information with all your senses.
2. Don't tell readers that your subject is funny; show her pulling a prank on a friend. Don't tell readers that the speaker was angry; show him pounding the lectern so hard he broke a finger.
3. Telling is story in outline; showing fills in the spaces between the lines.

Dialogue

Dialogue allows the narrator to recede and the characters to take center stage. When you use quotations, you — the writer — are telling the reader what the source said. The reader is listening to you relate the quotation instead of listening to the source speak. When you use dialogue, the writer disappears and the reader listens directly to the characters speaking. Compare these examples (the paraphrased material on the left and the corresponding quotations on the right are in italics):

Traditional Paraphrase	*Dialogue*
During the public hearing, *Henry Lathrop accused the council of wasting taxpayers' money.* "If you don't stop voting for all this spending, I am going to circulate a recall petition and get you all kicked off the council," he said. *Mayor Margorie Gold told Lathrop he was free to do as he wished.* "As for us," she said, "we will vote in the best interests of the city."	When Henry Lathrop spoke to the City Council during the public hearing, he pounded on the podium. *"You folks are wasting taxpayers' money.* If you don't stop voting for all this spending, I am going to circulate a recall petition and get you all kicked off the council." Mayor Margorie Gold slammed her gavel on her desk. *"Mr. Lathrop," she said as she tried to control the anger in her voice. She looked at him directly. "You are free to do as you wish.* As for us, we will vote in the best interests of the city."

In the traditional paraphrase on the left, the reporter is telling readers what was said instead of taking readers to the council chamber and letting them listen. In the dialogue on the right, Lathrop and Gold are speaking to each other. The dialogue gives readers the exchange without the intercession of the writer. Capturing the dialogue sometimes makes a story longer, but it is worth it.

When you do not witness the conversation, you have to ask enough questions to get the dialogue: "What did you say to your husband? What was his response? Then what happened? Where were you when that happened? Then what did you do?" Repeat the same questions to other participants until you are satisfied you know what happened.

Dialogue is a conversation between two or more people, none of whom normally is the reporter. Even though she wasn't in the room, O'Neill captured dialogue by careful interviews with the participants after the investigation ended. Let's listen in:

It was Tuesday, Feb. 4, 2003. At his desk at Mann Brothers Inc. in Elkhorn, the road construction company his great-grandfather had founded, Mann didn't know what to think.

"Hi Grandma," he began. "Sorry I missed your birthday. How are you?"

"I'm OK," she said, though her teeth were chattering as though she were cold. "I'm not worried about dying. At my age I thought I would have died a long time ago."

Mann frowned. Where was this coming from? Aside from having to take heart medicine every day, his grandmother was healthy, her mind sharp. She never rambled like this.

"Grandma, you're not dying. You're going to live a long time," he bellowed into the phone. "Where are you?"

"I'm in a dark place. I'm tied up. There's a man. . . . he's shining a light. . . . He says I'm going to die."

"What man? Put the man on the phone."

But all Mann heard was a muffled sound as the phone went dead.

Mann waited for a few minutes, wondering if she would call back.

Still puzzled, he phoned his aunt, Joan Wolfram, who lives a mile down the road from her parents.

"Something is wrong with Grandma Braun," he said.

Dialogue is a key element in re-creating scenes. A good reporter permits the characters to talk to one another. Be realistic, though. No one can accurately remember large chunks of conversation. If you weren't there to capture the dialogue, be careful about depending on the participants to remember exactly what they said.

Good writing uses figures of speech

1. Similes use "like" or "as" to compare the unknown to the known: "Her legs, wobbling like jelly, shook and then surrendered."
2. Metaphors equate one thing with another: "Michael is a lion with a gazelle's legs."
3. Allusions add value: "Osama bin Laden is a clear and present danger."
4. Personification allows you to breathe life into inanimate objects: "The houses have eyes."

Foreshadowing

Foreshadowing is the technique of advertising what's coming. Moviemakers tease you with the scenes they think will persuade you to buy a ticket. Broadcast journalists foreshadow to keep you from leaving during a commercial: "Coming up, there's a burglar prowling your neighborhood." Every lead foreshadows the story. The leads that not only tell but promise more good stuff to come are the most successful.

A student at Florida A&M University used foreshadowing to invite readers to continue the story:

A North Carolina family thought the worst was behind them when they were robbed Saturday morning at a gas station just off Interstate 95.

The worst was yet to come.

"The worst was yet to come." That's another way of saying, "Read on; it gets even more interesting." Here is a longer opening that is packed with promises of great things to come. It also was written by a college student, this one from the University of Missouri.

> Deena Borman's relationship with her roommate, Teresa, during her freshman year in college had shattered long before the wine bottle.
>
> Weeks had gone by with Teresa drawing further and further away from Deena. Finally, after repeatedly hearing Teresa talk about suicide, Deena says, "I kept telling her how silly she was to want to die."
>
> That made Teresa angry, so she threw a full wine bottle at Deena. It shattered against the wall and broke open the simmering conflict between them. That was when Deena tried to find out what had gone wrong with Teresa's life, and that was when Teresa told Deena that she wanted to do something to get rid of her.
>
> And that was when Deena began to be scared of her own roommate.

The writer is promising a great story. What is wrong with Teresa? Does Teresa really try to hurt Deena? Does Deena really have something to be scared about? There is a promise of great things to come. Would you keep reading?

O'Neill wrote her narrative in a four-part series. She used foreshadowing at the beginning and end of each segment. Here's how she used foreshadowing at the end of part 2:

> And so, at peace with her life and her Lord, Heddie Braun prepared to die.
>
> Yet, as she drifted into an uneasy sleep, she couldn't help but wonder, "How does he plan to kill me?"

Anecdotes

The ultimate treats, **anecdotes** are stories embedded in stories. They can be happy or sad, funny or serious. Whatever their tone, they should illustrate a point. You are likely to remember the anecdotes longer than anything else in the story. You probably remember the stories that your professors tell regardless of whether you remember the rest of the lecture. Long after you've forgotten this chapter, you'll probably remember Grandma Braun and some of the other examples. Facts inform. Anecdotes inform and entertain.

As befits something so valuable, anecdotes are hard to obtain. You can't get them by asking your source, "Got any good anecdotes?" But you can get them by asking your source for examples so you can re-create the story.

Be alert when your source alludes to stories. For instance, your source says: "Darren is like a one-man entertainment committee. He's always got something going on. And if nothing is going on, he'll hike up his pants really high and dance to the Jonas Brothers."

Good writing avoids sexism

1. Use gender-free terms like "flight attendant" and "firefighter."
2. Participate in the movement to avoid feminine endings: "comedian," "hero," "poet."
3. Make the subject plural: "Reporters must keep their minds open."
4. Rewrite to eliminate unnecessary allusions to gender: "A reporter must not prejudge."
5. Replace a sexist pronoun with an article: "A teacher must know what the students' interests are" (not "his students' interests").
6. Use the second person: "You must know what your students' interests are."

To turn this from a dry quote to an anecdote, you need to ask, "Can you give me an example of when he acted like an entertainment committee?" or "Tell me about the time he danced to the Jonas Brothers."

Some of the best anecdotal examples come from phrasing questions in the superlative: "What's the funniest thing that ever happened to you while you were standing in front of an audience?" "What's the worst case you've ever seen come into this emergency room?" "People tell me Rodney is always the first one they call when they need help on a project. Has he ever helped you?" "Can you give me an example?"

When leading bankers were summoned to the Treasury Department during the financial meltdown in the fall of 2008, journalists were not allowed in the meeting. Yet some were able to reconstruct the scene inside. Here's an anecdote set in a scene:

Good writing is coherent

1. Logical thinking produces logical story structures. If you don't know where you are going, readers won't know either. Construct an outline before you write a story.
2. Choose the proper sentence structure to show the relationship among ideas. Compound sentences equate ideas: "The river overflowed, and the crop was destroyed." Complex sentences show cause and effect or sequence: "When the river overflowed, the crop was destroyed."
3. Carefully construct transitions between paragraphs. Transitions are like road signs; they tell readers where you are going.

Drama Behind a $250 Billion Banking Deal
By Mark Landler and Eric Dash

WASHINGTON—The chief executives of the nine largest banks in the United States trooped into a gilded conference room at the Treasury Department at 3 p.m. Monday. To their astonishment, they were each handed a one-page document that said they agreed to sell shares to the government, then Treasury Secretary Henry M. Paulson Jr. said they must sign it before they left.

The chairman of JPMorgan Chase, Jamie Dimon, was receptive, saying he thought the deal looked pretty good once he ran the numbers through his head. The chairman of Wells Fargo, Richard M. Kovacevich, protested strongly that, unlike his New York rivals, his bank was not in trouble because of investments in exotic mortgages, and did not need a bailout, according to people briefed on the meeting.

But by 6:30, all nine chief executives had signed—setting in motion the largest government intervention in the American banking system since the Depression and retreating from the rescue plan Mr. Paulson had fought so hard to get through Congress only two weeks earlier.

All of these elements—writing in scenes, dialogue, foreshadowing and anecdotes—are the ingredients of narration. Most stories move between exposition and narration several times. Now let's look at the structures in which you can use these techniques.

Writers can organize narrative elements into a story in several ways. First, we will look at the news narrative, a hybrid of the inverted pyramid and a feature story. Then we will move further from the inverted pyramid when we look at the focus structure. From there, we will explore two other writing approaches: blogs and service journalism.

THE NEWS NARRATIVE STRUCTURE

In Chapter 6, you saw examples of inverted-pyramid stories that didn't have the news in the first paragraph. But as soon as the writer set the hook, the news lead appeared, and the writer arranged the rest of the story in the traditional descending order of importance. Further modification offers writers more choices.

When Jane Meinhardt of the *St. Petersburg Times* wrote about an unusual burglary ring, she started with a non-news lead, went to news and then went back to chronology, as her story, in Figure 7.1, shows. This is news, but it is presented as a story rather than as facts arranged in order of most to least important. The traditional lead isn't in the first paragraph, but it's not too deep in the story, either. And when the writer returns to the chronology, she uses a transition that signals a story to come: "The burglary ring unraveled Tuesday, Tita said." The transition has echoes of "Let me tell you how it happened." Journalists shouldn't be afraid to experiment with different story forms.

News Narrative with News Emphasis

The opening paragraphs set the scene with information that informs and is interesting. →

A traditional news lead gives "who," "what" and "when." →

The story continues with the breaking news for the next four paragraphs. →

PALM HARBOR—They carried knapsacks and bags to tote loot. They had a screwdriver to pry open doors and windows.

They used latex gloves.

They acted like professional criminals, but officials say they were teenage burglars coached and directed by a Palm Harbor woman whose son and daughter were part of her gang.

Pinellas County Sheriff's deputies arrested Rovana Sipe, two of her children and two other teens Wednesday after a series of home burglaries.

"She was the driver," said Sheriff's Sgt. Greg Tita. "She pointed out the houses. She's the one who said 'Do these.'"

Sipe, 38, of 2333 State Road 584, was charged with two counts of being a principal in burglary. She was held Thursday in lieu of $20,000 bail.

Her daughter, Jackie Shifflet, 16, was charged with grand theft. Her son, Ryan Shifflet, 15, was charged with two counts of burglary.

(continued)

← The writer supports the lead with a quote.

Figure 7.1
In news narratives with a news emphasis, the writer needs to establish some facts before giving the chronology. This format is associated with breaking news of significance, such as crime.

Figure 7.1
(continued)

> Charles Ruhe, 17, of 1600 Ensley Ave., in Safety Harbor, and Charles Taylor, 16, of 348 Jeru Blvd. in Tarpon Springs, also were held on four counts of burglary each.
>
> "They were very well-prepared to do burglaries, especially with the guidance they were given," Tita said. "We recovered thousands of dollars of stolen items. Anything that could be carried out, was."
>
> The burglary ring unraveled Tuesday, Tita said. A Palm Harbor woman saw a large, yellow car driven by a woman drop off three boys, he said. The three went to the back of her house.
>
> They put on gloves and started to pry open a window with a screwdriver, she said. When she tapped on a window, they ran.
>
> She called 911. As she waited for deputies, other neighbors saw the boys walk through a nearby neighborhood carrying bags.
>
> Deputies chased the boys and caught two. The third got into a large yellow car driven by a woman.
>
> The bags contained jewelry, a shotgun and other items deputies say were taken from another house in the neighborhood.
>
> Tita said the boys, later identified as Taylor and Ruhe, told detectives about other burglaries in Dunedin and Clearwater and who else was involved.
>
> At Sipe's house, detectives found stolen VCRs, televisions, camcorders and other valuables. They arrested the other two teens and Sipe.
>
> "We're very familiar with this family and its criminal history," Tita said. "We have found stolen property at the house in the past and made juvenile arrests."

← Now that the news has been established, instead of continuing to present the information in order of importance, the writer presents the rest of the story in chronological fashion. Note the important transition from inverted pyramid to chronology: "The burglary ring unraveled Tuesday, Tita said."

The story ends with a quote rather than a tie-back or summary.

THE FOCUS STRUCTURE

For centuries, writers have told stories by focusing on one individual or group that represents a bigger population. This approach allows the writer to make large institutions, complex issues and seven-digit numbers meaningful (see Figure 7.2). Not many of us can understand—let alone explain—the interaction of two or more pesticides. That's why one reporter told the story of an individual to tell a story of pesticide poisoning:

> Thomas Latimer used to be a vigorous, athletic man, a successful petroleum engineer with a bright future.
> Then he mowed the lawn.

Want to read on?

Even though former Soviet dictator Joseph Stalin was hardly talking about literary approaches, he summed up the impact of focusing on

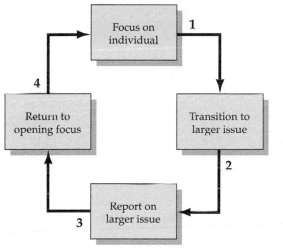

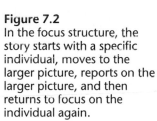

Figure 7.2
In the focus structure, the story starts with a specific individual, moves to the larger picture, reports on the larger picture, and then returns to focus on the individual again.

a part of the whole when he said, "Ten million deaths are a statistic; one death is a tragedy." Think about that the next time you hear about a hurricane that kills scores of people. If you can write a story of any tragedy by focusing on one of the victims, you have a better chance of emotionally involving your readers. Issues like health care, budget deficits and sexual harassment don't have much emotional appeal. You make them relevant when you discuss the issue by focusing on someone affected by it.

Writing the Lead

One college writer examining atypical hyperplasia found a specific person through whom she could tell the story:

Karen Elliott, 44, remembers the phone call from Dr. Jonathen Roberts, a general surgeon, as if it had happened yesterday. Dr. Roberts' nurse called one afternoon two years ago and told Karen to hold the line. She froze. She had just had a biopsy on her right breast because of a new lump. It's never good news when the doctor calls at home. Dr. Roberts cut to the chase.

"You have atypical hyperplasia," he said.

Being a nurse, Karen knew exactly what he meant. No number of breast self-exams could have detected this. Atypical hyperplasia is a lifelong condition characterized by abnormal cells. Affecting only 4 percent of the female population, it puts Karen and others at an increased risk for breast cancer. With her family history of the disease, her risk of breast cancer jumps sky-high.

What Karen didn't know was that her pleasant life in New Bloomfield would become a roller coaster of ups and downs for the next two years, a ride that nearly destroyed her. Her husband of 19 years, Bob, and

Good writing is concrete

1. Use familiar words: "highway," not "infrastructure"; "arena," not "facility"; "reading group," not "learning pod."
2. Be specific. "Big" or "loud" or "ugly" means something only in comparison to something else.
3. Replace generalities, such as "The business is downsizing," with concrete details, such as "The business is laying off 150 employees."

their two children, Bethany, 6, and Jordan, 8, could only watch as she struggled with the decision of whether to voluntarily have her breasts removed because Karen, and only Karen, could make that choice.

Karen is concrete; atypical hyperplasia is abstract. If the writer is skillful enough at creating Karen as a character instead of simply a source, readers will develop empathy for her and will read the story to see what choice she made.

Reporters working on local stories have just as many opportunities to apply the focus structure as those writing national and international stories. For example, instead of keeping score on the United Way fund drive, focus on the people who will benefit—or fail to benefit—from the campaign. If the streets in your city are bad, write about the problem from the point of view of a driver. The focus structure offers the writer a powerful method of reducing institutions, statistics and cosmic issues to a level readers can relate to and understand.

On the Job

Tips for Writing

Ken Fuson is a freelance writer who won awards as a writer at *The Des Moines Register* and *The Baltimore Sun*. He offers you this story:

I had a problem.

My editors at *The Sun* in Baltimore had generously agreed to let me write a series about the making of a high-school musical.

I went to every practice but one. Hung out with the students. Made friends with the adult directors.

But I had a problem. There were more than 40 students involved. I had detailed notes on two dozen or more. All were worthy and interesting, but I had to narrow the field to five or six main characters. Otherwise, readers would lose interest.

What to do? I asked my colleague, Lisa Pollak, and she gave me the best advice a storyteller could ever receive: "Choose the people with the most at stake."

No matter what the assignment, ask yourself: Who has the most at stake? Who has the most to win or lose? Who cares the most about this?

Find that person, and you have the potential for drama: Will this person get what he or she wants? And if you have the potential for drama, you're well on your way toward writing a story, a real story, and not just a forgettable article.

This applies to the most routine assignments. I guarantee, somebody out there cares deeply about the outcome of a spelling bee. Find that person. There's a story there.

With the musical series, I finally settled on the two girls who wanted the lead role of Maria in *West Side Story*; the male lead who didn't know what he would do after graduation; another boy with more guts than singing ability; and a young woman who decided to help direct because she wanted a career in the theater and thought a physical disability would prevent her from becoming an actress.

Thanks, Lisa.

Finishing the Setup

You've completed your lead that focuses on a person who illustrates the issue you are reporting. Now you must finish the setup to the story. In addition to the lead, the setup consists of as many as five elements: the transition to the nut paragraph, the nut paragraph, foreshadowing, the "so what" and the "to be sure."

The setup consists of

- The lead.
- The transition to the nut paragraph.
- The nut paragraph.
- Foreshadowing.
- The "so what."
- The "to be sure."

Add the Transition and the Nut Paragraph

When you open with a scene or an anecdote, you must construct a transition that explicitly makes the connection to the **nut paragraph**, sometimes known as the theme paragraph. "Explicitly" is the key word. If you fail to help readers understand the point of the opening, however interesting it may be, you risk losing them. The nut paragraph follows the transition, which is in italics in the following example:

> Anita Poore hit the rough pavement of the parking lot with a thud. She had never felt such intense, stabbing pain and could barely lift her heavy head. When she reached for the car door, a police officer stared at her and asked her husband, "Is she drunk?" A wave of nausea swept over her, and she vomited.
>
> "That's it. Get her out of here!" the officer demanded.
>
> Poore was not drunk. She avoided jail, but she faces a life sentence of pain. Now 25, she has suffered migraine headaches since she was in seventh grade.
>
> *Not that it is much comfort, but she's not alone.* Health officials estimate that Americans miss 157 million workdays a year because of migraines and spend more than $2 million a year on over-the-counter pain-killers for migraine, tension and cluster headaches. Researchers haven't found a cure, but they have found methods to lessen the pain.

The transition explicitly places Anita Poore among those who miss work, buy painkillers and are still waiting for a cure. What follows the transition is the theme.

Earlier in this chapter, you were introduced to wheat farmer Don Sheber. Here is how the writer used a transition (shown in italics) to the nut paragraph:

> In a normal year, Sheber's 600 acres of farmland in Kay County should be thick with nearly waist-high wheat stalks, and by harvest's end, his grain bins should be stuffed with 20,000 bushels of golden grain.
>
> *But this is not a normal year.* As Sheber finished his harvest early this week, he counted only 6,500 bushels from his shriveled crop, less than one-third his normal yield.

When you have involved the reader and successfully written the explicit transition to the nut paragraph, you are ready to build the rest of the setup.

Add Foreshadowing

Foreshadowing can be done in a single line ("The killing started early and ended late"), or it can be developed as part of several paragraphs. The goal is to assure readers they will be rewarded if they continue reading. This is what Susan Kinzie of *The (Raleigh) News & Observer* promised her readers in the opening to one in a series of stories about three generations of a family investigating whether they shared a DNA link to cancer:

Linda Brenner-David pushed up the sleeve of her sweater and looked away as the needle pierced her vein. Blood flowed into the vial, which the technician labeled and packed carefully into the foam of a white-and-red box.

That blood sample would be sent to a laboratory in Utah to tell Linda whether she, like her youngest sister, Marcy Brenner, had a genetic mutation that put her at higher risk for breast and ovarian cancer, whether she faced the threat of a disease that had almost killed her sister and may have killed her mother. Or whether she, like her other sister, Judi Coyne, had escaped the family legacy.

If Linda tested positive, that would set off another round of questions for her family. It could mean her 30-year-old daughter, Christine Morgan, had a higher risk of cancer, could mean her son did, could mean her 18-month-old grandson did, too. It could influence Christine's choices about having more children.

Kinzie tells readers that if they want to learn the results of the tests and how the women reacted to the news, they will have to read the full story.

Add the "So What"

The "so what" tells readers explicitly why they should care. Don Sheber's harvest dropped by two-thirds. So what? Anita Poore almost got arrested for having a migraine headache. Interesting, but so what? Reporters and editors know the "so what," or they wouldn't spend time on the story. Too often, however, they fail to tell it to readers.

Thomas Latimer was poisoned when he mowed his lawn. Latimer's story is interesting, but it's much more important when you are told why you should care. The italics identify the "so what" in the following example:

The makers of the pesticide, diazinon, and of Tagamet firmly deny that their products had anything to do with Mr. Latimer's condition. The pesticide maker says he doesn't even believe he was exposed to its product. And in fact, Mr. Latimer lost a lawsuit he filed against the companies.

Even so, the case intrigues scientists and regulators because it illustrates the need for better understanding of the complex interactions between such everyday chemicals as pesticides and prescription drugs.

Neither the Food and Drug Administration nor the Environmental Protection Agency conducts routine tests for such interactions. Indeed, the EPA doesn't even evaluate the synergy of two or more pesticides commonly used together. "We have not developed ways to test any of that," says an EPA spokesman. "We don't know how to do it." And a new congressional report says the FDA lacks both the resources and the enforcement powers to protect Americans from all kinds of poisons.

The "so what" is the impact—the relevance—to people who have no warning that two or more pesticides may interact to poison them. In other cases, the "so what" may be included in the theme statement.

Let's look at the migraine story again:

> (1) Not that it is much comfort, but she's not alone. (2) Health officials estimate that Americans miss 157 million workdays a year because of migraines and spend more than $2 million a year on over-the-counter pain-killers for migraine, tension and cluster headaches. (3) Researchers haven't found a cure, but they have found methods to lessen the pain.

Sentence 1 is the transition; sentence 2 is the "so what"; sentence 3 is the theme, which includes foreshadowing. The "so what" establishes the dimensions of the problem. When you define the "so what," you are establishing the story's impact.

Add the "To Be Sure"

To maintain an evenhanded approach, writers sometimes must acknowledge that there are two or more sides to the story. We've read in the pesticide story that the makers of the drugs and pesticides "firmly deny that their products had anything to do with Mr. Latimer's condition." We see the technique again in an article about the impact of gambling on Tunica, Miss.

Writer Jenny Deam opens with a scene in the mayor's store. The mayor says gambling is the best thing that ever happened to the town. At the front counter, a woman is asking for the $85 back she paid on furniture last week. She lost her grocery money gambling. What comes next is a combination theme and "to be sure" statement (italics added):

> And so is the paradox of this tiny Mississippi Delta county, now that the casinos have come to call.
>
> On the one hand, unemployment in a place the Rev. Jesse Jackson once called "America's Ethiopia" has dropped from nearly 24 percent to a low last fall of 5 percent. Anyone who wants a job has one with the casinos. There are more jobs than people to fill them. In a county of about 8,100 people, the number of food stamp recipients fell from 4,218 before the casinos to 2,907 now.
>
> *But there is another side. New problems never before seen.*
>
> Since the first casino opened in 1992, the number of DUI arrests has skyrocketed by 400 percent. U.S. Highway 61 leading to Memphis is constantly jammed. On a busy weekend as many as 28,000 cars head toward the nine casinos now open. The criminal court system is just as overloaded. In 1992, there

were 1,500 cases filed. A year later, 2,400. As of last month there had already been 6,800 cases filed for this year.

"Well," says the mayor, "it's just like anything else in life: You got to take the evil with the good."

Now that the story has been defined, the writer is ready to examine all sides of the issue.

And now that you have constructed the setup, you are ready to write the body of the story.

Writing the Body

Good writing is clear

1. Write more short sentences than long sentences, use more simple constructions than complicated constructions, and favor strong verbs over forms of "to be."
2. Know grammar as you would like your mechanic to know car parts. Learn the vocabulary of grammar and how grammatical structures work together.
3. If you respect and follow the rules of punctuation, you will not embarrass yourself.

Think of readers as people antsy to do something else. To maintain their interest, offer them frequent examples to support your main points. In narration, you use anecdotes, scenes and dialogue to move the story line. You mix exposition—the facts—with narration, the story line.

Every few paragraphs, Tina Smithers offered readers another story to keep them reading about atypical hyperplasia. Here's one of them:

Karen was walking downstairs to get the beach ball out of the summer box for Bethany's Hawaiian swim party at Kindercare. Suddenly, Karen fainted and fell down the stairs. She knew she had broken something.

Coming to, she blindly made her way upstairs and lay on the bed.

"The cat was staring me in the eyes," she mumbled as Bob, fresh from the shower, grabbed ice and a pillow.

Karen noticed Bethany crying in the doorway. At this point, Karen realized she had been shouting, "Call 9-1-1! Call 9-1-1!" She didn't want her daughter to see her lose control. She quieted down and told Bethany to come to her bed.

"It's okay, honey. Mommy broke her arm, but they'll be over soon to fix it."

In the ambulance, one of the paramedics tried to cut off her yellow Tommy Hilfiger sweater.

"It's brand new," Karen shouted. "Can't you pull it off?"

They gave one small yank, and Karen immediately changed her mind. Every bump along the way was agonizing. Karen pleaded for more morphine. Her wrist, it turned out, was broken in 20 places.

That anecdote helps show how the stress of dealing with atypical hyperplasia had weakened Karen.

Think of your story as an interstate highway. The highway is your story's infrastructure. In one story, the infrastructure might be chronology. In another, it might be movement from one location to another. At times, you need to exit the highway to introduce other examples and ideas. The exits should be smooth—easy off, easy on.

Writing the Ending

Stories should end, not just stop. One good technique, called a **tie-back**, marks one of the significant differences between the inverted pyramid and the focus structure. The inverted pyramid story diminishes in importance and interest as the story proceeds, so it can be cut from the end. The focus structure, in contrast, has an ending, so if the story has to be shortened, the writer or editor will have to delete something other than the ending.

Earlier in this chapter, you were introduced to Linda Brenner-David, who was being tested to see if she had a genetic disposition toward cancer. Eventually readers learned that Linda tested positive. The story ends with a scene that echoes the opening when Linda was being tested. The Brenners are asking the next question: What about Christine, Linda's daughter?

Down the hall at Duke, as she waited to get her blood drawn, Christine looked nervous and out of place, so young and healthy in a room full of old, sick people. "Now I'm in a whole 'nother box," she said. "Now it's 'what do we do for me?'" Thinking out loud in scraps of phrases, she wondered, too, what it would mean for her family.

A technician called her name, and she sat down in a small room surrounded by blinking machines and medical equipment. A sudden noise at her side made her jump. She rolled up the sleeve of her magenta turtleneck, made a fist and waited as a tube slowly filled with dark blood.

She took the white-and-red box back to Shelly, who put it in a FedEx envelope addressed to a lab in Utah.

Good writing is precise

1. Know the meaning of your words. Don't use "uninterested" when you mean "disinterested" or "allude" when you mean "refer."
2. Avoid insensitive or biased language. Write "protecting disabled employees" not "protecting the disabled."
3. Be specific. "City Council members favor . . ." is less specific than "Some City Council members favor . . ." unless you have polled all the members. Better yet: "Five City Council members . . ." Use conditional verbs when discussing proposals: "The bill would make it illegal . . ." (not "will make").

In Helen O'Neill's story about Grandma Braun's kidnapping, the ending, which is a tie-back, is a tease to the next story in the series. O'Neill concludes her story in the courtroom when the kidnapper is sentenced:

At the back of the courtroom Heddie Braun clutched the hand of her wheelchair-bound husband, Eddie, and listened. She didn't feel any joy, she said later. She was curious about what her kidnapper looked like without his black face mask. But mostly she felt sad for his wife and children.

Not Eddie. For Eddie, life in prison was not punishment enough for the monster who had taken his wife.

So he gave a grim smile when the judge sentenced Ravesteijn to 45 years for kidnapping, burglary and false imprisonment. Heddie let out a gasp.

Forty-five years? For kidnapping her?

But I'm just a nobody, she protested.

"No ma'am," Sheriff Graves said.

Her family thinks she may have suffered a mild stroke, brought on by the ordeal. Heddie says the pain in her foot wears her down, and that is why she seems so frail and tired.

She sleeps a lot these days, more than she used to.

Anecdotes, dialogue, scenes and good quotes all can end the story. What you must avoid is ending the last section of the story instead of wrapping up the story line.

WRITING FOR BLOGS

Blog entries range from short, inverted-pyramid stories, often written quickly by beat reporters, to essays. Where traditional journalism is formal, blogging is informal. Where traditional journalism is dispassionate, much of blogging is passionate. Where traditional journalism is third person ("he," "she," "they"), much of blogging is first person ("I," "we"). Where much of traditional writing is vetted by layers of editors, much of blogging goes straight from the writer to the reader.

Political bloggers capture a disproportionate amount of the attention, but there are respected bloggers, some of them independent, most of them working for startups or the traditional media, who blog on everything from travel to technology. Even some heads of companies are blogging. Public-relations professionals are doing it on behalf of their companies or organizations. The best blogs are conversational, based in specifics, full of comparisons, explanations, turns of phrases and links. While some Internet writers do not distinguish between fact and fiction, professional journalists must be meticulous about the facts in their blogs. Here are a few examples of good blogging.

Humor from Loretta Waldman of the *Hartford Courant* (**www .courant.com**):

Small Towns Need $ for Websites, but From Where?
By Loretta Waldman on October 30, 2008 12:44 PM

I set out to follow up on the status of the Harwinton town website the other day and out of habit, immediately went looking for it on the Internet.

Then I remembered they don't have a website.

A personal essay from Jeré Longman of *The New York Times* (**www.nytimes.com**):

EUNICE, La.— The electricity has been out since Hurricane Gustav blew through the Cajun prairie, but I still flick the light switch every time I walk into the kitchen or the bathroom.

My father, who is 76, has been shaving in a pail under the carport and making his coffee on the barbecue pit. "I'd walk a mile for a Camel and a mile for a cup of coffee," he said.

And passion from self-described libertarian Kevin Colby:

Congratulations, America! We are part owners of the new Yankee Stadium!

The federal government just gave America's richest sports team another gift.

For the second time in two years, the Internal Revenue Service has approved special rules that allow the Yankees to use additional tax-free bonds to pay the skyrocketing costs of the team's new stadium.

Dan Steinberg, who is a full-time sports blogger for *The Washington Post*, has two gripes about blogs. In an interview with *Gelf* magazine

(**GelfMagazine.com**), he says bloggers shouldn't steal good stuff from journalists who are doing the reporting. He also chafes at the traditional restrictions of taste imposed upon him by his newspaper. Steinberg, a former beat reporter, spends a lot of time in locker rooms. He would like to reflect some of the off-color talk, but his editors impose the same standards on him as they do the rest of the paper.

Other bloggers have more freedom. Steinberg is one of the few working for the traditional media who are full-time bloggers. Most are beat reporters who drop news tidbits or humorous observations into a blog about their beats. Some are primarily mini-aggregators. They monitor the Web for news of whatever specialty they cover and provide readers the links. From bursts to full-blown essays, bloggers use a variety of writing styles. There may not be rules or even best practices, but there is a worthwhile guideline: Be interesting and be accurate.

SERVICE JOURNALISM

In Chapter 1, you read that one of the criteria of news is usefulness. Many, if not most, of the magazines you find on the racks appeal to readers by presenting information they might find useful. More than that, they attempt to present this useful information in the most usable way. This approach to presenting information has been called **service journalism**. Often, you see it labeled "News you can use." Even television news stations boast of "news that works for you." Also, the best Web sites are those that provide usable information.

Newspapers, too, are doing more service journalism. Some sections, such as travel, food and entertainment, use many service journalism techniques. Front-page news stories also often contain elements of service journalism, such as a box listing a sequence of events or directing readers to a map, telephone numbers or e-mail addresses. Even in this textbook, you see examples of service journalism in the marginal elements that list the learning objectives for each chapter or highlight important points.

The techniques of service journalism require that you think about content and presentation even as you are reporting. Ask yourself, "What does the reader need to act on this information?" The answer might range from an address to a phone or fax number to instructions on how to fix a lawnmower or make a loaf of bread. It might include directions on how to travel to a festival or where and when to buy tickets. As these examples illustrate, you move from simply talking about something to providing the information the reader needs to act on your story.

Much of the basic service journalism information can be presented as sidebars or lists or boxed material. Figure 7.3 presents more information about service journalism in common service journalism presentation style.

Service Journalism

In today's microwave world, in-a-hurry readers want practical information presented in the most efficient and effective way.

What this means is that you must think not just of a message of words on paper. You also must think of how those words will appear on the page—the presentation.

• • • • • • • • • • • • • • • • • • • •

Basics

Service journalism is

- **Useful.** You must inform readers, but if you also find ways to demonstrate how the reader can use the information, you will be more successful. Emphasize WIIFM: "What's in it for me?" See how often you can get "you" in the first sentence of your copy.

- **Usable.** Whenever you can, make a list. Lists get more attention and are better understood and more easily retained. You don't have to write sentences. "Tips" is a magical word.

- **Used.** People stop paying attention to information they never use. You should be able to prove that your readers act on information. To get readers to respond, promise them something. Offer a prize; give them something free.

Refrigerator Journalism

10 tips to serve today's readers

1. **Save them time.**
2. **Help them make more money, save money or get something free.**
3. **Address different levels of news interest.**
4. **Address niche audiences more effectively.**
5. **Become more personally useful.**
6. **Make information more immediately usable.**
7. **Become more accessible.** Give readers your name, phone number, fax number and e-mail address.
8. **Become easier to use.** Learn to layer the news, use cross-references, put things in the same place, color-code, tell readers where to find things, use page numbers on contents blurbs—even on covers, use glossaries and show readers where to find more information.
9. **Become more visual and graphic.** Use photos and information graphics.
10. **Become more engaging and interactive.** Use contests, quizzes, crosswords, games—make your readers do things. They remember better if they do something. Give awards to those who send answers to you. Give a coffee mug to the reader with the best tip of the month. Readers involved in your publication are more likely to resubscribe.

Figure 7.3
Employing the common presentation devices of service journalism—such as boxes and sidebars— this example shows how to highlight information so readers can easily find it and use it.

Print is a hot, intense medium. Refrigerator journalism cools off a hot medium and invites access and participation.

Other Devices of Service Journalism

1. Use blurbs. After a title and before the article begins, write a summary/contents/benefit blurb. David Ogilvy says no one will read the small type without knowing the benefit upfront. Use the same benefit blurb in a table of contents or menu or briefs column. The best word in a benefit blurb is "how." How to, how you, how I did something. Be personal. Use people in your messages. Also, use internal blurbs, little summaries, pull quotes and tips to tease and coax readers on to the page.

2. Use subheads. Before you write, outline. Put the main points of the outline into the copy. Perhaps a better word than subhead is "entry point." Let readers enter the copy where they find something interesting.

3. Have a question-and-answer column. A Q&A format allows readers to save time by skipping over things they already know or are not interested in.

4. Repeat things in different ways for different people. Don't be afraid to say something in a box or a graphic that you have said elsewhere. Reinforcing a message aids retention.

"Never be above a gimmick."
—Dave Orman, ARCO

5. Think more visually. Stop using pictures and graphics that do not contain information. Make them useful. Remember, being effective and efficient is the only thing that matters. We used to write articles and then look for graphics or photos to enhance the message. Now, we put the information in the graphic (where it will get more attention and have more impact) and write a story to enhance the graphic.

The power of the box

When you can, put some information in a box. Boxes or sidebars, like lists, get more attention, increase comprehension and aid retention.

1. A reference box. "For more information, see, read, call . . ."

2. A note box. Take notes from your articles as if you were studying for an exam. Give them to your readers to complement your message.

3. A glossary box. Put unfamiliar or technical terms in a glossary box. Find a way to indicate which words are defined by putting them in color, setting them in a different typeface or underlining them. Also, teach readers how to pronounce difficult words.

4. A bio box. When you need to say something about where a person lived, went to school, and worked, put this information in a box so that your main story is not interrupted. If you have more than one person in the story, bio boxes are even more useful.

The **4** goals of the service journalist:

In a nutshell

1. Attention
2. Comprehension
3. Retention
4. Action

PR Tip

Newspapers, magazines and newsletters are doing more and more service journalism. "News You Can Use" and "Tips & Tactics" have become familiar heads. Both newspapers and magazines are becoming more visual. Yet most news releases sent out by PR professionals look the same as they did five and 50 years ago. Why not try refrigerator journalism techniques in your next news release?

Suggested Readings

Boynton, Robert S. *The New New Journalism: Conversations with America's Best Nonfiction Writers on Their Craft.* New York: Vintage Books, 2005.

Brooks, Terri. *Words' Worth: A Handbook on Writing and Selling Nonfiction.* Prospect Heights, Ill.: Waveland Press, 1999. Full of detailed advice and examples.

Franklin, Jon. *Writing for Story: Craft Secrets of Dramatic Nonfiction by a Two-Time Pulitzer Prize Winner.* New York: Plume, 1994. If you want to write nonfiction narration, this book is must reading.

Huang, Thomas, and Steve Myers, eds. *Best Newspaper Writing, 2008–2009.* St. Petersburg, Fla.: Poynter Institute, 2008. Each year the winning entries in the American Society of Newspaper Editors' writing contest are published in a book, which also contains interviews with the writers.

Kramer, Mark, and Wendy Call, eds. *Telling True Stories.* New York: Plume, 2007. Some of the nation's best writers offer advice on how to report, structure and write narrative stories.

Suggested Web Sites

www.asne.org   The American Society of Newspaper Editors conducts a prestigious writing contest every year. Winners are posted on the Web. Select "Archives," then "ASNE Awards," then "2005 Winners" to find the story of Grandma Braun and others.

www.inkstain.net/narrative   A great source of inspiration, this site posts narrative stories.

www.nieman.harvard.edu/reports.aspx   The Nieman Reports site is devoted to narrative writing.

www.poynter.org   Select "Reporting & Writing" to find scores of stories on these topics.

http://weblogs.about.com   Some great ideas for starting and maintaining a blog, from the folks at About.com.

Exercises

1. Write four to eight paragraphs about how you and your classmates learned to be reporters. Pick a scene from one of your classes and re-create it. Provide the transition into the body of the story and then stop.

2. Interview a student in your reporting class. Ask questions that elicit anecdotes. Write an anecdote about the person.

3. Using a chronology, write approximately eight paragraphs of a story about some aspect of your experience in the reporting class.

4. Choose a personal experience that is worth telling in a first-person story. Write two to three pages using chronology in the first person.

5. Find examples of service journalism from newspapers, magazines or Web sites, and analyze them. Find an example of a story that would have benefited from service journalism techniques. Tell what you would have done to make the information more usable.

6. Analyze a story using the focus structure. One good place to find such stories is the Nieman Reports Web site (**www.nieman.harvard.edu/reports.aspx**). How many elements of the setup can you identify? Find all the anecdotes. Identify any dialogue.

7. Write a blog on a subject about which you have a particular interest or expertise. Although you should use your own voice, follow the rules of grammar and punctuation.

8. Go to the ASNE Web site and read Helen O'Neill's story on Grandma Braun's kidnapping. Write a paper analyzing the techniques of narration used in the story.

8 Speeches, News Conferences and Meetings

American presidents know that reassuring the public is a critical component of their job, especially in times of crisis. When it works, it helps a nation heal. When it doesn't, it can harm a president's confidence rating or worse. No one knows that better than former President George W. Bush, whose inspiring speech at Ground Zero after the destruction of the Twin Towers in lower Manhattan was one of the high points of his presidency.

Later in his presidency, Bush didn't fare as well. After touring the Gulf Coast by air to view the catastrophic effects of Hurricane Katrina, he returned to Washington to address the nation. He had hoped to rally and inspire the country as he had done in Manhattan. It didn't work.

The New York Times wrote in an editorial that Bush "gave one of the worst speeches of his life." The *Los Angeles Times* wrote: "The dilatory performance of George Bush during the past week has been outrageous."

Then, in the waning days of his presidency, a massive economic crisis hit the U.S. and reverberated around the world. Bush again took to television to reassure the American public. The speech didn't help. The markets continued to tumble in the greatest economic crisis since the Great Depression. Bush's approval rating subsequently tumbled to 24 percent, one of the lowest ever recorded for a sitting president.

Most public officials — from mayors to governors to legislators — understand that speeches, news conferences and meetings are the staples of the news industry. Your first assignment as a beginning reporter is almost certain to involve one of these three basic story types. Your editor or news director will use these assignments to determine quickly how well-prepared you are for a career as a journalist.

Such stories are often routine and rarely of great importance. But because many of them involve elected or appointed officials, communities often elect and re-elect their leaders on the basis of their performance at these events. Communities are rallied to causes and nations to wars by speeches, news conferences and meetings.

Some argue that John F. Kennedy's display of intelligence and wit at news conferences got him elected and earned him respect as president. During President Bill Clinton's troubles with the Whitewater real estate deal, a *USA Today*/CNN/Gallup poll showed that the president's news conference raised his approval rating by 11 percentage points. President Ronald Reagan felt at home in front of cameras, and although he disliked news conferences, his televised speeches helped boost his image tremendously. And George W. Bush, though arguably not as comfortable in front of cameras as some of his predecessors, also knew how to use public addresses to gain popular support.

On the local level, every politician knows that the public will evaluate his or her performance on the basis of media reports of meetings where major decisions are made that affect everyone in the community.

It's important not to make the mistake of handling such stories with indifference. To the people of your community, and to the subject of every story, that story is the most important item in the newspaper, radio or television report of the day. Even the most routine speeches, news conferences and meetings require careful reporting and writing.

In this day of convergence, you may be asked to cover the events with a video camera, a digital camera or a digital recorder as well as your notebook. More and more frequently, your task will be not only to write a story but also to capture the mayor's statement about the subject so readers can listen for themselves on your Web site.

YOUR PREPARATION

Good reporters know that preparation makes covering a story much easier. A savvy television reporter unfamiliar with an assigned topic often will review video of previous stories on the subject. If that's not possible, a check of online information—from the local newspaper to national news Web sites to other online sources—may provide good background. A good starting point for a print reporter is the **morgue**— the newspaper or magazine library. There, you'll find all your publication has previously written about a subject. If you are assigned to cover a meeting or attend a press conference, a morgue check is likely to provide you with ample background. If it doesn't, a check in a national database such as LexisNexis should help. So might one of the many reference books you'll find in the news room. As we discussed in Chapter 4, most media libraries are computerized, so you'll probably be able to do most of the checking from your own computer.

Let's examine how to prepare for each of the basic story types.

Preparing for the Speech Story

Failure to get enough background on the speaker and on the topic almost guarantees failure to write a useful speech story. Not every speech you are assigned to cover will demand a lot of research. Many speakers and speeches will be dry and routine. The person giving the speech will be someone you know or someone you have covered before. At other times you may be given an assignment on short notice and may be forced to find background information after hearing the speech. Whatever the case, never take the speaker or the topic for granted.

The first step in your research is to identify the speaker correctly. Middle initials are important; sometimes even they are not enough. Sometimes checking the address is not enough. One reporter wrote

Think technical thoughts

Preparing to cover speeches, news conferences and meetings presents many technical questions for the television journalist. Here are three things to keep in mind:

- Think visuals. What will your backdrop be? Will there be signs, photos, samples, logos or flipcharts to help the story?
- Think sound. Will there be one microphone or a multi-box for you to insert your mike, or will you be free to set up your own microphone?
- Think light. Will the event take place outdoors or in a well-lit room, or must you bring your own lighting? How far is the camera throw (the distance from the event to your camera)? Will there be a camera platform or a set space, or will you be free to set up your camera anywhere?

about the wrong person because he did not know that a father and son shared the same name at the same address.

USA Today had to print a clarification when it reported that television celebrity Larry King had made a $1,000 donation to Bill Clinton's campaign. The donor was Larry L. King, author and playwright. A hospital in Boston was threatened with a lawsuit after telling relatives that Robert J. Oliver had died. His fiancée was surprised a few days later when Robert J. called her. It was Robert W. Oliver who had died. Robert W. was not listed in the phone book; Robert J. was.

Be sure you have the right person. Then, before doing research on the speaker, contact the group sponsoring the speech and ask for the topic. You might need to do some reading to help you understand the subject. If you're lucky, you may get an advance copy of the speech.

If the speech is important enough, you might want to contact the speaker ahead of time for a brief interview. If he or she is from out of town, you might plan for a meeting at the airport. You might also arrange ahead of time to interview the speaker after the speech. You may have some questions and some points to clarify.

For the radio or television reporter, a one-on-one interview with the speaker is important. Few things are more boring than lengthy video clips of a speech. You can avoid this problem by highlighting the key points of the speech in your report and perhaps interspersing a few choice quotes from the speech itself.

Not every speech will demand significant research, but even the most routine speech assignment requires some preparation. It might seem obvious, for instance, that the reason Gene Martin, director of the local library, is addressing the state Writer's Guild is to tell members how to use the library to write better stories. Not so. Gene Martin also is a successful "true confessions" writer who has been published dozens of times. He might be addressing the guild to tell members how he achieved his success.

Sooner or later you may be called on to cover speeches of major political candidates, perhaps even a speech by the U.S. president. For this task, too, you need background—lots of it. Being a journalist requires you to read the news and to know what is going on. You must keep abreast of current events by following television news, reading newspapers or reading Web sites every day.

Preparing for the News Conference Story

Preparing for a **news conference**—a public announcement designed to inform the public through the media—is similar to preparing to cover a speech. You must know the background of the person giving the news conference, and you must learn why the news conference is being held.

Bob Geldof (*left*), Kumi Naidoo and U2 singer Bono give a press conference for the Live 8 concert in summer 2005.

If the news is really important, the broadcast reporter may merely introduce the subject and broadcast the news conference live. Often the person holding the news conference has an announcement or an opening statement. Unless that statement is leaked to the media, you will not know its content ahead of time. But you can do some educated guessing. Check out rumors. Call the person's associates, friends or secretary. The more prepared you are, the better chance you have of coming away with a coherent story.

Every reporter at a news conference has a line of questions to pursue, particularly if the topic is known in advance. Your editor may want certain information, and other editors may want something else. You will not have time to think out your questions once you are there: The job of recording the responses to other reporters' questions will keep you too busy.

It may be impossible to arrange an interview before or after the news conference. If the person holding the news conference wanted to grant individual reporters interviews, he or she probably would not have called the news conference. But you can give it a try. You never know; you might end up with some exclusive information.

Preparing for the Meeting Story

You won't know exactly what to expect at a meeting unless an agenda is made available in advance. That's sometimes the case for meetings of city

To achieve total coverage of content and event, you must remember to

- Get the content correct. Digital recorders can be helpful, but always take good notes. Quote people exactly and in context.
- Note the background, personal characteristics and mannerisms of the main participants.
- Cover the event. Look around the edges—at the audience (size, reactions) and sometimes at what is happening outside the building.
- Get there early, position yourself and hang around afterward.

councils and zoning commissions. But if no agenda is available, you still must do your best to prepare for the meeting. Who are the people holding the meeting? What kind of an organization is it? Who are the key figures? What are the main issues to be discussed? Again, a database or your organization's morgue should be your first stop.

Contact some of the key figures to learn what the meeting is about. If you know the main subject to be discussed, you will be able to study and investigate the issues before arriving. Knowing what to expect and being familiar with the issues will make covering the meeting much easier.

A reporter with a regular **beat**—an assigned area of responsibility— usually covers the scheduled meetings of more important organizations and of groups like the city council, the school board or the county commission. (Beat reporting is discussed in detail in Chapter 10.) A beat reporter has ongoing familiarity with the organization and with the issues involved.

Even if you are not covering a beat but are assigned to the meeting as a general-assignment reporter, there are ways to prepare. Check the morgue for background. If the event involves a public body, open-meetings laws in most jurisdictions require advance notice not only of meetings but also of the topics to be discussed. If so, that will help.

Radio and television reporters often don't cover beats and are, in the best sense of the phrase, general-assignment reporters. Meetings of city councils are not regular fare for television reporters because video of a meeting can be exceedingly dull. As a result, television reporters in particular face some serious challenges in deciding how to portray the importance of what's coming out of the meeting.

The key is finding video to accompany the piece. If the city council is debating how to improve snow removal, for example, video footage of city trucks doing just that can add to the story. Because television is a visual medium, reporters have to be creative in finding ways to illustrate important but visually limited stories.

If you know snow removal will be a primary topic, someone back at the station can be searching for snow-removal footage while you're covering the meeting. Without good background work to determine the main theme of the meeting, such preparation is difficult or impossible.

COVERING THE STORY

An often-told story is that of a newspaper reporter who prepared well for a speech assignment, contacted the speaker, got an advance copy of the speech, wrote the story and spent the evening in a bar. He didn't know until after the speech story was handed in that the speech had been canceled.

Reporters take notes as Hillary Clinton, then U.S. senator from New York, speaks.

And then there's the story about the young reporter who was assigned to cover a meeting and came back to tell the city editor there was no story.

"Why not?" the city editor asked.

"Because the meeting was canceled."

"Why was that?"

"Well," replied the reporter, "when the meeting started, some of the board members got in this big argument. Finally, three of them walked out. The president then canceled the meeting because there was no quorum."

The reporter had been sent to cover a meeting. But the canceled meeting and the circumstances surrounding its cancellation probably were of more interest to readers than the meeting itself would have been.

Be Thorough and Accurate

Preparing to cover events is only the beginning. Knowing what to do when you get there is the next step. Remember this: Covering the content of a speech, news conference or meeting often is only part of the job — and sometimes the less important part. You must cover the entire event — the time, place, circumstances, number of people involved and possible consequences of what was said or of the actions taken.

Using a digital voice recorder

- Be familiar with the machine. *Practice using it. Make sure you understand its peculiarities. Check its sound capabilities.*
- Set it where you can see it's working. *If it has a digital counter, note the number when you hear a quote you want.*
- Take notes as if it's not working. *After all, it might not be.*

You need to develop your own shortcuts in note taking. Clear note taking is essential—but the notes need be clear only to you. That means you must develop a consistent habit, or you won't remember what your shortcuts mean when you start writing the story.

If you are a print or online reporter, you may find a digital voice recorder useful. Recorders often scare reporters, but they need not. Build confidence with the device by practicing with it beforehand. Use it again and again to become completely familiar with its idiosyncracies.

The most frequent complaint about digital recorders is that listening to the entire recording just to find a certain quote that you want to check takes too long. But you can avoid this problem if you have a recorder with a digital counter. At any point in a speech or a meeting when something of importance is said, note the number on the counter. Finding the quote later will be no problem.

Even when you record an event, you should take notes. Malfunctions can occur, even with the best machines, at the most inopportune times. Many veteran reporters wish they had taken a shorthand or speed-writing course early in their careers. You may find it useful to buy a speed-writing manual and become used to certain symbols. Every reporter sooner or later adopts or creates some shortcuts in note taking. You should do the same. Learn to abbreviate whenever you can (*wh* for "which," *th* for "that," *bk* for "book," *st* for "street," *bldg* for "building," etc.). Make up signs (*w/* for "with," *w/o* for "without," *acc/* for "according to").

You may be one of those fortunate people with a fantastic memory. Some reporters develop an incredible knack for re-creating short conversations with complete accuracy without taking a note. But you also may be one of those who takes reams of notes. If you are, take them as neatly as you can. Many of us cannot read our own handwriting at times—a nuisance, particularly when a proper name is involved.

Taking notes is most crucial when you wish to record direct quotes. As you learned in Chapter 3, putting someone's words in quotation marks means only one thing: You are quoting the person word for word, exactly as the person spoke. Almost all stories demand that you be able to record direct quotes. Your stories will be lifeless and lack credibility without them. A speech story, for example, should contain many direct quotes.

Be Thoughtful and Observant

Quoting the speaker at length or printing a speech in its entirety is recording, not reporting. The overall content of the speech may or may not be news. Sometimes context is missing. Sometimes the news may be what a speaker left unsaid. You must decide what is newsworthy, and to do that you must be well-prepared and knowledgeable about the subject you are covering.

A key to reporting any event is talking with as many sources and checking as many documents as possible. It's much better to leave out material you have collected than to leave questions unanswered. Without a doubt, the biggest single failure of inexperienced reporters is leaving gaps in a story. Your editor will ask the unanswered questions and force you to find answers. If you're smart, you'll do so before you are asked. Thorough reporting is the key.

In the process of gathering material, don't be a passive observer. You can vastly improve many a story by describing a person or place. Such reporting can help bring a story to life.

The television reporter has the luxury of recording the whole event. The challenge, then, is deciding which clips to use from the speech or meeting itself and how best to tell the story. Usually that involves a stand-up report by the reporter combined with clips of the speaker or speakers. In many ways, the television reporter's challenge is much greater than the one facing the newspaper reporter; the television reporter must report the same story in far fewer words.

One final point: More and more meetings are being televised on cable channels or replayed on the Web. Make sure you record quotes accurately and get your facts straight. If you don't, someone is sure to notice and call you to task.

WRITING THE STORY

As we discussed in Chapter 6, one of the most important parts of writing the story for any medium is the lead. Without a good lead, the reader or viewer won't be hooked, and the story will have been wasted. But crafting the lead is merely the beginning. In this section, we'll discuss some peculiarities about each type of story we cover in this chapter.

Writing the Speech Story

Although you may not be called upon to cover a speech by the U.S. president, you can learn a lot about how to write a speech story from the way the pros handle an important address. Figure 8.1 shows how writers for *The Washington Post* began their coverage of George W. Bush's speech on the nation's economic crisis in September 2008. The story leads with Bush's speech, but observe that the reporters quickly put it into context by noting the opposition in Congress to Bush's plan as well as the support of key congressional leaders.

Although that was the *Post*'s lead story, that day's edition contained more than a dozen related stories. You're unlikely to be tasked with covering such a big story as a beginning reporter, but you can learn a lot from noting how the *Post*'s reporters tackled such a complicated topic. Much of the detail about the bailout plan was provided in sidebars, supplementary stories adding particulars or taking another angle. That saved space in the main story for the essentials.

Bush Calls Bailout Vital to Economy, Will Meet With McCain and Obama
Proposal Takes Shape in Congress, but Broad Support Is Lacking

By Lori Montgomery and Paul Kane
Washington Post Staff Writers

The lead summarizes the key point of the president's message. →

President Bush said yesterday that the credit crisis that has seized world markets could devastate the U.S. economy unless Congress acts quickly to approve a $700 billion bailout plan for the nation's financial system, a message aimed at reluctant lawmakers as much as a deeply skeptical public.

← **The writer's point about "reluctant lawmakers" and "skeptical public" sets the context.**

"Our entire economy is in danger," Bush said in an address from the White House, emphasizing that the massive bailout was not targeted at "any individual company or industry. It is aimed at preserving America's overall economy."

← **Quotations continue the main point and help break up the monotony of the story.**

The phrase "from the White House" identifies where the speech was given. →

Warning that "America could slip into a financial panic," Bush blamed the crisis on "easy credit" in the housing market and "the faulty assumption that home values would continue to rise." As mortgage loans went bad and borrowers defaulted, he said, investors have succumbed to a "widespread loss of confidence" that threatens to shut down consumer lending, decimate the stock market, cause businesses and banks to fail—and cost millions of Americans their jobs.

← **Quoted phrases are integrated into the story's text throughout.**

"Ultimately, our country could experience a long and painful recession," Bush said. "Fellow citizens, we must not let this happen."

Background on prime-time speeches highlights this speech's importance. →

Bush delivered the prime-time speech, his first in over a year, after a clamor on Capitol Hill for him to acknowledge the most serious financial crisis in decades and to personally make the case for the government intervention his administration has proposed.

Five days after unveiling the bailout plan, which seeks to purchase troubled assets from faltering financial institutions, administration officials were still struggling to line up support among lawmakers appalled by its cost, doubtful of its methods and outraged by the speed with which they were being pushed to act. While the usually fractious Senate seemed to be coming together behind a version of the proposal, the administration had big trouble in the House, particularly among mistrustful Republicans who said the White House had failed to make a case for the bailout in terms ordinary people could understand.

← **Story returns to the wider context of the congressional debate.**

(continued)

Figure 8.1
A front-page story from *The Washington Post* of Sept. 25, 2008, reports on an important speech by President George W. Bush.

Figure 8.1
(continued)

Note that the
reporters conducted
an interview *before*
the speech was
delivered.

The writer provides
more context for the
drama unfolding.

"I'm seeking answers to two fundamental questions: Why this? And why now?" Rep. Deborah Pryce, R-Ohio, said before Bush delivered his remarks. "You can't make a move this large without the approval of the American people. And we don't have it, yet."

Despite such skepticism, top members of the House Financial Services and Senate Banking committees are slated to sit down this morning in an effort to draft the final details of a bipartisan bill. Bush also invited congressional leaders as well as presidential candidates John McCain and Barack Obama to meet with him at the White House today.

The president's top economic advisers were lobbying hard yesterday for passage of the bill. In testimony before the House Financial Services Committee, Treasury Secretary Henry M. Paulson Jr. said the White House would drop its resistance to lawmakers' demands for limits on executive compensation at companies that accept taxpayer money. Rep. Barney Frank, D-Mass., the committee's chairman, called that a "big step forward" and said he would push next year to apply those limits more broadly. . . .

The writer makes a
transition to a new
thought.

Writing the News Conference Story

Writing a news conference story may be a bit more challenging than writing a speech story. Because you will come to the conference with different questions in mind than your fellow reporters, you may come away with a different story. At the very least, your lead may be different from the leads of other reporters.

A news conference often covers a gamut of topics. It sometimes begins with a statement from the person who called the conference.

For example, when the mayor of Springfield holds a news conference to announce her candidacy for a second term, you can be sure she will begin with a statement to that effect. Although her candidacy might be news to some people, you may want to ask her questions about the location of a new landfill that the city is rumored to be planning. Most citizens will admit the need for landfills, but their location is always controversial. And then there's that tip you heard about the possibility of the city manager resigning to take a job in a large city.

Other reporters will come with other questions. Will there be further cuts in the city budget? Will the cuts mean that some city employees will lose their jobs? What happened to the plans to expand the city jail?

Many reporters today will first post a short summary of the news conference on their Web site. They may be required to post a recording of the event or even an audio or video news report. Then it's time to write the story for the newspaper or the television newscast.

However your report is distributed, when you come away from a news conference that covered many topics, you have the job of organizing the material in some logical, coherent order. Usually you will treat the most newsworthy subject first and deal with the other subjects in the order of their importance. Rarely would you report on them in the chronological order in which they were discussed.

Suppose you decided the location of the landfill was the most important item of the news conference — especially if the mayor revealed the location for the first time. You might begin your story this way:

> The city will construct its new landfill near the intersection of State Route 53 and Route E, four miles north of Springfield, Mayor Juanita Williams said today.
>
> "After nearly a year of discussion and the best advice we could obtain, we are certain the Route E location is best for all concerned," Williams said at a news conference.
>
> The mayor admitted there would be continued opposition to the site by citizens living in the general area, especially those in the Valley High Trailer Court. "No location will please everyone," Williams said.
>
> Williams called the news conference to make the expected announcement of her candidacy for a second term.

Now you have to find a way to treat the other topics of the conference. You may want to list them first with a series of bullets in this way:

> In other matters, Williams said:
> - City Manager Diane Lusby will not be resigning to take another post.
> - Budget constraints will not permit any new construction on the city jail this year.
> - Budget cuts will not cost any city employees their jobs. However, positions vacated by retiring personnel will not be filled.

After this list, you will either come back to your lead, giving more background and citing citizens or other city officials on the subject, or go on to treat, one at a time, the matters you listed. Pay particular attention to making proper transitions from paragraph to paragraph so that your story is coherent: "On other subjects, the mayor said . . . ," "The mayor defended her position on . . . ," "Again she stressed. . . ."

If one of the subjects is of special interest, you may want to write a sidebar. For this story, you may want to do a sidebar on the mayor's candidacy, her record, her possible opponents and so on.

With a longer or more complicated story, you may want to make a summary list of all the main topics covered and place it in a box or sidebar.

On the Job

Speeches, News Conferences and Meetings

After receiving a master's degree in journalism, Barry Murov worked as an associate editor of a Washington, D.C., newsletter, where he covered federal job programs. Then, after working for the *St. Louis Business Journal* for six years, first as a reporter, then as managing editor, Murov became editor of *St. Louis* magazine. He later joined Fleishman-Hillard Inc., an international public-relations firm. He's currently vice president of corporate communications at Reliv International, a marketer of nutritional supplements.

Murov has written and edited dozens of stories covering speeches, meetings and news conferences. Here are some tips he has for you:

"Always ask for a copy of the speech ahead of time," Murov says. "Even when you are lucky enough to get a copy, don't assume that the speaker will stick to the text."

As a former consultant for Fortune 500 corporations, Murov knows that "many executives tend to tinker with their speeches, even making significant changes, up until the final minute."

He recommends that you follow along in the text to note where the actual presentation differs. "You don't want your story to include a statement from the text that the speaker deleted. Also, you may find the real news nugget buried in the speech."

Don't leave a meeting or news conference immediately. "Go up to the spokesperson or the leader of the meeting and ask a question that hasn't been covered during the actual event.

"That can benefit in two ways: One, you will have something extra for your readers. Two, it helps you build a relationship with the spokesperson that may pay off in the future."

News conference stories can be tough for television reporters because it's impossible to mention all items discussed at the conference in a two-minute segment. Almost inevitably, a television reporter must select the single most important topic and highlight that. As a result, the typical report of a news conference will not touch on all the topics listed in the newspaper report, but the television reporter could include those details in his or her Web report.

A radio or television reporter at the news conference mentioned above probably would highlight the landfill story and skip most of the other items, perhaps mentioning only that the city manager is not resigning.

Writing the Meeting Story

Meetings are especially challenging for broadcast reporters. A discussion about setting tax rates for the coming year makes for boring television footage. But such news is important, and good television reporters find a way to make it interesting.

That often means finding a subject who is or will be affected by the change in the tax rate. If the city council is cutting support to the fine arts, for example, an interview with the head of the local arts council may be in order. Finding creative ways to include video is the key to a good broadcast report.

Readers and viewers expect reporters to take their place at a meeting. Let's look at a simple meeting story—in this case a meeting of a local school board:

Because three national corporations are protesting a formula used to compute their property taxes, more than $264,000 is being withheld from the Walnut School District's operating budget for the 2007–08 school year.

Superintendent Max Schmidt said at Monday's school board meeting that IBM Corp., ACR Corp. and Xerox are protesting that the method used in computing their 2004 property taxes was no longer valid. Nine California counties are involved in similar disputes.

The taxes, totaling $264,688, are being held in escrow by the county until the matter is resolved. Some or all of the money eventually may be returned to the district, but the administration cannot determine when or how much.

"If we take a quarter million dollars out of our program at this time, it could have a devastating effect," Schmidt said. "Once you've built that money into your budget and you lose it, you've lost a major source of income."

Mike Harper, the county prosecuting attorney, and Larry Woods, the school district attorney, advised board members to take a "wait-and-see attitude," Schmidt said. He said that one alternative would be to challenge the corporations in court. A final decision will be made later.

The board also delayed action on repayment of $80,000 to IBM in a separate tax dispute. The corporation claims the district owes it for overpaid 2003 property taxes. The county commission has ruled the claim is legitimate and must be repaid.

A possible source of additional income, however, could be House Bill 1002, Schmidt said. If passed, this appropriations bill would provide an additional $46 million for state education, approximately $250,000 of which could go to the Walnut School District.

The issue of the meeting was money problems—a subject that should concern every taxpayer. The writer jumped right into the subject in the lead and then in the second paragraph gave us the "who," "when" and "where." The reporter then dealt with specifics, naming names and citing figures, and quoted the key person at the meeting. In the last two paragraphs the writer dealt with other matters discussed in the meeting.

A television reporter might tackle the same story by interviewing a teacher faced with larger class sizes. Again, knowing what's on the agenda and doing advance work to find such a teacher requires thought and planning.

But the issues discussed at a meeting are not your only concerns in covering a meeting story. Remember, too, to cover the event. Who was there? Who represented the public? Did anyone have reactions after the meeting was over?

Reporter Jennifer Galloway of the *Columbia Missourian* began a meeting story in this way:

> Even though they are footing the bill, only one of Boone County's residents cared enough to attend a Tuesday night hearing on the county's budget for next year.
>
> With an audience of one citizen plus two reporters, County Auditor June Pitchford presented her official report on the $21 million budget to the Boone County Commission in a silent City Council chamber.

Even when covering routine, seemingly boring events, capture the pertinent ambience. Notice how the reporter's observation of a "silent . . . chamber" dramatized the reporting of "an audience of one citizen plus two reporters."

In addition to getting all the facts, your job is also to be interesting, to get people to read the story. Remember, one of the criteria of news is that it be unusual. Another is that it be interesting.

Remember, too, never to lead a story with something like this:

> The City Council met Tuesday . . .

What the council did is the news, not the fact that it met. When you're covering a meeting, your job is to tell what happened. And in the process, you are expected to write well.

Suggested Readings

Biography and Genealogy Master Index. Detroit: Gale Research Co., 1981 to present. A compilation of a large number of biographical directories with names of people whose biographies have been written. Indicates which date and volume of those reference books to consult for the actual biography.

Biography Index. New York: H.W. Wilson Co., 1946 to present. Helps you locate biographical articles that have appeared in 2,000 periodicals and journals, as well as in biographical books and chapters from collective biographies.

Carter, T. Barton, Marc A. Franklin and Jay B. Wright. *The First Amendment and the Fourth Estate.* Eagan, Minn.: West Group, 2008. A good explanation of the law of the press.

Houston, Brant, and Investigative Reporters and Editors, Inc. *The Investigative Reporter's Handbook.* 5th ed. New York: Bedford/St. Martin's, 2009. A guide to using government documents to find sources of information.

Suggested Web Sites

www.apme.com Associated Press Managing Editors is an organization that publishes advice useful to working editors.

www.asne.org The American Society of Newspaper Editors publishes a magazine called *The American Editor* (**http://tae.asne.org**) that often

contains useful stories to help reporters write better. Archives of these stories can be found at ASNE's Web site.

http://vlib.org The WWW Virtual Library helps reporters find online links to organizations useful for providing background information.

Exercises

1. Journalist Andrea Mitchell is coming to town to speak on the current U.S. president's relationship with the press. Prepare to cover the speech. Record the steps you will take to prepare for the speech and the information you have gathered on Mitchell.

2. You learn that actor Robert Redford is holding a news conference before speaking to a local group about environmental issues. You also learn that Redford is personally and actively involved in these issues. Using appropriate databanks, gather and record background information on Redford.

3. Find out when the Faculty Council or similar faculty representative group is having its next meeting. Record the steps you take to prepare for the meeting and the information you gather as you prepare. Then cover the meeting and write the story.

4. Former Vice President Al Gore spoke on global warming in July 2008 at D.A.R. Constitutional Hall in Washington, D.C. Read or listen to the speech at one of the following sites:

   www.npr.org/templates/story/story.php ?storyId=92638501

   www.youtube.com/watch?v=35jWlIknSFw

   Write a speech story as if you were reporting for the next day's newspaper.

5. Prepare for, cover and write a

   a. Speech story.
   b. News conference story.
   c. Meeting story.

   Then compare your stories to those appearing in the local paper.

9 Other Types of Basic Stories

When Hurricane Ike struck Galveston and the Texas Gulf Coast in September 2008, hundreds of reporters, both print and television, were pressed into service to cover the disaster. They employed lessons learned while covering small accidents and fires on their first jobs.

Consider this report filed the morning after for the CNN Web site:

GALVESTON, Texas (CNN)— Rescuers in Galveston were going door-to-door Saturday to check on the estimated 20,000 people who failed to flee Hurricane Ike, which has slowed to tropical storm status.

As of Saturday afternoon, the Galveston Fire Department had taken 27 people to a shelter in a high school on the coastal island, which was without electricity or water pressure.

No casualties had been discovered so far in the search and rescue efforts, which have been hampered by heavy flooding and scattered debris.

Galveston had ordered evacuation of the island, but Galveston City Manager Steve LeBlanc said about 40 percent of the city's 57,523 residents chose to stay.

LeBlanc said the island would be closed while authorities assess damages, including to the causeway, which was in "bad shape" because of debris and road damage.

"The road buckled in a number of places," LeBlanc said. "Even if we opened it up, you couldn't get through."

LeBlanc said 17 buildings on the island had been destroyed by fires, potent winds and a strong storm surge.

"We are in a recovery mode," Galveston Mayor Lyda Ann Thomas said in a press conference Saturday afternoon. "This eye came right over us, stayed a while and went on, but it brought a lot of damage to our city."

Ike was downgraded Saturday to a tropical storm 11 hours after it crashed ashore as a Texas-sized hurricane that walloped southeast Texas and southwest Louisiana.

In its wake, Ike—which smashed into the coast as a Category 2 hurricane—left four people dead, millions without power and destroyed homes and businesses along the Gulf Coast with powerful winds, rain and floodwaters.

President Bush declared 29 Texas counties and parts of Louisiana major disaster areas, making federal funds available for recovery from the storm.

Many people, like D.J. Knight of Pearlman, Texas, decided to ride out the storm at home, despite voluntary and mandatory orders issued across the region.

"The windows looked like they would explode," said Knight, a mother of two. "It just wouldn't stop."

Now, without electricity and surrounded by flooded roads and wreckage, Knight wonders whether it was worth enduring a sleepless night as the storm shook her home, located about halfway between Galveston and Houston.

"I didn't think it would be as bad as it was," she said. "It was horrible."

Knight is one of thousands waiting for assistance as the state rolls out the largest search and rescue operation in Texas history.

Gov. Rick Perry dispatched a 1,000-strong search and rescue team, including state troopers, pilots and members of the National Guard. Lines of National

Guard trucks and ambulances were deployed from San Antonio even as officials are trying to grasp the extent of damage and the number of Texans stranded by the storm.

However, flooding and debris have impeded rescue efforts in some areas, adding to the uncertainty about how many Texans actually survived the storm.

"We're obviously concerned that there may be people we find who didn't get out and who are going to be in the rubble of what we uncover," said Secretary of Homeland Security Michael Chertoff. "We hope for the best, but I do want to prepare people for the fact that we may have some fatalities."

Chertoff said 40,000 Texans were in 250 shelters, and that food and water would be distributed in about 20 coastal locations as rescue efforts continue. . . .

A basic story? Certainly not. But it is a story crafted by reporters well-grounded in the basics.

Information for such a report is gathered in many ways: through observation, by talking with public officials and by interviewing witnesses and, if possible, victims.

No one reporter covers an event of this magnitude. In both print and television, reports from multiple reporters are fed to someone back at the office who sifts through massive amounts of information in an attempt to help the public make sense of what happened. On television, that may be done on the fly by producers and anchors. At newspapers, writers meld reports from multiple reporters into a cohesive whole. On the front line, however, reporters are employing lessons learned long ago while covering fires or accidents on their first jobs.

THE VALUE OF EXPERIENCE

Nothing really prepares a reporter to cover something of the magnitude of Hurricane Ike or the World Trade Center collapse, so drawing upon coverage of earlier accidents, fires and disasters is about the best one can do. Similarly, nothing really prepares a reporter for the first time he or she encounters death on the job—a woman mangled in an automobile wreck or a child burned to death in an apartment fire. Some lessons are learned the hard way, but newspaper editors and television news directors agree on one thing: Good reporters know how to handle basic story types. Knowing how to handle basic stories is the best training for almost anything you will encounter on the job, including a task as daunting as covering Ike.

One of these basic story types is the obituary or life story, a staple of newspapers but also important to those in radio or television or at online sites. Most people's names appear in local newspapers only when they are born and when they die. When the latter occurs, newspapers try to take note. Although metropolitan papers often charge for obits, small and medium-sized papers still pay respects to local residents who die. Often, such stories are more than mere recitation of facts. They are stories about a person's life, and to family and friends they are extremely important. Such stories usually find their way into scrapbooks. Newspapers and television stations record major events in the life of a community, and these often involve reporting on crime, accidents, fires and court proceedings. And although television doesn't run a story on each person who dies in a community, the death of prominent individuals certainly gets play on the television or radio report. As a result, it's likely that as a beginning reporter—print, online or television—you will have a chance to cover such events. This chapter is designed to help prepare you to do so.

YOUR PREPARATION

When writing an obit or an account of a crime, an accident, a fire or a court proceeding, begin as you do any other story—with a check in a database or your publication's library. There you'll find background on the subject of the obit. Or you will learn whether a similar crime has occurred before, whether accidents are common at the location of the latest one, whether similar suspicious fires have occurred or whether a person charged with a crime has been in trouble before.

Preparing for an Obituary or Life Story

Sources for obits

- Mortuary forms.
- The newspaper.
- The newspaper's library.
- Interviews with family and friends of the deceased.

The newspaper library is the starting point for background research on someone who died. In all probability, your editor will have learned of the death from a death report issued by a local mortuary. Typically, mortuaries issue forms that contain all the basics you will need to write the story:

- The name and address of the deceased.
- The deceased's occupation and age.
- The cause, date and place of death.
- The names of relatives.
- The time and place of the funeral.
- The burial site.
- Biographical information.

The purpose of your search in the library is to find background material on the deceased to make the obituary more compelling to readers.

Some large newspapers use formula writing to produce obituaries, but more and more newspapers are treating these stories as real news—as life stories—worthy of extra reporting. A call to a close friend of the deceased, for example, might produce a more interesting story if you learn that the subject was an Olympic gold medalist in

1936. The library might reveal that achievement. A friend is almost certain to do so.

Television and online reporters often have access to files on prominent individuals. They also usually have online access to a nearby newspaper library. Again, that's a good place to start when writing an obituary or life story.

Preparing for a Crime Story

Crime reporting usually doesn't allow for much preparation. If the police radio reports a murder in your area, you may be dispatched to the scene as the story is breaking. At that point, no one will know who is involved or what happened. There will be no time to check the library, and you will have to do your initial reporting at the scene.

Most information about crimes comes from three sources:

- Police officials and their reports.
- The victim or victims.
- The witness or witnesses.

The circumstances of the crime, as well as when your editor assigns you to a crime story, will determine your primary sources. If you are dispatched to the scene of the crime as it happens or soon afterward, you will probably interview the victim and witnesses first. The police report will have to wait; most likely, it isn't even ready. But if you are assigned to write about a crime that occurred the night before, the police report is the starting point.

A police officer investigating a crime covers much of the same ground as you. The officer is interested in who was involved, what happened, when, where, why and how. These details are needed to complete the official report of the incident, and you need them for your story.

Regardless of any interviews you get, the police report always should be checked. It is often the source of basic information:

- A description of what happened.
- The location of the incident.
- The name, age and address of the victim.
- The name, age and address of the suspect, if any.
- The offense police believe the suspect has committed.
- The extent of injuries, if any.
- The names, ages and addresses of the witnesses.

The reporter who arrives at the scene of a crime as it takes place or immediately afterward has the advantage of being able to gather much of that information firsthand. When timely coverage is impossible, however, the police report allows the reporter to catch up quickly. The names of those with knowledge of the incident usually appear on the report, and the reporter uses that information to learn about the story.

Print and online reporters sometimes write crime stories from the police report alone. For routine stories, some editors view such reporting as sufficient. Good newspapers, however, demand more because police reports frequently are inaccurate. Most experienced reporters have read reports in which the names of those involved are misspelled, ages are incorrect and other basic information is inaccurate. Sometimes such errors are a result of sloppy reporting by the investigating officer or mistakes in transcribing notes into a formal report. Occasionally, an officer may lie in an attempt to cover up shortcomings in an investigation or misconduct at the scene of a crime. Whatever the reason, good reporters do their own reporting and do not depend solely on a police officer's account. Remember that good editors frown on single-source stories of any kind, basic or not. Your job is to do solid reporting, and you are expected to consult multiple sources.

Television reporters do extensive on-the-scene coverage of crime, which has become a common element on local newscasts. Live reporting from crime scenes is likely to be a key component of a beginning reporter's job because on-the-scene reporting is the only way to get good video for the story.

With crime stories, the background check in your publication's library often is done after you return to the office. Once you have the names of those involved, you can see whether the library reveals relevant material about them. Was the suspect arrested before? Was the store robbed before? The library might help provide the answers to these kinds of questions. So might public databases. In some jurisdictions, court records, including convictions, are now online and available to anyone.

Preparing for Accident and Fire Stories

If you are assigned to cover an accident or fire, you can expect some of the same problems you'd encounter covering a crime. Much depends on whether the police or fire report is available before or after you are assigned to the story.

If the accident or fire took place overnight, the report prepared by officials is the place to start. It will give you most of the basic information you need. It also will lead you to other sources.

If you are sent to the scene of an accident or fire, your job is to collect much of that information yourself. As with crimes, you will need basic information:

- A description of what happened.
- The location and time of the incident.
- The name, age, address and condition of the victim or victims.
- The extent of injuries, if any.

- The names, ages and addresses of the witnesses.
- The extent of any property damage or loss.

Preparing for a Court Story

Most court stories you are likely to cover will be follow-ups to earlier stories. If a murder suspect is appearing for a preliminary hearing, details of the crime probably were reported earlier. A library check may give you ample background information as you prepare for your visit to the courtroom. In the absence of that, a chat with the district attorney, the police chief or one of their assistants might provide sufficient background for writing the story.

Court stories are increasingly popular on television because most jurisdictions now allow cameras in the courtroom. There is plenty of opportunity for coverage in key local cases. In federal jurisdictions—which still prohibit cameras—print, online and television reporters often rely on artists' sketches of courtroom scenes to provide visuals.

Court stories often are difficult for beginners to write because it is difficult to understand the complex process of prosecuting criminals. In addition to criminal court cases, there are civil court proceedings—lawsuits that charge an individual or company with harming another. The legal system can be quite confusing. Here's our best advice on how to approach court stories: Ask plenty of questions of the judge and attorneys before or after the court proceeding or during recesses. It's much better to admit your lack of knowledge than to make a serious error because you didn't understand what was happening.

WRITING AN OBITUARY OR LIFE STORY

An obituary or life story is a news story. You should apply the same standards to crafting a lead and building the body of an obituary as you would for other stories. You begin by answering the questions you would answer in any news story: who (Michael Kelly, 70, of 1234 West St.), what (died), where (at Regional Hospital), when (Tuesday night), why (heart attack) and how (suffered while jogging). With this information, you are ready to start the story.

Creating a Lead

The fact that Kelly died of a heart attack suffered while jogging may be the lead, but the reporter does not know this until the rest of the information essential to every obituary is gathered. You also must know:

- Time and place of the funeral.
- Time and place of the burial.

Five safeguards for obit writers

1. Confirm the spelling of names.
2. Check addresses. If a telephone book or city directory lists a different address, contact the mortuary about the discrepancy.
3. Check the birth date against the age, noting whether the person's birthday was before or after the date of death.
4. Verify with the mortuary or family any obituary phoned or faxed to the newspaper.
5. Check your newspaper's library for stories about the deceased, but be sure you don't pull stories about someone else with the same name.

- Visitation time (if any).
- Survivors.
- Date and place of birth.
- Achievements.
- Occupation.
- Memberships.

Any of these items can yield the nugget that will appear in the lead. But if none of them yields notable information, the obituary probably will start like this:

> Michael Kelly, 70, of 1234 West St. died Tuesday night at Regional Hospital.

Later in the news cycle, another standard approach could be used:

> Funeral services for Michael Kelly, 70, of 1234 West St. will be at 2 p.m. Thursday at St. Catherine's Roman Catholic Church.

Good reporters, however, often mention a distinguishing characteristic of a person's life. It may be volunteer service, an unusual or important job, service in public office or even just having a name of historical significance. Whatever distinguishes a person can be the lead of the obituary. These leads demonstrate the technique:

> Miriam Makeba, the South African singer who wooed the world with her sultry voice but was banned from her own country for more than 30 years under apartheid, died after collapsing on stage in Italy. She was 76.

> Pulitzer Prize–winning author, radio host and activist Studs Terkel died in his Chicago home Friday. He was 96.

> Jimmy Carl Black, drummer, vocalist and self-anointed "Indian of the group" of Frank Zappa's The Mothers of Invention, has died at age 70.

Writing approaches can be as varied for obituaries and life stories as for any other news story. The following story emphasizes the personal reactions of individuals who knew the deceased:

> Few persons knew her name, but nearly everyone knew her face.
>
> For 43 years, Mary Jones, the city's cheerful cashier, made paying your utility bills a little easier.
>
> Tuesday morning after she failed to report to work, two fellow employees found her dead in her home at 432 East St., where she apparently suffered a heart attack. She was 66.
>
> By Tuesday afternoon, employees had placed a simple sign on the counter where Miss Jones had worked.
>
> "We regret to inform you that your favorite cashier, Mary Jones, died this morning. We all miss her."
>
> "She had a smile and a quip for everybody who came in here," said June Foster, a bookkeeper in the office.
>
> "She even made people who were mad about their bills go away laughing."

Building the Story

When the obituary is written straight from the standard mortuary form, this is usually what results:

Michael Kelly, 70, of 1234 West St., died Tuesday night at Regional Hospital.

Kelly collapsed while jogging and died apparently of a heart attack.

Services will be at 2 p.m. Thursday at St. Catherine's Roman Catholic Church. The Rev. Sherman Mitchell will officiate. Burial will be at Glendale Memorial Gardens in Springfield.

Friends may visit with the family at the Fenton Funeral Chapel from 7 to 9 p.m. Wednesday.

Born Dec. 20, 1935, in Boston to Nathan and Sarah Kelly, Kelly was a member of St. Catherine's Roman Catholic Church and a U.S. Navy veteran of the Korean War. He had been an independent insurance agent for the last 25 years.

He married Pauline Virginia Hatfield in Boston on May 5, 1954.

Survivors include his wife; a son, Kevin of Charlotte, N.C.; and a daughter, Mary, who is a student at the University of North Carolina at Chapel Hill.

Also surviving are a brother, John of Milwaukee, Wis., and a sister, Margaret Carter of Asheville, N.C.

The Kelly obituary is a dry biography, not a story of Michael Kelly's life. There is no hint of his impact on his friends, family or community. Here is an example of a life story built on good reporting:

Ila Watson Portwood died Sunday at the Candlelight Care Center of complications stemming from a stroke she suffered about two weeks earlier. She was 88.

She was born on Aug. 30, 1918, in Boone County. She graduated from Howard-Payne School in Howard County and attended the University of Michigan.

She was the former owner and operator of the Gem Drug Co. She and her late husband, Carl, started as employees in 1939 and bought the business in 1966. They retired in 1985 and sold the company to Harold Earnest.

"She was a total lady," Earnest said. "I've never seen her mistreat anyone. Just the sweetest lady anyone can meet."

Mrs. Portwood volunteered from 1984 to 1990 at the Cancer Research Center's Women's Cancer Control Program and was named volunteer of the year in 1987.

"She was a people person," said Rosetta Miller, program coordinator. "Her caring personalized her commitment to the staff and patients.". . .

Portwood was an ordinary person whose life affected others. An obituary should celebrate such a life rather than merely note the death.

Because much of the information in any obituary comes directly from the family, it generally is accurate. But you still should check the spelling of all names and addresses and the deceased's age against the birth date. You should never print an obituary based on information obtained by phone from someone purporting to be a funeral home

On the Job

Focus on a Dream

Major Garrett is a reporter for Fox News in Washington, D.C., who has covered the White House and presidential election campaigns. But there was one moment early in his career he has never forgotten.

"I had to call up the parents of a young boy who had just been killed by a drunk driver while riding his bike," Garrett says. "I didn't want to call these people. They were grieving for their son, and they had found out about his death while driving past the wreckage of his bike.

"I ended up writing the story about the son's life and his impact on the community, and eventually didn't think any more about it until six months later. I ran into the mother at the police station, which was my beat, and she immediately recognized me. I thought she was going to yell at me, or be angry with me, but she thanked me for being so true to detail and letting the community know who her son was. People think journalism is all about asking the president the big questions, but it's really about stories like these."

Garrett's advice to aspiring journalists? "The most important thing is to focus on a dream, not on a plan," he says. "Many reporters get frustrated because their career didn't follow their plan. They think, 'I should be working here within this time span.' There is no plan, only a direction. Also, the only way you get ready for the big stories everyone wants to cover is by working on the small stories. You play the way you practice."

representative. Too many newspapers have been the victims of hoaxes. Always call the funeral home to confirm the death.

Choosing Your Words

Avoid much of the language found on mortuary forms and in obituaries prepared by morticians. The phrasing often is more fitting for a eulogy than for a newspaper story.

Because of the sensitivity of the subject matter, euphemisms have crept into the vocabulary of obituary writers. "Loved ones," "passed away," "our dearly beloved brother and father," "the departed" and "remains" may be fine for eulogies, but such terms are out of place in a news story.

Watch your language, too, when you report the cause and circumstances of a death. Unless the doctor is at fault, a person usually dies not "as a result of an operation" but "following" or "after" one. Also, a person dies "unexpectedly" but not "suddenly" (all deaths are sudden). A person dies "of" cancer, not "from" it. Note, too, that a person dies "apparently of a heart attack" but not of "an apparent heart attack." And a person dies of injuries "suffered," not "received."

Be careful with religious terms. Catholics "celebrate" Mass. Jews worship in "synagogues," which are sometimes referred to as "temples" — check with the rabbi or office staff. An Episcopal priest who heads a parish is a "rector," not a "pastor." Followers of Islam are called "Muslims." Consult *The AP Stylebook* when you have a question.

The stylebook prescribes usage in other instances, too. A man is survived by his wife, not his widow, and a woman is survived by her husband, not her widower. Do you use courtesy titles such as "Mr." and "Mrs."? Many newspapers do in obits. Do you mention divorced spouses, deceased spouses or live-in companions? Do you identify pallbearers? Do you say that the family requests memorial contributions instead of flowers? You will need to consult your local stylebook often when you are writing an obit.

Giving Cause of Death

If the person who died is not a public figure and the family does not wish to divulge the cause of death, some newspapers and television stations will comply, though such a decision is questionable news judgment. The reader or viewer wants to know what caused the death. A reporter should call the mortuary, the family, the attending physician and the appropriate medical officer. Only if none of these sources will talk should the newspaper leave out the cause of death. Some newspapers, such as *The Des Moines Register, The Cincinnati Enquirer* and *The Detroit News*, require obituaries to include the cause of death, as do many television stations.

If the death is caused by cancer or a heart attack or is the result of an accident, most families will not object to including the cause in the obituary. But if the cause is, for example, cirrhosis of the liver brought on by heavy drinking, many families will object, and many media will not insist on giving the cause.

If the deceased was a public figure or a young person, most media organizations insist on the cause of death.

If the death is the result of suicide or foul play, reporters can obtain the information from the police or the medical examiner. Some newspapers and television and radio stations mention suicide as the cause of death in the obituary, others print it in a separate news story and still others ignore it altogether. This is one way to report it:

> Services for Gary O'Neal, 34, a local carpenters' union officer, will be at 9 a.m. Thursday at First Baptist Church. Coroner Mike Pardee ruled that Mr. O'Neal died Tuesday of a self-inflicted gunshot wound.

Handling Embarrassing Information

When the *St. Louis Post-Dispatch* reported in an obituary that the deceased had been disbarred and had been a key witness in a bribe scandal involving a well-known politician 13 years earlier, several callers complained. The paper's Reader's Advocate defended the decision to include that history in the obituary.

Obituary policy options

- Run an obituary that ignores any embarrassing information and, if necessary, leaves out the cause of death. If circumstances surrounding the death warrant a news story, run it separate from the obituary.
- Insist on including embarrassing details and the cause of death in all obituaries.
- Insist on including embarrassing details and the cause of death in the obituaries of public figures only.
- Put a limit on how far back in the person's life to use derogatory information like a conviction.
- Print everything newsworthy that is learned about public figures but not about private figures.
- Print everything newsworthy about both public and private figures.
- Decide each case as it comes up.

When author W. Somerset Maugham died, *The New York Times* reported that he was a homosexual even though the subject generally had not been discussed in public. When public figures die, newspapers sometimes make the first public mention of drinking problems in their obituaries. Acquired immune deficiency syndrome is one of the more recent causes of death to challenge editors. The death of actor Rock Hudson in 1985 brought AIDS to the attention of many who had never heard of the disease before. Because it was a stigmatized disease, many newspapers agonized over whether to say that Hudson had AIDS. However, as other public figures died of AIDS, it became almost routine to report the cause of death. Unfortunately, because society still regards AIDS negatively, some spokespeople go out of their way to mention the cause of death so people won't think AIDS was the cause. Yet history shows that the more often AIDS or any other disease is reported as a cause of death, the more accepted it becomes.

The crucial factor in determining what details of an individual's private life to report is whether the deceased was a public or private person. A public figure is someone who has been in the public eye — a participant in civic or social activities, a person who spoke out at public meetings or through the mass media, a performer, an author, a speaker. Public officials, individuals who have been elected or appointed to public office, are generally treated like public figures.

The decisions newspapers and television stations must make when dealing with an obituary are sensitive and complicated. It is the reporter's obligation to be aware of the newspaper or station policy. In the absence of a clear policy statement, the reporter should consult an editor.

WRITING A CRIME STORY

Sometimes the events of a crime are most effectively told in chronological order, particularly when the story is complex. More often, a traditional inverted-pyramid style is best. The amount of time the reporter has to file the story also influences the approach. Let's take a look at how the newspaper accounts of two crimes were developed and why different writing styles seemed appropriate for each.

The Chronologically Ordered Story

Gathering facts from the many sources available and sorting through conflicting information can be time-consuming tasks. Sometimes the reporter may have to write the story before all the facts are gathered. The result is a bare-bones account written to meet a deadline. Such circumstances often lead to poor crime stories. When there is time to learn the full story, readers or viewers get a complete account of what occurred:

James Phipps and Anthony Lilly, a pair of 17-year-olds from Kansas City, Kan., were heading west on Interstate 70 at 7:30 a.m. Friday, returning from a trip to Arkansas.

Within the next hour and a half, Phipps had used a sawed-off shotgun stolen in Arkansas to take Lilly hostage, and, after holding that shotgun to Lilly's head, was shot and killed by a Highway Patrol captain on the edge of a rugged wooded area south of Springfield.

As the episode ended, local officials had only begun to piece together a bizarre tragedy that involved a high-speed chase, airplane and helicopter surveillance, a march through a wooded ravine and the evacuation of several frightened citizens from their country homes.

As police reconstructed the incident, Phipps and Lilly decided to stop for gas at the Millersburg exit east of Springfield at about 7:30 a.m. With them in the van was Robert Paul Hudson Jr., a San Francisco-bound hitchhiker.

Hudson was not present at the shooting. He had fled Lilly's van at the Millersburg exit after he suspected trouble.

The trouble began when Lilly and Phipps openly plotted to steal some gasoline at Millersburg, Hudson told police. He said the pair had agreed to display the shotgun if trouble arose with station attendants.

Hudson said he persuaded Phipps to drop him off before they stopped for gas. He then caught a ride to Springfield and told his driver of the robbery plans he had overheard. After dropping Hudson off near the Providence Road exit, the driver called Springfield police, who picked up Hudson.

Meanwhile, Phipps and Lilly put $5.90 worth of gas in the van and drove off without paying. The station attendant notified authorities.

As he approached Springfield, Phipps turned onto U.S. 63 South, where he was spotted by Highway Patrol troopers Tom Halford and Greg Overfelt. They began a high-speed chase, which ended on a dead-end gravel road near Pierpont.

During the chase, which included a U-turn near Ashland, Phipps bumped the Highway Patrol car twice, forcing Halford to run into the highway's median.

Upon reaching the dead end, the suspects abandoned the van and ran into a nearby barn. At that point, Phipps, who Highway Patrol officers said was wanted in Kansas for escaping from a detention center, turned the shotgun on Lilly.

When Halford and Overfelt tried to talk with Phipps from outside the barn, they were met with obscenities. Phipps threatened to "blow (Lilly's) head off," and vowed not to be captured alive.

Phipps then left the barn and walked into a wooded area, pressing the gun against Lilly's head. Halford and Overfelt followed at a safe distance but were close enough to speak with Phipps.

While other officers from the Highway Patrol, the Lincoln County Sheriff's Department and Springfield police arrived at the scene, residents in the area were warned to evacuate their homes. A Highway Patrol plane and helicopter flew low over the woods, following the suspects and the troopers through the woods.

The four walked through a deep and densely wooded ravine. Upon seeing a partially constructed house in a nearby clearing, Phipps demanded of officers waiting in the clearing that his van be driven around to the house, at which time he would release his hostage. Halford said, "They disappeared up over the ridge. I heard some shouting (Phipps' demands), and then I heard the shot."

After entering the clearing from the woods, Phipps apparently had been briefly confused by the officers on either side of him and had lowered his gun for a moment.

That was long enough for Highway Patrol Capt. N.E. Tinnin to shoot Phipps in the abdomen with a high-powered rifle. It was about 8:45 a.m. Phipps was taken to Lincoln County Hospital, where he soon died.

The story is as complete as possible under the circumstances. The reporter who wrote it decided to describe the chain of events in chronological order both because of the complexity of the story and because the drama of the actual events is most vividly communicated in a chronological story form.

The story is also made effective by its wealth of detail, including the names of the troopers involved, details of the chase and more. To piece together this account, the reporter had to talk with many

On the Job

Lessons of the Police Beat

When *The San Diego Tribune* expanded its zoned editions in 1985, the paper hired journalism graduate James Grimaldi to cover El Cajon, Calif. His goal was to go from the suburbs to the city desk.

"The fastest way to the front page was police stories," Grimaldi says.

One Sunday, the El Cajon police discovered a quadruple homicide. Grimaldi volunteered to cover the story. By the end of the day, he had scored an exclusive jailhouse interview with the killer. Within six months, Grimaldi was promoted to police reporter.

He combed through hundreds of police reports looking for trend stories while covering the internal policies of the San Diego Police Department. At that time, the force was racked by a high officer death rate and embarrassed by a sensational, racially divisive trial of a black man acquitted of shooting to death a white police officer in what he said was self-defense.

Once, as coroners removed a charred body from a San Diego trash bin, Grimaldi was on the scene. He later was the first to report that the death probably was the work of a serial killer. He wrote about police corruption, mentioning the chief's use of city-owned video equipment to tape a TV show on bass fishing.

"There's no better way to learn how to report and write than covering crime," Grimaldi says. "It is the quickest way to explore any community. There's humor and pathos, politics and social issues. Every rookie reporter should spend some time covering crime."

From the *Tribune,* Grimaldi went to the *Orange County (Calif.) Register* in 1989. In 1994, Grimaldi was named the *Register's* bureau chief in Washington. He then landed at *The Washington Post,* where he won a Pulitzer Prize in 2006.

witnesses. The hard work paid off, however, in the form of an informative, readable story.

Notice how the third paragraph sets the scene and provides a transition into the chronological account. Such attention to the details of good writing helps the reader understand the story with minimal effort.

The Sidebar Story

If a number of people witnessed or were affected by a crime, the main story may be supplemented by a sidebar story that deals with the personal impact of the crime. The writer of the preceding chronological account decided to write a separate story on nearby residents, who had little to add to the main story but became part of the situation nonetheless:

In the grass at the edge of a woods near Pierpont Friday afternoon, the only remaining signs of James Phipps were a six-inch circle of blood, a doctor's syringe, a blood-stained button and the imprints in the mud where Phipps fell after he was shot by a Highway Patrol officer.

Elsewhere in the area, it was a quiet, sunny, spring day in a countryside dotted by farms and houses. But inside some of those houses, dwellers still were shaken by the morning's events that had forced a police order for them to evacuate their homes.

Mrs. James G. Thorne lives on Cheavens Road across the clearing from where Phipps was shot. Mrs. Thorne had not heard the evacuation notice, so when she saw area officers crouching with guns at the end of her driveway, she decided to investigate.

"I was the surprise they weren't expecting," she told a Highway Patrol officer Friday afternoon. "I walked out just before the excitement."

When the officers saw Mrs. Thorne "they were obviously very upset and shouted for me to get out of here," she said. "I was here alone and asked them how I was supposed to leave. All they said was, 'Just get out of here!'"

Down the road, Clarence Stallman had been warned of the situation by officers and noticed the circling airplane and helicopter. "I said, 'Are they headed this way soon?' and they said, 'They're here,'" said Stallman.

After Stallman notified his neighbors, he picked up Mrs. Thorne at her home and left the area just before the shooting.

On the next street over, Ronald Nichols had no intention of running.

"I didn't know what was happening," Nichols said. "The wife was scared to death and didn't know what to do. I grabbed my gun and looked for them."

Another neighbor, Mrs. Charles Emmons, first was alerted by the sound of the surveillance plane. "The plane was flying so low I thought it was going to come into the house," she said. "I was frightened. This is something you think will never happen to you."

Then Mrs. Emmons flashed a relieved smile. "It's been quite a morning," she said.

Annual crime statistics are a common source of stories. Reporters must take care when reporting them, however, if they involve small numbers. It is dramatic to say, "Murders increased by 200 percent in 2008," but it is misleading if the increase was from one murder to three.

To provide a more accurate picture, reporters can perform the equivalent of adding apples and oranges. "Unlike" items can be added, subtracted, multiplied and divided if they are grouped in a category that makes them "like" items.

For example, you can group murders, rapes, assaults and armed robberies in the category of "violent crimes." This can be useful if an individual category, such as murder, isn't large enough to provide much insight (as in many small towns). However, the larger category must be logical and meaningful.

The Inverted-Pyramid Account

The techniques of writing in chronological order and separating the accounts of witnesses from the main story worked well in the preceding case. More often, however, crime stories are written in the classic inverted-pyramid style because of time and space considerations:

A masked robber took $1,056 from a clerk at Gibson's Liquor Store Friday night, then eluded police in a chase through nearby alleys.

The clerk, Robert Simpson, 42, of 206 Fourth St., said a man wearing a red ski mask entered the store at about 7:35 p.m. The man displayed a pistol and demanded that Simpson empty the contents of the cash register into a brown grocery bag.

Simpson obeyed but managed to trigger a silent alarm button under the counter.

The robber ordered Simpson into a storage room in the rear of the building at 411 Fourth St.

Officer J.O. Holton, responding to the alarm, arrived at the store as the suspect left the building and fled south on foot.

Holton chased the man south on Fourth Street until he turned west into an alley near the corner of Olson Street. Holton said he followed the suspect for about four blocks until he lost sight of him.

Simpson said receipts showed that $1,056 was missing from the cash register. He described the robber as about 5 feet 11 inches with a bandage on his right thumb. He was wearing blue jeans and a black leather coat.

Police have no suspects.

Such an account is adequate and can be written directly from the police report. That, of course, would be a single-source story, so a good reporter would supplement the official version by taking the time to interview the clerk and police officer if deadlines permitted.

WRITING ACCIDENT AND FIRE STORIES

When covering an accident or a fire, you will gather many of the facts and all of the color at the scene. Being there will give you a clearer picture of what happened, so you will be able to write a better story. For a television reporter, being there is essential to getting the necessary video to tell the story.

Too many reporters cover accidents and fires as passive observers. Of course, you must observe. But you also must actively solicit information from people at the scene. Many of them, including those directly involved, you may never be able to find again.

The Scene of an Accident

When you are dispatched to the scene of an accident, move as quickly as possible to collect this information:

- The names, ages, addresses and conditions of the victims.
- Accounts of witnesses or police reconstructions of what happened.
- When the accident occurred.
- Where it occurred.
- Why or how it happened or who was at fault, as determined by officials in charge of the investigation.

If that list sounds familiar, it should. You could simplify it to read "who, what, when, where and why." As in any news story, that information is essential. You must gather it as quickly as possible after being assigned to the story.

If the accident has just taken place, a visit to the scene is crucial. Just as important is knowing what to do when you get there. These suggestions will help:

- *Question the person in charge of the investigation.* This individual will attempt to gather much of the same information you want. If you are able to establish a good relationship with the investigator, you may be able to secure much of the information you need from this one source, though single-source stories usually are inadequate.

  Remember that the spellings of names, addresses and similar facts must be verified later. Police officers and other public officials often make errors in recording the names of victims. To avoid such errors, call relatives of the victims, or consult the city directory or other sources to check your information.
- *Try to find and interview witnesses.* Police and other investigators may lead you directly to them. The most accurate account of what happened usually comes from witnesses, and the investigators will try to find them. You should, too. A good way to do that is to watch the investigators. Listen in as they interview a witness, or approach the witness after they are finished. If there is time, of course, try to find your own witnesses.
- *Try to find and interview friends or relatives of the victims.* These sources are helpful in piecing together information about the victims. Through them you often get tips about even better stories.
- *If possible, interview the victims.* Survivors of an accident may be badly shaken, but if they are able to talk, they can provide firsthand details that an official report cannot. Make every attempt to interview those involved.
- *Talk with others at the scene.* If someone has died or been injured at the scene of an accident, an ambulance paramedic or the medical examiner may be able to give you some indication of the cause. At least you can learn where the bodies or the injured will be taken; later the mortician or hospital officials may be able to provide information.
- *Be sensitive to victims and their families.* You have a job to do, and you must do it. That does not mean, however, that you can be insensitive to those involved in an accident.

Of course, your deadline will have a major impact on the amount of information you are able to gather. If you must meet a deadline soon after arriving at the scene, such as filing a story for your Web site, you

---

What to do at the scene of an accident

- Question the person in charge of the investigation.
- Try to find and interview witnesses.
- Try to find and interview friends or relatives of the victims.
- If possible, interview the victims.
- Talk with others at the scene.
- Be sensitive to victims and their families.

Visiting the scene of an accident, such as this train derailment in Alabama, is essential to gathering crucial information and writing an effective story.

probably will be forced to stick to the basics of who, what, when, where, why and how. Thus it is important to gather this information first. Then, if you have time, you can concentrate on more detailed and vivid information to make the story highly readable.

The First Story

The following account of a tractor-trailer accident was produced in a race against the clock by the staff of an afternoon newspaper:

A truck driver was killed and a woman was injured this morning when a tractor-trailer believed to be hauling gasoline overturned and exploded on Interstate 70, turning the highway into a conflagration.

Both lanes of I-70 were backed up for miles after an eastbound car glanced off a pickup truck, hurdled the concrete median and collided with a tanker truck heading west.

The explosion was immediate, witnesses said. Residents along Texas Avenue reported the initial fireball reached the north side of the street, which is about 300 yards from the scene of the accident. A wooded area was scorched, but no houses were damaged.

Police evacuated the 600 block of Texas Avenue for fear that the fire would spread, but residents were returning to their homes at 12:35 p.m., about an hour after the collision. Authorities also unsuccessfully attempted to hold back the onlookers who gravitated to a nearby shopping center parking lot to view the blaze.

Police did not identify the driver of the truck, which was owned by a Tulsa, Okla., firm named Transport Delivery Co.

"Apparently it was gasoline," said Steve Paulsell, chief of the County Fire Protection District. "That's what it smelled like." Other officials reported the truck may have been hauling fuel oil or diesel fuel.

For an afternoon newspaper with an early afternoon deadline, such a story presents major problems, particularly when it occurs, as this one did, at about 11:30 a.m. Four reporters were dispatched to the scene; all of them called in information to a writer back at the office. There was little time to interview eyewitnesses. Because of the pressing deadline, the reporters were forced to gather most of their information from fire and police officials at the scene.

The Follow-Up Story

Writers for the morning newspaper or daily Web site, by comparison, had plenty of time to gather rich detail to tell the story in human terms. Much of the breaking news value was diminished by the next day because of intense coverage by afternoon newspapers, radio and television stations and updated Web sites. It was time to tell the story of a hero:

Witnesses credited an off-duty fireman with saving a woman's life Monday following a spectacular four-vehicle collision on Interstate 70 just east of its intersection with Business Loop 70.

The driver of a gasoline truck involved in the fiery crash was not so lucky. Bill Borgmeyer, 62, of Jefferson City died in the cab of his rig, which jackknifed, overturned and exploded in flames when he swerved in a futile attempt to avoid hitting a car driven by Leta Hanes, 33, of Nelson, Mo.

Hanes, who was thrown from her auto by the impact, was lying unconscious within 10 feet of the blazing fuel when firefighter Richard Walden arrived at the crash scene.

"I knew what was going on," Walden recalled, "and I knew I had to get her away from there." Despite the intense heat, Walden dragged the woman to safety.

"She had some scrapes, a cut on her knee and was beat around a little bit," Walden said. "Other than that, she was fine."

Hanes was taken to Boone Hospital Center, where she was reported in satisfactory condition Monday night.

Smoke billowing from the accident scene reportedly was visible 30 miles away. Westbound interstate traffic was backed up as far as five miles. Several city streets became snarled for several hours when traffic was diverted to Business Loop 70. The eastbound lane of I-70 was reopened about 2 p.m.; the westbound lane was not reopened until 3 p.m. . . .

The richness of detail in the second account and the eyewitness descriptions of what happened make the follow-up story more interesting than the first one.

The Scene of a Fire

Accidents and fires present similar problems for the reporter, but at a fire of any size you can expect more confusion than at the scene of an accident. One major difference is that the officer in charge at a fire will be busier. At the scene of an accident the damage has been done and the authorities usually are free to concentrate on their investigation. At a fire the officer in charge is busy directing firefighters and probably will be unable to talk with you. The investigation will not even begin until the fire is extinguished. In many cases the cause of the fire will not be known for hours, days or weeks. In fact, it may never be known. Seldom is that the case in an accident, except perhaps for air accidents.

Fire scenes generally provide plenty of opportunities for newspaper and online photographers and television videographers. Reporters help their visual counterparts gather information to accompany the images.

One potential problem is that you may not have access to the immediate area of the fire. Barriers often are erected to keep the public—and representatives of the news media—from coming too close to a burning structure. The obvious reason is safety, but such barriers may hamper your reporting. You may not be able to come close enough to firefighters to learn about the problems they are having or to obtain the quotes you need to improve your story.

Hazards at the scene of a disaster, such as this fire resulting from a Los Angeles–area earthquake, can make a reporter's job difficult and dangerous.

Getting Information

Despite the difficulties, you cover a fire much as you would an accident, interviewing officials and witnesses at the scene. You also should try to interview the property owner. Moreover, because the official investigation will not have begun, you must conduct your own.

When covering any fire, you must learn these facts:

- The location of the fire.
- The names, ages and addresses of those killed, injured or missing.
- The name of the building's owner or, in the case of a grass fire or forest fire, the name of the landowner.
- The value of the building and its contents or the value of the land.
- Whether the building and contents were insured for fire damage. (Open land seldom is.)
- The time the fire started, who reported it, and how many firefighters and pieces of equipment were called to the scene.
- What caused the fire, if known.

As in any story, the basics are who, what, when, where, why and how. Of primary importance is whether life is endangered. If it is not, the amount of property damage becomes the major emphasis of the story.

Was arson involved? Was the building insured for its full value? Was there an earlier fire in the building? Did the building comply with the fire codes? Were any rare or extremely valuable objects inside? Were there explosives inside that complicated fighting the fire and posed an even greater threat than the fire itself?

You will be able to obtain some information later from the official fire reports if they are ready before your story deadline. But most of the answers will come from interviews that you conduct at the scene with the best available sources. Finding your sources may not be easy, but you can begin by looking for the highest-ranking fire official. Large fire departments may have a press officer whose job is to deal with you and other reporters.

Another important source in covering fire stories is the fire marshal, whose job is to determine the cause of the fire and, if arson is involved, to bring charges against the arsonist. You should make every effort to talk with the fire marshal at the scene, if he or she is available.

Doing Follow-Up Interviews

In most cases, though, the fire marshal will be the primary source of a second-day story. As in covering any **spot news**—a story in which news is breaking quickly—deadlines will determine how much you can do at the scene of a fire. If your deadline is hours away, you can concentrate on the event and individuals connected with it. You will have time to find the little boy whose puppy was killed in the fire or to interview the first firefighter who entered the building. But if you have only minutes until your deadline, you may have to press the fire official in charge for information. You may have to coax from that person every tidbit, even making a nuisance of yourself, to gather the information you need. Through it all, you can expect confusion. There is little order to be found in the chaos of a fire.

WRITING A COURT STORY

Throughout a complicated court procedure, a reporter has opportunities to write or broadcast several stories, probably while also posting to the Web. The extent to which the reporter does so, of course, depends on the importance of the case and the amount of local interest in it. In a major case, the filing of every motion may prompt a story; in other cases, only the verdict may be important. As in any type of reporting, news value is the determining factor.

Also, as in any form of reporting, accuracy is important. Perhaps no other area of writing requires as much caution as the reporting of crime and court news. The potential for libel is great.

Avoiding Libelous Statements

Libel is damage to a person's reputation caused by a written statement that makes the person an object of hatred, contempt or ridicule, or that injures his or her business or occupational pursuits (see Chapter 14). Reporters must be extremely careful about what they write. One of the greatest dangers is the possibility of writing that someone is charged with a crime more serious than is the case.

After checking clippings in the newspaper library, for example, one reporter wrote:

> The rape trial of John L. Duncan, 25, of 3925 Oak St. has been set for Dec. 10 in Jefferson County Circuit Court.
> Duncan is charged in connection with the June 6 rape of a Melton High School girl near Fletcher Park.

Duncan had been charged with rape following his arrest, but the prosecutor later determined the evidence was insufficient to win a rape conviction. The charge had been reduced to assault, and the newspaper had to print a correction.

Any story involving arrests should raise caution flags. You must have a sound working knowledge of libel law and what you can and cannot write about an incident. The reporter who writes the following, for example, is asking for trouble:

> John R. Milton, 35, of 206 East St. was arrested Monday on a charge of assaulting a police officer.

Only a prosecutor, not a police officer, may file charges. In many cases, a police officer arrests a person with the intent of asking the prosecutor to file a certain charge, but the prosecutor who examines the evidence finds that it warrants a lesser charge or none at all. For that reason, most newspaper editors prefer to print the name of an arrested person only after a charge has been filed. Unfortunately, when deadline constraints make that impossible, many newspapers publish the names of arrested individuals before charges are filed.

A decision to publish a name in such circumstances requires extreme caution. If an individual is arrested in connection with a rape and the newspaper prints that information but later learns that the prosecutor has filed a charge of assault, a libel suit could result. Many states, however, give journalists a **qualified privilege** to write fair and accurate news stories based on police reports.

Once the charge is filed, the lead should be written like this:

> John R. Milton, 35, of 206 East St. was charged Monday with assaulting a police officer. Prosecutor Steve Rodriguez said . . .

By wording the lead this way, the reporter shows not only that Milton was arrested but also that the prosecutor charged him with a crime.

Reporters who cover court news are not trained as attorneys, and it takes time to develop a sound working knowledge of legal proceedings. The only recourse is to ask as many questions as necessary when a point of law is not clear. It is far better to display ignorance of the law openly than to commit a serious error that harms the reputation of the accused and opens the newspaper to costly libel litigation.

However, it is also important to know that anything said in open court is fair game for reporters. If, in an opening statement, a prosecutor says the defendant is "nothing but scum, a smut peddler bent on polluting the mind of every child in the city," then by all means report the remark in context in your story. But if a spectator makes that same statement in the hallway during a recess, you probably would not report it. Courts do not extend the qualified privilege to report court proceedings beyond the context of the official proceeding.

Continuing Coverage of the Prosecution

With the preceding points in mind, let's trace a criminal case from the time of arrest through the trial to show how a newspaper might report each step.

A Typical First Story

The following straightforward account of an arrest was filed on deadline. Later the reporter interviewed neighbors about the subject's personality and wrote an expanded story for other editions. This bare-bones story, however, provides a glimpse of several key points in covering arrest stories.

An unemployed carpenter was arrested today and charged with the Aug. 6 murder of Springfield resident Anne Compton.

Lester L. Rivers, 32, of 209 E. Dillow Lane was charged with first-degree murder, Prosecuting Attorney Mel Singleton said.

Chief of Detectives E.L. Hall said Rivers was arrested on a warrant after a three-month investigation by a team of three detectives. He declined to comment on what led investigators to Rivers.

Compton's body was found in the Peabody River by two fishermen on the morning of Aug. 7. She had been beaten to death with a blunt instrument, according to Dr. Ronald R. Miller, the county medical examiner.

Notice that the reporter carefully chose the words "arrested . . . and charged with" rather than "arrested for," a phrase that may carry a connotation of guilt.

Another important element of all crime and court coverage is the tie-back, a sentence or sentences that relate a story to events covered in a previous story—in this case, the report of the crime itself. It is important to state clearly—and near the beginning of the story—which crime is involved and to provide enough information about it so that the reader recognizes it. Clarification of the crime is important even in major stories with ready identification in the community. This story does that by recounting when and where Compton's body was found and by whom. It also tells that she died after being hit with a blunt instrument.

Follow-Up Story: First Court Appearance

The following morning the suspect was taken to Magistrate Court for his initial court appearance. Here is part of the story that resulted:

Lester L. Rivers appeared in Magistrate Court today charged with first-degree murder in connection with the Aug. 6 beating death of Springfield resident Anne Compton.

Judge Howard D. Robbins scheduled a preliminary hearing for Nov. 10 and set bail at $10,000. Robbins assigned Public Defender Ogden Ball to represent Rivers, 32, of 209 E. Dillow Lane.

Rivers said nothing during the 10-minute session as the judge informed him of his right to remain silent and his right to an attorney. Ball asked Robbins to set the bail at a "reasonable amount for a man who is unemployed." Rivers is a carpenter who was fired from his last job in June. Despite the seriousness of the charge, it is essential that Rivers be free to help prepare his defense, Ball said.

Police have said nothing about a possible connection between Rivers and Compton, whose body was found in the Peabody River by two fishermen on the morning of Aug. 7. She had been beaten to death.

> *"To make inroads into the mind-set that 'if the press reported it, it must be true' is the lawyer's most challenging task."*
>
> —**Robert Shapiro**, *attorney*

The reporter clearly outlined the exact charge and reported on key points of the brief hearing. Again, the link to the crime is important, to inform the reader about which murder is involved.

Follow-Up Story: Preliminary Hearing

Next came the preliminary hearing, where the first evidence linking the defendant to the crime was revealed:

Lester L. Rivers will be tried in Jefferson County Circuit Court for the Aug. 6 murder of Springfield resident Anne Compton.

Magistrate Judge Howard D. Robbins ruled today that there is probable cause to believe that a crime was committed and probable cause that Rivers did it. Rivers was bound over for trial in Circuit Court.

Rivers, 32, of 209 E. Dillow Lane is being held in Jefferson County Jail. He has been unable to post bail of $10,000.

At today's preliminary hearing, Medical Examiner Ronald R. Miller testified that a tire tool recovered from Rivers' car at the time of his arrest "could have been used in the beating death of Miss Compton." Her body was found floating in the Peabody River Aug. 7.

James L. Mullaney, a lab technician for the FBI crime laboratory in Washington, D.C., testified that "traces of blood on the tire tool matched Miss Compton's blood type."

In reporting such testimony, the reporter was careful to use direct quotes and not to overstate the facts. The medical examiner testified that the tire tool *could* have been used in the murder. If he had said it *was* used, a stronger lead would have been needed.

Defense attorneys usually use such hearings to learn about the evidence against their clients and do not present any witnesses. This apparently was the motive here, because neither the police nor the prosecutor had made a public statement on evidence in the case. They probably were being careful not to release prejudicial information that could be grounds for a new trial.

Follow-Up Story: Arraignment

The prosecutor then filed an *information*, as state law required. (In other states, a grand jury would have been asked to determine whether the evidence warranted a trial.) The defendant was arraigned in Circuit Court, and the result was a routine story that began as follows:

Circuit Judge John L. Lee refused today to reduce the bail of Lester L. Rivers, who is charged with first-degree murder in the Aug. 6 death of Springfield resident Anne Compton. Rivers pleaded not guilty. Repeating a request he made earlier in Magistrate Court, Public Defender Ogden Ball urged that Rivers' bail be reduced from $10,000 so he could be freed to assist in preparing his defense.

The not-guilty plea was expected, so the reporter concentrated on a more interesting aspect of the hearing—the renewed request for reduced bail.

Follow-Up Story: First Day of the Trial

Finally, after a series of motions was reported routinely, the trial began:

Jury selection began today in the first-degree murder trial of Lester L. Rivers, who is charged with the Aug. 6 beating death of Springfield resident Anne Compton.

Public Defender Ogden Ball, Rivers' attorney, and Prosecuting Attorney Mel Singleton both expect jury selection to be complete by 5 p.m.

The selection process started after court convened at 10 a.m. The only incident occurred just before the lunch break as Singleton was questioning prospective juror Jerome B. Tinker, 33, of 408 Woodland Terrace.

"I went to school with that guy," said Tinker, pointing to Rivers, who was seated in the courtroom. "He wouldn't hurt nobody."

Singleton immediately asked that Tinker be removed from the jury panel, and Circuit Judge John L. Lee agreed.

Rivers smiled as Tinker made his statement, but otherwise sat quietly, occasionally conferring with Ball.

The testimony is about to begin, so the reporter sets the stage here, describing the courtroom scene. Jury selection often is routine and becomes newsworthy only in important or interesting cases.

Follow-Up Story: Trial Testimony

Trial coverage can be tedious, but when the case is an interesting one, the stories are easy to write. The reporter picks the most interesting testimony for leads as the trial progresses:

A service station owner testified today that Lester L. Rivers offered a ride to Springfield resident Anne Compton less than an hour before she was beaten to death Aug. 6.

Ralph R. Eagle, the station owner, was a witness at the first-degree murder trial of Rivers in Jefferson County Circuit Court.

"I told her I'd call a cab," Eagle testified, "but Rivers offered her a ride to her boyfriend's house." Compton had gone to the service station after her car broke down nearby. Under cross-examination, Public Defender Ogden Ball, Rivers' attorney, questioned whether Rivers was the man who offered the ride.

"If it wasn't him, it was his twin brother," Eagle said.

"Then you're not really sure it was Mr. Rivers, are you?" Ball asked.

"I sure am," Eagle replied.

"You think you're sure, Mr. Eagle, but you really didn't get a good look at him, did you?"

"I sold him some gas and got a good look at him when I took the money."

"But it was night, wasn't it, Mr. Eagle?" Ball asked.

"That place doesn't have the best lighting in the world, but I saw him all right."

The reporter focused on the key testimony of the trial by capturing it in the words of the participants. Good note-taking ability becomes important here, because trial coverage is greatly enhanced with direct quotation of key exchanges.

Long exchanges may necessitate the use of the question-and-answer format:

Ball: In fact, a lot of the lights above those gas pumps are out, aren't they, Mr. Eagle?

Eagle: Yes, but I stood right by him.

Q. I have no doubt you thought you saw Mr. Rivers, but there's always the possibility it could have been someone else. Isn't that true?

A. No, it looked just like him.

Q. It appeared to be him, but it may not have been because you really couldn't see him that well, could you?

A. Well, it was kind of dark out there.

Follow-Up Story: Verdict

Finally, there is the verdict story, which usually is one of the easiest to write:

Lester L. Rivers was found guilty of first-degree murder today in the Aug. 6 beating death of Springfield resident Anne Compton.

Rivers stood motionless in Jefferson County Circuit Court as the jury foreman returned the verdict. Judge John L. Lee set sentencing for Dec. 10.

Rivers, 32, of 209 E. Dillow Lane could be sentenced to death in the electric chair or life imprisonment in the State Penitentiary.

Public Defender Ogden Ball, Rivers' attorney, said he will appeal.

After the verdict was announced, Mr. and Mrs. Lilborn O. Compton, the victim's parents, were escorted from the courtroom by friends. Both refused to talk with reporters.

Many other types of stories could have been written about such a trial. Lengthy jury deliberations, for example, might prompt stories about the anxiety of the defendant and attorneys and their speculations about the cause of the delay.

The Free Press/Fair Trial Controversy

Covering the courts is not a simple task. If done poorly, it inevitably leads to criticism of the press, as evidenced by the 1954 murder trial of Dr. Samuel Sheppard in Cleveland. Sheppard was accused of murdering his wife. News coverage in the Cleveland newspapers, which included front-page editorials, was intense. In 1966, the Supreme Court said the trial judge had not fulfilled his duty to protect the jury from the news coverage that saturated the community and to control disruptive influences in the courtroom.

This case more than any other ignited what is known as the **free press/fair trial controversy**. It is a controversy that continues. On numerous occasions, Judge Lance Ito, the judge in the murder trial of former football star O.J. Simpson, threatened to end television coverage of court proceedings to protect Simpson's rights during his criminal trial. Lawyers charged that the media ignored the Sixth Amendment right of the accused to an impartial jury, and the media countered with charges that lawyers ignored the First Amendment.

Editors realize that coverage of a crime can make it difficult to impanel an impartial jury, but they argue that courts have available many remedies other than restricting the flow of information. In the Sheppard case, for example, the Supreme Court justices said a **change of venue**, which moves the trial to a location where publicity is not as intense, could have been ordered. Other remedies suggested by the court in such cases are to continue (delay) the trial, to grant a new trial or to head off possible outside influences during the trial by sequestering the jury. Editors argue also that acquittals have been won in some of the most publicized cases in recent years.

When cameras are banned from the courtroom, reporters often rely on artists' sketches to provide a visual element for their stories. Timothy McVeigh and Terry Nichols, who were eventually convicted in the bombing of the Alfred P. Murrah Federal Building in Oklahoma City, Okla., in 1995, are shown at the trial with their attorneys.

Despite the remedies the Supreme Court offered in the Sheppard case, trial judges continued to be concerned about impaneling impartial juries. Judges issued hundreds of gag orders in the wake of the Sheppard case. Finally, in 1976, in the landmark case of Nebraska Press Association v. Stuart, the Supreme Court ruled that a gag order is an unconstitutional prior restraint that violates the First Amendment to the Constitution. The justices did not go so far as to rule that all gag orders are invalid. But in each case, the trial judge has to prove that an order restraining publication would protect the rights of the accused and that there are no alternatives that would be less damaging to First Amendment rights.

Suggested Readings

Buchanan, Edna. *The Corpse Had a Familiar Face*. New York: Pocket Books, 1994. One of many books by one of America's best crime reporters.

Buchanan, Edna. *Never Let Them See You Cry*. New York: Random House, 1992. An excellent description of covering crime in Miami.

Houston, Brant, and Investigative Reporters and Editors, Inc. *The Investigative Reporter's Handbook*. 5th ed. New York: Bedford/St. Martin's, 2009. A guide to using government documents to find sources of information.

Singer, Eleanor, and Phyllis M. Endreny. *Reporting on Risk: How the Mass Media Portray Accidents, Diseases, Disasters and Other Hazards*. New York: Russell Sage Foundation, 1993. A critical look at media reporting of accidents and disasters.

Suggested Web Sites

www.ap.org   Excellent examples of how to write obituaries and crime, accident, fire and court stories can be found on the Associated Press Web site.

www.nna.org   Small newspapers are served by the National Newspaper Association. Its members are more likely than metro papers to write obituaries as news stories rather than paid advertisements.

www.nsc.org   The National Safety Council Web site offers accident statistics, information on safety and links to other sites.

Exercises

1. Which elements are missing from the following obituary information?
   a. John Peterson died Saturday at Springfield Hospital. Funeral services will be at 1:30 p.m. Tuesday. Friends may call at the Restwell Funeral Home, 2560 Walnut St., from 6 to 9 p.m. Monday. The Rev. William Thomas will officiate at services in the First Baptist Church. Burial will be at City Cemetery.
   b. Richard G. Tindall, Springfield, a retired U.S. Army brigadier general, died at his daughter's home in Summit, N.J. Graveside services will be at 2 p.m. July 3 at Arlington National Cemetery in Arlington, Va.

2. Write a lead for an obituary from the following information:

   Martha Sattiewhite, born July 2, 1979, to Don and Mattie Sattiewhite, in Springfield. Martha was killed in a car accident June 30, 2008. Funeral services will be July 6. She was president of her Springfield High School senior class and of the sophomore class at the University of Oklahoma.

3. An obituary notice comes from a local mortuary. It contains the basic information, but under achievements it lists only "former member of Lion's Club." Your city editor tells you to find out more about the deceased. Whom would you call, and why?

4. If George Thomas, private citizen, committed suicide while alone in his home, would you include the cause of death in his obituary? Why or why not?

5. A few newspapers write obituaries of notable people in advance because the time between the death and publication can be short. Some papers even interview the subject. Write a two-page advance obituary of one of the following: Benjamin Chavis Muhammad, Henry Cisneros or Madonna. At the end, list your sources.

6. Find an accident story in a local newspaper. List all the obvious sources the reporter used in obtaining information for the story. List additional sources you would have checked.

7. Talk with a firefighter in your local fire department about the department's media policy at fire scenes. Based on what you learn, write instructions for your fellow reporters on what to expect at fires in your city or town.

8. Make a list of at least 10 federal agencies that may be of help in reporting accident, fire and disaster stories. Also list the telephone numbers of the agency offices nearest to you.

9. Cover a session of your local municipal court. Write a story based on the most interesting case of the day.

10. Find a court story in a local newspaper. Determine what sources the reporter used in the story, and explain how the story could have been improved.

10 Beat Reporting

Derrick Goold's beat is baseball. He covers the Cardinals for the *St. Louis Post-Dispatch*. He loves the work, but that's what it is—work. The demands of covering his beat in the age of convergence require him to be fast and flexible. Here's how he describes his job:

> The species of journalist known as beat reporter has two habitats: on deadline and online. For those of us out in the field—working the beats and breaking news—spending the day wired has taken on an entirely new and noncaffeinated meaning. As readers have become increasingly more plugged in, reporting has become increasingly more real-time and information increasingly more available and desired.
>
> As a baseball writer, my days include a variety of vehicles for reporting. There is the newsletter to write for subscribers in the morning, the blog for the midday traffic, the news update when news needs updating, the radio appearance in the afternoon and the pregame television spot.
>
> I often liken the job of a sports beat writer to spinning plates. You work many stories at the same time while trying to make sure the only thing that crashes is the computer.

Other beats may not offer the excitement of game time, but all beats now include meeting the real-time requirements of the Web, and often television or radio as well. As Derrick points out, "Reporters have never been more accessible to their readers. There's interaction, accountability, and a 24-hour news cycle."

He has an important caution for newcomers to the world of multimedia multitasking:

"A beat writer has to know when it's time to stop writing, stop blogging, stop appearing and get back to the bedrock job of reporting. Step off the hamster wheel and remember that good output requires better input. As many avenues as these platforms have opened up for our writing, they have also made it possible for our reporting to be deeper, more inventive and more instructive.

"It is also reporting that sets a beat writer apart. A beat writer's chats, blogs, hits, updates and tweets have gravity because of reporting. Content may be the coal of this new media engine. Reporting is still the fire."

Beat reporting—with Derrick's emphasis on "reporting"—is still the core of daily journalism. More than the technology is changing. We saw in Chapter 1 how the definition of news itself is broadening. This change broadens the range of beats. They now often include—along with such standard beats as local government, police, business and sports—cultural beats that reflect the interests and activities of a changing America. Some beat reporters now cover shopping malls. Some cover commuting. Some cover spiritual life. Some cover the Internet.

BEAT REPORTING IN THE 21st CENTURY

Increasingly, beat reporters tell their audiences not only what is happening but how to get involved. Stories include the telephone numbers and e-mail addresses as well as the names of decision makers. Much of the most useful reporting is done in advance of public meetings, with the goal of enabling citizens to become participants instead of passive onlookers. Readers are regularly invited to comment, question, even criticize coverage, and to speak up on public issues via e-mail or by participating in online chat rooms. Reporters post original documents online as well as additional photographs, audio and video that won't or can't be published in newsprint.

Blogs, some of them sponsored by news organizations, others independently created, provide a whole new avenue of two-way communication. Journalists write regular personal journals on their organization's Web site. Readers and critics—"citizen journalists"—provide their own take on the news, often with original reporting and almost always with a viewpoint different from that of professional, objective reporters.

Despite these changes, beat reporters remain the eyes and ears of their communities. They are surrogates for their readers, keeping track of government, education, police, business and other powerful institutions that shape readers' lives.

Traditionally, beat reporting has been mainly the province of daily newspapers. Its value is so obvious, however, that increasingly television reporters are assigned to beats. Because television staffs typically are much smaller than newspaper staffs, however, another benefit of convergence is that it expands the hard-pressed staff of the cooperating television station and enriches the news content.

The principles of good reporting apply to the coverage of any beat. The same principles also apply to specialized publications, including those aimed at particular ethnic groups, industries or professions. A reporter for *Women's Wear Daily* may cover designers. A reporter for *Diario Las Americas* in Miami may cover Cuban exile politics. But each is doing the same job: discovering and writing news that's relevant and useful to the publication's readers.

Important as it is, beat reporting is under pressure as hard economic times force many news organizations to reduce their staffs, including their number of beat reporters. The cuts are forcing reporters to take on more than one beat. For instance, police reporters are assigned to cover courts as well. Lower and higher education beats are combined, as are city and county government beats. Added to the requirements of multimedia, these broadened assignments often reduce the time reporters have for developing sources or doing in-depth stories. Still, beats remain central to good coverage, and the principles of effective beat reporting have become even more important.

Editors and audiences still expect reporters to provide information and understanding that will help readers and viewers improve the quality of their lives. That's important work. It's rewarding work. But it's not easy.

PRINCIPLES FOR REPORTERS ON A BEAT

The successful beat reporter is

- Prepared.
- Alert.
- Persistent.
- There.
- Wary.

Whether the beat you cover is the public library or the Pentagon, the county courthouse or the White House, the principles of covering it are the same. If you want to succeed as a reporter on that beat, you must be prepared, alert, persistent, there and wary. Let's take a closer look at what each of these rules means in practice.

Be Prepared

Where should preparation begin? For you, it has already begun. To work effectively, any journalist needs a basic understanding of the workings of society and its various governments. You need to know at least the rudiments of psychology, economics and history. That is why the best education for a journalist is a broad-based one, providing exposure to the widest possible sampling of human knowledge. But that exposure will not be enough when you face an important source on your first beat. You will need more specific information, which you can acquire by familiarizing yourself with written accounts or records or by talking to sources.

Reading for Background

In preparing to cover a beat, any beat, your first stop should be the news room library (see Chapter 4). Most news room libraries have computer access not only to material that has appeared in that newspaper but also to worldwide networks of information on nearly any topic. You can access the contents of major newspapers, magazines, research publications and other reference libraries. Use the **Internet** to acquire background information and to understand the context of local events and issues. For example, if you're new to the medical beat or the science beat, you might begin with the Web site of the Association of Health Care Journalists (**www.ahcj.umn.edu**) or the National Association of Science Writers (**www.nasw.org**).

In your local research, make notes of what appear to be continuing issues, questions left dangling in previous stories or ideas for stories to come. Go back several years in your preparation. History may not repeat itself, but a knowledge of it helps you assess the significance of current events and provides clues to what you can expect in the future.

The library is only the start of your preparation. You must become familiar with the laws governing the institution you cover. If a governmental organization is your beat, find the state statutes or the city charter that created the agency you will be covering. Learn the powers, duties and limitations of each official. You may be surprised to discover that someone is failing to do all that the law requires. Someone else may be doing more than the law allows.

Look at your state's open-meetings and open-records laws, too. Every state has such laws, though they vary widely in scope and effectiveness. Knowing what information is open to the public by law can be a valuable tool for a reporter dealing with officials who may find it more convenient to govern privately.

Identifying Sources

Now you're ready to start talking to people. Your first interviews should be conducted in the news room with your predecessor on the beat, your city editor and any veterans who can shed light on the kinds of things that rarely appear in statute books or newspaper stories. Who have been good sources in the past? Who will lie to you? Who drinks to excess? Who seems to be living extravagantly? Whose friends are big land developers? Who wants to run for statewide or national office? Who has been hired, fired or promoted? Who has moved to a competing company? Remember that you are hearing gossip, filtered through the biases of those relating it. Be skeptical.

Some understanding of the workings of your own news room won't hurt, either. Was your predecessor on the beat promoted, or was he or she transferred because of unsatisfactory job performance? Will an introduction from your predecessor help you or hurt you with your sources? And what are your city editor's expectations? Is your assignment to report practically every activity of government, or will you have time to do some investigative work and analysis? Trying to live up to your boss's expectations is easier if you know in advance what they are.

Establishing Relationships with Sources

Only after gaining as much background as possible are you ready to face the people you will be covering. A quick handshake and a superficial question or two may be all you have time for in the first encounter, but within a week you should arrange for sit-down conversations with your most important sources. These are get-acquainted sessions. You are trying to get to know the sources, but don't forget that they need to know you, too, if they are going to respect and trust you.

You may have noticed that the preparation for covering a beat is similar to the preparation for an interview or for a single-story assignment (see Chapter 3). The important difference is that preparing for a beat is more detailed and requires more time and work. Instead of just preparing for a short-term task, you are laying the foundation for an important part of your career. A beat assignment nearly always lasts at least six months and often two years or more. That understanding helps shape your first round of meetings with sources.

A story may emerge from these first interviews, but their purpose is much broader. You are trying to establish a relationship, trying to convert strangers into helpful partners in news gathering. To do this, you should demonstrate an interest in the sources as people as well as officials. Ask about their families, their interests, their philosophy, their goals. Make clear with your questions that you are interested rather than ignorant. (Don't ask if the source is married. You should already know that. Say, "I understand your daughter is in law school. Is she going into politics, too?" Similarly, don't ask if your source has any hobbies. Find that out beforehand. Say, "So you collect comic books. Sure takes your mind off the budget, doesn't it?")

And be prepared to give something of yourself. If you both like to fish, or you both went to Vassar, or you both have children about the same age, seize on these ties. All of us feel comfortable with people who have something in common with us. This is the time, too, to let your sources know that you know something about their work and that you're interested in it.

Solid preparation will help you avoid asking stupid questions. More important, it will help you make sure you ask the right questions. And because you have taken the trouble to get to know your sources, you are more likely to come away with responsive answers to the questions you ask.

Be Alert

Important stories are seldom labeled as such. In many cases the people involved may not realize the significance of what they are doing. Probably more often they realize it but hope nobody else will. The motivation for secrecy may be dishonesty, the desire to protect an image or a conviction that the public will misunderstand.

If your beat is a government agency, you will find that many public officials and public employees think they know more about what is good for the public than the public does. The theory of democratic government is that an informed citizenry can make decisions or elect representatives to make those decisions in its own best interests. If you are the reporter assigned to city hall, the school board or the courthouse, you carry a heavy responsibility for helping your readers put that theory into practice. To discharge that responsibility, you must probe beneath the surface of events in search of the "whys" and "hows" that lead to understanding.

When you are presented with a news release or hear an announcement or cover a vote, ask yourself these questions before passing the event off in a few paragraphs:

- *Who will benefit from this, and who will be hurt?* If the tentative answer to the first part suggests private interests, or the answer to the second part is the public, some digging is in order.
- *How important is this?* An event that is likely to affect many people for good or ill usually deserves more explanation than one affecting only a handful.
- *Who is for this, and who is against it?* When you know the answers to these questions, the answers to the first two questions usually become clearer.
- *How much will this activity cost, and who will pay?* An architect's design for renovating the downtown may look less attractive when the price tag is attached. The chamber of commerce's drive to lure new industry may require taxpayers to pay for new roads, sewers, fire protection, even schools and other services for an increased population.

Once you have asked the questions and gotten answers, the story may turn out to be about no more than it appeared to be on the surface. But if you don't ask them, you — and your readers — may find out too late that more was there than met the eye. The answers allow you to judge that most important element of news value: impact.

Be Persistent

Persistence means two things to a reporter on a beat. First, it means that when you ask a question, you cannot give up until you get an answer. Second, it means that you must keep track of slow-developing projects or problems.

Insisting on a Responsive Answer

One of the most common faults of beginning reporters is that they give up too easily. They settle for answers that are unresponsive to their questions, or they return to the news room not sure they understand what they were told. In either case the result is an incomplete, confusing story.

"Why is it that our fourth-graders score below average on these reading tests?" you ask the school superintendent.

He may reply, "Let me first conceptualize the parameters of the socioeconomic context for you."

The real answer probably is, "I only wish I knew."

Your job is to cut through the jargon and the evasions in search of substance. Often that is not an easy task. Many experts, or people who want to be regarded as experts, are so caught up in the technical language of their special field that they find it almost impossible to

> To evaluate a story, ask yourself
>
> - Who will benefit from this, and who will be hurt?
> - How important is this?
> - Who is for this, and who is against it?
> - How much will this activity cost, and who will pay?

Skilled reporters are persistent interviewers and insist on responsive answers.
Make sure your questions are answered satisfactorily.

communicate clearly. Many others seek refuge in gobbledygook or resort to evasion when they don't know an answer or find the answer embarrassing. Educators and lawyers are particularly adept at such tactics.

Listen politely for a few minutes while the school superintendent
conceptualizes his parameters. Then, when he finishes or pauses for
breath, lead him back toward where you want to go. One way is to say,
"It sounds to me as if you're saying . . . ," and then rephrase in plain
English what he told you. At those times when you are in the dark—
and that may be often— confess your puzzlement and ask for a translation. And keep coming back to the point: "But how does all that
affect reading scores?" "How can the problem be solved?" "What are
you doing about it?"

The techniques you have learned for preparing for interviews and
conducting them will help you. Your preparation for the beat will help,
too. Probably most helpful, though, are the questions you keep asking
yourself rather than your source: "Does that make sense to me?" "Can I
make it make sense to my readers?" Don't quit until the answer is yes.
You should not be obnoxious, but you do have to be persistent.

Following Up Slow Developments

Persistence is also required when you are following the course of slow-developing events. Gardeners do not sit and watch a seed germinate. Their eyes would glaze over long before any change was apparent. Gardeners do, however, check every few days, looking for the green shoots that indicate the process is taking place as it should. If the shoots are late, they dig in to investigate.

Beat reporting works much the same way. A downtown redevelopment plan, say, or a revision in a school's curriculum is announced. The story covers the plans and the hoped-for benefits. The seed is planted. If it is planted on your beat, make a note to yourself to check on it in a week or two. And a week or two after that. And a month after that. Start a file of reminders so you won't forget. Such a file often is called a **tickler** because it serves to tickle your memory.

Like seeds, important projects of government or business take time to develop. Often what happens during the long, out-of-public-view development is more important than the announcements at the occasional news conferences or the promises of the promotional brochures. Compromises are made. Public money is spent. The public interest may be served, or it may not.

Sometimes the story is that nothing is happening. At other times the story may be that the wrong things are happening. Even if nothing improper is taking place, the persistent reporter will give readers an occasional update. At stake, after all, is the public's money and welfare.

Be There

In beat reporting there is no substitute for personal contact. Trying to cover a beat by telephone or e-mail won't work. The only way to do it is to be there — every day, if possible. Joking with the secretaries, talking politics with council members and lawyers, worrying over the budget or trading gossip with the professional staff — you must make yourself a part of the community you are covering.

Remember that the sources who are most important to you probably are in great demand by others, too. They have jobs to do. Maneuver to get as much of their time as you need, but don't demand too much. Do your homework first. Don't expect a school superintendent to explain basic concepts of education. You can learn that information from an aide or from reading. What you need to learn from the superintendent is how he or she intends to apply those concepts, or why they seem to be inapplicable here. Find out what Class I felonies are before asking the police chief why they are increasing. You will get the time you need more readily if busy sources know their time will not be wasted.

Maintaining Your Connections with Sources

There are other simple techniques you can use to build and maintain good relationships with the people on your beat. Here are some of them:

- *Do a favor when you can.* As a reporter you spend much of your time asking other people to do favors for you—giving you their time, sharing information they need not share, looking up records and figures. If a source wants a favor in return, don't refuse unless granting the favor would be unethical. The favors asked usually are small things, such as getting a daughter's engagement picture in the paper or procuring a print of a picture taken with the governor to decorate the official's wall.
- *Don't shun good news.* One ill-founded but common complaint is that the news media report nothing but bad news. Admittedly, there is usually no story when people are doing what they are supposed to do. Sometimes there should be, if they do their duty uncommonly well or have done it for a very long time or do it under the burden of some handicap.
- *Protect your sources.* Many people in government—politicians and bureaucrats alike—are willing to tell a reporter things they are not willing to have their names attached to in print or otherwise. The same is true of people in private business, who may fear reprisals from their employer, co-workers or competitors. Sometimes such would-be anonymous sources are trying to use you to enhance their own positions. You have to protect yourself and your readers against that possibility. Confer with an editor if you have doubts. Most papers are properly wary of relying on unnamed sources. Sometimes, though, requests for anonymity are valid, necessary to protect the source's career. Once you have agreed to protect a source, you must do it. Don't tell anyone but your editor. An inability to keep your mouth shut can cost you more than a source. It can cost you your reputation. (The protection of sources has legal as well as ethical implications. So-called **shield laws** in some states offer journalists limited exemptions from legal requirements to disclose sources. See Chapter 14. But there are no blanket exemptions.)
- *Above all, be accurate.* Inaccurate reporting leads first to loss of respect from sources, then to loss of the sources themselves and finally to loss of the job. If you are a good, tough reporter, not all of the contacts on your beat will love you. But if you are an accurate reporter, they will respect you.

Ensuring Accuracy

The best way to ensure accuracy is to check and double-check. Many of the stories you will write are likely to be complicated. You will be expected to digest budgets, master plans, legal opinions and complicated discussions, and to translate these into language your readers can understand. When in doubt, ask somebody.

If you are unclear about the city manager's explanation of the budget before the council, arrange a meeting afterward and go over it.

On the Job

Newer, Faster, Better

Sonja Bjelland's beat is cops and courts for *The Press-Enterprise* in Riverside, Calif. Here's her day:

"I am constantly juggling multiple technologies and demands: Web story updates and thoughtful newspaper pieces, notebooks and video cameras, cell phones and computers.

"Demands from the Internet require reporters to write numerous leads throughout the day and sometimes two or more full stories on the same topic. The last version of the story needs to provide scope and context not available in quick Web items from earlier in the day. Often, I'm marking in my notes what I might want to include and prewriting my story in a notebook while still covering an event."

In the few years since she finished school, technology has changed the demands of the job. "Technology has also made some parts of the job easier," Sonja says. "I can quickly search someone's background, track court records and find their friends through MySpace or Facebook. I also try to post to the Web documents used in the story so the readers can see it for themselves."

At *The Press-Enterprise*, she says, they have started daily blogs focusing on homicide and general crime while occasionally blogging from ongoing trials.

In Sonja's case, covering a trial requires posting updates at every break, and writing both a midday story and a wrap-up for the print edition. Communication between editor and reporter is even more important as instant decisions are made.

"I use my J School skills and operate under the same high standards, just faster," she says.

If a company's brief in a legal case has you confused, call the lawyer who wrote it. If the new master land-use plan strikes you as vague, consult with the planner. If you are writing a story on a subject you feel tentative about, arrange to read it back to the sources when it is complete. Not all experts relish being asked to translate their jargon into English, so in some cases you will have to insist, politely. The best persuader is the assurance that it is far better for your sources to take a few minutes to explain now than to see themselves misrepresented in print.

Remember, beat reporting is a lot like gardening. Both require you to be in the field every day, cultivating. And in both, the amount of the harvest is directly proportional to the amount of labor invested.

Be Wary

The point of all this effort—the preparation, perceptiveness, persistence and personal contact—is to keep your readers informed. That is an obvious statement, but it needs to be made because every reporter on a beat is under pressures that can obscure the readers' importance. You must be wary of this problem.

You will have little contact with 99.9 percent of your readers. They will not write you notes when you have done a story they like or call you when they dislike what you have written. They will not offer to buy you a cup of coffee or lunch, or stop you in the hall to urge you to see things their way. But your sources will.

If you write that city council members are thinking about raising the property tax rate, you probably will hear complaints from council members about premature disclosure. If you write that the CEO of a major business is looking for a new job, chances are he or she will deny it even though the story is true.

All sources have points of view, programs to sell, careers to advance, opponents to undercut. It is likely and legitimate that they will try to persuade you of the merit of their viewpoint, try to sell their programs through the columns of your newspaper, or try to shape the news to help their career.

Be wary of sources' efforts to use you. You can lose the critical distance a reporter must maintain from those being covered. When that happens, you start thinking like a participant rather than an observer. You begin writing for your sources rather than your audience. This is a real danger. No one can spend as much time with sources as a reporter on a beat does, or devote as much effort to understanding them, without becoming sympathetic. When you associate so closely with the insiders, you may forget that you are writing for the outsiders.

CONVERGED COVERAGE

"Working in a converged news room requires a spirit of collaboration and a willingness to adapt to new technologies," says Sophia Maines, who covers higher education in Lawrence, Kan. "This may seem simple, but it does require a change of mind-set for reporters accustomed to working in a traditional news room." Her news room is far from traditional. It includes a newspaper, a Web site and a cable television station. Her work feeds all three outlets.

The basics don't change. She cultivates sources, develops story ideas and then writes the stories. Often, they wind up on Page One of the *Lawrence Journal-World*. But just as often, they also show up on the 6 p.m. newscast on television. And invariably they're posted on LJWorld.com, frequently with supporting materials and video the newspaper couldn't accommodate.

Sophia explains, "In our news room, many reporters work in teams. As an education writer, I work closely with a television reporter who covers the same beat. I may work with my convergence partner on story development, or we may conduct interviews together. If I am free, I may take a television camera to an interview and tape it for a broadcast story. For convergence to work, it's vital that reporters develop synergy."

"Synergy" means that contributions from several sources—or reporters—yield products (stories) that are better than any single contributor could produce. It's a term that helps explain the value of convergence.

Convergence isn't always smooth, of course.

Sophia again: "This relationship has its ups and downs. When one of my fellow reporters recently moved to another beat at the newspaper and stopped working with his broadcast counterpart, he joked that he was having a tough time with the 'convergence divorce.' Teams in a converged news room can seem like marriages, with similar trials, compromises and memorable moments. Like marriages, the teams succeed when the partners work at them."

For newspaper reporters, convergence means a high-tech return to the distant days of multiple editions, when instead of one deadline a

With cell phones, digital cameras and laptop computers, reporters can and do post stories online as they unfold.

day journalists had many. For radio and television reporters, the online opportunities match those of live reporting over the air. Research shows that increasing numbers of online readers rely on Web sites to stay in touch with news as it happens.

You'll be expected to gather and present to readers more information, more detail and more points of view than either print or broadcast now permits. Readers who care enough to follow an issue online will want and expect to see the source documents you use—and those the policy-makers use. They'll want and expect links to other Web sites that offer related information or further background.

And, increasingly, readers and viewers react to your reporting. Newspapers, television and magazines provide great depth and variety. But they don't provide the opportunity for their readers to converse with either the people in the news or the writers. Online readers can—and expect to—do just that. So online reporters must be prepared to answer questions, respond to criticisms, elaborate on their written words—not just to editors or sources, but to readers.

Bloggers are likely to add their own perspective. A blog nearly always includes the writer's opinions. Many also include original reporting, sometimes with specialized expertise a reporter doesn't have. Many traditional reporters find this prospect terrifying. They're more comfortable in a world of one-way communication, reporter to reader. That world still exists, but anyone preparing to enter the new world of convergence should understand that it demands more of reporters. The public conversation is richer and more complex than ever before.

For more on writing online, read the sections in this chapter and see Chapter 13, "Writing Online."

COVERING IMPORTANT LOCAL BEATS

Crucial factors and practical principles for beat reporters

- *Power:* Information is power.
- *Money:* The budget is the blueprint.
- *Politics:* Distributing power and money is politics.

Your political science courses will introduce you to the structure of government, but from a reporter's viewpoint, function usually is even more important than structure. You must learn who holds the real power, who has the most influence on the power holders and who are the most likely sources of accurate information. Power, money and politics are the crucial factors to watch in any beat reporting. These general principles will help you in covering any state or local institution.

Information Is Power

The holder of information may be a professional administrator—the city manager, school superintendent, police chief or court clerk—or may be an elected official: the mayor, chair of the county commission or chair of the school board. The job title is unimportant. Find the person who knows in detail how the organization really works, where the money goes and how decisions are made. Get to know that person because he or she will be the most important person on your beat.

The Budget Is the Blueprint

This principle is a corollary of the first. Just as detailed knowledge of how an organization works is the key to controlling that organization, a budget is the blueprint for the organization's activities. The budget tells where the money comes from and where it goes. It tells how many people are on the payroll and how much they are paid. It tells what programs are planned for the year and how much they will cost. Over several years' time, the budget tells where the budget makers' priorities are and what they see as their organization's role in the community.

Find copies of the last two or three years' budgets for your beat. Try to decipher them. Learn all you can from your predecessor and from newspaper clips. Then find the architect who drew up this blueprint — the budget director or the clerk or the assistant superintendent — and get a translation. Ask all the questions you can think of. Write down the answers.

When budget-making time arrives, follow every step. Attend every public hearing and every private discussion session you can. In those dollar figures are some of the most important stories you will write — stories of how much your readers will be paying for schools and roads and garbage pickup, stories of what they will get for their money. You'll find a guide to understanding budgets in Chapter 5.

Distributing Power and Money Is Politics

At any organizational level in any form, power and money go hand in hand with politics. Politics provides the mechanisms through which limited resources are allocated among many competing groups. Neither elections nor political parties are necessary for politics. You will have to learn to spot more subtle forms of political maneuvering.

If you are covering city hall, for example, pay close attention while the city budget is being drafted. You may find the mayor's pet project being written in by the city manager. Nobody elects the city manager, but it is good politics for him or her to keep the mayor happy. Are the builders influential in town? If so, you will probably find plenty of road and sewer projects in the budget. Are the city employees unionized? Look for healthy wage and benefit increases if they are. None of these projects is necessarily bad just because it is political. But you and your readers ought to know who is getting what and why.

Writing for Readers

What does it mean to write for your readers instead of your sources? It means that you must follow several important guidelines:

Translate. The language of bureaucrats, educators, scientists or lawyers is not the same language most people speak. You need to learn the jargon of your sources, but you also need to learn how to translate it into standard English for your readers. The city planning consultant might say, "Preliminarily, the concept appeared to permit attainment of all our criteria; but, when we cost it out we have to question its economic viability." Your lead could translate that to:

> The proposed plan for downtown redevelopment looks good on paper, but it may cost too much, the city's planning consultant said today.

Make your writing human. In big government and big business, humanity often gets lost in numbers. Your readers want and need to know the impact of these numbers on real people. How many people will be displaced by a new highway? Who are they? Who will be affected by a school closing or a welfare cut? When a police report announced that burglaries were up 35 percent in the last two months, an enterprising reporter told the story through the eyes of a victim. It began this way:

> Viola Patterson picked her way through the shattered glass from her front door, passed the table where her television used to sit, and stopped before the cabinet that had held her family silver.
>
> She wept.
>
> Mrs. Patterson, 72, is one of the more than 75 people victimized by burglars in the last two months.

Think of the public pocketbook. If the tax rate is going up 14 cents, how much will it cost the average homeowner? If employees of a firm are seeking a 10 percent raise, how much will that cost the employer? How much of that increase will be passed on to customers? If garbage collection fees are about to be increased, how do they compare to fees in comparable cities?

The city manager proposed "adjusting" the price of electricity to lower the cost to industrial customers and raise rates to private homes. The city hall reporter did a quick survey of comparable cities around the state. Then she wrote:

> City residents, who already pay more for their electricity than residents of eight similar-sized cities around the state, would be charged an average of $4 per month more under a proposal announced Tuesday by City Manager Barry Kovac.
>
> Industrial users, whose rate now is about average among the nine cities, would enjoy the second-lowest rate under Kovac's proposal.
>
> Kovac defended his plan as "equitable and necessary to ensure continued economic growth for the city."

Get out of the office. City council votes are important, but far more people will have personal contact with government in the form of a police officer, a clerk or a bus driver than with a council member. Go to where government meets its constituents. Ride a bus. Visit a classroom. Patrol with a police officer. Not only will you get a reader's-eye view of your beat, but you may also find some unexpected stories.

Ask the readers' questions. "Why?" "How much will it cost me?" "What will I get out of it?" You are the public's ombudsman.

Remember, a good beat reporter has to be prepared, be alert, be persistent and be there. If you keep in mind, too, who you are writing for, you'll keep the customers—and the editors—satisfied.

CITY AND COUNTY GOVERNMENT

Most medium-sized cities have council-manager governments. The mayor and council members hire a professional administrator to manage the day-to-day affairs of the city. The manager, in turn, hires the police and fire chiefs, the public-works director and other department heads. Under the city charter, the council is supposed to make policy and leave its implementation to the manager. Council members usually are forbidden to meddle in the affairs of any department.

Some small towns and a decreasing number of big cities have governments in which the mayor serves as chief administrator. Rudy Giuliani, mayor of New York during the terrorist attacks of Sept. 11, 2001, became a national hero for his take-charge approach. Whatever the structure, you will have a range of good sources to draw on.

Subordinate Administrators

Lower-level administrators know the details of budgets, planning and zoning, and personnel matters. They are seldom in the spotlight, so many of them welcome a reporter's attention as long as the reporter does not get them into trouble. Many are bright and ambitious, willing to second-guess their superiors and gossip about politics, again providing you can assure them that the risk is low.

Council Members

Politicians, as a rule, love to talk. What they say is not always believable, and you have to be wary of their attempts to use you, but they will talk. Like most of us, politicians are more likely to tell someone else's secret or expose the other guy's deal. So ask one council member about the political forces behind another member's pet project, and ask the other about the first's mayoral ambitions. That way you probably will learn all there is to know.

Pressure Groups

You can get an expert view of the city's land-use policies from land developers and a different view from conservationists. The manager or the personnel director will tell one side of the labor-management story. The head of the employees' union will tell the other. How about the school board's record in hiring minorities? Get to know the head of the local NAACP or Urban League chapter. Public officials respond to pressure. As a reporter, you need to understand those pressures and who applies them.

Public Citizens

Consumer advocate Ralph Nader made the term "public citizens" popular, but every town has people — lawyers, homemakers, business executives, retirees — who serve on charter commissions, head bond campaigns, work in elections and advise behind the scenes. Such people can be sources of sound background information and useful assessments of officeholders.

Opponents

The best way to find out the weaknesses of any person or program is to talk with an opponent. Seek out the board member who wants to fire the school superintendent. Look up the police captain demoted by the new chief. Chat with the leader of the opposition to the new hospital. There are at least two sides to every public question and every public figure. Your job is to explore them all.

Once you have found your sources, keep looking, listening and asking for tips, for explanations, for reactions, for stories. The fun is just starting.

EDUCATION

Keeping up with issues on the education beat

- Subscribe to trade newsletters and magazines.
- Remember the most important part of the beat — what goes on in the classroom.
- Understand what standard test scores mean.
- Get to know teachers, administrators, parents and students.

No institution is more important to any community than its schools. None is covered more poorly. And none is more demanding of or rewarding to a reporter. The issues that arise on the education beat are among the most important in our society. If it is your beat, be prepared to write about racial tensions, drug abuse, obscenity versus free speech, religious conflict, crime, labor-management disputes, politics, sex — and yes, education.

Whether the classrooms hold kindergartners or college students, the principles for covering education remain the same. For the most part, so do the issues. When the schools are private rather than public, you have fewer rights of access.

The Schools

The classroom is not an easy place to cover. You may have trouble getting into one. Administrators frequently turn down such requests on the grounds that a reporter's presence would be disruptive. It would, at first. But a good teacher and an unobtrusive reporter can overcome that drawback easily. Many newspapers, at the start of the school year, assign a reporter to an elementary school classroom. He or she visits frequently, gets to know the teacher and pupils, becomes part of the furniture. And that reporter captures for readers much of the sight and sound and feeling of schooling.

There are other ways, too, of letting readers in on how well — or how badly — the schools are doing their job:

- *Examine standardized test scores.* Every school system administers some kind of standard tests designed to measure how well its students compare either with a set standard or with other students. The results of such tests are or ought to be public information. Insist on learning about them. Test scores are an inadequate measure of school quality, but they are good indicators. When you base a story on them, be sure you understand what is really being compared and what factors outside the schools may affect the scores. Find out what decisions are made on the basis of standardized test scores. For example, do schools with relatively low average scores get additions to their faculty? Do they get special education teachers?
- *Be alert to other indicators of school quality.* You can find out how many graduates of your school system go to college, how many win scholarships and what colleges they attend. You can find out how your school system measures up to the standards set by the state department of education. Does it hold the highest classification? If not, why not? National organizations of teachers, librarians and administrators also publish standards they think schools should meet. How close do your schools come?
- *In education, you get what you pay for.* How does the pay of teachers in your district compare with pay in similar-sized districts? How does the tax rate compare? What is the turnover among teachers?
- *Get to know as many teachers, administrators, parents and students as possible.* You can learn to pick out the teachers who really care about children and learning. One way to do that is to encourage them to talk about their jobs. A good teacher's warmth will come through.

One reason schools are covered poorly is that the beat often does not produce the obvious, easy stories of politics, personalities and conflict that the city hall or police beats yield. School board meetings usually produce a spark only when a side issue intrudes. Most school board members are more comfortable talking about issues other than education itself, which often is left to the professionals.

The politics and the budgets of schools are very much like those of other institutions. The uniquely important things about schools are the classrooms and what happens inside them. Your reporting will suffer if you forget that fact. So will your readers.

Colleges and Universities

Look around you. Relevant and useful stories are everywhere. From the next meeting of the governing board to the classroom of a popular professor, the same principles that apply to coverage of elementary schools can be applied on the campus.

Politics, economics, pedagogy and all the subjects in the course catalog are also prime prospects for examination. Politics may be partisan, especially in public universities with elected or appointed governing boards, or it may be bureaucratic, as individuals or departments compete for power and prestige. The economics of higher education translates to budgets, salaries and tuition levels. Pedagogy, the art and science of teaching, is often overlooked by reporters, but it is really the point of the enterprise.

The Chronicle of Higher Education and campus newsletters are required background reading—the former for insights into national issues and trends, the latter for the nitty-gritty of local developments.

Suppose, for example, that *The Chronicle* reports a dramatic rise in tuition costs across the nation. The obvious local story is what's happening on your campus and how that compares with the situation at peer institutions. A less obvious story may be how students are scraping up that tuition money. And an even better, though more difficult, story would be how rising costs affect who can afford to attend, and therefore the composition—by race, ethnicity, social class, even geography—of the student body.

To cover your campus, you'll have to overcome the natural hesitancy of many students to challenge professors, administrators and other authority figures. Try to think of them not as superior beings, but as sources and possible subjects of stories. Then treat them respectfully but not obsequiously, as you would any public official. If your campus is state-supported, they are public officials, after all. That means, among other things, that state laws governing open meetings and records apply.

Here are a few of the issues that should yield good stories on most campuses:

- *Politics.* How are members of the governing board chosen? Who are the members, anyway? What's their agenda? Within the campus, which are the favored departments? How strong is the fraternity and sorority system? How much clout does the athletic department wield with the campus administration or alumni? In an institution founded on free inquiry, just how free is speech for students, faculty and staff?
- *Economics.* How much do the president, the faculty and the janitors get paid? Where does the money to support the institution really come from—the state, tuition, alumni giving, research grants and contracts? Where does that money go? How much is spent on intercollegiate athletics? How much on the English and history departments?
- *Pedagogy.* Who are the best (and worst) teachers on campus? Is good teaching rewarded as much as research is? Among the faculty, who gets tenure, and who doesn't? Who does the teaching, anyway—senior faculty, graduate students, part-timers?

You can practice good reporting without leaving your campus.

THE POLICE BEAT

The police beat probably produces more good, readable stories per hour of reporter time than any other beat. It also produces some of the worst, laziest reporting and generates many of our most serious legal and ethical problems. It is the beat many cub reporters start on and the beat many veterans stay on until they have almost become part of the force. It offers great frustration and great opportunity. All these contradictions arise from the nature of police work and of reporting.

How to cover the cops

- Educate yourself in police lore.
- Try to fit in.
- Lend a sympathetic ear.
- Encourage gossip.
- Talk with other police watchers.

If you are going to be a police reporter—and nearly every reporter is, at least briefly—the first thing you have to understand is what police officers are and what they do. We hire police officers to protect us from each other. We require them to deal every day with the dregs of society. Abuse and danger are parts of the job, as is boredom. We pay police officers mediocre wages and accord them little status. We ask them to be brave but compassionate, stern but tolerant. What we get very often is less what we ask for than what we should expect. Police work seldom attracts saints. Police officers are frequently cynical, often prejudiced, occasionally dishonest.

When you walk into a police station as a reporter for the first time, expect to be met with some suspicion, even hostility. Young reporters often are perceived by police as being radical, unkempt, anti-authority. How closely does that description fit you or your classmates? How many of you are pro-cop?

Police departments are quasi-military organizations, with strict chains of command and strong discipline. Their members are sworn to uphold the status quo. The reasons that police officers and young reporters are mutually suspicious should be clear by now.

Then, how do you cover these people? You do so by using the same tricks of the trade you ply at city hall or in the schools:

- *Educate yourself in police lore.* Take a course in law enforcement, if you can, or take a course in constitutional law. You also might read Joseph Wambaugh's novels for a realistic portrait of the police.
- *Try to fit in.* Men should consider getting a conservative haircut. Men and women should dress conservatively too—and learn the language of the police force. Remember that police officers, like the rest of us, usually are quicker to trust people who look and act the way they do.
- *Lend a sympathetic ear.* You enjoy talking about yourself to somebody who seems to be interested; so do most police officers. They know they have a tough job, and they like to be appreciated. Open your mind, and try to understand points of view with which you may disagree strongly.
- *Encourage gossip.* Police officers may gossip even more than reporters do. Encourage such talk over a cup of coffee at the station, while tagging along in a patrol car or over a beer after the shift. The stories will be one-sided and exaggerated, but you may learn a lot. Just don't print anything you haven't verified.

- *Talk with other police watchers.* Lawyers can be good sources, especially the prosecutors and public defenders who associate every day with the police. Other law enforcement sources are good, too. Sheriff's deputies, for example, may be eager to talk about dishonesty or inefficiency in the city police department, and city police may be eager to reciprocate.

One important reason for all this work is that little of the information you need and want as a police reporter is material you are entitled to under public-records laws. By law you are entitled to see only the arrest sheet (also called the arrest log, or the **blotter**). This record tells you only the identity of the person arrested, the charge and when the arrest took place. You are not entitled by law to see the arrest report or to interview the officers involved.

Writing a story depends on securing more than the bare-bones information. Finding out details depends on the goodwill you have generated with the desk sergeant, the shift commander and the officers on the case. The dangers—of being unfair, of damaging your and your paper's or Web site's reputation—are ever-present. Good reporting requires that you know what the dangers are and how to try to avoid them.

The greatest danger arises from the one-sidedness and frequent inaccuracy of arrest reports. At best, they represent the officer's viewpoint. Particularly in cases involving violence, danger, confusion or possible repercussions, there may be plausible viewpoints different from that of the police officer. Conflicting interpretations of the same situation lead many times to the dropping of charges.

To protect yourself, and to be fair to the accused, always be skeptical. Attribute any accusatory statement to the officer who made it. If the room for doubt is great enough, talk to the accused, his or her relatives or lawyer, and any witnesses you can find.

THE COURTS

A skeptic's guide to the courts

- Never trust a lawyer unless you know him or her very well.
- A judge's word may be law, but it isn't gospel.
- Truth and justice do not always prevail.

One way to begin trying to understand the American judicial system is to think of it as a kind of game. The opposing players in a criminal case are the state, which is the accuser, and the defendant, who is the accused. In a civil case the opponents are the plaintiff and the defendant. Each player is represented by a lawyer, who does everything possible to win for his or her client. The judge referees the contest, insisting that all players abide by the rules. At the end, the judge (sometimes with a jury) decides who won.

Such an irreverent description grossly oversimplifies a system that, because of its independence and usual honesty, stands second only to a free press in protecting the liberty of Americans. But it may help in demystifying a system that can overawe a beginning reporter.

There is a great deal in courts and the law to inspire awe. Black-robed judges and learned attorneys speak a language full of Latin phrases and highly specialized terms. Written motions, arguments and decisions are laden with convoluted sentences and references unintelligible to the uninitiated. A court can protect your money or your freedom or deprive you of both.

You can hardly cover the courts aggressively while standing awe-struck, though, so here are some tips that may help restore your working skepticism:

- *Never trust a lawyer unless you know him or her very well.* Although most lawyers are honest, all lawyers are advocates. Consequently, everything they write or say must be interpreted as being designed to help their client and hurt their opponent. This is true whether the lawyer represents the defense or the prosecution in a criminal case or represents either side in a civil lawsuit. Bar association codes of ethics forbid it, but many lawyers will try to use reporters to win some advantage. Be suspicious.
- *A judge's word may be law, but it isn't gospel.* Not every judge is a legal scholar. Most judges are, or have been, politicians. All judges are human. They are subject to error, capable of prejudice. Some are even dishonest.
- *Truth and justice do not always prevail.* Prosecutors sometimes conceal evidence favorable to the defense. Defense lawyers sometimes seize on technicalities or rely on witnesses they know to be unreliable in order to win acquittals. Judges sometimes misinterpret the rules or ignore them. Innocent people do go to jail, and guilty ones go free. Courts are no more perfect than newspapers. The two combined can produce frightening scenes. Sometimes the press helps correct miscarriages of justice. Reporter Gene Miller won two Pulitzer Prizes for winning freedom for people wrongfully imprisoned after unjust murder convictions.

The judicial system is not exempt from honest and critical reporting. And the sources of that reporting — just as in city hall or the police station — are records and people.

Court Records

Whenever a case is filed in court — whether it is a criminal charge or a civil lawsuit — the court clerk assigns it a number. It also has a title. In the case of a criminal charge, the title will be State v. Joe Doakes, or something similar. (The "v." is short for "versus," the Latin word meaning "against.") A civil case — a lawsuit seeking damages, for example — could be Joe Doakes v. John Doe. Doakes would be the plaintiff, the party filing the suit. Doe would be the defendant. To secure the records from the court clerk, you must know the case number or case title, which lawyers also call the "style" of the case.

You can follow a case by checking the case file. At least in the more important criminal cases, however, you usually keep track by checking with the prosecutor and defense lawyers.

Once a civil suit has been filed, the defense files a reply. The plaintiff may file a motion seeking information. The defense may file a motion to dismiss the suit, which the plaintiff will answer. The judge rules on each motion. You can follow it all by checking the file regularly. Except in rare cases, all motions and information filed with the court become public records. Often information from lawsuits can provide you with interesting insights into the otherwise private affairs of prominent persons or businesses.

Many lawsuits never go to trial before judge or jury. It is common procedure for lawyers to struggle for advantage over a period of months, filing motions and countermotions to gain the best position or to sound out the other side's strength. Then, after a trial date has been set, one side or the other will propose a settlement, which is negotiated. The case is dropped. One reason for this course of action is that the details of an out-of-court settlement need not be made public, unlike the outcome of a trial.

Human Sources

Human sources in court

- Lawyers.
- Judges.
- Other court functionaries.

If a case goes to trial, you cover civil and criminal proceedings in much the same way. You must listen to testimony and, during breaks, corner lawyers for each side to seek explanation and elaboration, while filling in the background from court records and your news room library. Your personal contacts are important sources of information during this process.

Lawyers

The best sources on the court beat are likely to be lawyers. Every courthouse reporter needs to win the confidence and goodwill of the prosecutor and his or her staff. Not only can they keep you abreast of developments in criminal prosecution, but they often can—because assistant prosecutors generally are young, political and ambitious—keep you tuned in to all sorts of interesting and useful courthouse gossip. They are good sources for tips on who the best and worst judges are, which local officials may be on the take, which defense lawyers are less than upright. Like all gossip, such tips need careful handling and thorough checking.

Lawyers in private practice can be grouped, from a reporter's viewpoint, into two classes: those who will talk and those who won't. The former class usually includes young lawyers, politically ambitious lawyers and criminal defense lawyers, all of whom often find publicity helpful. Cultivate them. Lawyers have egos only slightly smaller than those of reporters. Feed those egos. Encourage them to talk about themselves, their triumphs, their ambitions.

Judges

Don't ignore judges as sources, either. Some are so conscious of their dignity and their image that they have no time for reporters. Remember, though, that most judges in most states are elected to their jobs. That makes them politicians, and it is a rare politician who slams the door on a friendly reporter. Even many federal judges, who are appointed by the president, have done a stint in politics and still have a taste for newspaper ink. Judges' egos may be even bigger than reporters'. Treat every judge accordingly.

Other Court Functionaries

Many other court functionaries can be helpful sources. Police officers and sheriff's deputies or U.S. marshals assigned to court duty often are underworked and eager for a chance to talk about whatever they know, which may turn out to be good backstage stuff. The bailiffs who shout for order in the court and help the judge on with a robe may be retired police officers or small-time politicians and also talkative. And secretaries, as everywhere, are good to know and even better to have know you.

THE ENVIRONMENT, SCIENCE AND MEDICINE

In surveys, newspaper readers say they want more and better coverage of the environment. This desire is especially strong among younger readers (and nonreaders, too). Top-quality environment coverage wins important awards and brings prestige to news organizations. For example, a series on threats to the world's fisheries won *The (New Orleans) Times-Picayune* a Pulitzer Prize and an immediate boost in reputation. A report by *The (Spokane, Wash.) Spokesman-Review* on the bungled cleanup of a nuclear-waste site not only won national prizes but led to federal investigations and reforms.

Environment stories are as close as your city parks, the public landfill or the local water supply. Expert sources are as close as the nearest university or state natural resources agency. Well-informed,

From covering the preservation of wetlands and the protection of endangered species to investigating abandoned city buildings and polluting sewer systems, reporters working the environment beat find a multitude of challenging and rewarding stories.

passionate advocates are as close as the local chapter of the Sierra Club, the Audubon Society or nearly any developer of subdivisions or defender of property rights.

Learning the Beat

Emilia Askari, then president of the Society of Environmental Journalists, prepared some suggestions for editors on responding to reader interest. Her tips offer useful starting points for would-be environment writers:

- *Define the beat broadly.* The environment includes urban as well as wilderness issues. Think of abandoned buildings, old service stations and sewer systems as well as wetlands and endangered species.
- *Spend time on the beat.* Cultivate sources among experts and activists. Read what they read.

- *Expect pressure and controversy.* Land use, preservation, property rights and economics all can generate emotion as well as interest. You'll be under critical scrutiny by all sides of every issue you cover.
- *Look beyond purely local issues.* Such broader issues as global warming, deforestation and overfishing have local angles as close as the weather and the grocery store.
- *Educate yourself.* Look for opportunities to attend conferences on topics and techniques. Learn computer-assisted reporting. Take a course or more at the nearest college.
- *Write for kids.* They're interested; they're active; they're the readers and the citizens of tomorrow. Besides, there's no better way to make sure you really understand a complex issue than to explain it successfully to a youngster.
- *Watch for reports of scientific studies and translate them into everyday language.* Many of the best environment stories begin with research reports in scientific journals. Often these reports are picked up first in the specialized publications mentioned below. Make sure you know, and tell readers, the funding sources and any other possible bias in the studies you report.

SEJ is a good source of information and professional guidance. The SEJ home page can be found at **www.sej.org**. Information from and about the quarterly *SEJournal* can be accessed from this site.

Finding Stories

Many of the techniques, the problems and the possibilities of environment reporting are paralleled in reporting on science and medicine. On these beats there will be fewer meetings to attend or offices to visit than on a city hall or school beat. More of the stories here are likely to be generated by your own enterprise or by applying the local touch to a national story. You can find out what a new pesticide ban will mean to local farmers. Or you can determine whether local doctors are using a new arthritis treatment, or what a researcher at the state university is learning about the effects of alcohol on rats.

Where can you look for story ideas? Specialized publications are good places to start. Read the *Journal of the American Medical Association*, the *New England Journal of Medicine* and *Medical World Journal*. New developments and issues in medicine are covered in news stories. *Scientific American* and *Science News* are informed but readable sources of ideas in all the sciences. For environmental issues, read *Natural History* magazine. Your state's conservation department may put out a publication. Get on the mailing lists of the National Wildlife Federation, the Sierra Club, the Audubon Society and Friends of the Earth.

Nearly every community has human sources, too. In medicine, these include members of the local medical association, the administrator of the hospital and public health officials. In the sciences, look for local school or college faculty, employees of government agencies like extension or research centers, even interested amateurs like those in astronomy societies. In the area of the environment, there is no shortage of advocacy groups or of industries that want to defend their interests. State and federal regulatory and research agencies are helpful, too.

Dealing with Special Issues

The special problems posed by scientific beats begin with the language your sources use. It is a language full of Latin phrases, technical terms and numbers. You will have to learn enough of it both to ask intelligent questions and to translate the answers for your readers. A good medical dictionary and science dictionary are invaluable. Use them and continue asking for explanations until you are sure you understand.

Another problem may be convincing scientists and physicians to talk to you in any language. Many of them have had little contact with reporters. Much of the contact they have had probably has been unpleasant, either because it arose from some controversy or because the reporter was unprepared. Reluctant sources are much more likely to cooperate if you demonstrate that you have done your homework so you have at least some idea of what they are talking about. Promise to check your story with the sources. Accuracy is as much your goal as theirs.

In medicine a concern for privacy may deter some sources from talking freely. A physician's allegiance is, and should be, to the patient. As a reporter you have no legal right to know a patient's condition or ailment. This is true even if the patient is a public official. In fact, most information about a person's medical history and condition is protected by law from disclosure by government recordkeepers.

Sources also may be guarded in comments about their work. Most researchers in medicine and science are cautious in making any claims about the significance or certainty of their work. Some are not so cautious. You must be. Before describing any development as "important" or "dramatic" or "frightening," check and double-check with the researcher involved and others knowledgeable in the field.

Sometimes a researcher will be reluctant to discuss his or her work until it has been published in a professional journal or reported at a convention. Such presentation may be more important to the scientist than any newspaper publicity. Funding and fame are high-stakes issues for research scientists. Many, justifiably afraid of having unscrupulous fellow researchers claim credit for their work, maintain secrecy until a study is complete. A researcher's agreement to give you first notice when he or she is ready to go public may be the best you can hope for in this circumstance.

Despite difficulties, the coverage of science, medicine or the environment offers great challenges and rewards. The challenge is to discover and explain developments and issues that are important to your readers. The rewards, as in all other areas of reporting, can be prizes, pay raises or—most important—recognition by your sources and peers of a job well done.

SPORTS

Before you ever thought about sports reporting, chances are you were reading, watching and playing sports. In that sense, at least, preparing to be a sports reporter is easier than preparing to cover city hall. But there is more to preparation than immersing yourself in sports. Competition pushes people to their limits, bringing out their best and worst. So you need to know some psychology. Sports has played a major role in the struggles of blacks and women for equality. So you need to know some sociology and history. Sports, professional and amateur, is big business. So you need a background in economics. Some of our greatest writers have portrayed life through sports. So you need to explore literature.

Looking Beyond the Clichés

"It's the writer's responsibility to come up with a different approach," says Peter St. Onge, a reporter and columnist at *The Charlotte (N.C.) Observer.* In his own words, this is how he does it:

> When my editor sent me to a PGA golf tournament, I sat at the most popular spectator hole—one that some pros could drive—and wrote about why the fans loved it. When my editor wanted a Super Bowl preview story, I went around town trying to find someone who truly believed Buffalo would beat Dallas (I didn't find anyone, which made the story even better). When a minor-league baseball player from town got called up to the big leagues, I talked to his high school coach, college coach and best friend and asked them about the moment they got the phone call from the player—and what their thoughts were.

Let's take a quick look at the story that resulted from one of those different approaches. If you read sports, you've read the story of the rookie getting summoned to the big leagues. Often the story is one long cliché, from the obligatory "aw shucks" quote of the athlete to the recitation of statistics. A different approach yields a different and better story. Here's St. Onge's opening:

The best friend got the call Wednesday, just before midnight, the phone's jangle jarring him from sleep.

"He called me about two minutes after he got out of his coach's office," Mark Adams remembers. "He said, 'You wanted me to call you when I got called up.'

"Then he said, 'I'm there.'"

The Red Sox. The big leagues. How many times had they talked about this moment? At college, on road trips, on the lake with fishing poles in their hands?

They had both been star players, both good enough for a chance at professional baseball. But only one had the opportunity.

Once, Tim VanEgmond had said that he was nervous about being called up. That when he finally stepped on a major-league mound, he might feel more loneliness than anything.

"I told Tim not to worry," the best friend says. "I told him, 'You're not just playing for you. You're also playing for me.'"

After recounting the reactions and recollections of the two coaches, St. Onge summarizes both the story and the relationships:

Today, they will all be thinking of him, for all their own reasons. The best friend, the junior college coach and the college coach will try to find satellite dishes somewhere and lock onto a Boston or Milwaukee station.

But even if they can't, that's OK. The phone will ring again

soon, and it will be Tim Van-Egmond, the one they saw grow up, the one they grew up with. He'll give them all the real details then. He always does. It's their moment, too.

That story entertains while it informs. It shows readers something of the character of an athlete and the nature of friendship. Here are a few tips to help you be alert to stories that go beyond the cliché:

- *Look for the losers.* Losing may not—as football coaches and other philosophers like to assert—build character, but it certainly bares character. Winners are likely to be full of confidence, champagne and clichés. Losers are likely to be full of self-doubt, second-guessing and surliness. Winners' dressing rooms are magnets for sportswriters, but you usually can tell your readers more about the game and those who play it by seeking out the losers.
- *Look for the bench warmers.* Talk to the would-be football player who has spent four years practicing but never gets into a game. Talk to the woman who dreams of being a professional golfer but is not yet good enough. Talk to the baseball player who is growing old in the minor leagues. If you do, you may find people who both love their sport more and understand it better than do the stars. You may find less press agentry and more humanity.
- *Look beyond the crowds.* Some of the best, and most important, sports stories draw neither crowds of reporters nor crowds of fans. The growth of women's sports is one example. Under the pressure of federal law—

the "Title IX" you read and hear about—the traditional male dominance of facilities and money in school and college athletics has given way to nearly equal treatment for women. From junior high schools to major universities, women's teams now compete in nearly every sport except football. The results of this revolution are likely to be felt far beyond the playing fields, just as the earlier admission of blacks to athletic equality advanced blacks' standing in other areas.

So-called minor sports and participant sports are other largely untapped sources of good stories. More Americans watch birds than play football. More hunt or fish than play basketball. More watch stock-car races than watch track meets.

But these and similar sports are usually covered—if at all—by the newest or least talented reporter on the staff. Get out of the press box. Drop by a bowling alley, a skeet-shooting range or the local college's Frisbee-throwing tournament.

Developing Contacts

Being there is half the fun of sports reporting. You're there at the big games, matches and meets. You're there in the locker rooms, on team buses and planes, with an inside view of athletics and athletes that few fans ever get. If you are to answer your readers' questions, if you are to provide insight and anecdote, you must be there, most of the time.

Sometimes you should try being where the fans are. Write about a football game from the average fan's point of view in the end zone. Cover a baseball game from the bleachers. Cold hot dogs and warm beer are as much a part of the event as a double play. Watch one of those weekend sports shows on television, and compare the way a track meet or a fishing trip is presented with the way it is in person. Join a city league softball team or a bowling league for a different kind of inside view.

A sports reporter must develop and cherish sources just as a city hall reporter must. You look for the same kinds of sources on both beats. Players, coaches and administrators—like city council members and city managers—are obvious sources. Go beyond them. Trainers and equipment managers have insiders' views and sometimes lack the fierce protectiveness that often keeps players, for example, from talking candidly.

Alumni can be excellent sources for high school and college sports stories. If a coach is about to be fired or a new fund drive is being planned, important alumni are sure to be involved. You can find out who they are by checking with the alumni association or by examining the list of major contributors that every college proudly compiles. The business managers and secretaries who handle the money can be invaluable for much-needed but seldom-done stories about the finances of sports at all levels. Former players sometimes will talk more candidly than those who are still involved in a program. As on any beat, look for people who may be disgruntled—a fired assistant coach, a benched star, a big contributor to a losing team. And when you find good sources, cherish them. Keep in contact, flatter them, protect them. They are your lifeline.

Unfortunately, being where a reporter needs to be isn't always easy or pleasant. Many women, and some men, have found themselves victims of harassment by athletes, coaches or fans. Sports reporters, especially women, may find their professionalism tested in ways—and in surroundings—seldom encountered by colleagues on beats that usually are considered more serious.

Digging for the Real Story

It is even harder for a sports reporter than it is for a political or police reporter to maintain a critical distance from the beat. The most obvious reason is that most of the people who become sports reporters do so because they are sports fans.

The Negative Influence of Celebrity

To be a fan is precisely the opposite of being a dispassionate, critical observer. In addition, athletics—especially big-time athletics—is glamorous and exciting. The sports reporter associates daily with the stars and the coaches whom others, including cynical city hall reporters and hard-bitten managing editors, pay to admire at a distance.

Anywhere athletics is taken seriously, from the high schools of Texas to the stadiums of the National Football League, athletes and coaches are used to being given special treatment. Many think of themselves as being somehow different from and better than ordinary people. Many fans agree. Good reporters, though, regard sports as a beat, not a love affair.

The Problem with Financial Incentives

Sports figures ranging from high school coaches to owners of professional baseball teams deliberately and persistently seek to buy the favor of the reporters who cover their sports. We are taught from childhood that it is disgraceful to bite the hand that feeds you. Professional teams and many college teams routinely feed reporters.

Sports journalism used to be even more parasitic toward the teams it covered than is the case now. At one time, reporters routinely traveled with a team at the team's expense. Good newspapers pay their own way today.

Even today, however, many reporters find it rewarding monetarily as well as psychologically to stay in favor with the teams and athletes they cover. Many teams pay reporters to write promotional pieces for game programs. And writing personality profiles or "inside" accounts for the dozens of sports magazines can be a profitable sideline.

Most sports reporters, and the editors who permit such activities, argue that they are not corrupted by what they are given. Most surely are not. But temptation is there for those who would succumb. Beyond that, any writer who takes more than information from those he or she covers is also likely to receive pressure, however subtle, from the givers.

Allegiance to the Reader

Good sports reporters maintain their distance from the people they cover, just as reporters on other beats do, by keeping their readers in mind. Readers want to know who won and how. But they also want to know about other sides of sports, sides that may require some digging to expose. Readers' questions about sports financing and the story behind the story too often go unanswered.

Sports stories behind the story

- Money.
- The real "why."
- The real "who."

- *Money.* Accountants have become as essential to sports as athletes and trainers. Readers have a legitimate interest in everything from ticket prices to the impact of money on the actual contests.
- *The real "why."* When a key player is traded, as much as when a city manager is fired, readers want to know why. When athletes leave school without graduating, find out why. When the public is asked to pay for the expansion of a stadium, tell the public why. One of the attractions of sports is that when the contest is over, the spectators can see who won and how. Often that is not true of struggles in government or business.
- *The real "who."* Sports figures often appear to their fans, and sometimes to reporters, to be larger than life. In fact, athletics is an intensely human activity. Its participants have greater physical skills, and larger bank accounts, than most other people, but they are people.

Suggested Readings

Houston, Brant, and Investigative Reporters and Editors, Inc. *The Investigative Reporter's Handbook.* 5th ed. New York: Bedford/St. Martin's, 2009. A guide to using government documents to find sources of information.

Royko, Mike. *Boss.* New York. New American Library, 1971. A classic, brilliantly written study of urban machine politics.

Sports Illustrated. Features the best continuing examples of how sports should be reported.

Suggested Web Sites

www.espn.com   As every sports fan knows, here you'll find multimedia reporting, commentary, statistics and lots of good story ideas.

www.ire.org   Investigative Reporters and Editors is the most important source of continuing education for public-affairs reporters. Among other things, IRE maintains an extensive library of some of the best stories done on nearly every topic, both print and broadcast. Also, it is a great place to begin networking with some of the most accomplished professional journalists.

www.journalismnet.com   A great resource for journalists. You'll find sources for almost any subject.

www.newslab.org   Useful tips for beat reporters, with an emphasis on broadcast—especially television—reporting.

www.opensecrets.org   An invaluable source for reporters covering elections, this site includes searchable campaign donation data from the nonpartisan Center for Responsive Politics.

www.powerreporting.com   A very helpful site, sponsored by the *Columbia Journalism Review*, and full of relevant resources.

www.poynter.org   We list this site repeatedly because it is so useful in so many ways. One feature is its links to nearly every professional journalism organization. The home page also includes a regular column of Web tips and sources.

www.pulitzer.org   Go to the "Beat Reporting" section and you'll find the winners of journalism's most important prize, with selections of their award-winning work.

www.scout.cs.wisc.edu   *The Scout Report* is a weekly publication offering a selection of new and newly discovered Internet sources of interest to researchers and educators.

Exercises

1. You've been assigned to cover your campus. Do some background research. Then write a memo describing what you expect to be the most important issues on your new beat and whom you expect to be your most important human sources.

2. Now venture off campus and prepare to cover your city government. Go to a city council meeting, and take careful notes on the issues discussed. Pick just one issue and research it. Write a story that introduces this issue to a newcomer.

3. Examine how two or three major news organizations cover a national beat, such as Congress or a federal agency. What similarities and differences do you see between that work and local coverage? The topics will be different, but what about sources? Do you see any different focus on reader interests?

4. Analyze a local news story about science, medicine or the environment. Identify the sources. If you were reporting this story, what other sources would you consult? What specific questions would you try to get answered?

5. Assume that you've been assigned to cover your school's basketball or other sports program. Drawing on sources suggested above and favorites such as ESPN.com and SI.com, write a memo describing at least five story ideas. Identify the best sources for each.

11 Writing News for Radio and Television

Two billion people watched. On Aug. 8, 2008, two billion people—a third of the world's population—watched the opening of the Olympics in Beijing.

And after that opening night, an NBC survey revealed that 76 percent of the people in the U.S. had stayed up later than usual to watch the Olympics. Thirty-nine million people watched American swimmer Michael Phelps win his record seventh gold medal.

During the 2008 Olympics, television did what it does best: It told the world the details of what happened. Moreover, television journalists were able to repeat their reports and update their audience as the news developed. If you tuned in to NBC, you not only saw what happened and listened to commentary, but you also were able to see headlines under the picture and, under that, other news streaming by like a ticker tape. Somewhat like online news, you could pay attention to the news you were most interested in, and you had the feeling you were up-to-date about what was happening. At times you probably heard the anchor on television say that you could go to the network's Web site for more information.

Of course, radio and television are not always present to record the news while it is happening. Much of the time, these journalists must write and report news after it has occurred. Many, if not most, radio and television stations provide at least some news written for them by journalists working for the wire services or who are employed by the stations themselves.

Selecting and writing news for these media is different from selecting and writing news for print. This chapter explores the differences and discusses news reporting and newswriting for television and radio. Even if your primary emphasis is not radio and television news, in this day of converging media in news rooms, you may be called on to work with radio and television reporters or even to prepare copy for their reports. And if you are writing for radio or television news, almost certainly you will be called on to contribute to the station's Web site. Radio and television stations have expanded their news operations to give background for stories they have no time for on air. Rather than interrupt programming when new facts arrive on a developing story, they often send listeners and viewers to their Web sites. CNN and MSNBC, for example, not only send viewers to their Web sites; they also offer instantaneous e-mails from Twitter to keep viewers informed. In the new world of convergence, you may well be expected to be able to write radio and television copy as well as online copy.

CRITERIA FOR SELECTING RADIO AND TELEVISION NEWS

All of the news criteria you have learned so far apply to the selection of print, radio and television news. Four criteria distinguish radio and television news from print news: These newswriters emphasize *timeliness* above all other news values, *information* more than explanation, news with *audio or visual impact*, and *people* more than concepts.

Emphases of radio and television news

- Timeliness.
- Information.
- Audio or visual impact.
- People.

Timeliness

The radio and television newswriter emphasizes one criterion of news value—timeliness—more than any other. *When* something happens often determines whether a news item will be used in a newscast. The breaking story receives top priority.

Radio and television news "goes to press" many times a day. If an event is significant enough, regular programming can be interrupted. The sense of immediacy influences everything in radio news, from what is reported to how it is reported. Often this is also true of television news. Even when television and radio air documentaries or in-depth segments, they typically try to infuse a sense of urgency, a strong feeling of the present, an emphasis on what's happening now.

Information

Timeliness often determines why a news item is broadcast; time, or lack of it, determines *how* it is reported. Because airtime is so precious, radio and television reporters are generally more concerned with information than with explanation. Most stories must be told in 20 to 30 seconds; rarely does a story run longer than two minutes. A minute of news read aloud is only 15 lines of copy, or about 150 words. After you subtract time for commercials, a half-hour newscast has only 22 minutes of news, which amounts to about one-half of the front page of a newspaper. Although these newswriters may never assume that their audience knows anything about a story, they may often have to assume that listeners or viewers will turn to newspapers, newsmagazines or the Internet for further background and details.

Of course, because of the long success of *60 Minutes* and because of relatively low production costs, television newsmagazines such as *20/20* and *Dateline NBC* continue to be popular. Newsmagazines represent a somewhat different challenge to television newswriters, but even in a newsmagazine format, the writing resembles that done for television news.

"Good television journalism presents news in the most attractive and lucid form yet devised by man."

—Bill Small,
veteran broadcaster,
former president of CBS News

Audio or Visual Impact

Another difference between radio and television news and print news results from the technologies involved. Some news is selected for radio because a reporter has recorded an on-the-scene audio report. Some news is selected for television because it is visually appealing or exciting. For this reason, news of accidents or of fires that may get attention only in the records column of the newspaper may get important play on a television newscast. If a television crew returns with good pictures of an event, that event often will receive prominence in the next newscast.

In today's world of convergence journalism, whether you work for a news organization, for a public-relations firm or in organization communications, you may have to decide which of the media will best carry your messages and attract the most attention from your audience.

People

Another important difference between radio and television news selection and print news selection is that radio and television more often attempt to tell the news through people. They follow the classic writing formula described by Rudolf Flesch in *The Art of Readable Writing*: Find a problem, find a person who is dealing with the problem, and tell us how he or she is doing. These journalists look for a representative person or family, someone who is affected by the story or who is a chief player. Thus, rather than using abstract concepts with no sound or visuals, television in particular humanizes the story. You can't shoot video of an issue, but you can show visually the impact on people.

WRITING RADIO AND TELEVISION NEWS

Radio and television newswriting emphasizes certain characteristics that newspaper and online writing do not, and story structure may vary.

Characteristics of Radio and Television Newswriting

Radio and television newswriting

- Emphasizes immediacy.
- Has a conversational style.
- Is tightly phrased.
- Is clear.

Because of the emphasis on timeliness, radio and television newswriters, like online writers, must emphasize immediacy and try to write very tightly and clearly. However, radio and television newswriters must work harder at achieving a conversational style.

Immediacy

Radio and television newswriters achieve a sense of immediacy in part by using the present tense as much as possible. Note the use of

Some all-news radio stations serve their communities with news and commentary 24 hours a day. Many allow listeners to voice their opinions.

present and present perfect tense verbs (italicized) in this Associated Press story:

EPA Grants Ill. Incinerator Key Permit

SAUGET, Ill. (AP)—The U.S. Environmental Protection Agency *has given* a Metro East hazardous-waste incinerator a key permit, and environmentalists *aren't* happy about it.

The EPA gave Veolia Environmental Services its long-awaited Title V operational permit last week for the company's incinerator of toxic medical and chemical waste in Sauget (SAW-zhay).

That's despite legal challenges by environmental groups including the Sierra Club and the American Bottom Conservancy.

The incinerator, when it was under different ownership, applied for the license more than a decade ago and *has been allowed* to operate under permits it *has held* since then.

Environmentalist Kathy Andria *says it's* unclear if they'll appeal. But she *says* such an incinerator *has* no business being in a metropolitan area.

Notice the present perfect tense ("has given") in the lead. The present perfect tense designates past action continuing in the present. The second verb in the lead ("aren't") is in the present tense.

The action in the second paragraph happened "last week," so the verb "gave" is in the past tense.

The third paragraph begins with the contraction "That's," also in the present tense. In a print story, "That was" might have been used instead.

The fourth paragraph has two verbs in the present perfect tense ("has been allowed" and "has held"). Two other verbs ("was" and "applied") are in the past tense.

The last paragraph has two occurrences of "says," an "it's" and a "has," all in the present tense. In a print story, "said" would probably be used both times in place of "says."

The story has a sense of immediacy partly because the writer used present and present perfect tenses where a print writer might have used the past tense.

Sometimes you stress immediacy by saying "just minutes ago" or, on a morning newscast, "this morning." If there is no danger of inaccuracy or of deceit, though, you can omit references to time. For example, if something happened yesterday, you may report it today like this:

> The latest rash of fires in southern California is under control.

But if you use the past tense in a lead, include the time element.

> The legislature sent a welfare reform bill to the governor late last night,
> finishing just in time before the spring recess.

The best way to avoid the past tense is to update yesterday's story. By leading with a new development or a new fact, you may be able to use the present tense.

Remember, radio and television are "live." Your copy must convey that important characteristic.

Conversational Style

"Write the way you talk" is questionable advice for most kinds of writing; however, with some exceptions, it is imperative for radio and television writing. "Read your copy aloud" is good advice for most kinds of writing; for radio and television writing, that's what it's all about.

Write so that your copy sounds good. Use simple, short sentences, written with transitive verbs in the active voice. Transitive verbs do things to things; they demand an object ("The Senate passed the bill").

People rarely use verbs in the passive voice when they talk; it usually sounds cumbersome and awkward. You don't go around saying, "Guess what I was just told by somebody." The verb "was told" is in the passive voice; the subject is acted upon. The preposition "by" also tells you the verb is in the passive voice. "Guess what somebody just told me" is active and more natural, less wordy and stronger. The verb "told" is in the active voice; the subject is doing the acting.

Because casual speech contains contractions, an occasional contraction is OK, too, as long as your pronunciation is clear. The negative "not" is more clearly understood than the contraction "n't." Conversational style also permits the use of occasional fragments. Sentences are sometimes strung together loosely with dashes and sometimes begin with the conjunction "and" or "but," as in the following example from the Associated Press:

> SPRING LAKE, N.C. (AP)—Aubrey Cox keeps giving police the slip. *But* he's had lots of practice—he's been doing it for 41 years.

Notice how the use of contractions gives this Associated Press story a conversational tone:

Absentee Ranch Owner Accused in Deaths of 32 Bison

FAIRPLAY, Colo. (AP)—A software executive who owns a luxury home outside the old Colorado mining town of Fairplay is being accused of foul play.

Prosecutors will try next week to convince a judge *there's* enough evidence against Jeff Hawn to go to trial.

Hawn is charged with theft and 32 counts of aggravated animal cruelty in connection with the deaths of 32 bison belonging to a neighboring rancher. Authorities say Hawn and the rancher feuded over the bison roaming onto Hawn's property.

Hawn, *it's* alleged, invited 14 hunters to shoot any bison on his land last March. Investigators believe Hawn may have shot some of the bison himself.

The case has outraged many in Fairplay, a town of about 700 founded by gold prospectors in 1859. *It's* also drawn attention to Colorado's "open range" laws and the local politics of fencing.

Writing in a conversational style does not mean using slang or colloquialisms or incorrect grammar. Nor does it mean using vulgar or off-color expressions. Remember that your audience includes people of all ages, backgrounds and sensitivities.

Tight Phrasing

You must learn to write in a conversational style without being wordy. That means you must condense. Cut down on adjectives and adverbs. Eliminating the passive voice will get rid of a couple of words. Make each word count.

Keeping it short means selecting facts carefully because often you don't have time for the whole story. Radio and television newscasters want good, tight writing that is easy to follow. Let's look at how a wire

"Short words are best, and old words, when short, are best of all."

—Winston Churchill

story written for newspapers can be condensed for radio and television. First read this AP story written for print and published in the *St. Louis Post-Dispatch*:

Former Prosecutor's Husband Faces Drug Charge
By Valerie Schremp Hahn

ST. CHARLES—The husband of a former St. Charles County prosecutor faces a drug charge after police said he was growing 359 marijuana plants in the basement of their Portage des Sioux home.

Max Conley, 42, of the 900 block of Pawnee Drive, was charged Tuesday with producing a controlled substance, a felony. He is married to Ella Boone Conley, who was put on administrative leave on Aug. 25, pending the results of the investigation. She resigned on Sept. 26 and now works for a law firm in St. Peters.

Her attorney has said she didn't know about the marijuana and was only living there part time because of problems between the couple.

The investigation began after the St. Charles County Regional Drug Task Force got information that Max Conley was growing marijuana. A detective went to the house on Aug. 24, and Conley gave him permission to search the home. The detective found the plants in the basement "in various stages of growth," according to court documents, and he also found lights, wiring, chemicals, potting soil and pots being used to grow the plants.

The court documents said Conley admitted growing the marijuana.

A warrant was issued Tuesday for his arrest, and bail was set at $25,000. At the request of St. Charles County Prosecuting Attorney Jack Banas, a special prosecutor from the St. Louis circuit attorney's office, Jeannette Graviss, headed the investigation.

Graviss said Tuesday that there was not enough evidence to charge Ella Boone Conley and that she was not home when police went to the house. She said Max Conley did not have a job.

Banas did not want to talk about specifics of the case but said it was Boone Conley's decision to resign from his office. He also said the entire situation has been difficult to deal with.

Boone Conley's attorney, Joe Green, said in an interview in September that she resigned to protect the integrity of the St. Charles County prosecuting attorney's office. He also said she was planning to file for divorce. She had filed for divorce in 2002, but the case was later dismissed.

Conley's attorney, Joe McCulloch, said Conley would turn himself in this morning but would not comment further.

Green and Boone Conley could not be reached for comment Tuesday. Conley also could not be reached.

Boone Conley, 44, had worked as an assistant prosecutor in St. Charles County for 13 years and ran unsuccessfully for the Republican nomination for associate circuit judge in the Aug. 8 primary.

Most recently, she had headed the child support enforcement unit.

Here's how the story appeared on the Associated Press broadcast wire in its entirety:

Husband of Prosecutor Found Growing 359 Marijuana Plants

ST. CHARLES, Mo. (AP) — The husband of a former St. Charles County prosecutor is accused of growing 359 marijuana plants in the basement of their home.

Forty-two-year-old Max Conley was charged yesterday with the felony of producing a controlled substance. Conley's attorney says he plans to turn himself in this morning.

He is married to Ella Boone Conley, who resigned from the prosecutor's office September 26th amid the investigation. She ran unsuccessfully for the Republican nomination for associate circuit judge in the August eighth primary and now works for a law firm in St. Peters.

Her attorney says she was unaware of the marijuana and was only living in the home part time because of domestic problems. Ella Boone Conley has not been charged in the case.

In the broadcast version, the audience is given just the bare facts. They must turn to their newspapers or online news source for the details and background. One newspaper story is often equivalent to two or three broadcast stories or even a half dozen online stories.

In radio and television news, tight writing is important even when there is more time. Strive to waste no words, even in television documentaries, which provide in-depth coverage of events.

On the Job

Writing News for Radio and Television

Bernard Choi joined King 5 Television in Seattle in 2004 as a reporter. Before that he worked as the government reporter and fill-in anchor for KWCH (CBS) in Wichita, Kans., after spending two years on the education beat there. During the summer of his sophomore year of college, he interned at WPSD (NBC) in Paducah, Ky. There he won first place in the Randolph Hearst Journalism Awards in television news. He also won first place in the Education Writers Association's Television Hard News category.

"I was a wide-eyed reporter straight out of college," Choi says. "When my new boss offered me a full-time on-air reporting position, I jumped at the chance. I had never covered a beat. I didn't know what covering a beat entailed."

Three years, two beats and countless mistakes later, Choi realizes he was in way over his head. "But, I'm glad no one caught on and that they gave me the chance to discover the most rewarding type of journalism. It allows you to dig the story up from the ground before it appears in a news release or the news wires."

The most important thing he learned was to talk to people. "I'm generally a shy person with people I don't know," he says. "I had to force myself to walk up to strangers and chat. Stories are about people, and what better way to find a story than to talk to people. More often than not, you will get a story from someone who is plugged in a lot faster than trying to search public records."

Of course, you have to do that, too, he says.

Choi's final bit of advice: Journalists should say thanks every now and then.

Clarity

Unlike newspaper and Internet news readers, television and radio news audiences can't go back over the copy. They see or hear it only once, and their attention waxes and wanes. So you must try hard to be clear and precise. However, all the emphasis on condensing and writing tightly is useless if the message is not understood.

Clarity demands that you write simply, in short sentences filled with nickel-and-dime words. Don't look for synonyms. Don't be afraid to repeat words or phrases. Oral communication needs reinforcement. Avoid foreign words and phrases. Avoid phrases like "the former" and "the latter." Repeat proper names in the story rather than use pronouns. The listener can easily forget the name of the person to whom the pronoun refers.

When you are tempted to write a dependent clause in a sentence, make it an independent clause instead. Keep the subject close to the verb. Close the gap between the doer and the activity. This version doesn't do that:

> A man flagged down a Highway Patrol officer near Braden, Tennessee, today and told him a convict was hiding in his house. The prisoner, one of five who escaped from the Fort Pillow Prison on Saturday, surrendered peacefully.

The second sentence contains 12 words between the subject, "prisoner," and the main verb, "surrendered." By the time the broadcaster reaches the verb, many listeners will have forgotten what the subject was. The story is easier to understand this way:

> A man flagged down a Highway Patrol officer near Braden, Tennessee, today and told him a convict was hiding in his house. The prisoner surrendered peacefully. He's one of five who escaped from the Fort Pillow Prison on Saturday.

The third sentence is still a complex sentence ("who escaped . . ." is the dependent clause), but it is easily understood. The complex sentence is often just that—complex—only more so in oral communication.

Clarity also requires that you resist a clever turn of phrase. Viewers and listeners probably are intelligent enough to understand it, but a good figure of speech takes time to savor. If listeners pause to savor it (if they grasped it in the first place), they will not hear what follows. Clever columnists often fail as radio commentators.

Even more dangerous than figures of speech are numerical figures. Don't barrage the listener or viewer with a series of numbers. If you must use statistics, break them down so that they are understandable. For example, it is better to say that nearly one of every four adult Americans smokes than to say how many million smokers there are in the United States. You may be tempted to say how many billion dollars a federal program will cost, but you will help listeners understand if you say that it will cost the average wage earner $73 for each of the next five years.

Story Structure

Now that you know the characteristics of radio and television writing, let's examine the story structure. Writers must craft television and radio leads somewhat differently from the way they cast print and online leads. They also must construct special introductions and conclusions to video or audio segments and synchronize their words with taped segments.

Writing the Radio and Television Lead

Like newspaper reporters, television and radio reporters must grab the attention of their audience. Much of what you learned in Chapters 6 and 7 applies to radio and television leads. But be aware that people tend to be doing other things when listening to radio or watching television, so when you write for them, you strive to attract their attention in different ways.

One way is by preparing your audience for what is to come. You cue listeners to make sure they are tuned in. You introduce the story with a general statement, something that will pique the interest of the audience; then you go to the specifics. For example:

General statement	Things are far from settled for Springfield's teacher strike.
Specifics	School officials and union representatives did not agree on a contract yesterday. They will not meet again for at least a week.

Sometimes the opening sentence will cover a number of news items:

> There were several accidents in the Springfield vicinity today.

"Cuing in" is only one method of opening a radio or television story. Other leads go immediately into the "what" and the "who," the "where" and the "when." In radio or television news the "what" is most important, followed by "who" did "what." The time and place may be included in the lead, but seldom is the "why" or the "how." If time permits, the "why" and the "how" may come later in the story, but often they are omitted.

The first words of the lead are the most important. Don't keep the listener guessing what the story is about. Don't begin with a dependent clause or with prepositional phrases, as in this example:

> With the strong backing of Governor Minner, a second state spending-limit
> bill is scheduled for final Senate action today.

The opening words are meaningless without what comes later. The listener may not know what you are talking about. Here is a better way to introduce this story:

> The Senate will vote today to make deeper cuts in state spending — with
> the strong backing of Governor Minner.

Be sure to "tee up," or identify, an unfamiliar name. By introducing a person, you prepare listeners for the name they otherwise may miss. Do it this way:

> Veteran Kansas City, Kansas, businessman and civic leader Kenneth Durban
> died yesterday in a nursing home at age 83.

Don't mislead. The opening words must set the proper tone and mood for the story. Attract attention; tease a little. Answer questions, but don't ask them. Lead the listener into your story.

Writing Lead-Ins and Wrap-Ups

Radio and television journalists must learn how to write a **lead-in** that introduces a recorded excerpt from a news source or from another reporter. The functions of a lead-in are to set the scene by briefly telling the "where," the "when" and sometimes the "what," and to identify the source or reporter. The lead-in should contain something substantive. Here's an example:

> A grand jury has decided not to charge a Springfield teenager in the killing
> of his father. Jan Morrow reports the panel believes the death was an
> accident.

Lead-ins should generate interest. Sometimes several sentences are used to provide background, as in the following:

> We'll all be getting the official word this morning on how much less our dol-
> lars bought last month. The consumer price index for March is expected to
> show another sharp rise in retail prices. The rate of inflation was one percent
> in January and one-point-two percent in February. Here's more on our infla-
> tion woes from Bill McKinney.

Be careful not to include in the lead-in what is in the story. Just as a headline should not steal word for word the lead of a newspaper story, the lead-in should not rob the opening words of the correspondent. The writer must know the contents of the audio report in order to write a proper lead-in.

After the recorded report, you may want to wrap up the story before going on to the next item. The **wrap-up** is especially important in radio copy because there are no visuals to identify the person just heard. If the story reported by Evelyn Turner was about a meeting to settle a strike, you might wrap up Turner's report by adding information:

> Turner reports negotiations will resume tomorrow.

A wrap-up such as this gives your story an ending and clearly separates it from the next story.

Writing to the Video

Writing to the video (the industry continues to use the word "video" in our digital age) means letting the video dictate what you write and how much you write. To do this, you must learn a whole new approach for your writing.

"Writing a silence is as important as writing words. We don't rely on video enough."

—John Hart, veteran NBC broadcaster

Writing for a video report begins with the selection of the subject and deciding how it is to be shot. The writing continues through the editing process and is done with the pictures clearly in mind.

Words and pictures must be complementary, never interfering with each other, never ignoring each other. Your first responsibility is to relate the words to the pictures. If you do not, viewers will not get the message because they will be wondering what the pictures are about.

You can, however, stick too closely to the pictures by pointing out the obvious in a blow-by-blow account. You need to avoid both extremes and use what Russ Bensley, formerly of CBS News, calls the "hit-and-run" technique. This means that at the beginning of a scene or when a scene changes, you must tell the viewer where you are or what is happening. Once you are into the scene, the script may be more general and less closely tied to the pictures. Some refer to this as "touch-and-go" writing.

Suppose the report concerns the continuation of a hospital workers' strike and the opening scene shows picketers outside the hospital. You can explain the tape by saying:

> Union members are still picketing Mercy Hospital today as the hospital
> workers' strike enters its third week.

Viewers now know two things about the scene that are not obvious on the video: who is picketing and where. If the video switches to people sitting around a table negotiating, you must again set the scene for viewers:

> Meanwhile, hospital administrators and union leaders are continuing their
> meetings — apparently without success.

Once you have related the words to the pictures, you may add other details of the strike. You must not only comment on the video but complete it as well. Part of completing it is giving the report a wrap-up, or a strong ending. Don't be cute or obvious, though. Here's one possible ending for the strike story:

> Strikers, administrators, patients and their families agree on one sure effect
> of the strike — it's a bad time to be sick.

Now that you know some principles of writing radio and television news, let's learn how to prepare the copy.

PREPARING RADIO AND TELEVISION COPY

Preparing copy to be read by a newscaster is different from preparing it for a typesetter. Your goals are to make the copy easy for the newscaster to read and easy for the audience to understand. What follows will help you accomplish these two goals.

Format

Most radio and television news editors want triple-spaced copy. Leave two to three inches on the top of the page and one to two inches on the bottom.

For radio copy, set your margins so that you have 70 characters to a line (see Figure 11.1). Each line will average about 10 words, and the newscaster will average 15 lines per minute. Start each story on a separate piece of paper. That way, the order of the stories can be rearranged, and stories can be added or dropped easily. If a story goes more than one page, write "MORE" in parentheses at the bottom of the page.

Write television copy on the right half of the page in a 40-character line (see Figure 11.2). Each line will average about six words, and the newscaster will average about 25 lines per minute. Use the left side of the copy for audio or video information. This information, which is not to be read by the newscaster, is usually typed in all caps. The copy that is read generally appears in upper- and lowercase.

In television copy, number the stories, and start each story on a separate page. If a story goes more than one page, write "MORE" in parentheses at the bottom of the page.

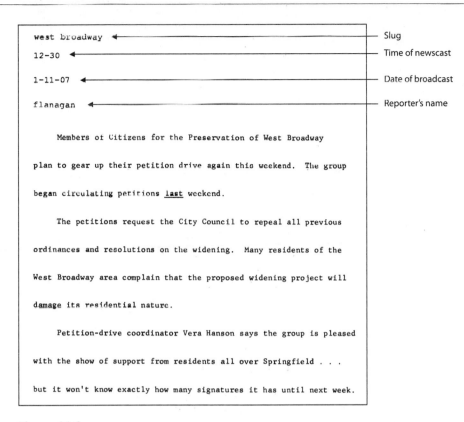

Figure 11.1
Radio copy averages 70 characters, or about 10 words, to the line.

Do not hyphenate words, and be sure to end a page with a complete sentence or, if possible, with a complete paragraph. Then if the next page should be missing in the middle of a newscast, the newscaster can at least end with a complete sentence or paragraph.

At many stations, you prepare copy for a **videoprompter**, an electronic device that projects the copy over the camera lens so the newscaster can read it while appearing to look straight into the lens.

Date the first page of your script, and type your last name in the upper left-hand corner of every page. Stations vary regarding these directions. The newscast producer determines the **slug**—the identifying word or phrase—for a story and its placement. Some producers insist that the slug contain the time of the broadcast. If a story continues to a second page, write under the slug "first **add**" or "second add," or "page 2," "page 3" and so forth.

Stations with computerized news rooms may use scripting software that alters these formats somewhat.

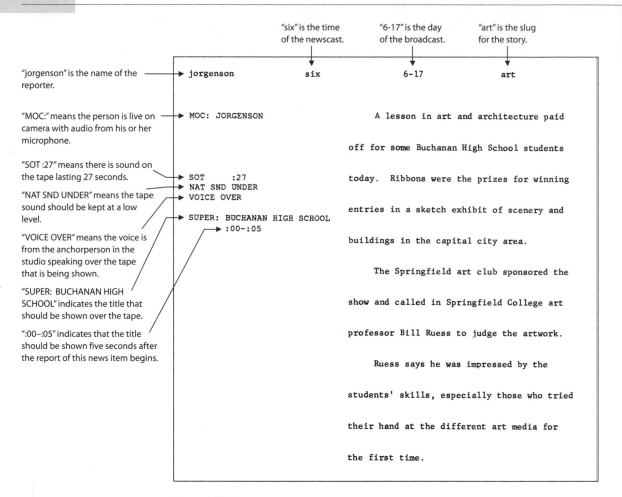

"six" is the time of the newscast.

"6-17" is the day of the broadcast.

"art" is the slug for the story.

"jorgenson" is the name of the reporter.

jorgenson   six   6-17   art

"MOC:" means the person is live on camera with audio from his or her microphone.

MOC: JORGENSON

A lesson in art and architecture paid off for some Buchanan High School students today. Ribbons were the prizes for winning entries in a sketch exhibit of scenery and buildings in the capital city area.

"SOT :27" means there is sound on the tape lasting 27 seconds.

SOT   :27

"NAT SND UNDER" means the tape sound should be kept at a low level.

NAT SND UNDER
VOICE OVER

"VOICE OVER" means the voice is from the anchorperson in the studio speaking over the tape that is being shown.

SUPER: BUCHANAN HIGH SCHOOL
       :00-:05

"SUPER: BUCHANAN HIGH SCHOOL" indicates the title that should be shown over the tape.

":00-:05" indicates that the title should be shown five seconds after the report of this news item begins.

The Springfield art club sponsored the show and called in Springfield College art professor Bill Ruess to judge the artwork.

Ruess says he was impressed by the students' skills, especially those who tried their hand at the different art media for the first time.

Figure 11.2
Television copy is typed in two columns: one for text to be read and the other for audio and video directions.

Names and Titles

In radio and television style, unlike that followed by newspapers, well-known names are not given in full, even on first reference. You may say "Senator McCaskill of Missouri" or "Governor Brewer of Arizona." Don't use middle initials unless they are a widely recognized part of someone's name (Edward R. Murrow) or unless they are necessary to distinguish two people with the same first and last names, as with George W. Bush and his father George H. W. Bush.

Titles should always precede names so that listeners are better prepared to hear the name. When you use titles, omit the first name and middle initial. For example, you would say "Federal Reserve Chairman Bernanke" and "Justice Ginsburg."

Pronunciation

You must help the newscaster pronounce the names of people and places correctly. To do this, write out difficult names phonetically in parentheses. MSNBC has its own reference list, and many individual stations have their own handbooks. Look up difficult names in unabridged dictionaries. If you don't find the name there, call the person's office, or the consulate or embassy. If the name is of a U.S. town, try calling someone in that town. There is no rhyme or reason to the way some people pronounce their names or to the way some place-names are pronounced. Never assume. Never try to figure it out. Find out. Here's an example of how you should write out difficult names:

> There's been another deadly bombing in the Philippines.
>> A bomb exploded near a Roman Catholic church in the southern city of Zamboanga (zahm-BWAHNG-gah), killing one person and injuring 12.

Perhaps most people would know how to pronounce "Lima" (LEE-mah), Peru, but not everyone would correctly pronounce "Lima" (LIE-mah), Ohio. You must note the difference between "NEW-erk," N.J., and "new-ARK," Del., both spelled "Newark." And who would guess that "Pago Pago" is pronounced "PAHNG-oh PAHNG-oh"?

Abbreviations

Generally, you do not use abbreviations in radio and television copy. It is easier to read a word written out than to read its abbreviation. Do not abbreviate the names of states, countries, months, days of the week or military titles.

When you do abbreviate a name or phrase, use hyphens instead of periods to prevent the newscaster from mistaking the final period in the abbreviation for the period at the end of the sentence. You may abbreviate the names of well-known entities: "the U-S," "the U-N," "the G-O-P" and "the F-B-I." Do not use hyphens in acronyms (abbreviations such as "NATO" and "HUD" that are pronounced as one word).

You may use the abbreviations "Dr.," "Mr.," "Mrs." and "Ms.," and "a.m." and "p.m."

Symbols and Numbers

Do not use symbols in your copy because newscasters can read a word more easily than they can interpret a symbol. Never use such symbols as the dollar sign ($) and the percent sign (%). Don't even use the abbreviation for number ("no.").

Numbers can be a problem for both the announcer and the listener. As in newspaper style, write out numbers one through nine. Also write out eleven, because 11 might not be easily recognized as a number. Use figures for 10 and from 12 to 999. The eye can easily take in a three-digit number, but write out the words "thousand," "million" and "billion"—for example, "3,800,000" becomes "three million, 800 thousand." Write out fractions ("two-and-a-half million dollars") and decimal points ("three-point-two percent").

Some stations have exceptions. Figures often are used to give the time ("3:20 a.m."), sports scores ("ahead 5 to 2") and statistics, market reports ("an increase in the Dow Jones Industrial Average of 2-point-8 points"), and addresses ("3-0-0-2 Grand Street"; in common speech no one would give an address as "three thousand two").

Ordinarily, you may round off big numbers. Thus "48-point-3 percent" should be written "nearly half." But when dealing with human beings, don't say "more than one hundred" if 104 people died in an earthquake.

Use "st," "nd," "rd" and "th" after dates: August 1st, September 2nd, October 3rd, November 4th. Make the date easy to pronounce: June 9th, 1973.

Quotations and Attributions

Rarely use direct quotations and quotation marks. Because it is difficult and awkward to indicate to listeners which words are being quoted, use indirect quotes or a paraphrase instead.

If it is important for listeners to know the exact words of a quotation (as when the quoted words are startling, uncomplimentary or possibly libelous), introduce the quote by saying "in his words," "with these words," "what she called" or "he put it this way." Most writers prefer to avoid the formal "quote" and "unquote," though "quote" is used more often than "unquote." Here's an example:

> In Smith's words, quote, "There is no way to undo the harm done."

When you must use a direct quotation, the attribution always should precede the quotation. Because listeners cannot see the quotation marks, they will have no way of knowing the words are a direct quote. If by chance they did recognize the words as a quote, they would have no idea who was being quoted. For the same reason, the attribution should precede an indirect quote as well.

If you must use a direct quotation, keep it short. If the quote is long and using it is important, use a recording of the person saying it. If you are compelled to use a quote of more than a sentence in your copy, break it up with phrases such as "Smith went on to say" or "and still quoting the senator." For television, put longer or more complicated quotes on a full-screen graphic display as you read it.

Punctuation

In radio and television copy, less punctuation is good punctuation. The one exception is the comma. Commas help the newscaster pause at appropriate places. Use commas, for example, after introductory phrases referring to time and place, as in the following:

> In Paris, three Americans on holiday met their death today when their car overturned and caught fire.

> Last August, beef prices reached an all-time low.

Sometimes three periods are used in place of a comma. Three periods also take the place of parentheses and semicolons. They signal a pause and are easily visible. The same is true of the dash, as in the following example:

> But the judge grumbled about the news coverage, and most prospective jurors agreed — saying the news coverage has been prone to overstatement, sensationalism and errors.

The only punctuation marks you need are the period, comma, question mark, dash, hyphen and, rarely, quotation marks. To make the copy easier to read, add the hyphen to some words even when the dictionary does not use it: anti-discrimination, co-equal, non-aggression.

Stations vary in writing style and in the preparation of copy. But if you learn what is presented here, you will be well-prepared. Differences will be small, and you will adapt to them easily.

One final note. You may be called on to do standup, on-the-scene reporting in front of a camera. You need to practice the art of speaking without a script. You might consider taking a course in public speaking.

Suggested Readings

Bliss, Edward Jr., and James L. Hoyt. *Writing News for Broadcast*, 3rd ed. New York: Columbia University Press, 1994. A classic text that excels in good writing.

Block, Mervin. *Writing Broadcast News — Shorter, Sharper, Stronger*, 2nd ed. Chicago: Bonus Books, 1997. An excellent book by a former network newswriter.

Freedman, Wayne. *It Takes More Than Good Looks.* Chicago: Bonus Books, 2003. A book packed with practical, down-to-earth advice by a man called "the best local TV news feature reporter in the country."

Schultz, Brad. *Broadcast News Producing.* Thousand Oaks, Calif.: Sage, 2004. A text that teaches how to put together a newscast.

Stephens, Mitchell. *Broadcast News*, 4th ed. New York: Holt, Rinehart and Winston, 2004. Covers all aspects of broadcast writing and the business of broadcast news.

White, Ted. *Broadcast News Writing, Reporting and Producing*, 4th ed. Burlington, Mass.: Elsevier/Focal Press, 2005. The best book on all aspects of broadcast newswriting.

Suggested Web Sites

www.nab.org Site of the 75-year-old National Association of Broadcasters. A wonderful resource for all kinds of radio- and television-related information, including a career center.

www.newscript.com This site aims to help radio journalists improve their skills as writers and anchors.

www.newstrench.com This "Thunder and Lightning News Service" calls itself "the site for TV news gathering . . . and the people who do it." Offers resources for gathering television news.

www.rtnda.org The Radio and Television News Directors Foundation promotes excellence in electronic journalism through research, education and professional training. Excellent reports, useful links.

www.tvrundown.com Provides news links to many specialized areas, such as medical news. Subscribers can delve into case histories.

http://writing.umn.edu/docs/publications/irving%20fang.pdf "Writing Style Differences in Newspaper, Radio, and Television News," a monograph by renowned author Professor Irving Fang of the University of Minnesota. A clear discussion, along with examples of stories demonstrating the differences in style.

Exercises

1. Watch a local evening television newscast. Make a simple list of the news stories. Then try to find these stories in the next morning's local newspaper, and compare the coverage.

2. Does the following AP story follow acceptable broadcast style? Is it technically correct? Does it emphasize immediacy? Change the copy where you think necessary.

   JEFFERSON CITY, Mo. (AP) — Missouri is tapping into its prison system budget to make a more than $4 million payment to probation and parole officers whom [sic] a court ruled were wrongly excluded from a pay raise.

   The state is using Department of Corrections money that was expected to be left over during the current fiscal year, which ends in July 2009.

   Office of Administration Commissioner Larry Schepker says he cautioned Gov. Matt Blunt's office about using that money for the back pay. But Schepker adds it should not be a problem, based on Missouri's current trend in male prison population.

   The Service Employees International Union had sued on claims that probation and parole workers were wrongly denied a $1,200 pay raise given to most other Missouri employees in 2004. The courts agreed.

3. Rewrite the following AP newspaper brief in broadcast writing style. Assume that the news is current and that you have time for a couple of paragraphs of the story.

AGENCY, Mo. (AP)—Buchanan County Sheriff's deputies answering a domestic disturbance call this week instead discovered a pair of monkeys reported stolen almost a year ago from a Kansas City man.

Sgt. Mark Brock said the pigtailed macaques, named Abby and Nicholas, were found late Thursday while deputies investigated the call at a residence in rural Agency. After spotting the monkeys, the deputies got a search warrant and came back to take a closer look at them.

The sheriff's department said it received a tip that the monkeys could be found at a family residence.

"They had cages and whatnot, like any other family pet," said Brock, who has experience with exotic pets cases in the past, including monkeys.

Catherine M. Montes has been charged and is scheduled to appear next month in court.

The animals were reunited with their owner, Dana Savorelli, who identified them through microchips implanted under their skin. He said the two appeared in good health although Abby was suffering from a cold with a raspy cough and is taking antibiotics.

"We're wore out," he said. "It was kind of a fluke" the monkeys were found during the deputies' initial disturbance call. "We had them go up and search that place before."

Savorelli, who owns the Monkey Island Rescue and Zoological Sanctuary in Kansas City, said three monkeys were stolen in October, when video surveillance showed a woman appearing to drug the animals and then take them.

He said the third monkey, Melissa, hasn't been found and Thursday's arrest didn't find any clues to her whereabouts. No charges have been filed in Jackson County.

Lunchtime diners at Woody's Grocery Store in Agency Friday were bemused by news of the monkey discovery nearby.

"Why would you want to steal a monkey?" unless it was valuable, said Terry Batchelder, a loader operator at Everett Quarry.

12 Writing for Public Relations

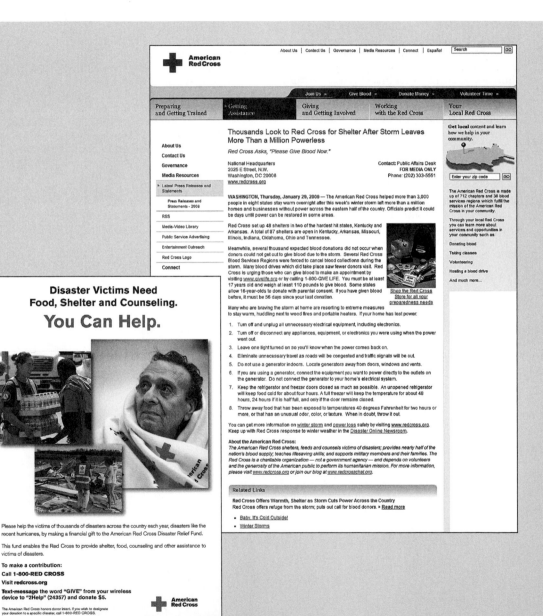

Y ou work for an over-the-counter drug company. A company vice president walks into your public-relations office and tells you that tiny fragments of metal have been found in a small number of your company's 500-milligram acetaminophen caplets.

You learn from the company's quality-control department that about one in 400,000 caplets might contain traces of the particulates. According to the Food and Drug Administration, the possibility of adverse effects is remote. Your company has 100 percent of the initial product batch that originally caused the investigation.

Now company managers want your opinion. Would you advise recalling 11 million bottles of 500-milligram acetaminophen caplets?

You may confront issues and decisions like this if you choose a career in public relations.

You may not be planning a career in news. You may know already that you are headed toward some area of public relations. Or, as happens to many people, perhaps you will work in news organizations for a while, but at some point you may decide to switch to public relations. Perhaps you already are writing for public relations.

Professionals agree that the skill most required of public-relations people is good writing. Your writing skills should include newswriting, and you should be familiar with the way news operations work. That's why journalism schools traditionally require a course in newswriting

In this chapter you will learn:
1. Various types of public-relations writing.
2. Guidelines for persuasive writing.
3. Different approaches to writing news releases.

Public-Relations Tasks

Public Relations: Strategies and Tactics, by Dennis L. Wilcox and Glen T. Cameron, lists the following activities as common to those who work in public relations. Notice how many involve writing either directly or indirectly.

Advise management on policy	Write speeches for others
Plan and conduct meetings	Write letters
Participate in policy decisions	Obtain speakers for organizational
Prepare publicity items	meetings
Plan public-relations programs	Plan and write booklets, leaflets,
Talk to editors and reporters	reports and bulletins
Sell programs to top management	Attend meetings
Hold press conferences	Design posters
Get cooperation from middle	Plan films and videotapes
management	Greet visitors
Write feature articles	Plan and prepare slide presentations
Get cooperation from other	Screen charity requests
employees	Plan and produce exhibits
Research public opinion	Evaluate public-relations programs
Listen to speeches	Take pictures or supervise
Plan and manage events	photographers
Make speeches	Conduct fund-raising drives
Conduct tours	Give awards

for students interested in public relations, and that's why many public-relations professionals like to hire people with some news experience. Only by studying news and how news organizations handle it will you be successful in public relations or in offices of public information. Knowing how reporters are taught to deal with news releases will help you write better releases. Of course, studying news also helps you enormously in the advertising world and in what is now frequently called strategic marketing or strategic communication.

Skilled public-relations or public-information practitioners know how to write news, and they apply all the principles of good newswriting in their news releases. A good news release meets the criteria of a good news story.

These same professionals know that working for an organization and doing internal and external communications demands a different perspective and, in many cases, a different kind of writing. In many ways, of course, good writing is good writing, and what you have learned so far applies to public-relations writing. But you also will be called upon to do writing that is different from the kinds of writing done by those who work for news organizations.

PUBLIC-RELATIONS WRITING: A DIFFERENT APPROACH

Rex Harlow, called by some the "father of public-relations research" and perhaps the first full-time public-relations educator, claimed to have found 472 definitions of public relations. The 1978 World Assembly of Public Relations in Mexico came up with this definition: "Public relations is the art and social science of analyzing trends, predicting their consequences, counseling organization leaders and implementing planned programs of action which will serve both the organization's and public interest."

In *Public Relations: Strategies and Tactics*, authors Dennis L. Wilcox and Glen T. Cameron claim these key words are found in all the definitions of public relations:

- *Deliberate:* the "activity is intentional . . . designed to influence, gain understanding, provide feedback, and obtain feedback."
- *Planned:* "organized . . . systematic, requiring research and analysis."
- *Performance:* "based on actual policies."
- *Public interest:* "mutually beneficial to the organization and to the public."
- *Two-way communication:* "equally important to solicit feedback."
- *Management function:* "an integral part of decision-making by top management."

Public relations, then, is not just publicity, which seeks to get the media to respond to an organization's interests. Nor is it advertising, which pays to get the attention of the public, or marketing, which combines a whole host of activities to sell a product, service or idea. Advertising and marketing are concerned with sales.

A Range of Interests

If you wish to write in the field of public relations, you have many areas from which to choose. Here are some of the specialties:

- *Media relations:* seeking publicity and answering questions posed by the media.
- *Government affairs:* spending time with legislatures and regulatory agencies and doing some lobbying.
- *Public affairs:* engaging in matters of public policy.
- *Industry relations:* relating to other firms in an industry and with trade associations.
- *Investor or financial or shareholder relations:* working to maintain investor confidence and good relationships with the financial world.

And the list goes on. Whoever said public-relations writing was dull knew nothing of the various worlds these professionals inhabit.

One more term must be introduced before proceeding. More and more today you see the term "**strategic communication**" replacing "public relations." Some say that one simple reason for this change is that the term "public relations" has always suffered a "PR" problem. But, of course, the reasons are much more serious than that.

The demands made of public-relations professionals are greater today than they were a generation ago. As Ronald Smith explains in *Strategic Planning for Public Relations,*

> No longer is it enough merely to know *how* to do things. Now the effective communicator needs to know *what* to do, *why* and how to *evaluate* its effectiveness. Public relations professionals used to be called upon mainly for tasks such as writing news releases, making speeches, producing videos, publishing newsletters, organizing displays and so on. Now the profession demands competency in conducting research, making decisions and solving problems. The call now is for strategic communicators.

In short, the strategic communicator must take a more scientific approach, do some research, make careful choices, and when finished, evaluate the effectiveness of the completed program. Such a communicator would certainly be expected to write clearly and precisely, but differently from reporters.

Objectivity and Public-Relations Writing

Journalists will debate forever whether anyone can be truly objective when writing a story. Most settle the argument by saying what is demanded is fairness. Nevertheless, in traditional reporting, writers should strive not to have a point of view. Reporters should not set out to prove something. Certainly they should not be an advocate for a point of view. They should get the facts, and let the facts speak for themselves.

By contrast, columnists have a point of view, and good ones find ways to support it convincingly. Editorial writers use facts to persuade people to change their minds, or to confirm their opinions, or to get people to do something or to stop doing something.

That's also what public-relations writers do. Though sometimes they wish only to inform their audiences, they most often want to do what editorial writers do—persuade the audience to a particular position.

However, there's one major difference. Journalists serve the public. Public-relations writers work for an organization or for a client other than a news operation. Their job is to make that organization or client appear in the best possible light. Effective public-relations writers do not ignore facts, even when they are harmful or detrimental to the cause they are promoting. But they are promoting a cause or looking out for the best interests of the people for whom they are working. As a result, they will interpret all news, even bad news, in the most favorable light.

Public-relations writers work much the way attorneys work for clients—as advocates. They don't lie or distort, but perhaps they play down certain facts and emphasize others. In its "official statement of public relations," the Public Relations Society of America states:

> Public relations helps our complex, pluralistic society to reach decisions and function more effectively by contributing to mutual understanding among groups and institutions. It serves to bring private and public policies into harmony. . . . The public-relations practitioner acts as a counselor to management and as a mediator, helping to translate private aims into reasonable, publicly acceptable policy and action.

For a good discussion of what public relations is, check the Web site of the Public Relations Student Society of America at www.prssa.org. The Public Relations Society of America has a code of ethics for the practice of public relations. The code requires members to "adhere to the highest standard of accuracy and truth," avoiding extravagant claims or unfair comparisons and giving credit for ideas and words borrowed from others. It also requires members not to "knowingly disseminate false or misleading information." See **www.prsa.org** for the rest of the code.

PUBLIC-RELATIONS WRITING: A DIVERSITY OF TASKS

Public-relations personnel are concerned with three things: the message, the audience and the media to deliver the message.

The Message

You must know the message your organization wants to send. That message may be a product, a program or the organization itself. For every message you work on, you must first know what you hope to accomplish, even if your purpose is just to inform.

That's why it is so important for you to be a reporter first, to know how to gather information and to do so quickly. Like any reporter, you may be called on in an instant to deal with a crisis in the company for which you work. When meat from a Toronto-based company killed 12 people and sickened dozens more all over Canada, there was work to do. Naturally, the price of the company's stock dropped.

Ways to Get Noticed

Journalists, especially television journalists, are sometimes accused of creating stories by their very presence, or at least of fanning the flames. While creating news is not in the journalist's job description, a large part of public relations is doing exactly that. Here's a list of how to create news from Wilcox and Cameron's *Public Relations: Strategies and Tactics*:

1. Tie in with news events of the day.
2. Cooperate with another organization on a joint project.
3. Tie in with a newspaper or broadcast station on a mutual project.
4. Conduct a poll or survey.
5. Issue a report.
6. Arrange an interview with a celebrity.
7. Take part in a controversy.
8. Arrange for a testimonial.
9. Arrange for a speech.
10. Make an analysis or prediction.
11. Form and announce names for committees.
12. Hold an election.
13. Announce an appointment.
14. Celebrate an anniversary.
15. Issue a summary of facts.
16. Tie in with a holiday.
17. Make a trip.
18. Give an award.
19. Hold a contest.
20. Pass a resolution.
21. Appear before a public body.
22. Stage a special event.
23. Write a letter.
24. Release a letter you received (with permission).
25. Adapt national reports and surveys for local use.
26. Stage a debate.
27. Tie in to a well-known week or day.
28. Honor an institution.
29. Organize a tour.
30. Inspect a project.
31. Issue a commendation.
32. Issue a protest.

The recall cost the firm more than $20 million. Nevertheless, Maple Leaf Food, Inc., which employs nearly 23,000 people, is surviving—mainly because of excellent communications.

From the beginning of the crisis, company president Michael McCain took full blame for the crisis and regularly apologized to all victims. In a Sept. 5, 2008, news release, for example, he said, "We deeply regret this incident and the impact it has had on people's lives." The release clearly outlined four immediate steps the company had taken. It assured readers that the company was doing everything possible to determine the cause of the contamination and to prevent it from ever happening again.

You might not have a boss as enlightened as Michael McCain, but as the public-relations person, it is your job to try to be candid and truthful with the press and the public. In this case, an editorial in the *Calgary Herald* praised Maple Leaf Foods for its "show of openness and accountability."

The Audience

Almost as important as knowing all you can about the message is knowing the audience to whom you are directing it. The better you target your audience, the more effective you will be. As in advertising, demographics and psychographics determine the way you write your message, the language you choose, and the simplicity or complexity of the piece you are creating.

Who are these people, what are their attitudes, what do they do for work and recreation? You will answer these questions somewhat differently if you write for internal audiences (employees or the managers of those employees) or external audiences (the media, shareholders, constituents, volunteers, consumers or donors).

In the public-relations crisis suffered by JetBlue Airways on Valentine's Day 2007, Todd Burke, JetBlue's vice president of corporate communications, found himself dealing more with employees than with the public. He told Kevin J. Allen of Ragan.com: "An interesting thing happened. I now found myself having to manage internal audience almost as much as I did external."

Not that the external audience was ignored. The communications team put together a "Passenger Bill of Rights," and they persuaded then-CEO David Neeleman to do a YouTube video in which he apologized to customers.

The Media

Once you have mastered the message or product and targeted the audience, you then have to choose the best medium by which to deliver the message to the audience.

Television, Radio and Newsstand Publications

For a message that nearly everyone wants or needs to know, television may be your best medium. Procter & Gamble spends millions advertising soap on television because everyone needs soap. Television offers color and motion; television can show rather than tell.

Radio listeners usually are loyal to one radio station. They will listen to your message over and over. The more often they hear it, the more likely they are to retain it.

Print media such as newspapers and magazines are better for complicated messages and sometimes for delicate messages. Some argue that print still has more credibility than other media and that people can come back again and again to a print message.

The Internet: An All-in-One Medium

Perhaps the best place to do public relations today is online. More and more people are getting the information and products they need online. Here you have all the media in one medium. Remember, people who are online generally are better educated and more affluent than those who are not. They love the control they have over the messages they find there. They can "click here" on only the information they want, and they can do so in any order they choose. They can be involved and engaged and respond to one another.

What is so challenging about "new" media is the high degree of individualization; you are in the world of "mass customization." You must present the message at different levels to different people so that they feel they have choices, so that everyone feels as if you are writing only to him or her. It's all about individual choices and involving your readers so they will interact with you. As expert Jakob Nielsen puts it, online readers are "selfish, lazy and ruthless." You will study more about writing online in Chapter 13. Just remember, communicating online means ideally that you have the means of communicating in a number of ways—via print, video and audio—all in one medium.

Social-Networking Media

JetBlue's use of YouTube is just one example of using online video to reach an audience. When the rising Mississippi continued to flood and wreak havoc on thousands of victims in June 2008, American Red Cross public-affairs team member Jeffery Biggs used only a Twitter feed—a social-networking service that sends messages in real time—to keep people informed.

Wendy Harman, the American Red Cross's director of new media integration, had been training her team "on how to use the social media for some time." As reported in *O'Dwyer's PR Report* by Darby C. Doll,

"Harman established what she calls 'the online newsroom,' consisting of a Word Press blog, Google Maps, Facebook page, YouTube channel and Flickr album, in addition to the Twitter Feed."

In his article, Doll goes on to talk about other forms of micro-blogging that can be of enormous help to public-relations professionals:

- Jaiku (**jaiku.com**): Share photos and music; text Jaikus from your smartphone.
- Plurk (**plurk.com**): "Share your life easily with friends, family and fans."
- Tumblr (**tumblr.com**): "Post anything: Customize everything."
- Identi.ca (**identi.ca**): Calls itself a "public timeline."

Then, of course, you have the huge social-media giants, Facebook and MySpace, which have micro-blogging features. LinkedIn has become enormously popular among corporate and other business users.

All of this has developed very fast, and most believe that we've seen only the beginning. Print will not disappear, but the arrival of the micro-blog may change the way we write nearly everything.

Internal Publications, Brochures and Billboards

If you work in internal communications, you may decide to publish a newsletter or magazine. A large number of corporations are now communicating with employees throughout the day via an intranet, an internal online service accessible only to them. As a result, a surprisingly large number of organizations have abandoned their regularly published, internal print publications.

For messages that need more explanation, such as health-care matters, perhaps a printed brochure will do the job best. Externally, for matters that may concern the community, you may want to use billboards in addition to paid ads in publications or radio and television ads. Or you may choose to write news releases and leave it to others to interpret your message. (See Figure 12.1 for a sample news release.)

Sometimes, however, there's no quick fix. What took a long time to build can come tumbling down quickly, and then a long rebuilding process is necessary.

THE MEDIA CAMPAIGN

Research shows that the more media you use, the better chance you have to succeed. That's why effective public-relations people, like those in advertising, think in terms of campaigns and strategies. A campaign assumes that you can't just tell an audience once what you want them to learn, retain and act on. You need a strategy to reach a goal that may take days, weeks, months or even years to attain. Which media do

Contact: Mary Ann Beahon
Director of University Relations
(573) 592-1127
mbeahon@williamwoods.edu
www.thewoods.edu

December 3, 2008
FOR IMMEDIATE RELEASE

William Woods Senior Art Students Showcase Work

FULTON, Mo. — Demonstrating what they've learned during the past four years, three William Woods University seniors are displaying their talents at the annual Senior Art Show. The show runs through Dec. 12 in the Mildred Cox Gallery of the Gladys Woods Kemper Center for the Arts.

The exhibit features the work of Hillary Reed of Castle Rock, Colo.; Adam Dresden of Granite City, Ill., and Kelly Trustee of Huntsville, Mo. Included in the show are examples of ceramics, oil painting, charcoal, pencil, watercolor and graphic design.

The Mildred Cox Gallery is open 9-4 p.m. Monday through Friday, and 1-4 p.m. Saturday and Sunday. Admission is free and open to the public. For more information about the exhibit, call (573) 592-4245.

###

Figure 12.1
A traditional news release is double-spaced and follows AP style. Note the line "For Immediate Release," the date and the name of the contact. Note also the contact's title, phone number and e-mail address and the school's Web site address.

you use to introduce the subject? Which media will you engage for follow-up and details? Which aspects of the message are best suited for which media? You accomplish little by sending out the message once and in only one medium. It's far more effective to send the message in a mix of media in a carefully timed or orchestrated way.

Public-relations writers adapt messages to the whole spectrum of media available. To do this, you must learn what each medium does best. Perhaps the cultural critic Marshall McLuhan was exaggerating when he wrote that the medium is the message, but no one doubts there is a great deal of truth to his statement. Think of what this means now that you have all of the new media and social media available to you. The public-relations campaign, as practiced by the American Red Cross, takes on a whole new meaning.

You may be hired as a speechwriter or do something as specialized as writing the organization's annual report. Corporations and institutions such as hospitals and universities hire thousands of communicators to get their messages out to the public. Or you may work for a public-relations agency that is hired to do this work for organizations.

Regardless of the means or media you choose to use, your job is to have good relations with the public. You do that best by trying to establish mutually beneficial relationships and situations. All of this is best achieved when you make it possible for two-way communications. You must allow and encourage your various publics to have a voice in what you are trying to accomplish. If you involve your audience in what you are trying to achieve, your chances of achieving it increase. Establishing a Web site is an excellent way to get people's ideas and reactions. Of course, you must find ways (notices on bulletin boards, brochures, newsletters, etc.) to make your Web site known.

PUBLIC-RELATIONS WRITING: A MATTER OF PERSUASION

"If you don't understand good journalistic style and format (who, what, when, where and why) for writing a press release, you harm your company and yourself."

— *G.A. Marken,*
president of Marken
Communications,
Public Relations Quarterly

Most of the time, your writing will attempt to persuade people. You need to study the techniques of persuasion and to use them carefully.

Your Attitude

To persuade people, you need to believe three things:

1. *People are essentially good.* You need to be convinced of this and to appeal to people's basic goodness and fairness.
2. *People are intelligent or at least educable.* Don't talk down to people; don't assume that you can trick or fool them. Of course, don't assume that just because they are intelligent and educated, they know the subject matter as well as you do. A good rule: Never underestimate the intelligence of your audience; never overestimate what they know. A college professor with a Ph.D. in philosophy or history may be brilliant in those areas but might know nothing about the financial markets.
3. *People are changeable.* You must believe not only that people are changeable but also that you can change them.

Credibility and Trust

More than anything else, you need to establish and maintain your credibility and the credibility of the organization you represent. Aristotle wrote that the character of the speaker is the most essential and powerful component of persuasion. Without a doubt, character is the most important attribute public-relations people need to have and to develop. A sterling reputation takes a long time to build—and can be lost in an instant.

In addition, you must assume good will on the part of your audience. You cannot persuade people by beating up on them, by calling them names or by considering them the enemy. This is particularly true regarding your attitude toward the press. Too many public-relations professionals consider the press the enemy, not to be trusted with the truth, to be stonewalled at every opportunity.

Consider this example of working with the media. Americans care about what their pets eat. If they can't trust what they feed these beloved family members, what are they to do? Congress knows what people care about, and sometimes congressional leaders act on that knowledge. In 2007, after a recall of pet foods, Congress called Duane Ekedahl, president of the Pet Food Institute, to testify. That's scary. But the Pet Food Institute was ready. Gene Grabowski reported in *O'Dwyer's PR Report* that staffers "were in daily communication with officials of the FDA and in frequent contact with key congressional aides." By having the staff do some groundwork and then testifying before Congress, Ekedahl ensured that his message was heard around the world, and people became less concerned about the biggest recall in pet-food history. The institute also established the National Pet Food Commission and advertised it that morning in *The New York Times* and *The Washington Post*. Pet owners could rest easier.

Another example of using good sense and trust is how the University of North Carolina–Chapel Hill handled the situation when it learned that People for the Ethical Treatment of Animals had planted a spy in one of its animal-research facilities. The woman had worked there for eight months and had secretly videotaped animals and the staff at work. PETA's goal was to defeat the Helms amendment to the 2002 farm bill that would have extended USDA authority for animal welfare to cover laboratory mice, rats and birds. That change, according to those opposed to it, would have meant a great deal more paperwork for the research team and little improvement in animal care. PETA held a press conference and set up a Web site showing lurid photos and making claims of animal cruelty and neglect.

The university's response was rapid, candid and forthright. On the day PETA broke the story, Tony Waldrop, vice chancellor for research, and other university officials held a press conference, promised a thorough investigation and opened the facility in question to reporters. The university did not attempt to deny or discredit PETA's claims. The press had no hint of a cover-up to feed on, and university officials, at least, considered media coverage to be fair and factual. The story faded from the news in a couple of days. The farm bill passed with the Helms amendment intact.

> *"Employers want people who can write and communicate ideas—who can pull complex or fragmented ideas together into coherent messages. This requires not only technical skill but also intelligence. It also requires a love of writing."*
>
> — *Thomas H. Bivins,*
> Public Relations Writing

Many corporations and organizations publish newsletters and magazines for internal and external audiences. These outstanding publications are from Staffing Industry Analysts Inc. in Los Altos, Calif.

Meanwhile, the university lived up to its promise to investigate. It spent several thousand hours in internal investigations, and Waldrop commissioned a panel of three outside experts to do an independent review. The university then presented a 40-page report to the federal Office of Laboratory Animal Welfare, and the local press summarized it — again, in a fair, evenhanded manner. The report was then published in the university's research magazine: a candid account of what PETA claimed, what the university found in its investigations and what it did to correct the problem.

That's how public relations can, should and does work.

In *O'Dwyer's PR Report* (Oct. 2006), Bill Huey, president of Strategic Communications in Atlanta, writes: "The next time you become incensed about something the media has done — or you want to go on a crusade, call your travel agent and go on a golfing vacation instead."

WRITING NEWS RELEASES THAT GET ATTENTION

Earlier in this chapter you read that good writing is the most important skill for a public-relations professional. You also read about all of the various positions you can hold as a public-relations person. Each demands a great variety of writing skills directed at different audiences. If you write copy for brochures or for your organization's newsletter, magazine, Web site or annual report, if you write for print or broadcast or film, the quality of what you produce reflects directly on your organization.

Perhaps nothing that you will be called on to write is more important than news releases. Even the smallest newspaper and radio or television station gets dozens of news releases daily. How do you break through the clutter and get listened to or looked at by the gatekeepers on the news desks? If you send news releases online, your problem is still the same.

Here are some guidelines to help you get your messages to your intended audiences.

Know What News Is and How to Write It

If you are headed toward a career in public relations or public information, you're probably taking this newswriting course to help you understand the principles of news. The news media will not pay attention to copy that is laced with opinion or self-serving quotations. Worse, they will ridicule your work and discard it immediately. Avoid statements such as this: "Monroe College is recognized as the foremost and most prestigious college of liberal arts in the entire Midwest." Who says?

To write for most publications, certainly for newspapers, you need to know Associated Press style. (See Appendix 2 for a summary of the style followed by most news publications.) Correct spelling, usage and grammar are essential, of course, but just as important is AP style. Why should news editors take you seriously if you don't bother to write in the style of their publications?

News releases are notoriously inaccurate and inconsistent in style and grammar. How ironic that people so concerned with image can be so careless in the way they present themselves to the public.

Know the Structure and Operations of News Rooms

If you do not get actual experience in a news room in college, find ways to spend some time in one. In Chapter 2, you studied how news rooms are organized. Now use your public-relations skills to get inside one and to experience what goes on there.

The simplest and most important thing you can learn about news rooms is that they have deadlines. Learn the deadlines of the media in your area, and respect those deadlines. This means you cannot call in a story to a television news station a half-hour before broadcast time. Not only will the station not use your story, but station employees will resent you and not forget the interruption at a critical time. News organizations will tell you what time you must submit a story to make the news that day.

Know the People in the News Media and the Jobs They Hold

It's especially important to know people and their jobs in newspapers you contact. Sending a release addressed simply to a newspaper can be a waste of time and make you look as if you do not know what you are doing. Sending a release to the business editor or to the features editor makes more sense. Addressing by name the editor of the section in which you wish the release to appear works best.

At a packed meeting of the Publicity Club of New York, Faye Penn, then features editor of the *New York Post*, told her audience to stop sending her news releases. First she said she could not possibly read them all; then she said that many of them were about things her section never covered. Later, she admitted she looked to see who had sent them.

If people in the news media know and trust you, they are more likely to read your releases. Sometimes you can call them with a story idea and let them write their own stories. There's nothing writers like more than to get wind of good stories. At that same Publicity Club meeting, features editor Barbara Schuler of *Newsday* warned that she never answers her phone but does read all news releases and faxes. She stressed the importance of getting the release into the right hands and handed out a sheet with the names, phone numbers and beat assignments of the reporters at *Newsday*. You need that list for each medium you cover.

Remember, your job is to help reporters write good stories. If you can help them do that and at the same time serve your client's interests, you will be a successful public-relations practitioner.

Know the Style of Writing That Fits the Medium

Do not make the mistake of sending to a radio or television station the same news release that you send to a newspaper. Do not expect busy newspeople to translate your newspaper release into broadcast copy. If you can write radio or television copy (see Chapter 11), you have a much better chance of getting the copy read over the air.

Also, be aware that just as some newspapers will use your news releases almost verbatim, some radio and television stations will use your audio and video. The Center for Media and Democracy's 2006 report of a six-month investigation revealed that 46 stations in 22 states inserted video news releases into their newscasts. Moreover,

News Releases That Get Used

Fraser P. Seitel, author, communications consultant and teacher, identifies the following as the eight topics of news releases that are most likely to be used:

1. New products or projects
2. Personnel promotions—at least of important people
3. Trends
4. Conflict
5. Topicality—"relating your news to pressing issues of the day"
6. Local heritage—tying news to community roots or history
7. Human interest
8. Insanity—the truly bizarre or unusual

nearly 90 percent did not give the slightest hint to viewers that these were VNRs, even though some of them dealt with controversial subjects such as global warming.

Know How to Distribute Information Online

Of course, not even the largest newspapers or radio or television networks can reach as many people as online media. Millions of Web sites know practically no limits. First, you must establish your own credible, up-to-date, interactive Web site. Second, you must be thoroughly familiar with Web sites such as **www.online-pr.com**, **www.prnewswire .com** and **www.medialink.com** so that you can distribute your releases online and keep up with what's happening in public relations. Third, you yourself must become expert at using the new media to get across your organization's messages (see Chapter 13).

APPROACHES TO WRITING NEWS RELEASES

To be effective in their jobs, writers of news releases need to learn all the techniques that journalists use in writing news stories.

The Inverted Pyramid

The straight, no-nonsense inverted-pyramid news release remains the staple of the public-relations professional. Many believe that any other approach will not be taken seriously by news professionals. (See Chapter 6 for more on the inverted pyramid.)

Here's an example. Notice that the release begins with the name, address and phone number of the organization putting out the release and the name of a contact person. If the news is for immediate release, say so. Otherwise, indicate a release date. (To learn how a release is formatted, see Figure 12.1.)

NEWS

Missouri Department of Natural Resources
P.O. Box 176, Jefferson City, Missouri 65102
For further information contact: Mary Schwartz (573-751-3443)
(For immediate release)

JEFFERSON CITY, MO., FEB. 25, 2008—The winter solitude of Roaring River, Bennett Spring and Montauk state parks will be shattered by about 8,000 fishing enthusiasts expected to participate in the annual trout opening March 1 in Missouri State Parks.

The start of trout-fishing season in these parks marks the beginning of the vacation season in Missouri State Parks, which are administered by the Missouri Department of Natural Resources. The Department also administers 30 other state parks and 22 historic sites, which officially open on April 15.

"Trout opening is definitely a big event for fishermen in Missouri," said John Karel, director of state parks. "But, it's also a big day for state parks since it traditionally marks the beginning of the upcoming vacation season."

Karel notes that park visitors to Montauk, Roaring River and Bennett Spring state parks will be greeted by a number of new construction and major renovation projects. . . .

The release goes on to talk about the projects and about how many trout tags were sold. It's a traditional approach, although the lead attempts to be a bit creative with "winter solitude" being "shattered." The lead jumps to a quote from an authority, John Karel, the director of the state parks, and uses him as the source throughout.

Going Beyond the Inverted Pyramid

Let's look now at a different approach; some would call it a feature approach. (See Chapter 7 for more on variations in story structure.) In the following example, the information heading at the top of the release stays the same.

When the siren sounds at 6:30 a.m. March 1 in Bennett Spring State Park near Lebanon, Bill Brooks will be there. He'll be standing knee-deep in icy water as he's done every March 1 since 1990.

Brooks, known in fishing circles as Big Trout, will join an expected 8,000 other Missouri fishing enthusiasts for the opening of trout-fishing season in Missouri State Parks. Missouri's other trout-fishing state parks are Roaring River, near Cassville, and Montauk, near Salem.

Brooks can't imagine anything, short of a death in the family, that would keep him away. "This is just a tradition for me. I'm already making wagers and getting together my equipment."

As an extra measure, Brooks has made a special trip from his Marshfield home to the park just to check stream conditions.

Tips for writers of news releases

1. Follow an accepted journalistic style of writing. Use AP style.
2. Go easy on length. Hold it to two double-spaced, typewritten pages.
3. Avoid breaks. Don't hyphenate words at the ends of lines, and don't split a sentence at the bottom of a page.
4. Write clearly. Avoid corporate jargon, legalese or other alien language.
5. Remember the pyramid. But don't put all the w's in the lead.
6. Beware of adjectives. Especially avoid superlatives.
7. Make it local.
8. Attribute news to a person—not to a company or organization.
9. Indent the paragraphs.

— *Carole Howard and Wilma Mathews,* On Deadline: Managing Media Relations

On the Job

News Releases

After Brad Whitworth received his journalism degree, he joined the staff of a small magazine covering Illinois politics. When the magazine folded abruptly six months later, he moved into corporate communications, where he worked first for a small association and then for a large insurance company.

Whitworth has spent the past 25 years doing public relations, speechwriting and internal communications for Silicon Valley companies, including high-tech giants Hewlett-Packard and Cisco. For 10 of those years his work took him to Asia Pacific, Canada, Latin America and Europe.

"For global audiences, it's important to keep your words and sentences as simple as possible," says Whitworth. "In fact, the more complex or technical your subject matter, the simpler your words need to be.

"It's a good thing the language for doing business around the world is English. But for many audiences, it's their second language. Everything I learned in journalism school about making writing clear, concise, consistent and complete is even more critical when communicating with co-workers or customers halfway around the world."

Throughout his career, Whitworth has relied on the International Association of Business Communicators for his professional development and networking. "I landed my job at Hewlett-Packard through IABC's job bank and have hired dozens more through the network." He's given back to IABC, too, serving as president of two local chapters and as the youngest-ever chairman of the 16,000-member not-for-profit organization.

"It's really important to stay connected with others who are doing the same kind of work," he says. "You can share best practices, learn about job opportunities and take part in seminars, conferences and workshops. Your learning shouldn't stop when you leave campus."

After 18 years of opening days, Brooks has seen some changes. "I guess you could say they've gotten stricter on us. Things used to be a lot wilder down there in the old days, until they stopped us from gambling and stopped selling beer. . . ."

The release then introduces fishing expert Jim Rogers, who runs concessions at both Bennett Spring and Roaring River. Rogers tells with specific numbers how he has sold more than double the number of trout tags that he sold just eight years ago.

In this approach, the writer uses a "real person," a long-time fisherman, to introduce the story—rather than a person in authority. By using Brooks and Rogers, the writer tells a story and still gives important information, but in an interesting and appealing way. This approach is described in Chapter 7 as the focus structure.

Now suppose the writer accompanied this story with a photo from the year before of Big Trout standing knee-deep in icy water. Public-relations professionals know that releases accompanied by photos or art of some kind get more attention and more play.

This photo, provided by the Missouri State Department of Conservation, can accompany news releases promoting trout fishing in Missouri.

Some professionals have also begun to place attention-grabbing headlines on top of their releases. Others accompany the head with a summary/contents/benefit blurb. Why should the editor or the intended audience have to read the entire release to find out what it's about?

You might want to go a step further. Why not do some service journalism? Put the parks, their locations and the opening dates in a separate box. How about a map of how to get there? Perhaps you could make a list of the top-10 things to remember on opening day. Maybe you could create an infographic indicating where to get trout tags. Some news organizations will use just one sidebar or graphic of what you send. But the important thing is that if you give them choices, you have a better chance of getting some of your information used.

In the past, some public-relations professionals shied away from what they thought of as gimmicks, for fear that editors would not take them seriously. What they didn't see was the way newspapers were changing, especially some sections.

Why not experiment? Attention is harder and harder to get. Don't be afraid to try a "you" lead or even a question. For example, "Are you ready for opening day at Bennett Springs?" Remember to get to the "so what" quickly—not the "so what" of your organization but rather the "so what" of the audience. What's in it for the reader or listener? Most readers don't care whether AT&T has announced the purchase of another cellphone company. (Some companies seem never to do anything but "announce" things in news releases.) Readers do care about how this purchase might affect them and their phone bills.

Remember, too, that a film clip of Big Trout will more likely be used by a television news producer than will a written release, and a recorded interview might get played on your local radio station or on the Web.

Even if none of these media uses your material as you presented it, perhaps you will succeed in grabbing the attention of an editor or reporter. If that person is inspired to pursue the story, you'll still get the information to the public.

Be sure that you make yourself available—by phone, e-mail, fax, Web site, or in person—24 hours a day. A reporter on deadline will write the story with or without you. It's better that you talk—it's always better that you talk—to the reporter.

Remember, your job is not just to write news releases. Your job is to get information from your organization to the public. Writing news releases is only one means to that end. As a public-relations writer, you will use your writing skills in myriad ways in all media to serve your clients.

Suggested Readings

Bivins, Thomas H. *Public-Relations Writing*, 4th ed. Lincolnwood, Ill.: NTC/Contemporary Publishing, 1999. Covers the wide variety of writing expected of public-relations professionals.

Holtz, Shel. *Public Relations on the Net*. New York: Amacom, 1999. Anything Shel Holtz says or writes about online subjects is worth paying attention to. See also **http://blog.holtz.com**.

Horton, James L. *Online Public Relations: A Handbook for Practitioners* Westport, Conn.: Quorum Books, 2001. A superb primer and more, it begins by explaining terminology and ends with 85 industry and general information topics to place news and to gather information.

Howard, Carole, and Wilma Mathews. *On Deadline: Managing Media Relations*, 4th ed. Prospect Heights, Ill.: Waveland Press, 2006. A practical book on how organizations should deal with the news media.

Huey, Bill. "'Incensed' About Something the Media Has Done? Get Over It." *O'Dwyer's PR Report* (October 2006): 37. Excellent advice for public-relations professionals on how to deal with what they perceive as bad press.

Newsom, Doug, and Jim Haynes. *Public-Relations Writing: Form and Style*, 8th ed. Belmont, Calif.: Wadsworth, 2007. A truly thorough classic. It even has a section on grammar, spelling and punctuation.

Seitel, Fraser P. *The Practice of Public Relations*, 10th ed. New York: Prentice Hall, 2006. You can tell Seitel has been a teacher. He writes simply, clearly and engagingly.

Seitel, Fraser P. "'Used' News Releases." *O'Dwyer's PR Report* (September 2006): 31, 42. Seitel's columns on "Professional Development" appear regularly in this publication.

Wilcox, Dennis L. *Public-Relations Writing and Media Techniques*, 6th ed. New York: Longman, 2008. Filled with practical tips in all areas of public-relations writing, plus handy boxes and sidebars.

Suggested Web Sites

www.instituteforpr.com   Offers information about public-relations research, measurement, programs, seminars, publications, scholarship, etc., from the Institute for Public Relations, which provides "the science beneath the art of public relations."

www.odwyerpr.com   You must subscribe to this Web site, but when you do, you also receive *O'Dwyer's PR Report*, an excellent monthly publication that devotes each issue to a public-relations specialty field.

www.online-pr.com   An amazingly helpful site for anyone interested in public relations. A source for loads of useful Web sites.

www.prsa.org   Site of the Public Relations Society of America. Has general information about the society, lists its chapters and sections, and offers information on publications, membership and accreditation, recognition and awards, conferences and seminars.

www.prwatch.org   Web site of the Center for Media and Democracy. Investigates "public-relations spin and propaganda." This site sends out more than 1,000 news releases each day.

Exercises

1. Visit the public-relations or public-affairs department of a local college, hospital, corporation or association, and investigate thoroughly its public-relations program. Interview people in various positions about their jobs and experience, and write a 1,000-word report.

2. A classmate was killed in a car accident. A few thousand dollars has been raised to set up a scholarship to honor his memory, but much more money is needed to endow the scholarship. Several students in the class have been training to run in the Chicago marathon. A group decides to solicit money for each mile the students complete. Organize a campaign on your campus to get people to pledge or donate money. Answer these questions:

   a. What are your target audiences?
   b. Which media will you use?
   c. What print, video and audio materials will you develop?

   Then write a news release for the local print media.

3. Read the following news release, and note any deviations from AP style. Also note any content that news organizations might object to.

   NEWS RELEASE

   "Chest Pains", an excellent film in the HEALTH-CARE series produced by the American College of Physicians, will be shown from 7:00-8:30 P.M., Wednesday, October 22, at St. Mary's Health Center. Springfield internist, Dr. Harold Kanagawa, will host a question-and-answer period following the film.

   Although most people assume that chest pains signify a heart attack, the public is less aware that other conditions—hiatal hernia, ulcers, viral infections of the heart's membranes—can also cause pains that require prompt diagnosis and appropriate medical treatment. Designed to help increase awareness of the symptoms and their possible significance, "Chest Pains" features an internist and actual patients as they work together to resolve underlying medical problems.

   Through a warm and engaging human-interest style of presentation, each twenty-five-minute documentary encourages people to take an increased responsibility for their own well-being by establishing healthy habits and assuming a more active role in disease prevention.

The HEALTHCARE series is produced under an educational grant from the Elsworth Company of Midland, Michigan. Other films in this superb, highly acclaimed series cover "Aches, Pains and Arthritis", "Diabetes", and "Abdominal Discomfort".

Doctor Kanagawa, a renowned specialist in internal medicine, is 1 of fifty-thousand members of the American College of Physicians. Founded in 1915, the College is the largest medical specialty society in the U.S. and one of the most prestigious. It represents doctors of internal medicine, related non-surgical specialists, and physicians-in-training.

To register or for more information, contact the Women's Life Center.

4. Interview a student at your college or university who comes from a small town. Then write a news release about his or her life and activities at school, and send it to the town's newspaper.

5. Study the Web site of the college or university you attend. List five things about it that you think are excellent and five things that you would like to see improved.

13 Writing Online

D uring Barack Obama's presidential campaign in 2008, he recognized that mainstream media were far from the only way of reaching supporters and would-be supporters. Obama's sophisticated Web site allowed people to donate in record numbers and in record amounts, sold Obama coffee mugs and T-shirts, and helped supporters send pro-Obama messages to their friends.

It didn't stop there. The Web site also provided registered volunteers with a detailed script and a list of voters to call in swing states. There was also an Obama-Biden tax calculator to help you determine how much you would gain from the candidates' plans. Elsewhere, there was an Obama YouTube channel; Facebook, MySpace and LinkedIn sites; and even an iPhone applet, issued just days after the iPhone 3G upgrade hit the market.

Obama's opponent, John McCain, while launching a somewhat less-sophisticated effort in cyberspace, still managed to have his own YouTube channel, a Facebook site and an impressive Web site.

Clearly, both campaigns were well-aware that the media landscape had changed. No longer were candidates dependent on big media to get out their messages. Nevertheless, although these new channels

Students and faculty used the Futures Lab's many technologies during election night, Nov. 4, 2008, at the Donald W. Reynolds Journalism Institute (RJI). Election watch parties such as these were an attempt to rebuild public trust in the media.

were important, professional journalists were still essential to the public in making sense of what was happening. And journalists did just that by describing in great detail the shift in direction of the political winds.

There was a big story to tell, and for the most part, the public turned to mainstream journalists to make sense of it all. Journalists responded by writing news for newspapers, magazines, radio, television and the Web. Those who wrote for the Web did so with clarity and purpose and with a newfound sense of what writing for online media is all about.

Like the candidates, journalists also used the Web in innovative ways. In Columbia, Mo., the *Columbia Missourian*; KOMU, the local NBC affiliate; and KBIA Radio, an NPR affiliate, joined forces to produce a four-hour webcast as the election results poured in. Wrapped around it was a watch party to which citizens of all political stripes were invited. Other news sites offered election results on demand. For instance, *The New York Times* had a map with voting results broken down to the county and parish level for the entire nation.

All of this demonstrates the increasing importance of the Web in our society's media mix. Although professional journalists work alongside citizen journalists in that arena, to maintain their role as important contributors to the public dialogue, journalists must learn to harness the Web to the best of their ability. In this chapter, we examine the peculiarities of writing for online media and see what sets it apart from writing for traditional media.

THE LESSON OF KATRINA

"Computers can:

- *Look things up for us.*
- *Navigate for us ('Please turn to page . . .').*
- *Link words to other words.*
- *Remember where we were and take us back there.*
- *Play audio, video and animation.*
- *Organize and present information according to a nonlinear structure."*

— Andrew Bonime and Ken C. Pohlmann,
Writing for New Media

It's no stretch to argue that the mainstream media really began to understand the power of online media only when disaster struck in the form of Hurricane Katrina in 2005. No story better illustrates the power of online journalism in the wake of Katrina than that of NOLA .com, the online site of *The (New Orleans) Times-Picayune*. Floodwaters idled the newspaper's printing plant, making publication impossible, but NOLA.com became a primary source of information. It did so with great distinction. (See Figure 13.1.)

Mark Glaser writes in *Online Journalism Review*:

The NOLA.com news blog became *the* source for news on hurricane damage and recovery efforts—including updates from various reporters on the ground and even full columns and news stories.

The blog actually became the paper, and it had to because the newspaper's readership was in diaspora, spread around the country in shelters and homes of families and friends. The newspaper staff was transformed into citizen journalists, with arts reviewers doing disaster

Figure 13.1
When Hurricane Katrina displaced a community and suspended the function of
other media sources, NOLA.com provided thorough, accessible information
about the situation to those displaced and without other means of
communication.

coverage and personal stories running alongside hard-hitting journalism. In a time of tragedy and loss, the raw guts of the organization were
exposed for us to see.

Glaser writes that NOLA.com editor Jon Donley turned over his
blog to his readers, who sent in dozens of calls for help. Most came
through text messaging because mobile telephone towers and land-
lines were downed and inoperable. The calls for help were relayed onto
the blog, which rescuers monitored to know where to go. As a result,
NOLA.com not only provided information but also saved lives.

Across the country, newspapers and other media noticed. They
began to realize the power of online journalism and set about the task
of giving it its own place in the media landscape.

THE WEB AS ITS OWN MEDIA FORM

The 69-year-old Associated Press Managing Editors association amended its bylaws in 2001 to fill one seat of its board of directors with a supervisor of an online news operation. In 2002 Ken Sands, interactive editor of *The Spokesman-Review*, Spokane, Wash., was elected to the board.

Newspaper Web sites are expanding the reach of their publications in unprecedented ways. According to the Newspaper Association of America, in 2008, unique visitors to newspaper Web sites represented on average more than 41 percent (66 million) of all Internet users over the course of a month.

Online journalism wasn't always so powerful, and in its infancy few knew how to use it. Indeed, when it first appeared, online journalism followed a familiar pattern—one established when radio began to yield to television. As television became established in the post–World War II era, news reports consisted almost entirely of someone sitting at a desk reading written-for-radio news. Similarly, when the World Wide Web appeared in the mid-1990s, media organizations quickly adopted it but merely regurgitated news written for traditional media—newspapers, magazines, and radio and television stations. Sites operated by traditional media contained little more than stories that already had appeared in print or on the air.

As the Internet evolved, that began to change. One reason it changed is that citizen journalism began to flourish—as it did in New Orleans—challenging the dominance of traditional media in the process of disseminating news. Anyone, it seemed, could become a journalist or even a publisher.

Recognizing that the media landscape had changed, traditional publishers began to embrace blogs, the instant messaging of news alerts and even citizen journalism itself. Those developments led editors and publishers of traditional media to understand that the Web is an entirely new medium that demands a fresh approach, one that takes advantage of the Internet's ability to deliver links to other sites, to link people with two-way communication and, with high-speed connections, to provide not only text, photos and graphics but also audio and video on demand.

When the Web first came along, no one knew how to make money with it, an essential ingredient in a country in which the media are not state-supported. All that has changed. In 2007, online advertising revenue exceeded $21.2 billion, a 26 percent increase from the previous year. No other medium was experiencing revenue growth of that magnitude. And *Folio:*, the trade publication of the magazine industry, reported that some publications were now using online revenue to make up for lost print revenue, effectively underwriting their older siblings. Clearly, Web businesses based on news are here to stay, and that requires us to study the best ways of producing both advertising and news for them.

Just as writing for television evolved from its early iterations, so too is writing for the Web evolving. Most now recognize that writing for the Web is different from writing for television or newspapers. The Web is clearly a unique medium that requires a new approach, but that approach is still evolving as journalists learn new ways to communicate online. Let's take a look at the conventional wisdom on writing for the Web as we know it today.

HOW TO WRITE FOR THE WEB

Even if you plan to work at a newspaper, magazine, or radio or television station, you will need to know how to write for online media. At a growing number of newspapers, even veteran journalists are being asked to turn in two versions of their stories, one for the newspaper and one for the paper's Web site. At the St. Paul *Pioneer Press*, all print reporters must file a Web story within 30 minutes after witnessing an event or learning about the news. In the old days, newspapers would print several editions a day and would occasionally come out with an "extra." Today cyberspace has turned newspapers into 24-hour, competitive news machines, and "print reporters" are rapidly becoming a disappearing species.

Of course, online writing isn't just about writing. It's about determining the best way to tell a story and then using all media forms — text, audio, video and graphics — to deliver it. That requires at least a basic understanding of audio and video production and the use of information graphics. Writing, though, is at the heart of all media, including the Web.

Good online writing has many of the characteristics of other forms of effective writing. Much of what you have read so far about newswriting applies to online journalism; what you've learned about news gathering and news reporting for print, radio or television applies here. The demand for accurate, simple, clear and concise writing is the same for all the media.

Nevertheless, the online journalist must be aware of some fundamental differences between online and traditional media. These distinctions increasingly result in stories that look quite different from those published on paper or broadcast. One sure way to drive away online readers is to give them **shovelware** — stories as they appeared in print. Hundreds of publications continue to do that, but it's now clear that most online readers refuse to be buried in the dirt created by shovelware — unless they have a real need for in-depth information.

To be sure, there are readers who want the stories as they appear in the newspaper, not rewritten in some other form. They want those stories because they want to know what other readers are seeing. Readers of *The New York Times'* online edition, who are scattered around the world, undoubtedly want to see what the print readers have read. *The Times* and many other newspapers now produce downloadable versions that look exactly like the newspaper edition. There's a market for that. But most readers want stories tailored to take advantage of the Web's considerable power. They want links, and they want graphics, audio and even video to accompany the text.

To write effectively for the Web, you need to learn a unique way of thinking about writing. Let's begin with these three principles:

Newspapers own seven of the top 22 national news and information Web sites and provide a strong draw for younger audiences, according to the Newspaper Association of America.

1. The reader rules.
2. The writing is nonlinear.
3. Structure is everything.

The Reader Rules

"Hypertext and hypermedia have the following characteristics:

- *They present ideas nonsequentially.*
- *They follow the thought process.*
- *They allow users to choose individual pathways through the information.*
- *They allow information to transcend individual documents.*
- *They link text with pictures, audio, and video."*

— *Andrew Bonime and Ken C. Pohlmann,* Writing for New Media

Unlike print journalists writing for newspapers and magazines, where narrative works fine, journalists writing for online sites should keep no secrets from readers; they should not try to withhold information until later in the story. In short, when writing online, you should surrender to readers' control of the story's sequence. Online, authors lose their "position of central authority," writes David Weinberger, author and editor of the *Journal of the Hyperlinked Organization*, a newsletter that considers the Web's effect on how business works. Every reader is different; every reader has different needs. Every reader, therefore, not only will select what to read but also will choose a path that best meets those needs.

Also, readers can come from anywhere in the world, not just from a local audience. And because of the enormous archival capability of the Internet, readers can come in at any time. As Professor Phill Brooks of the Missouri School of Journalism tells his students, "Today becomes yesterday tomorrow." In other words, he says, you are writing history to an international audience.

You should think of different ways to present different information for different people at different times. Unlike newspapers and magazines, which must decide how long to make a story, online media should layer information in such a way that readers can choose the amount they need on each visit to the site.

You have learned to write an inverted-pyramid story. This much of the traditional news story remains the same. The headline and lead in an online story become even more important because the lead may be all that appears on the screen. Readers may have to click to get more of the story, so if the headline and lead are not compelling, the story probably will not be read. The lead must nail the "what" or the "so what?" to get the full attention of the reader. In that respect, there's a striking similarity to the anchor's introduction to a television news story.

The lead is also important because for most search engines, the lead will be the only information provided as a link to the story. You would be wise to include keywords such as "Maine" and "governor" in the lead about a story concerning the Maine governor. See Figure 13.2 for an example of a site using searchable terms.

Sometimes the lead appears like an extended headline, followed by two or three statements that also read as headlines. After the lead, little is the same as in the traditional news story. Readers often can click on the hyperlinked headlines to read the full version of the story on another page within the Web site.

Figure 13.2
The Seattle Times (**http://seattletimes.nwsource.com**) used the inverted pyramid in its story on the arrest of Illinois Gov. Rod Blagojevich on federal corruption charges involving the "selling" of Barack Obama's newly vacated Senate seat. Note the use of searchable keywords like "Illinois," "governor" and "Gov." in the headline and lead, as well as clickable links to related stories in a separate box.

As a result, the reader interacts actively, not passively, with the story. Steve Outing writes on Poynter Online:

> If I gave you an assignment to look at the content of 100 news Web sites, you'd probably find that 95 percent of them don't ever go beyond routine presentation of text, images, and the occasional audio or video clip. It's still the rare few that craft content in such ways that go beyond what would be possible in print or broadcast. Rare is the story that uses online interactive techniques that help the user understand the story best by letting him or her interact with and manipulate elements of the story — to experience it, not just read about it.

Outing writes that good Internet writing says to the reader, "Don't read — do!" It does this because it plays to the essential nature of the Internet: It is interactive.

The Writing Is Nonlinear

Because most people don't think linearly, writing online is more in line with the way people think. It's even more in line with the way today's readers read. Break the story into short, digestible pieces. Rather than stringing together a long story and trying to get readers to read the whole thing in the order in which you presented it, keep in mind that many readers don't want to read everything you have to tell them. You must give them choices and let them decide what to read and in what order.

Stories that require multiple continuous screens turn off many readers immediately. Many readers hate to scroll on screen. Some exit even before they get to the bottom of the screen. Few will take the time to read a lot of text in one clump. Note, of course, that this is not true of highly motivated readers who crave your information. At times you may want to send them to reliable databases, where they can read the whole story and get all the facts—preferably, of course, within your own site.

Structure Is Everything

Some who write online forget entirely about structure, and that's a mistake. Even though an online story ideally takes an entirely different structure than a print story, it still must be organized in a logical, coherent way. Many experts argue that the online writer should present information in layers. Remember: No two readers are alike. You may present the same information with different degrees of detail and support. The first layer is information that is immediately available to readers—no action or effort is demanded. A second layer, a more substantial read, could be reachable easily by moving the cursor or by scrolling. A third layer may require readers to click on a link that opens up still more information, perhaps audio, video or a source document.

The reality is that stories are almost never rewritten for the Web once written for print or television. So, while sophisticated layering of the story in shorter snippets may be ideal, time constraints often dictate that the story run much as it was written for print. Then, audio, video and graphics are added to make the story more appealing for an online audience. Web producers are getting more and more sophisticated as they learn how to do that.

A great example appeared in *The New York Times* as it covered the debt crisis in the U.S. following the 2008 economic collapse. (See Figure 13.3.) Graphics and photos were used to lead readers into the text of the series "The Debt Trap," and audio and video complemented the piece about the ease with which people can amass huge sums of personal debt. You can read the series here: www.nytimes .com/interactive/2008/07/20/business/20debt-trap.html.

Similarly, "The Girl in the Window" by writer Lane DeGregory and photographer Melissa Lyttle, on the *St. Petersburg Times* site, used a marvelous collection of multimedia objects to tell the story of a young girl left to fend for herself without family: www.tampabay.com/ specials/2008/reports/danielle.

Figure 13.3
A rotating set of large photos on the opening page of *The New York Times'* special series on debt helps bring readers into the text (**http://nytimes.com**).

Multimedia stories like these can keep a reader hooked for extended periods of time. They can be much more effective than print stories or even television.

So, while relatively few Web sites write specifically for the Web, when doing so you should consider taking a different approach. When you write for print, you need to be concerned with continuity, with themes, with working in all aspects of the story while keeping the writing clear and coherent. When you write online, you need to worry not about the structure or flow of the whole piece but rather about the relationships of the levels and parts. You need to help readers navigate from place to place to get the information they want. That means you must have clear entrances and exits.

Sometimes you have to give clear directions. For example, if you include a hyperlink in your story, more readers will "click here" if you tell them to do so than if you don't. Sometimes you may take readers down one path that branches into several others. Some call this technique "threading." The story of a plane crash can lead to various threads: the airline and its record of crashes, the plane itself and the record of that type of plane, the place of the accident, the people involved and so forth.

You need not be concerned about repetition. Remember, readers choose what parts to read. Besides, a certain amount of repetition or of stating things in different ways, perhaps visually, increases retention. Different readers, online or elsewhere, process information differently.

GUIDELINES FOR WRITING ONLINE

Readers online are surfers or scanners, much more so than readers of print, perhaps because it takes 25 percent longer to read online than it does in print. Researchers Jakob Nielsen and John Morkes found that 79 percent of those they tested scanned a new page they came across; only 16 percent read the copy word for word. You can find their study at **www.useit.com/alertbox/9710a.html**.

Online expert Shel Holtz says you want readers to dive, not to surf. Surfing is what frustrated readers do. Here are 10 ways to make divers of surfers—or at least to hold their attention long enough to get your message across.

Think Immediacy

Although you must first make sure what you write is accurate, the Internet can deliver news when it is brand new. Writing online is like writing for the wire services. Everyone on the Internet now consumes information the way a wire-service subscriber does. Keeping readers with you means keeping readers up-to-the-minute. You must update breaking stories quickly and add depth whenever it is available.

But just because you can easily correct your mistakes, that does not mean you are allowed to make them. Reporter David Broder of

Figure 13.4
South Florida's news site, SunSentinel.com, delivers links to new, breaking stories on its home page.

The Washington Post warned at an annual national roundtable sponsored by the Scripps Howard Foundation that posting news too quickly and without verification could sacrifice quality and damage credibility.

While attempting to exercise such care, newspapers are now using their Web sites to break news. For example, when the *Financial Times* learned that Iranian security forces held a son of Osama bin Laden, it reported that news on its Web site on Saturday because it doesn't publish on Sunday. The Ft. Lauderdale, Fla., *Sun Sentinel* partners with radio and television, and it may break a story in any of those media, occasionally even scooping itself. Time usually is the deciding factor. (See Figure 13.4.)

Save Readers' Time

What most readers do not have is time. Whatever you can do to save readers' time is worthwhile. It's been said by various people in different ways since the philosopher Blaise Pascal first said it: "Excuse me for this long letter; I don't have time to write a short one." For many stories, if not most, perhaps your chief concern should be this: Have I presented this information in such a way as to cost readers the least amount of time?

The best way to save readers' time is to be clear. Choose the simple word; vary the length of sentences but keep them short; write short paragraphs. Help readers. Emphasize key words by highlighting them or by putting them in color.

Another reason to write simply, using simple words and simple sentences, is to enable the auto-translation programs used by some search engines to translate a page. The simpler the words and sentences, the more likely a foreign-language translation of the story will be accurate and understandable.

Provide Information That's Quick and Easy to Get

The overall organization of your story must say to the reader that getting this information is going to be quick and easy. Online readers have zero tolerance for confusion and no time at all to be led astray. It's too easy to click on something else.

Don't get carried away by your own eloquence. Be guided by what your readers want or need to know. Make it easy for them. Write short paragraphs with one idea per paragraph.

On the Job

An Online Career

Troy Wolverton says that when he was studying journalism in graduate school, he "quickly fell in love with the Internet." He took every course available in new media, as well as newspaper reporting, basic photojournalism and broadcast journalism. He freelanced for *The New York Times* Web site and taught a class in Internet basics. He left graduate school to take a job at the *San Jose Mercury News* as an online editor.

After two years, he began working as a reporter for CNET News.com, a technology-news Web site. There he covered e-commerce companies such as Amazon, online auctioneer eBay and online brokerage E-Trade. Wolverton is now on his third online job, as a reporter at TheStreet.com, where he covers the retail industry both online and off.

"I was trying to figure out where I wanted to go when I left CNET," he says. "Many online reporters I know—the few of us that are left—have a desire to get back to print. In fact that's the route several of my former News.com colleagues have taken.

"I probably wouldn't turn down *The New York Times* if they came calling, but I really enjoy working online. I love the immediacy of the medium. By the time a newspaper is delivered to a reader's door, many of the stories in it have been online for hours.

"Writing for an online publication brings you closer to your readers. When I wrote for a newspaper, I felt as if my stories were floating out into the ether. I had no idea whether people were reading them. I know how much people are reading my News.com articles by how many e-mail responses I receive."

Think Both Verbally and Visually

In the past, writers for print thought little about how their stories were going to appear. Their job was to write the story—period. The designer's job was to make the story fit on the page in some meaningful way. Writers did not worry about headlines, subheads, summary quotes, photos, illustrations or anything else. The story was king.

Television newswriters know that they must write to the pictures. Good television has good video; a visual medium tries to show rather than to tell. Words complement pictures; they say what the pictures do not. Many times, of course, the writer does not make the pictures and is not responsible for getting them. But the writer still must consider the best way to tell the story; sometimes visuals convey information as no amount of text could possibly do.

As an online journalist, you may or may not have to do it all yourself, but you definitely must *think* both verbally and visually. From the outset, you must be concerned about the most effective and efficient way for the information to appear on the screen. You have to think not only about the organization of the page but also about ways to use graphics, to be interactive and to use online tools.

No one doubts that photos and graphics grab readers' attention. That's why you see more icons and infographics in magazines and newspapers, and that's why you must think, perhaps with the help of graphic designers, of ways to use graphic elements online.

Then there is the matter of video, the use of which is growing rapidly on Web sites around the world. A great example may be found at Newsy.com, which compares the coverage of news from various traditional media outlets.

In short, if you are writing online, you have to be much more than a wordsmith. You must have a pocketful of other skills. Writing online demands a great deal of collaboration and not just with other writers. Working closely with individuals more expert than you in design, photography and videography is crucial from the outset. All those elements must work together, and no one does it better than variety.com, shown in Figure 13.5.

Cut Copy in Half

You probably don't have to be told that online writing must be concise. But you do need to be told to cut your copy in half. Years ago, writing expert William Zinsser recommended that writers take their eight pages and cut them to four. Then comes the difficult part, he wrote—cutting them to three. And that was for print!

Most online readers simply will not read long stories. Even veteran computer users find reading text on a screen somewhat difficult, even

Mark Deuze and Christina Dimoudi of the Amsterdam School of Communications Research conclude from their study that online journalism is really a fourth kind of journalism after print, radio and television. Its main characteristic is "empowering audiences as active participants in the daily news." Online journalists have "an interactive relationship with their audience" and a "strong element of audience orientation" and are "more aware of their publics and service function in society than their colleagues elsewhere."

Figure 13.5
To a greater extent than most sites, variety.com uses hyperlinks throughout its stories. The hyperlinks lead readers to related stories, entertainer profiles and industry information.

unpleasant, says Jakob Nielsen. Perhaps this will change when larger, high-resolution screens become less expensive and thus more common.

Studies contradict one another about people's aversion to scrolling. In the not-so-distant past, some experts advised getting the whole story on one screen. Because some screens are small, they advised not writing more than 20 lines of text. Now, because of the proliferation of larger and less-irritating screens, some readers are finding it easier and less frustrating to scroll for more information. As in writing for radio and television, there's little room online to be cute or even literary. Be crisp and clear.

Use Lots of Lists and Bullets

Often you can cut copy by putting information into lists. Whenever you can make a list, do so. Lists get more attention and allow for better comprehension and more retention than ordinary sentences and paragraphs. Bulleted or numbered lists are scannable. Readers can grasp them immediately. Think of information on the Web as a database. That's how people use their computers, and that's how they use the Web.

Nielsen tested five versions of the same information for usability. Look first at the longest version, what he calls "promotional writing," his control condition:

> Nebraska is filled with internationally recognized attractions that draw large crowds of people every year, without fail. In a recent year, some of the most popular places were Fort Robinson State Park (355,000 visitors), Scotts Bluff National Monument (132,126 visitors), Arbor Lodge State Historical Park & Museum (100,000), *Carhenge* (85,598), Stuhr Museum of the Prairie Pioneer (60,002), and Buffalo Bill Ranch State Historical Park (28,446).

Now look at this same material in list form:

> In a recent year, six of the most-visited places in Nebraska were:
> - Fort Robinson State Park.
> - Scotts Bluff National Monument.
> - Arbor Lodge State Historical Park & Museum.
> - *Carhenge*.
> - Stuhr Museum of the Prairie Pioneer.
> - Buffalo Bill Ranch State Historical Park.

The list version of the information scored a 124 percent usability improvement over the first version.

Write in Chunks

When you can't put material into lists, you can still organize it into chunks of information. Put information into sidebars or boxes. Readers will read more, not less, if you break up the information into small bites. Research has shown that putting some information in a sidebar can result in better comprehension of the subject. But the main objective is to write for diverse readers who want to get only the information they want in the order in which they want to receive it.

Think of your story as having parts. When writing a story for a newspaper, you need to think of ways to join the various parts of the story. You also should craft transitions carefully, and you may even add subheads. When writing a story online, instead of writing subheads, make each segment of the story a separate story. Be sure that each part can stand on its own and be comprehensible and make your point. Again, remember the importance of a strong lead in the best inverted-pyramid form.

Use Hyperlinks

To understand the Web, think of a spiderweb. The Web, says David Weinberger, is a place of connection; it is a connective place; it is a

"We have derived three main content-oriented conclusions from our four years of Web usability studies:

- *Users do not read on the Web; instead they scan the pages, trying to pick out a few sentences or even parts of sentences to get the information they want.*
- *Users do not like long, scrolling pages; they prefer the text to be short and to the point.*
- *Users detest anything that seems like marketing fluff or overly hyped language ('marketese') and prefer factual information."*

—John Morkes and Jakob Nielsen, "Concise, Scannable, and Objective: How to Write for the Web," useit.com, 1997

The 3-2-2-1 Format

After spending 25 years as a professional newsman, the last four of those as a general manager, Associate Professor Clyde Bentley now teaches classes in online journalism and other courses at the University of Missouri. In one class, students take stories from the newspaper and rewrite them for the Web. Bentley calls the students online "producers" rather than reporters.

"I was surprised at the resistance my students had to changing the copy of reporters," Bentley says. "They preferred the 'shovelware' concept so they would not tamper with the prose of their friends."

In frustration, he instituted what he called a "3-2-2-1" format. "It was a way to force my young journalists to take on a new process."

Here's what the numbers mean:

3 Subheads
By inserting three subheads, the producers "chunk" the story into four pieces. "This is easier to read than one long, scrollable piece of text," Bentley says. The subdivisions can be as simple as "who, what, when. . . ."

2 External Links
These are directions to further information posted outside the story (to the left of the text on the *Columbia Missourian* site, often at the bottom on other sites). "For instance, in a story about the local dog pound, we might have external links to the ASPCA and the American Kennel Club."

2 Internal Links
These are explanatory links tied to text within the story. "In the pound story," Bentley explains, "the word 'Doberman' might be a link that takes one to a breeder's site that explains the Doberman pinscher."

1 Piece of Art Not Available in the Print Edition
Print publications limit art primarily because of space limitations. There are no such limits on the Web. "If a photographer shoots 20 shots, we can run more than one," Bentley says. "More commonly, however, the producers insert mug shots of people mentioned in the story. There is no reason not to run mugs of everyone who is mentioned."

place where we go to connect. Users of the Internet feel connected. If you want them to read your copy and come back for more, you must satisfy and enhance that sense of being connected.

Being connected means being interactive. Web users want to be actively involved in what they are reading. They are not passive observers. Like video-game players, they want to be in control of where they are going and how they get there. Your copy must be interactive both internally and externally. See Figure 13.6 for an example.

Figure 13.6
MercuryNews.com offers a wide range of hyperlinks, organized by topic. It provides direct article links with descriptive captions, as well as links to various other subjects of interest.

Internal Connections

The most challenging and necessary aspect of online writing is making the copy interactive. You begin that process by streamlining your copy — not including everything. Create **hyperlinks**, and allow readers to click on information elsewhere on your site.

One of the most perplexing problems writers face is deciding when to include the definition of a word. Will you insult some readers by including the definition? Will you leave others behind if you do not define the term? A similar problem is whether to tell who a person is. Many readers may wonder how stupid you think they are for telling them that actor Fred Thompson is a former Republican senator from Tennessee. Other readers may need or want that information.

The online writer can simply make the word or name a hot spot or a link and hyperlink it to a different "page." Readers need only click on the word to find its meaning or read more about it. No longer do writers have to write, "For more information, see. . . ." Academic writers use footnotes. Hypertext and hypermedia, linking readers to audio, video and pictures, are much more convenient.

Among other rules for writing online, Ellen Schindler, a senior account executive at Berry Associates, recommends the following:

- Double-space between paragraphs. Leave two spaces after periods.
- Avoid serif type. Serifs get lost on the screen.
- Make the text black. It's easier to read.
- Simple is best.

Writing concisely has never been easier. Rather than defining words, going into long explanations, giving examples or elaborating on the story itself, you can stick to the essentials and make the rest of the story available to readers who need or want it. A story about a homicide can link to a map of where the crime took place, to a chart showing the numbers of homicides this year as compared with last year, to a piece about friends of the victim, to information about violent crimes nationally, and so forth.

Remember, too, that unlike the newspaper where you may be short of space, and unlike radio and television where you may be short of time, online you have unlimited space and time to run photos and aspects of stories that could be of real interest to some readers. Sports fans, for example, would probably enjoy seeing a whole gallery of shots from Saturday's championship game. They would read interviews from all of the stars of the victory — or of the defeat.

External Connections

Of course, you can do much more. You can hyperlink to different Web sites. Academic writers include bibliographies. Print journalists often identify sources in their stories. Other writers simply say to readers: That's all I know about the subject, I'm not going to tell you where I obtained my information, and I'm not telling you where you can find more information. Hypertext and hypermedia have changed all that. Not only can you hyperlink online, but readers expect you to do so.

Obviously, you are not expected to draw readers away from your site to a competitor, especially on a breaking story. Nevertheless, readers will come to rely on your site to help them find more information about subjects that interest them greatly.

To find appropriate external hyperlinks, you need to know how to use search engines like Yahoo (**www.yahoo.com**) and Google (**www.google.com**).

Give Readers a Chance to Talk Back

A big part of being interactive is allowing readers to talk back. The Internet has leveled the playing field. Everyone is an owner or a publisher. Everyone feels the right and often the need to write back — if not to the writer of the piece, then to other readers in chat rooms or blogs. The wonderful thing about allowing readers to talk back is that they do. When they do, they will revisit the site again and again. Online readers want to be part of the process. Readers love it when newspapers like *The Miami Herald* include the reporter's e-mail address in the byline, and many of them respond.

A word of caution: Including e-mail addresses on the Web leaves you open to operations that use a program called an e-mail "syphon" that scans Web site pages for e-mail addresses that are then used for spam. Depending on your mail-server provider's anti-spamming capabilities, putting your e-mail address in a news story or magazine article can subject you to a deluge of spam. Rather than revealing your permanent personal address, one alternative is to use an address provided by your employer solely for this purpose.

Never has it been easier to find out what is on the minds of your readers. Print and broadcast have always been mainly one-way communication. Now, not only can you get opinions easily and quickly, but you can incorporate them into your story or at least hyperlink to them. Letters to the editor have always been among the best-read sections in newspapers and magazines. (See Figure 13.7.) Many readers, especially those reading online, not only want to express their own opinions but love to read the opinions of others. Be sure, however, to use the same strict standards for publishing others' remarks on your Web site that

Figure 13.7
Blogs allow journalists, pundits and ordinary citizens to post their thoughts online as often as they like. On his blog, "Talking Points Memo" (**www.talkingpointsmemo.com**), journalist Joshua Micah Marshall comments on politics, culture and foreign affairs throughout the day.

you use for publishing in your newspaper or magazine. Even e-mail polls can be and have been flooded by advocacy groups. Reporting their results can be meaningless and misleading and certainly unprofessional unless they are monitored carefully.

Don't Forget the Human Touch

Veteran Washington correspondent Helen Thomas told a convention of newspaper interactive editors: "I do hope the human touch remains in the robotic scheme of things. Human beings still count."

Remember, people make the news. Facts are just facts unless you relate them to people.

WRITING WITH SEARCH ENGINES IN MIND

It's almost impossible to overemphasize one major consideration in writing for online media: If your online story cannot be found, it won't be read. That's why editors of Web sites place great emphasis on *search-engine optimization*, the process of making sure your story will be found when someone searches for its topic on sites such as Google or Yahoo. Generally, the better job you do getting key terms into the lead, the more likely your story will appear near the top of the search results for that topic.

Newspapers and magazines are notorious for writing baseball stories that never mention the word "baseball" and hockey stories that never use the word "hockey." That's OK if the user searches for the team name, such as Atlanta Braves. She'll find your story even if the word "baseball" is not included. But what if the user searches for "baseball"? Your story will not be found unless it contains metadata—that is, tagging information—that includes that search term. Understanding that is the key to making sure that all possible search terms appear either in the metadata accompanying the story or in the story itself.

Many Web sites have protocols for ensuring that the proper terms are used, and several companies now offer services that ensure content is maximized for search engines. That can be a wise investment for the site looking to increase readership.

LEGAL AND ETHICAL CONCERNS

Online journalists have the same legal and ethical concerns as other journalists (see Chapters 14 and 15). Libel is still libel, and plagiarism is still plagiarism. Just because you are not "in print" doesn't mean you can destroy someone's reputation or distort the truth. You also must always be aware that what is on the Internet is not yours, even though the very design of it allows you to download words and images easily. If you use someone else's words, put quotation marks around them and cite the source.

Although the Internet makes it easier to find and steal someone else's work, it also makes it easier to get caught doing so. In several cases Web readers of local columnists or reviewers have turned in a writer for plagiarism.

Plagiarism is not the only danger. Some areas of ethics are even more difficult for online journalists to solve.

Privacy

There are Web sites that have files on nearly everyone. Some allow you to see what anyone has ever posted in a chat room. What may journalists use? Most everyone agrees that private e-mail is off-limits. But what about material sent to corporate intranets?

Advertising

Newspapers and magazines generally try to label advertising as advertising, and they have rules that require ads to use typefaces different from those the publication uses for news and other articles. There also are rules about the placement of ads. Online ads regularly break up the copy of news stories or pop up over news stories. There is no separation of ads from editorial content and no attempt to make any separation.

Why don't the rules that apply to print apply online? They should. Note what the code of the American Society of Magazine Editors says:

> The same ASME principles that mandate distinct treatment of editorial content, advertisements, and special advertisements, and special advertising sections ("advertorials") in print publications also apply to online editorial projects bearing the names of print magazines or offering themselves as electronic magazines. The dynamic technology of electronic pages and hypertext links creates a high potential for reader confusion. Permitting such confusion betrays reader trust and undermines the credibility not only of the offending online publication or editorial product, but also of the publisher itself. It is therefore the responsibility of each online publication to make clear to its readers which online content is editorial and which is advertising, and to prevent any juxtaposition that gives the impression that editorial material was created for — or influenced by — advertisers.

The ASME code then goes on to spell out 10 specific ways to carry out these general guidelines.

The code of the American Society of Business Press Editors says simply: "On all such papers, editors should ensure that a clear distinction is made between advertising and editorial content. This may involve typefaces, layout/design, labeling and juxtaposition of the editorial materials and the advertisement." The ASBPE code adds this important sentence: "Editors should directly supervise and control all links that appear with the editorial portion of the site."

Manipulating Photos

The print media have not dealt well with the problem of identifying manipulated photos either. *New York Times* photographer Fred Ritchin proposed using an icon to flag a digitally altered photo. But how will readers know how much it has been altered? Will readers trust what they see?

Concealing Your Identity

It's very easy to conceal your identity as a reporter on the Web. At times you may be doing undercover investigative reporting, but usually the time to reveal yourself as a reporter is at the outset of your questioning people online, not after you have gotten to a certain point in your story.

Corrections

Some online news sites act as if they never make mistakes. They simply post new stories with updated information. Surely you owe it to readers to tell them that the story has changed or has been updated with new information and how that was done. Such notice of correction or updating will not be done unless the news site has a clear policy requiring it.

Forbes.com erroneously quoted Disney Chairman Michael Eisner as saying he didn't think his company's network, ABC, would be operating "in four to five years." In the update to the story, the changed headline read, "Clarification: Eisner Discusses the ABC Brand and Other Brands." In addition to correcting the story, Forbes.com put asterisks next to the changed sentences and included explanations at the bottom of the story, like this one: "The original version of this story incorrectly stated that Eisner did not see the third-ranked network being around in four to five years." In his column in *The Washington Post*, Howard Kurtz reported that Forbes.com editor Paul Maidment said his reporter had "extrapolated" without the "broader context."

Hyperlinks to External Sites

Is raw data journalism? How much and how often may you use raw data, and with what warnings or interpretations? There's little doubt that readers appreciate links to source data so they can make judgments for themselves. At the same time, good Web sites help readers navigate that information. Journalists are still trying to find the right balance between the two.

TOMORROW'S READERS

Print has been around for centuries, and we are still figuring out ways to use it effectively. In contrast, writing online is in its infancy. Like all good writers, online journalists must be students of writing. Both writers and readers are still learning the most effective uses of the newest medium, which is a sum of all media that is greater than its parts. The new media are more about showing than telling, about the audience experiencing rather than witnessing, about the audience participating actively rather than passively, about the audience doing rather than merely reading. Perhaps never have writers been more challenged.

Suggested Readings

Craig, Richard. *Online Journalism: Reporting, Writing, and Editing for New Media*. Stamford, Conn.: Wadsworth-Thomson Learning, 2005. A comprehensive source of information about writing for the Web.

McAdams, Mindy. *Flash Journalism: How to Create Multimedia News Packages*. Burlington, Mass.: Folio Press, 2005. Flash is a key player in delivering video for the Web, and this book shows users how to incorporate it.

Rosales, Rey. *The Elements of Online Journalism*. Lincoln, Neb.: iUniverse, 2006. A good primer on writing for the Web.

Suggested Web Sites

www.commercialappeal.com Like many daily newspapers, *The (Memphis, Tenn.) Commercial Appeal*'s online edition includes most of the stories from its print edition, along with additional online-only posts.

http://espn.go.com One of the best and most extensive Internet sites for sports fans, ESPN.com was an early leader in the use of audio and video.

www.mercurynews.com This Web site, one of the first comprehensive sites for local news, includes area news courtesy of the *San Jose Mercury News*.

www.msnbc.msn.com This companion site to the cable news channel offers a wealth of news resources. Its opinions section includes, among other things, links to top stories; stories from Slate.com, another Microsoft Web site; and opinion pieces and blogs—online journals written by pundits and journalists.

www.newsy.com This innovative, video-heavy site compares how various media around the world covered major stories.

www.useit.com This is expert Jakob Nielsen's site. You won't find anyone more knowledgeable and up-to-date on the research in the field of online writing than Nielsen.

Exercises

1. Choose a major national story from a recent news-paper or newsmagazine. Then visit two newspaper Web sites, and compare their treatment of the story. Write a 300-word critique of the writing techniques that the Web sites used.

2. Visit your local newspaper or television station, and interview individuals who report the news online. Find out how they were trained and what major challenges they face.

3. Your professor will assign you a newspaper story. Rewrite it for online use, and indicate any hyper-links that you might include.

4. Visit five newspaper or magazine Web sites. Then pick the one that does the best job of using online writing techniques, and write a 200-word report on your findings.

5. Find a Web site that does a good job of linking read-ers to original source material. Evaluate the use of that technique, and explain why the technique works in this case.

14 Law

"The government's power to censor the press was abolished so the press would remain forever free to censure the government."

— *Hugo Black, Supreme Court justice*

T he First Amendment to the U.S. Constitution states:

Congress shall make no law respecting an establishment of religion, or prohibiting the free exercise thereof; or abridging the freedom of speech, or of the press; or the right of the people peaceably to assemble, and to petition the Government for a redress of grievances.

Read that again: "Congress shall make no law . . . abridging the freedom of . . . the press." No other business in the United States enjoys that specific constitutional protection, unless you count religion as a business.

Why should there be such protection for the press? The Supreme Court gave an eloquent answer to this question in a 1957 obscenity decision. The press is protected, the Court ruled, to ensure the "unfettered interchange of ideas for bringing about the political and social changes desired by the people." The free flow of ideas is necessary in a democracy because people who govern themselves need to know about their government and those who run it, as well as about the social and economic institutions that greatly affect their day-to-day lives. Most people get that information through newspapers, the Internet, radio and television.

In 1966 Congress passed the **Freedom of Information Act** to assist anyone in finding out what is happening in federal agencies. This act, amended in 1996 by the Electronic Freedom of Information Act to improve access to computerized government records and again on New Year's Eve 2007 to improve the process, makes it easier for you to learn about government business. All 50 states have similar **open-records laws**. The federal government and all the states also have **open-meetings laws** requiring that the public's business be conducted in public. However, all of these access laws contain exemptions that keep some meetings private.

The First Amendment and laws on access to information demonstrate America's basic concern for citizen access to the information needed for the "unfettered interchange of ideas." Nevertheless, there are laws that reduce the scope of freedom of the press.

LIBEL

Traditionally, most of the laws limiting the absolute freedom of the press have dealt with libel, the damage to a person's reputation caused by making the person an object of hatred, contempt or ridicule in the eyes of a substantial and respectable group. These laws result from the desire of legislatures and courts to help individuals protect their reputations. Their importance was explained by U.S. Supreme Court Justice Potter Stewart in a libel case (parentheses added):

The right of a man (or woman) to the protection of his (or her) own reputation from unjustified invasion and wrongful hurt reflects no more
than our basic concept of the essential dignity and worth of every human
being—a concept at the root of any decent system of ordered liberty.

Protection for reputations dates back centuries. In 17th-century
England, individuals were imprisoned and even disfigured for making
libelous statements. One objective was to prevent criticism of the government. Another was to maintain the peace by avoiding duels. Duels
are rare today, and government is freely criticized, but the desire to
protect an individual's reputation is just as strong.

A case concerning an Israeli general is helpful in understanding
libel. The extensively covered trial was held in the winter of 1984–
1985 in the federal courthouse in Manhattan. The case was based on a
1983 *Time* magazine cover story, "Verdict on the Massacre," about
Israel's 1982 judicial inquiry into the massacre of several hundred civil-
ians in two Palestinian refugee camps in Lebanon.

The *Time* article suggested that Ariel Sharon, then Israel's defense
minister and later its prime minister, had cooperated with the Leba-
nese militia that had carried out the massacre. Sharon sued *Time*. His
attorneys knew they would have to show that their client had suffered
hatred, contempt or ridicule because these statements were serious
attacks on their client's reputation and not just unpleasant comments.

The jury's decision was in three parts. The first part of the verdict
was in answer to this question: Was the paragraph concerning Sharon
defamatory? The jury said it was. This meant the *Time* article had damaged Sharon's reputation and had brought him into hatred, contempt
or ridicule.

The second question for the jury was this: Was the paragraph concerning Sharon false? Again the jury answered affirmatively. If the
answer had been no, the case would have ended there. Truth is a complete defense for libel.

The third question for the jury was this: Was the paragraph published with "actual malice"—with knowledge that it was false or with
reckless disregard for whether it was false ("serious doubt" that it was
true)? The jury answered no. Thus the trial ended in favor of *Time* magazine, despite the jury's ruling that the article was defamatory.

Courts use four categories to help jurors like those in the Sharon
case decide if someone's reputation has been damaged because he or
she has been brought into hatred, contempt or ridicule:

1. *Accusing someone of a crime.* This may have been the basis in the Sharon
   case.
2. *Damaging a person in his or her public office, profession or occupation.*
   Although the statements by *Time* against Sharon did not accuse him
   of crimes, they did damage him in his profession as a military man.

*"Journalists don't believe
. . . the Freedom of Information Act was created
to be turned on us as an
excuse to hide information."*
—*Sarah Overstreet,*
columnist

3. *Accusing a person of serious immorality.* The example lawyers often use is accusing a woman of being unchaste. Many states have statutes that make an accusation of unchastity a cause of action in a libel suit.
4. *Accusing someone of having a loathsome (contagious) disease.* This category was fading as an area of defamation; however, the AIDS epidemic helped it reappear.

This does not mean you can never say a person committed a crime, was unethical in business, was adulterous or had a loathsome disease. It does mean you must be certain that what you write is true.

Libel Suit Defenses

There are three traditional defenses against libel: truth, privilege, and fair comment and criticism. Two other constitutional defenses—the actual malice and negligence tests—also help libel defendants.

Truth

Truth is the best defense against libel. In libel cases involving matters of public concern, the burden of proof is on the plaintiff. This placement of the burden, however, does not change the reporter's responsibility to seek the truth in every possible way.

You cannot be certain, for example, whether a person charged with arson actually started the fire. Who told you Joe Jones started the fire? The first source to check is the police or fire report. If a police officer or fire marshal says that Jones started a fire, you can report not that Jones did it but that he has been *accused* of doing it. Unless you have information you would be willing to present in court, you should go no further. Be sure to report no more than what you know is true.

When a newspaper in Oklahoma reported that a wrestling coach had been accused of requiring a sixth-grader, who wanted to rejoin the team, to submit to a whipping by his fellow students while crawling naked through the legs of team members, the coach sued. He claimed damage to his reputation.

In cases like this, the reporter has to be certain not just that one or more participants told of the incident but also that their statements were true. In court, some participants might testify to an occurrence; others might testify the incident never took place. A jury would have to decide on the credibility of the participants.

Although you must always strive for absolute truth in all of your stories, the courts will settle for what is known as **substantial truth** in most cases. This means that you must be able to prove the essential elements of all you write.

On the Job

The Keys to Avoiding Libel

Ken Paulson earned a law degree after graduating from journalism school. He then practiced journalism for 18 years. After serving as senior vice president of the Freedom Forum in Arlington, Va., and executive director of The First Amendment Center at Vanderbilt University, he returned to the news room as editor of *USA Today*. Now he has moved again, to head the Newseum in Washington, D.C.

"Having a law degree has been helpful as a journalist," he says, "but the key to avoiding libel suits really boils down to a few fundamentals."

The keys to avoiding a libel suit are rooted in professionalism and common sense. Paulson suggests that journalists ask themselves these questions:

- Have I reported fully?
- Have I reported factually?
- Have I reported fairly?
- Have I reported in good faith?

"If you can answer those four questions in the affirmative, the law will take care of itself," he says. Paulson joined the Gannett Company in 1978. He has been executive editor of *Florida Today* in Melbourne, Fla.; editor of the *Green Bay (Wis.) Press-Gazette*; managing editor of the *Bridgewater (N.J.) Courier-News* and executive editor of Gannett Suburban Newspapers in the New York counties of Westchester, Rockland and Putnam.

Privilege

In addition to truth, the courts traditionally have allowed another defense against libel: **privilege**. This defense applies when you are covering any of the three branches of government. The courts allow legislators, judges and government executives the **absolute privilege** to say anything—true or false—when acting in their official capacities. The rationale is that the public interest is served when an official is allowed to speak freely and fearlessly about making laws, carrying them out or punishing those who do not obey them. Similarly, a participant in a judicial proceeding, such as an attorney, court clerk or judge, is absolutely privileged to make false and even defamatory statements about another person during that proceeding.

In the executive branch it isn't always clear whose statements are privileged and under what conditions. The head of state and the major officers of executive departments of the federal and state governments are covered. However, minor officials might not enjoy the protection of absolute privilege.

As a reporter you have a qualified privilege, sometimes called *neutral reporting* or *conditional privilege*, to report what public officials say. Your privilege is conditional on your report's providing full, fair and accurate coverage of the court session, the legislative session or the president's press conference, even if any of the participants made defamatory statements. The privilege is also conditional on clear attribution to the session or press conference. You can quote anything the president of the United States says without fear of losing a libel suit, even if the president is not acting in an official capacity. Reporters have a qualified privilege to report unofficial presidential statements. But there are many other levels of executives in federal, state and local government. Mayors of small towns, for instance, often hold part-time positions. Although you are conditionally privileged to report on what these officials say when they are acting in their official capacities, a problem can arise when a part-time mayor says something defamatory when not acting in an official capacity. Some jurisdictions might grant a neutral reporting privilege; others might not.

Fair Comment and Criticism

In some writing you may be commenting or criticizing rather than reporting. The courts have protected writers who comment on or criticize the public offerings of anyone in the public eye. Individuals included in this category are actors, sports figures, public officials and other newsworthy people. Most often, such writing occurs in reviews of plays, books or movies, or in commentary on service in hotels and restaurants.

The courts call this **fair comment and criticism**. You are protected as long as you do not misstate any of the facts on which you base your comments or criticism, and as long as you do not wrongly imply that you possess undisclosed, damaging information that forms the basis for your opinion. Merely labeling a statement as an opinion will not result in opinion protection, the U.S. Supreme Court ruled in 1990.

The Actual Malice Test

It was a small but momentous step from fair comment and criticism to the case of *The New York Times* v. Sullivan. In 1964 the U.S. Supreme Court decided that First Amendment protection was broader than just the traditional defenses of truth and privilege and that the press needed even greater freedom in coverage of public officials.

The case started with an advertisement for funds in *The New York Times* of March 29, 1960, by the Committee to Defend Martin Luther King Jr. and the Struggle for Freedom in the South. The advertisement contained factual errors concerning the police, according to Montgomery, Ala., Commissioner L.B. Sullivan. He thought the errors damaged his reputation, and he won a half-million-dollar judgment against *The New York Times* in an Alabama trial court.

The Supreme Court said it was considering the case "against the background of a profound national commitment to the principle that debate on public issues should be uninhibited, robust and wide open." Thus Justice William Brennan wrote that the Constitution requires a federal rule prohibiting a public official from recovering damages from the press for a defamatory falsehood relating to his or her official conduct, unless the public official can prove the press had knowledge that what was printed was false or that the story was printed with reckless disregard for whether it was false or not.

The justices called this the **actual malice test**.

The decision in the Sharon case discussed earlier in the chapter is an example of the burden of proving **actual malice** by the press. The jury decided that *Time* did not know at the time of publication that its statement about Sharon was false.

In 1991, the Supreme Court decided Masson v. *The New Yorker*, the so-called "fabricated quotes" case. Masson, a psychotherapist, had sued the magazine and journalist Janet Malcolm, accusing them of making up quotes he never said. Overruling a lower court's decision that journalists could fictionalize quotations by making rational interpretations of speakers' remarks, the Supreme Court protected the sanctity of quotation marks. But the Court also made it clear that not every deliberate change in a quotation is libelous. Only a "material change in the meaning conveyed by a statement" poses a problem.

Although Masson won the right to try his case, he lost against all defendants. Malcolm won in 1994.

Standards Applicable to Public Figures

The actual malice protection was expanded in two cases in 1967 to include not only public officials but also public figures—those in the public eye but not in public office.

The first case stemmed from a *Saturday Evening Post* article that accused Coach Wally Butts of conspiring to fix a 1962 football game between Georgia and Alabama. At the time of the article, Butts was the athletic director of the University of Georgia. The article, titled "The Story of a College Football Fix," was prefaced by a note from the editors of the *Post* stating:

> Not since the Chicago White Sox threw the 1919 World Series has there been a sports story as shocking as this one. . . . Before the University of Georgia played the University of Alabama . . . Wally Butts . . . gave (to Alabama's coach) . . . Georgia's plays, defensive patterns, all the significant secrets Georgia's football team possessed.

The *Post* reported that, because of an electronic error about a week before the game, George Burnett, an Atlanta insurance salesman, accidentally had overheard a telephone conversation between Butts and the head coach of Alabama, Paul Bryant.

Coach Butts sued Curtis Publishing, publishers of the *Post*, and won a verdict for $60,000 in general damages and $3 million in punitive damages. Curtis Publishing appealed the case to the Supreme Court and lost. The trial judge reduced the amount of the damages to $460,000.

The second case was decided the same day. Edwin Walker sued the Associated Press for distributing a news dispatch giving an eyewitness account by an AP staffer on the campus of the University of Mississippi in the fall of 1962. The AP reported that Walker personally had led a student charge against federal marshals during a riot on the Mississippi campus. The marshals were attempting to enforce a court decree ordering the enrollment of a black student.

Walker was a retired U.S. Army general at the time of the publication. He had won a $2 million libel suit in a trial court. However, the Supreme Court ruled against him.

In both cases the stories were wrong. In both, the actual malice test was applied. What was the difference between the Butts and Walker cases? The justices said the football story was in no sense "hot news." They noted that the person who said he had heard the conversation was on probation in connection with bad-check charges and that *Post* personnel had not viewed his notes before publication. The Court also said, as evidence of actual malice on the part of the *Post*, that no one looked at the game films to see if the information was accurate; that a regular staffer, instead of a football expert, was assigned to the story; and that no check was made with someone knowledgeable in the sport. In short, the *Post* had not done an adequate job of reporting.

The evidence in the Walker case was considerably different. The Court said the news in the Walker case required immediate dissemination because of the riot on campus. The justices noted that the AP received the information from a correspondent who was present on campus and gave every indication of being trustworthy and competent.

In the Butts and Walker cases the Court used two definitions of a public figure. The first, like Butts, is a person who has assumed a role of special prominence in the affairs of society — someone who has pervasive power and influence in a community. The second, like Walker, is a person who has thrust himself into the forefront of a particular public controversy in order to influence the resolution of the issues involved.

In the 1970s the Supreme Court decided three cases that help journalists determine who is and who is not a public figure. The first case involved Mary Alice Firestone, who sued for libel after *Time* magazine reported that her husband's divorce petition had been granted on grounds of extreme cruelty and adultery. Mrs. Firestone, who had married Russell A. Firestone Jr. of the Firestone Tire and Rubber Co. family, claimed that those were not the grounds for the divorce. She also insisted that she was not a public figure with the burden of proving actual malice. The Supreme Court agreed. Even though she had held press conferences and hired a clipping service, the Court ruled that she had not thrust herself into the forefront of a public controversy in an attempt to influence the resolution of the issues involved. The Court admitted that marital difficulties of extremely wealthy individuals may be of some interest to some portion of the reading public but added that Firestone had not freely chosen to publicize private matters about her married life. The justices said she was compelled to go to court to "obtain legal release from the bonds of matrimony." They said she assumed no "special prominence in the resolution of public questions." The case was sent back to Florida for a finding of fault, and a new trial was ordered. Mrs. Firestone remarried, and the case was settled out of court.

The second case involved Sen. William Proxmire of Wisconsin, who had started what he called the Golden Fleece Award. Each month he announced a winner who, in his opinion, had wasted government money. One such winner was Ronald Hutchinson, a behavioral scientist who had received federal funding for research designed to determine why animals clench their teeth. Hutchinson had published articles about his research in professional publications. In deciding that Hutchinson was not a public figure, the Court ruled that he "did not thrust himself or his views into public controversy to influence others." The Court admitted there may have been legitimate concerns about the way public funds were being spent but said this was not enough to make Hutchinson a public figure.

The third case concerned an individual found guilty of contempt of court in 1958 for his failure to appear before a grand jury investigating Soviet espionage in the U.S. In a 1974 book published by the Reader's Digest Association, Ilya Wolston's name was included in a list of people indicted for serving as Soviet agents. Wolston, however, had not been indicted, and he sued.

The Supreme Court, in deciding that he was not a public figure, found that Wolston had played only a minor role in whatever public controversy there may have been concerning the investigation of Soviet espionage. The Court added that a private individual is not automatically transformed into a public figure merely by becoming involved in or being associated with a matter that attracts public attention.

As a journalist, do you have the same protection from a libel action when you write about a person somewhat connected with a news event as you do when you are certain a person is a public figure or public official? A 1974 Supreme Court decision says the answer usually is no. In the landmark Gertz v. Welch case, the justices said states could give more protection to private individuals if a newspaper or radio or television station damaged their reputations than if the reputations of either public officials or public figures were damaged. Generally, you have protection from a libel action when you write about people who have thrust themselves into the forefront of a controversy or event, as long as your reporting stays generally on the topic at hand.

Standards Applicable to Private Citizens

Private citizens who sue for punitive, or punishment, damages must meet the same actual malice test as public officials and public figures. Because of the Gertz case, states have been allowed to set their own standards for libel cases involving private citizens who sue only for actual damages. A majority of states and the District of Columbia have adopted a negligence test, which requires you to use the same care in gathering facts and writing your story as any reasonable reporter would use under the same or similar circumstances. If you made every effort to be fair and answer all the questions a reasonable person might ask, you probably would pass the negligence test.

One state, New York, has adopted a gross irresponsibility test. A few states have established a more stringent standard that requires private citizens to prove actual malice. Some states simply require a jury to find "fault."

The Continuing Danger

Despite all the available defenses, libel remains a serious risk to journalists' financial health, as the following example demonstrates: In 1997, a Texas jury awarded a record $222.7 million to a defunct bond-brokerage firm against Dow Jones & Co., which publishes *The Wall Street Journal*. The judge threw out $200 million in punitive damages but let stand the $22.7 million in actual damages for a *Journal* story about "bond daddies."

Libel and the Internet

Individuals who libel others over the Internet can be held liable. But the Internet raises the interesting question of whether an online service provider like America Online or MSN can be held liable for the libelous messages of their users.

In 1991, CompuServe successfully defended itself against a libel suit in a New York federal trial court. CompuServe had made a contract with another company to provide an electronic bulletin board in the form of a newsletter about journalism. The second company then used a third company to create the newsletter. Because CompuServe did not try to exercise any editorial control over the newsletter, the court let CompuServe off the hook for libel. The court also reasoned that no library can be held responsible if a book that the librarian has not reviewed contains libel. CompuServe, the court said, was providing an "electronic, for-profit library."

In 1995, however, Prodigy lost a similar libel case. To promote itself as a family-oriented Internet service provider, Prodigy controlled the content of its computer bulletin boards by using screening software to look for forbidden words, and its editorial staff censored allegedly offensive posts. Unfortunately for Prodigy, no list of software-generated words could screen for libel. A New York trial court said that by holding itself out as exercising editorial control, Prodigy was "expressly differentiating itself from its competition and expressly likening itself to a newspaper." Thus the court treated Prodigy like a newspaper and held it liable for the libel posted on one of its bulletin boards.

Congress did not agree with the Prodigy decision, however, and in 1996 passed a law providing "protection for 'Good Samaritan' blocking and screening of offensive material." Congress obviously did not support the idea that failure to screen meant protection from libel but that any screening meant liability. That law has been repeatedly upheld in courts.

Blogging has not produced court rulings yet. It seems reasonable to expect, however, that the developing field of Internet law will apply, with independent bloggers being held responsible for their own writings and commercial Web sites that host blogs being covered by the law and the rulings discussed above.

INVASION OF PRIVACY

Libel is damage to an individual's reputation. **Invasion of privacy** is a violation of a person's right to be left alone.

As a reporter, you may be risking an invasion-of-privacy suit under any of the following circumstances:

- You physically intrude into a private area to get a story or picture—an act closely related to trespass.
- You publish a story or photograph about someone that is misleading and thus portray that person in a "false light."
- You disclose something about an individual's private affairs that is true but also is highly offensive to individuals of ordinary sensibilities.

Invasion of privacy may also be claimed if someone's name or picture is used in an advertisement or for similar purposes of trade. Called *appropriation*, this does not affect you when you are performing your reporting duties.

"There are only two occasions when Americans respect privacy. . . . Those are prayer and fishing."

—**Herbert Hoover,**
*31st president
of the United States*

Consent is a basic defense in invasion-of-privacy suits. Make sure, however, that your use of the material does not exceed the consent given.

Another basic defense in an invasion-of-privacy suit is that you're a reporter covering a newsworthy situation. The courts usually protect the press against invasion-of-privacy suits when it is reporting matters of legitimate public interest. There are three exceptions, however.

Trespassing

You may be committing invasion of privacy by

- Trespassing on private property.
- Portraying someone in a "false light."
- Causing unwanted publicity that is offensive to a person of ordinary sensibilities.

One exception arises when you invade someone's privacy by entering private property to get a story. You cannot trespass on private property to get a story or take a picture, even if it is newsworthy. The courts will not protect you when you are a trespasser. Two *Life* magazine staffers lost an invasion-of-privacy suit because, with one posing as a patient, they went into a man's home to get a story about a faith healer. They lost the case even though they were working with the district attorney and the state board of health. You may enter private property only when you are invited by the owner or renter. Tagging along with the authorities, even with their permission, gives you no right to enter private property without the property owner's permission.

Portraying in a "False Light"

The court also will not protect you if you invade someone's privacy by publishing misleading information about that person. For example, a legal problem arises if a photograph or information from a true story about a careful pedestrian struck by a careless driver is used again in connection with a story, say, about careless pedestrians. The pedestrian who was hit could file a lawsuit charging libel, "false light" invasion of privacy or even both in some states.

Some states do not recognize "false light" invasion of privacy and insist that libel is the appropriate form of suit. But "false light" suits can cover situations where a picture or story is misleading but not defamatory. Even flattering material can place a person in an unwanted, false light. Legal observers say that "false light" claims are on the rise nationally, at least in part because of the high hurdles that libel plaintiffs face.

Causing Unwanted Publicity Offensive to a Person of Ordinary Sensibilities

The third category of invasion of privacy that the courts recognize — unwanted publicity — concerns stories about incidents that, because they are true, cannot be defamatory but can be highly offensive to a person of ordinary sensibilities. An example is a picture published by

Sports Illustrated in which a football fan's pants zipper was open. The fan sued for invasion of privacy but lost. Also in the area of unwanted publicity, the Supreme Court held in 1975 and again in 1989 that truthfully reporting the name of a rape victim is permitted. In 1976 and in 1979 the justices upheld the right of the press to publish the names of juveniles involved with the law because the information was truthful and of public significance.

The courts say that in order for privacy to be invaded, there must be a morbid and sensational prying into private lives. Merely being the subject of an unflattering and embarrassing article is not enough.

PROTECTION OF SOURCES AND NOTES

Another area you must know about is your ability — or inability — to protect your sources and notes. The problem may arise in various situations. A grand jury that is investigating a murder may ask you to reveal the source of a story you wrote about the murder. You may be asked to testify at a criminal or civil trial.

The conflict here is between a reporter's need to protect sources of information and the duty of every citizen to testify to help the courts determine justice. Because of the nature of your work as a reporter, you will be at the scene of events that are important and newsworthy. Anyone wanting the facts about an event can subpoena you to bring in all the details. Journalists usually resist. They work for their newspaper or radio or television station, not a law-enforcement agency. Their ability to gather information would be compromised if the sources knew that their identities or their information would go to the police.

By 2009 some protection against testifying — shield laws — had been adopted by 33 states and the District of Columbia. The states are:

> *"(The media) seek to maintain a balance on the constantly shifting tightrope of personal privacy, access to information and government accountability."*
>
> —*John R. Finnegan Sr.,*
> *former newspaper editor*

Alabama	Illinois	New Mexico
Alaska	Indiana	New York
Arizona	Kentucky	North Carolina
Arkansas	Louisiana	North Dakota
California	Maryland	Ohio
Colorado	Michigan	Oklahoma
Connecticut	Minnesota	Oregon
Delaware	Montana	Pennsylvania
Florida	Nebraska	Rhode Island
Georgia	Nevada	South Carolina
Hawaii	New Jersey	Tennessee

Shield law protection is important because, without it, journalists do go to jail. In 2001–2002, Vanessa Leggett, a freelance journalist in

Houston, Texas, spent a record 168 days in jail for refusing to hand over notes and tapes of interviews she had made while writing a book about the murder of a Houston socialite. Texas has no shield law. In 2004–2005, Jim Taricani, a broadcast reporter in Providence, R.I., spent four months under house arrest for refusing to tell who gave him an FBI videotape that showed a Providence official taking a bribe from an undercover FBI agent. A federal judge had ordered Taricani to reveal his source. Although Rhode Island has a shield law, the federal government does not.

Perhaps *New York Times* reporter Judith Miller has garnered the most publicity for being jailed. Her saga started when conservative columnist Robert Novak revealed the name of a CIA undercover agent, Valerie Plame. This occurred after Plame's husband, retired diplomat Joseph Wilson, had said the administration of George W. Bush misrepresented that Saddam Hussein had tried to buy depleted uranium from Niger. Although Miller did not write about Plame, she went to jail on July 6, 2005, for refusing to reveal the source who provided her with information about Plame.

Because it is a violation of federal law for an official to reveal the identity of an undercover CIA agent, a special prosecutor was assigned to investigate the leak. Several other journalists, including Novak, did testify after receiving permission from their sources to reveal the sources' names. Miller and her bosses at the *Times* took the position that her promise to hold confidential her sources' names was not one she could break. The U.S. Supreme Court refused to hear her appeal. Although her imprisonment inspired bills in Congress calling for a federal shield law, Congress has not yet passed such a law.

After 85 days in jail, Miller obtained permission from her source — who turned out to be the top aide to Vice President Dick Cheney — and testified before the grand jury. She was freed from jail, but the problem of confidential sources remains unsolved. However, Congress did pass the **Privacy Protection Act** of 1980. Under that act, federal, state and local enforcement officers generally may not use a search warrant to search news rooms. Instead, they must get a subpoena for documents, which tells the reporters to hand over the material. Officers may use a warrant to search news rooms only if they suspect a reporter of being involved in a crime or if immediate action is needed to prevent bodily harm, loss of life or destruction of the material.

The difference between a search warrant and a subpoena is important. Officers with a search warrant can knock on the door, enter the news room and search on their own. A subpoena does not permit officers to search the news room. A subpoena for documents requires reporters to turn over the material to authorities at a predetermined time and place. In addition, it gives reporters time to challenge in court the necessity of surrendering the material.

Even in states with shield laws, judges in most criminal cases involving grand juries will not allow you to keep your sources secret. In other criminal cases, courts may allow confidentiality if a three-part test is met. Supreme Court Justice Potter Stewart suggested this test in his dissent in Branzburg v. Hayes:

> Government officials must, therefore, demonstrate that the information sought is clearly relevant to a precisely defined subject of government inquiry. . . . They must demonstrate that it is reasonable to think the witness in question has that information. . . . And they must show that there is not any means of obtaining the information less destructive of First Amendment liberties. . . .

In civil litigation you may be permitted to keep sources confidential in most cases unless the court finds that the information sought is unavailable from other sources and is highly relevant to the underlying litigation or is of such critical importance to the lawsuit that it goes to the heart of the plaintiff's claim.

If you are sued for libel, you will find it very difficult both to protect your sources and win the lawsuit. The court might very well rule against you on whether a statement is true or false if the statement came from a source you refuse to name.

The best way to avoid such confrontation with the courts is not to promise a source you will keep his or her name confidential. Only for the most compelling reason should you promise confidentiality.

In 1991, the U.S. Supreme Court ruled in Cohen v. Cowles Media Company that the First Amendment does not prevent a source from suing a news organization if a reporter has promised the source confidentiality but the newspaper publishes the source's name anyway.

ACCESS TO COURTS

The Supreme Court held in 1979 that "members of the public have no constitutional right" under the Sixth Amendment to attend criminal trials. In a reversal exactly one year later, the justices held that the public and the press have a First Amendment right to attend criminal trials. The justices said the right was not absolute but that trial judges could close criminal trials only when there was an "overriding interest" to justify such closure. The basic concern of judges when they close trials is to protect the accused person's Sixth Amendment right to an "impartial jury"—often translated by attorneys into "a fair trial."

In addition, the First Amendment prevents the government from conducting business—even trials—in secret. In the Richmond Newspapers case in 1980, Chief Justice Warren Burger traced the unbroken and uncontradicted history of open judicial proceedings in England and the United States. He concluded that there is a "presumption of openness" in criminal trials and pointed out the important role of the news media as representatives of the public.

By 1984 the Supreme Court had decided that openness in criminal trials "enhances both the basic fairness of the criminal trial and the appearance of fairness so essential to public confidence in the system." Public proceedings vindicate the concerns of victims and the community in knowing that offenders are being brought to account for their criminal conduct "by jurors fairly and openly selected." Proceedings of jury selection could be closed, the chief justice said, only when a trial judge finds that closure preserves an "overriding interest" and is narrowly tailored to serve that interest.

Judges are using that option. For instance, when John Gotti was convicted of organized crime activities in New York, the jurors' names were kept secret. Gotti's attorneys unsuccessfully challenged the anonymity. Jurors' names in the Rodney King and Reginald Denny cases in Los Angeles also were withheld. Both of those cases involved allegations, supported by videotape evidence, of racial violence.

In 1986 the Supreme Court said only an overriding interest found by a trial judge can overcome the presumption of openness of criminal proceedings. Today, 47 states allow cameras in at least some state courtrooms. Cameras are permitted in some lower federal courts but are excluded from the Supreme Court.

COPYRIGHT AND FAIR USE

The purpose of copyright law is to ensure compensation to authors for contributing to the common good by publishing their works. The Constitution provides for this in Article 1, Section 8, by giving Congress the power to secure "for limited times to authors and inventors the exclusive right to their respective writing and discoveries." The same section indicates that this provision is intended "to promote the progress of science and useful arts" for the benefit of the public. Copyright laws protect your work and prohibit you from using significant amounts of others' writings without permission, which sometimes requires payment of a fee.

Key elements of copyright law include the following:

- Copyrightable works are protected from the moment they are fixed in tangible form, whether published or unpublished.
- Copyright protection begins with a work's "creation and . . . endures for a term consisting of the life of the author and 70 years after the author's death."
- Works for hire and anonymous and pseudonymous works are protected for 95 years from publication or 100 years from creation, whichever is shorter.

- There is a "fair use" limitation on the exclusive rights of copyright owners. In other words, it may be permissible to use small excerpts from a copyrighted work without permission. According to the Supreme Court, these factors govern fair use:
  1. The purpose and character of the use.
  2. The nature of the copyrighted work.
  3. The substantiality of the portion used in relationship to the copyrighted work as a whole.
  4. The effect on the potential market for or value of the copyrighted work.

Although a work is copyrighted from the moment it is fixed in tangible form, the copyright statute says certain steps are necessary for the work to receive statutory protection. The author or publisher must:

- Publish or reproduce the work with the word "copyright" or the symbol ©, the name of the copyright owner and the year of publication.
- Register the work at the Library of Congress by filling out a form supplied by the Copyright Office and sending the form, a specified number of copies (usually one copy of an unpublished work and two copies of a published work), and a fee to the Copyright Office. The copies and registration fee may be sent together and usually are.

Copyright law has a special provision for broadcasters of live programs. Broadcasters need only make a simultaneous tape of their live broadcasts in order to receive copyright protection. The tape fulfills the requirement that a work be in a "fixed" form for copyright protection. Because a digital form is a "fixed" form, editors of electronic newspapers already meet that copyright requirement.

Some aspects of U.S. copyright law changed in 1989, when the U.S. finally joined the 100-year-old Berne Convention, an international copyright treaty, primarily to prevent the pirating of American film productions in other countries. The changes include the following:

- *Placing a copyright notice on a work is no longer necessary to preserve a copyright after publication.* This is in line with the Berne Convention principle that the exercise of a copyright should not be subject to formalities. Nevertheless, the copyright notice is still useful because it acts as a bar to an infringer's claim of innocent infringement.
- *Copyright registration is no longer a prerequisite for access to the federal courts for an infringement action.* But registration is required for a copyright owner to recover statutory damages. (Without registration, the copyright owner can recover only the damages he or she can prove, court costs and "reasonable" attorney's fees.) The amount of statutory damages, generally between $750 and $30,000, is determined by the judge. If the infringer was not aware he or she was infringing a copyright, the court may award as little as $200. If the infringement was willful, the court can award up to $150,000. Thus, like the copyright notice, copyright registration remains highly advisable.

Suggested Readings

Carter, T. Barton, Marc A. Franklin, and Jay B. Wright. *The First Amendment and the Fourth Estate*, 6th ed. Westbury, N.Y.: Foundation Press, 1994.

Gilmour, Donald M., Jerome A. Barron, Todd F. Simon, and Herbert A. Terry. *Mass Communications Law*, 5th ed. New York: West, 1990.

Holsinger, Ralph, and Jon Paul Dills. *Media Law*, 3rd ed. New York: McGraw-Hill, 1987.

Middleton, Kent R., and Bill F. Chamberlin. *The Law of Public Communication*, 3rd ed. New York: Longman, 1994.

Overbeck, Wayne. *Major Principles of Media Law*. Fort Worth, Texas: Harcourt Brace, 1993.

Pember, Don R. *Mass Media Law*, 6th ed. Dubuque, Iowa: McGraw-Hill, 1993.

Siegel, Paul. *Communication Law in America*. New York: Rowman and Littlefield, 2007.

Teeter, Dwight L. Jr., and Don R. Le Duc. *Law of Mass Communications*, 7th ed. Westbury, N.Y.: Foundation Press, 1995.

Zelensky, John D. *Communications Law*. Belmont, Calif.: Wadsworth, 1993.

Suggested Web Sites

www.firstamendmentcenter.org   You'll find here a wonderful chronology of the "significant historical events, court cases, and ideas that have shaped our current system of constitutional First Amendment jurisprudence," presented by the Freedom Forum. Also, stories, commentaries and roundups of First Amendment disputes.

www.rcfp.org   The Reporters Committee for Freedom of the Press maintains online "publications and topical guides on First Amendment and Freedom of Information issues." Current hot stories, plus archives and much more.

www.medialaw.org   Media Law Resource Center, formerly the Libel Defense Resource Center, is "a non-profit information clearinghouse organized in 1980 by leading media groups to monitor and promote First Amendment rights, in the libel, privacy, and related fields of law." Includes a 50-state survey of media libel law, 1998–1999.

Exercises

1. The Internet is, of course, international. Suppose you write something in Florida. Can you be sued for libel in Australia? Explain.

2. *The New York Times* v. Sullivan was significant as a landmark decision in favor of the press. Discuss the consequences for the press if the decision had been different.

3. You are on an assignment with your photographer, who enters a house without permission and photographs the sale of illegal drugs. Discuss the issues raised by the circumstances, and explain why you would or would not publish the pictures.

4. Using the Lexis database, determine how the U.S. Supreme Court has used Richmond Newspapers v. Virginia, 448 U.S. 555 (1980), in later cases dealing with openness in criminal proceedings.

5. Decisions of the North Dakota Supreme Court are seldom relevant to student journalists outside that state. The case of Wagner v. Miskin is an exception. Why?

15 Ethics

WE ARE PHOTOGRAPHERS
NOT
ASSASSINS

C onsider the following:

- *Vancouver Province* sports columnist David Pratt plagiarized material from an eight-year-old *Sports Illustrated* article. CBS News quoted Pratt as saying, "It was a Saturday, and I wanted to get out of (the office) before noon." He was fired.
- Shinika Sykes, who reported on higher education for *The Salt Lake Tribune*, plagiarized material from the University of Utah's student newspaper. She was fired.
- *The (Spokane, Wash.) Spokesman-Review* reported that it used a forensic computer expert posing as an 18-year-old man in a gay chat room to ascertain whether Spokane Mayor Jim West was using his public position to proposition young men on a gay Web site. Is it ethical for journalists to hire undercover people to get a story?
- The *Corpus Christi Caller-Times* used a reporter to pose as a prostitute to lead police to the arrest of several johns. Said editor Libby Averyt, "Having a reporter become involved in law enforcement activities was a mistake and will not happen again."
- Jessica Heslam reported in BostonHerald.com that a *Herald* reviewer had found "almost three dozen instances of direct quotes and other material lifted from numerous newspaper articles without any attribution" in Jon Keller's book *The Bluest State*. Keller works at WBZ-TV in Boston as a political analyst.
- Diana Griego Erwin quit her position as a three-times-a-week columnist for *The Sacramento Bee* when, among other things, the editors discovered that they were "unable to verify the existence of 43 people she named in her columns."
- Fox 2 Detroit paid Fanchon Stinger more than $300,000 a year to anchor its morning show. Then it was reported that Stinger's media company placed ads in connection with a city sludge company that was under FBI investigation. She was suspended.
- In her third column in *The Daily Tar Heel*, the student newspaper of the University of North Carolina at Chapel Hill, Jillian Bandes wrote, "I want all Arabs to be stripped naked and cavity-searched if they get within 100 yards of an airport. I don't care if they're being inconvenienced. I don't care if it seems as though their rights are being violated." She was fired.
- Cultural critic Lee Siegel of *The New Republic* magazine started using a pseudonym for a culture blog in the magazine in which he praised himself and attacked others. When readers got on him concerning what he had written about comedian Jon Stewart, Siegel wrote: "Siegel is brave, brilliant, and wittier than Stewart will ever be. Take that, you bunch of immature, abusive sheep."
- *The New York Times* did not publish a story for an entire year about the government's engagement in domestic spying. *The Times'* editors said they gave in to national security arguments by the Bush administration.
- Randy Cohen wrote in *The Salt Lake Tribune*'s Web site about a journalism major in college who, as an intern at a national magazine, was asked

to write comments on one of the magazine's blogs. The intern was told to be sure not to mention that he was connected to the magazine and to write in the style of a reader.

This is just a small list of recent, well-known decisions of journalists that have ethical implications. No wonder that Cherie Blair, wife of former British Prime Minister Tony Blair, could say to an audience of students at Roehampton University that there "is no professional morality in journalism," that journalism is "not a noble calling" and that it has "no ethics."

And yet, arguably, journalism has never been practiced in a more ethical way in this country and in a host of other countries around the globe. How can that be? Some of the credit belongs to bloggers who are serving as watchdogs of the press and to a whole lot of other citizens on the Internet who are calling attention to every irregularity they see in journalism. As a result, journalists have responded by becoming much more transparent, by discussing their mistakes and failings. It's safe to say that, unlike in the past, nearly every practicing journalist is concerned about ethics.

Nevertheless, journalism as a profession has been slow to establish a mandatory and enforced code of ethics because of a fear that such a code might in some way infringe on freedom of the press.

In other professions, enforcing a code of ethics means the profession must have the power to keep people from practicing unless they have membership or a license to practice. That also means that the profession must have the power to suspend a license and to keep members from practicing if they violate the code of the profession.

For some professions, the state requires a license to practice. If, as a condition of keeping that license, people may not express certain ideas, that is a form of censorship. Because journalists are not licensed by states, it is difficult to determine who is a journalist. In fact, the Supreme Court has said that it does not want to define a journalist.

Therefore, the U.S. government does not keep anyone from practicing journalism, although individual news organizations have established and enforced codes of ethics that have restricted journalists in their work. As you read in some of the opening examples, journalists who have plagiarized have been suspended or fired from their news organizations.

Because of the wide range of the First Amendment and its relatively few legal restraints, journalism, perhaps more than any other profession, needs to discuss proper conduct. As the Commission on Freedom of the Press concluded in 1947, unless journalists set their own limits on what is acceptable and responsible, government will eventually and inevitably do it for them. Journalists too often and too easily justify all of their actions by citing the First Amendment.

"If bloggers had no ethics, blogging would have failed, but it didn't. So let's get a clue."

—*Jay Rosen*, media critic, author, scholar

Like other professional groups, associations of journalists like the Society of Professional Journalists have codes of conduct. Of course, journalists do not have to belong to such organizations to practice their profession. A majority of newspapers and television stations now have written codes of ethics. Large news organizations are most likely to have them. Organizations such as the Public Relations Society of America, the International Association of Business Communicators, the American Society of Business Writers and Editors, the American Society of Magazine Editors, the American Business Press and dozens of others all have codes of ethics. CyberJournalist.net has a model bloggers' Code of Ethics that is similar to the code of the Society of Professional Journalists.

Some critics condemn codes of ethics either for being hopelessly general and therefore ineffective or for being too restrictive. Some argue that strict codes help improve journalists' credibility; others say they merely make journalists easy targets for libel suits.

Your organization may or may not have a code of ethics. Either way, you should devise your own ethical values and principles. Your upbringing, and perhaps your religious training and your education, have already helped prepare you to do this.

THREE ETHICAL PHILOSOPHIES

"Ethics is a system of principles, a morality or code of conduct. It is the values and rules of life recognized by an individual, group or culture seeking guidelines to human conduct and what is good or bad, right or wrong."

— Conrad C. Fink,
media ethics professor

Your personal ethics may derive from the way you answer one fundamental question: Does the end justify the means? Should you ever do something that is not good in itself in order to achieve a goal that you think is good?

If you answer no to that question, you are in some sense at least an *absolutist* or a legalist, and you would most likely subscribe to *deontological ethics*. If you answer yes to that question, you are more of a *relativist* and would subscribe to *teleological ethics*. If you answer maybe or sometimes, you would subscribe to a form of *situation ethics*.

Don't be put off by the jargon of philosophers. To understand ethical thinking, to be able to discuss ethics and to solve ethical problems that arise on the job, you need to learn the vocabulary of ethicists.

Deontological Ethics

Deontological ethics is the ethics of duty. According to this philosophy, you have a duty to do what is right. Deontologists believe that some actions are always right, some always wrong; that there exists in nature (or, for those with religious faith, in divine revelation) a fixed set of principles or laws from which there should be no deviation. For a

Ethics in the Blogosphere

Jay Rosen, media critic, author and scholar, has written that journalists have their ethics and bloggers have theirs. Here's what he wrote about ethics for bloggers on his blog, PRESSthink, Sept. 15, 2008:

- Good bloggers observe the *ethic of the link*. (That is, they make a point of inserting relevant links in their blogs so that readers can connect to one another and to other information about the blog's topic.)
- They correct themselves early, easily and often.
- They don't claim neutrality, but they do practice transparency.
- They aren't remote; they habitually converse.
- They give you their site, but also other sites as a proper frame of reference. . . .
- When they grab on to something, they don't let go but "track" it.

deontologist, the end never justifies the means. That belief is why some refer to this ethical philosophy as **absolutism** or legalism.

An absolutist or legalist sees one clear duty: to discover the rules and to follow them. For example, if it is wrong to lie, it always is wrong to lie. Suppose someone comes to your door and asks where your roommates are so that he or she can murder them. If you were an absolutist, you would not lie to save their lives.

One such absolutist was Immanuel Kant (1724–1804). Kant proposed the "categorical imperative," a moral law that obliges you to do only those things that you would be willing to have everyone do as a matter of universal law. Once you make that decision, you must regard your decision as "categorical" and without exception, and you must do what you decide.

Many people draw support for their absolutism from their religious beliefs. They cite the Bible, the Koran or another religious source. If they themselves cannot resolve an ethical dilemma, they may turn to a minister, priest, rabbi, imam or guru for the answer. The absolutist is concerned only with doing what is right and needs only to discover what that is.

The absolutist journalist is concerned only with whether an event is newsworthy. If an event is interesting, timely, significant or important, it is to be reported, regardless of the consequences. The duty of the journalist is to report the news. Period. Walter Cronkite once said that if journalists worried about all the possible consequences of reporting something, they would never report anything.

People rely on the news media to keep them informed. That is why journalists enjoy First Amendment privileges. Charles A. Dana, who in 1868 began a 29-year career as editor of *The (New York) Sun*, said, "Whatever God in his infinite wisdom has allowed to happen, I am not too proud to print."

"I tell the honest truth in my paper, and I leave the consequences to God."

—*James Gordon Bennett, newspaper publisher, 1836*

Absolutists discount any criticism of the press for any stories it delivers to the public. Stop blaming the messenger, they say. We don't make events happen; we just report them.

Teleological Ethics

Teleological ethics is the ethics of final ends. According to this philosophy, what makes an act ethical is not the act itself but the consequences of the act. Teleologists believe that the end can and often does justify the means. In this philosophy, ethics are more relativistic than absolutist.

From a teleological perspective, stealing, for example, may not always be wrong: A mother who steals food for her starving child would be performing a virtuous act. Similarly, a teleologist would say, a person who lies to save someone's life would be acting ethically, and a person who kills to protect his or her own life would be acting morally.

An important consideration in teleological ethics is the intention of the person performing the act. What one person would declare unethical, another person would do for a good purpose or a good reason. For example, police often work undercover, concealing their identity to

On the Job

Ethics in Reporting

Jean McHale earned her bachelor's degree in magazine journalism in 1986. She began her career editing the quarterly magazine for a not-for-profit civic service organization. She next held increasingly responsible positions at a self-storage insurance magazine. In the mid-1990s she joined the employee communications department at a multistate bank, where she coordinated an award-winning redesign of the employee newsletter. A bank merger prompted her to leave the corporate sector, and for the next five years she worked as a public-information specialist for the Arizona Supreme Court. During that time she was part of the inaugural effort to publish court decisions on the Arizona Judicial Department Web site.

McHale's next career transition took place when she landed a public-relations position at a graduate school for health professions and dentistry. Following her stint in higher education, she joined the staff of a nonprofit professional association. She currently works in public relations at the Institute for Supply Management.

"My career spans a range of organizations, as well as the public and private sectors," McHale says. "I'm glad that early in my career I joined several professional associations and learned to reach out to fellow members and colleagues for perspective on ethical issues, career advice and best practices.

"I've worked in highly regulated industries such as insurance and banking. And I've worked to support other professions with strong ethical codes—medicine, our justice system and supply management, for example. Ethics in my career is defined by many moments, rather than just one or two defining moments. My journalism education was one of the earliest tools I had to start a lifelong career that requires making ethical choices and decisions every day."

apprehend criminals. In the course of this work, if they must lie or even get involved in criminal activity, the teleological response would be "So be it." Their purpose is to protect the public; their intention is to work for the good of society. The end justifies the means.

Some journalists would not hesitate to do the same. Some might require that some conditions be in place before they would steal or use deceit, but then they would proceed. They believe their purpose is to be the watchdog of government, to protect the common good, to keep the public fully informed. Whatever they must do to accomplish these goals, they argue, is clearly ethical.

Situation Ethics

Situation ethics is the ethics of specific acts. When asked whether the end justifies the means, a person subscribing to situation ethics would reply, "It all depends." Here are five philosophies that make use of some form of situation ethics.

Antinomianism

Antinomianism is the belief that there are no moral absolutes and that there is only one operative principle: Every person and every situation are unique, and to resolve an ethical dilemma by applying principles held by others or principles that apply in other cases is unethical. An antinomian believes that because each situation is unique, each ethical problem must be judged entirely on its own merits.

Love of Neighbor

Another type of situation ethics has been described by Joseph Fletcher (1905–1991). Fletcher bases his philosophy on love of neighbor as articulated in the Golden Rule and the maxim "You shall love your neighbor as yourself." He presents his ethic from a Christian per- spective with roots in Judaic teaching, but one need not profess Chris- tianity to share the conviction that all principles are relative to one absolute: love of neighbor. Indeed, most religions, as well as secular humanism, hold human values as the highest good.

Although people who subscribe to this belief understand and accept other ethical maxims and weigh them carefully when facing an ethical decision, they must be prepared to set them aside completely if love of neighbor demands it. In the broad sense, followers of Fletcher's form of situation ethics always place people first. In every ethical dilemma, they always do what is best for people. Sometimes they must choose between love for one person and love for a larger community of people.

Utilitarianism

The thinking that Fletcher advocates leads to another form of situation ethics: utilitarianism. From the utilitarian perspective, your choices are ethical if you always choose the action that is likely to bring the most happiness to the greatest number of people. This theory, formulated by John Stuart Mill (1806–1873) and Jeremy Bentham (1748–1832), was later modified to emphasize the greatest good rather than the greatest happiness. Some utilitarians also add the words "over a long period of time," because some actions may seem wrong if one looks merely at the present situation.

Most journalists probably subscribe to a utilitarian philosophy. They know, for example, that publishing a story about the infidelities of a public official may destroy the person's reputation, hurt his or her family and perhaps even lead to suicide, but, taking a utilitarian view, they decide that for the greater good, the public should have this information. The decision to publish would seem even more justifiable if the public official were involved in embezzlement or bribery.

John Rawls' Veil of Ignorance

Political theorist John Rawls (1921–2002) would have you treat all people the same, as if all differences in social or economic status were concealed behind a "veil of ignorance." Behind the veil, all people would be equal, regardless of their race, gender, age or looks. If there were any unequal treatment, it would benefit the least advantaged person or persons.

Rawls argued that these considerations would make people act more in tune with their rational self-interest. People would be more likely to look out for themselves if they placed themselves in the position of others.

In our society, research indicates that wealthy white men and poor African-American men who commit the same crimes seldom receive the same sentences. The "veil of ignorance" would help judges and juries disregard racial and other differences.

Journalists often treat famous people, especially politicians, more harshly than they treat average citizens. If journalists placed themselves with politicians behind the veil, perhaps their adversarial attitude would dissipate somewhat.

Aristotle's Golden Mean

Another form of situation ethics derives from Aristotle's (384–322 BCE) notion of the **Golden Mean,** a moderate moral position that avoids either of two extremes. Aristotle stated that after considering the extremes, a person is likely to find a rational and moral position somewhere in between—though not necessarily in the middle.

Journalists make choices ranging from running no photographs of a crime to running the most graphic images of a violent death. A person who subscribes to the ethics of the Golden Mean would try to run a photo that indicates the horror of the tragedy without offending the sensibilities of the audience or of the victim's family.

RESOLVING ETHICAL ISSUES

Unless you are an absolutist, ethical reasoning can take many forms. You may adopt one or more ethical stances, and they will guide your day-to-day ethical decision making. What is paramount is that you engage in **principled reasoning**. You must deliberate by reflecting on ethical principles—principles that will help you decide on proper or moral ways to act.

Principled reasoning assumes that you are not acting ethically if you do something simply because you have been told to do it or because that's what everyone else does. You are not ethical if you report a story just to beat the competition.

To help journalists and others make ethical decisions, ethicists Clifford Christians, Kim Rotzoll and Mark Fackler have adapted a model of moral reasoning devised by Dr. Ralph Potter of the Harvard Divinity School. Called the Potter Box (see Figure 15.1), the model has four elements:

1. *Appraising the situation*. Making a good ethical decision begins with good reporting. You need all the facts from a variety of sources. Reaching a decision without trying to know all the facts makes any ethical decision impossible. Many questioned the decision of *The New York Times* to print a story based on two anonymous former advisers alleging that Sen. John McCain had had an affair with a lobbyist. If *The Times* had any further evidence of the alleged affair, it did not cite any in the story.
2. *Identifying values*. What are your personal values, your news organization's values, your community's values, the nation's values? For example, you may place high value on your personal credibility and that of your news organization. Certainly, freedom of the press is a value prized by many in this nation.
3. *Appealing to ethical principles*. You need to look at the various ethical principles discussed previously. The principles are not meant to be a shopping list from which you choose items that serve your personal interest. To be ethical, you may have to choose a principle or principles that are far from expedient.

"Journalists demean themselves and damage their credibility when they misrepresent themselves and their work to news sources and, in turn, to the public at large."

—*Everette E. Dennis,*
Felix E. Larkin Distinguished
Professor of Communication
and Media Management at
Fordham University, where
he heads the Center for
Communication

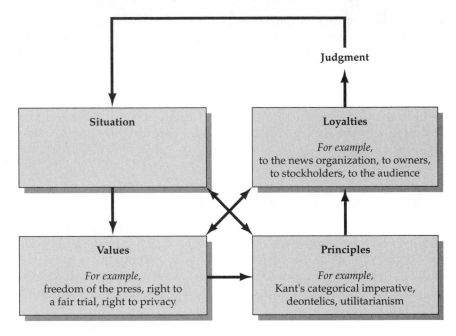

Figure 15.1
The Potter Box can help journalists analyze and resolve ethical problems.

4. *Choosing loyalties.* You owe a certain loyalty to your news organization, yes, but you also must be loyal to your own principles and values and to your readers, listeners or viewers. And what about loyalty to your sources and to the people about whom you are reporting? Finally, some would argue that you also must consider your loyalty to your station's owners and stockholders. If your news agency is not profitable, it will cease to exist.

One thing is certain about making ethical decisions. Doing so assumes that people are absolutely free to choose. As Sir Harold Evans, the British-born journalist and former editor of *The Sunday Times* and of *The Times*, has written, "The whole of ethics is based on the presumption of free will and the freedom to make choices." Nevertheless, and perhaps for that reason, there is no one clear answer to an ethical dilemma. Seldom do the most reasonable and experienced news veterans agree completely. But principled reasoning at least makes an ethical decision possible.

The four elements in the Potter Box need not be considered in any particular order. Also, don't stop reasoning after you have touched on the four elements. Principled reasoning should continue, even to another discussion of another ethical dilemma.

This continuing ethical dialectic or dialogue helps create ethical journalism and ethical journalists. Journalists should not simply reflect society. They should present a reasoned reflection. Journalism should be done by people who make informed, intelligent and prudent choices.

The main objection to the Potter Box is that using it takes too much time and is impractical in the deadline business of journalism. However, as you become better acquainted with ethical principles and more practiced at principled reasoning, you will be able to make ethical decisions much more quickly and reasonably.

Although each case is different and you always must know the situation, you need not always start from the beginning. After a while you will know what your values are, where your loyalties lie and which principles will most likely apply.

ETHICAL PROBLEMS

Because of the First Amendment, society has relatively few "rules" for journalists in spite of the special problems they face. In the following sections, we discuss some of these problems.

Deceit

Perhaps the most bothersome ethical problem facing journalists involves using deceit to get a story. Deceit covers a wide range of practices. When may you lie, misrepresent yourself, use a hidden voice recorder or camera? When may you steal documents? For absolutists, the answer is simple: Never! For others, the answer is not easy.

When may a newspaper hire someone to "catch" or verify a rumor, as *The Spokesman-Review* did to find out whether the mayor was using his position to lure young men on a gay Web site?

A group of journalists in an ethical decision-making seminar at the Poynter Institute for Media Studies devised a list of criteria to justify the use of deceit. The box "Conditions Justifying the Use of Deceit by Journalists," on page 334, synthesizes their conclusions. All the conditions listed there must be present to justify deceit.

Conflicts of Interest

Reporting generally assumes that reporters start out with no point of view, that they are not out to get someone or to get something from the story. This basic assumption is the foundation of all credibility.

Most news-media codes of ethics devote the bulk of their substance to determining what constitutes a conflict of interest. And well they should.

Ethical problems faced by journalists

- Deceit.
- Conflicts of interest.
- Friendship.
- Payola.
- Freebies.
- Checkbook journalism.
- Participation in the news.
- Advertising pressure.
- Invasion of privacy.
- Withholding information.
- Plagiarism.

Conditions Justifying the Use of Deceit by Journalists

- An issue of profound public importance:
  — of vital public interest, revealing system failure at high levels.
  — a preventive measure against profound harm to individuals.
- All other alternatives exhausted.
- Eventual full disclosure of the deception and the reason for it.
- Full commitment to the story by everyone involved.
- The harm prevented outweighs any harm caused.
- A meaningful, collaborative and deliberative decision-making process that takes into account:
  — short- and long-term consequences of the deception.
  — the impact on credibility.
  — motivations for actions.
  — congruence between the deceptive act and the organization's editorial mission.
  — legal implications.
  — consistency of reasoning and action.

Friendship

Perhaps the most obvious, most frequent, yet most overlooked conflict of interest confronting journalists is friendship. Friendship may be the greatest obstacle to the flow of information.

No one knows whether friendship causes more stories to be reported or more stories to be killed. Either way, it sets up a powerful conflict of interest.

If you ever find yourself covering a story that involves a personal acquaintance, ask your supervisor to assign the story to someone else.

This is even more important if family relationships are involved. The *Columbia Journalism Review* questioned whether veteran NBC News correspondent Andrea Mitchell should be on the air at all during a time of great financial crisis. Mitchell, who is married to Alan Greenspan, former chairman of the Federal Reserve, apparently never mentions his name in her reporting. *The New York Times* reported that the president of NBC News, Steve Capus, called the *Review*'s article "simplistic," but the network did not allow Mitchell to take the lead in covering congressional hearings about the economy.

Payola

Journalists may not accept payment for a story other than from their employer. Also, news organizations frown upon reporters doing promotional work for people they cover. Other conflicts of interest are not as obvious. Should architecture critic Edward Gunts have told the editors of *The Baltimore Sun* that he was reviewing architecture in areas where he owned property? The *San Jose Mercury News* prohibits its business news reporters and editors from owning stock in local companies.

Will news agencies prohibit journalists from accepting speakers' fees? Will Congress attempt to legislate full disclosure of journalists' income and associations?

Freebies

When journalists accept free gifts from people they cover, the gifts always come with a price:

- Can reporters remain objective?
- Do reporters write stories they otherwise would not write?
- Does the public perceive the reporter who accepted or is suspected of accepting freebies as objective?

The perception of conflict of interest is what bothers most news organizations. Some argue that the least reporters must do is disclose prominently in their stories any freebies they accepted. As in any case of deceit, reporters must disclose how they were able to get the story and why accepting freebies was necessary.

For example, travel writers are offered free trips, free cruises, free hotel accommodations and other freebies by companies that expect them to write about what they experience. Many small news outlets cannot afford to send their travel writers on expensive tours. Travel writers who accept freebies should mention doing so in their stories and let readers decide whether to trust the reporting.

Most news organizations have rules against accepting freebies. The Scripps-Howard newspaper group says, "When the gifts exceed the limits of propriety, they should be returned." The Society of Professional Journalists says, "Nothing of value shall be accepted." Is a cup of coffee something of value? The Associated Press expects its staff members to return gifts of "nominal value." Is a baseball cap of nominal value?

You must learn the ethics code of your news organization. Sometimes, your personal code may be more stringent than the code of your organization. In that case, follow your own code. Remember, you may not think a freebie will influence your reporting. But does your audience think that it might?

If you choose a career in public relations, remember that the code of the Public Relations Society of America states that you are to do nothing that tempts news professionals to violate their codes.

Checkbook Journalism

"But I don't believe that paying sources is unethical, as long as it's disclosed to the reader; in some cases I think it makes for better journalism. It gives a fair share of the profits to sources who spend time and take risks."

—*John Tierney,*
from "Newsworthy," reprinted
from The New York Times
Magazine

Will the audience believe your story if you paid your source for it? Should you always report that you had a paid source? Is it ethical to pay a source for an exclusive story? Should newspeople be in the business of preventing other newspeople from getting a story? Are paid sources likely to have an ax to grind? Do they come forward only for financial gain?

The terrible consequence of checkbook journalism is that even legitimate news professionals may be cut off from sources who want and expect pay. Some sources have begun asking for a fee even for good news. The increase in tabloid journalism, both in print and in broadcast, has brought the opportunists out in droves. The networks say that they do not pay for interviews, but the tabloids say payments are disguised as consultant fees, writes Richard Zoglin in *Time* magazine. Should sources be paid for contributing to a commercial product?

Surely, good reporting demands that you pay sources only when necessary and only if you can get other sources to corroborate your findings. You'd also better be sure that your bosses know that you're doing it.

Participation in the News

"If you're not involved in the community at all and you're totally neutralized, you end up not knowing enough about the community, not being able to get enough leads and so on in order to do your job."

—*Tony Case,*
quoting ethicist Louis W. Hodges
in Editor & Publisher

You'd also better let your bosses know which organizations you belong to. *The Washington Post* issued a memo to staffers that barred any reporters who had participated in a pro-abortion rights march in Washington "from any future participation in coverage of the abortion issue." Don Kowet reported in *The Washington Times* that the same memo prohibited any "news room professional" from participating in such a protest.

But what about participating in a political campaign? And must a religion reporter be an atheist?

According to Kowet, Richard Harwood, *Washington Post* ombudsman at the time, told a conference of journalists: "You have every right in the world to run for office, or participate in a political activity or lobbying activity. You don't have the 'right' to work for *The Washington Post*."

Nevertheless, some worry that uninvolved journalists will be uninformed journalists, an unconnected group of elitists. The problem is compounded when editors and even news organizations are involved in community projects. May the editor join the yacht club? May the station support the United Way? Is *The New York Times* coverage of the Metropolitan Museum of Art influenced by its generous support of that institution? May an HIV-positive journalist report on AIDS?

Finally, should journalists demand of themselves what they demand of politicians: full disclosure of their financial investments and memberships, as well as public knowledge of their personal tastes, preferences and lifestyles?

Advertising Pressure

It's likely you won't work long at a news organization before you realize some subjects are taboo to write about and others are highly encouraged. If you are lucky, you will work for a paper, station or magazine with a solid wall of separation between editorial and advertising, sometimes referred to as the separation of "church" and "state."

The Influence of Advertisers

However, in some places, advertising salespeople are allowed to peek over that wall and see what stories the publication or station is planning to run. That information might help sell some advertising. Some say, What could be wrong with that?

The next step is for the advertising department to climb over the wall and suggest that editorial do a story on some subject so that advertising can be sold.

And then the next step isn't too far away. Advertising begins to suggest or even to dictate what must and must not be printed or said on radio or shown on television. In print media, advertising may want the layout, design and type of their ads or sections to look like the publication's normal design. Advertisers may also insist that the word "advertising" appear in small print, or at the bottom of the page or be dropped altogether. Some advertisers prefer the term "sponsored by" as softening the pure sales pitch of their message.

Conflicts and Policies in Print Media

Seldom does a paper have a policy as blatant as that of the *Palo Alto Daily News*, a free paper: "In addition to covering business as a news beat, (the reporter) must also cover local business from the perspective of the business owner, or, as their partner. This means promoting the business as their own. This is the key to early and continued success. If we embrace our advertisers and help them promote with good writing and photos, they will become our strongest supporters."

Although some newspaper companies have allowed advertising and news personnel to become a bit chummier, some magazines have gone much further. The Southern Progress Corp., for example, a big moneymaker for Time Warner and publisher of *Southern Living, Southern Accents, Sunset, Cooking Light* and other successful magazines, has stopped worrying about the separation of advertising and editorial. In a *Wall Street Journal* story by Matthew Rose, former Southern Progress editor Michael Carlton said, "There is no church and state. They all sit in the same church, maybe in different pews." In the same story, another former chief executive of the Southern Progress unit is quoted as saying, "For me, the acid test was: Am I serving the reader well?"

Not only does Southern Progress tip off advertisers as to what editorial is going to do, they also sometimes allow advertisers into planning sessions and to make suggestions.

With Southern Progress boasting high renewal rates and high profits, is this the future? Currently the Meredith and Hearst magazine corporations have not followed suit.

Conflicts and Policies in Other Media

The question of advertisements online is dealt with in Chapter 13. Radio newscasters generally separate themselves from the commercials. Yet the late popular long-time commentator Paul Harvey and, more recently, Rush Limbaugh and Charles Osgood have not refrained from reading the commercials with the same gusto with which they say everything else. What has it done to their credibility? Television suffers the same advertising pressures as print, with the added problem that there are only so many minutes in a newscast. Is it ethical to cut a complicated international story to 90 seconds to make time for one more commercial?

Invasion of Privacy

Most journalists would cry out against an invasion of their own privacy. Yet many of them argue for a vague "right to know" when they report on others, especially if those others are public officials or public figures. The head-on collision of the right to know and the right to privacy will confront you every day of your reporting life. The Constitution mentions neither "right."

Crime Victims and Suspects

The most obvious and talked-about issue dealing with the right to privacy is naming crime survivors, especially rape and abuse survivors. Florida legislated against publishing rape survivors' names, only to have the law struck down by a Florida District Court. The Supreme Court has held that news agencies cannot be punished for publishing lawfully obtained information or information from a public record. Meanwhile, legislators in many states are looking for ways to close the records on rape and to punish police, hospitals, court clerks and other officials for releasing survivors' names.

So the issue comes down to a matter of ethics, and as usual, there is no complete agreement. Not publishing the name continues the stigma that somehow the rape was the survivor's fault. Publishing the survivor's name is heaping more suffering on that person. Few news outlets would publish a rape survivor's name without the survivor's approval.

Do we name the accused? What if the accusation is false? A 17-year-old girl cried rape in Palos Heights, Ill., but five days later she admitted she made the whole thing up. According to a report by Kim Janssen on SouthtownStar.com, everyone knew who she was. Janssen reported that Northwestern University journalism ethics professor Jack Doppelt said he would print her name. Kelly McBride of the Poynter Institute said she wouldn't but would not blame editors who would.

Juvenile Offenders

A similar problem arises with publishing the names of juvenile offenders. News agencies traditionally have not published them because they have held that juveniles are entitled to make juvenile mistakes, even if those mistakes are crimes. After all, juvenile court records are sealed. The courts have upheld the right to publish juvenile offenders' names that are on the public record.

Some media critics, such as *The Fresno Bee*'s former editor and ombudsman Lynne Enders Glaser, have applauded the publication of the names of juvenile offenders. Glaser wrote: "It doesn't take a rocket scientist to figure out that more and more violent crimes are being committed by young people. And in increasing numbers, *Bee* readers have challenged the law and the media to stop protecting the identity of criminals because of their age."

However, in addition to the stigma forever attached to the juvenile offender's name and the embarrassment caused his or her parents and family, some worry that in some groups a youth's notoriety will encourage other young people to violate the law. Others argue that shame will stop other juveniles from committing crimes.

Public Figures

Reporting on crime victims and reporting on juvenile crimes raise just two of the myriad privacy issues you will face. Journalists are still protected when writing about public officials and public figures — most of the time. But what about the children of politicians or celebrities? Noelle Bush was in the national news when she tried to use a fake prescription to buy the anti-anxiety drug Xanax and again when she was found with a piece of crack cocaine in her shoe while in an Orlando treatment center. Why? Because she is the daughter of then Florida Gov. Jeb Bush, the brother of then President George W. Bush.

Photos and Video

Photographers and videographers must be especially concerned with privacy. How often and under what circumstances should they stick cameras into people's grieving and anxious faces? When should they comply with government requests not to photograph, such as when they were forbidden to take pictures of the coffins of troops returning from Iraq or when the Federal Emergency Management Agency asked them not to photograph the dead in Katrina's wake?

Sometimes matters of privacy and ethics are more a matter of good taste. When contract photographer Rick Wilking took a picture of then President George W. Bush writing a note at the United Nations, he did not know what the note said. Gary Hershorn, a Reuters' news editor for pictures, zoomed in on the page and found the message: "I think I may need a bathroom break. Is this possible?" The note, written to then Secretary of State Condoleezza Rice, was transmitted to Reuters' clients. Hardly unethical. But was it in good taste?

Withholding Information

May you ever withhold information from the news organization for which you work? If you are writing what you hope to be a best-selling book, may you save some "news" until after the book is published?

If you work as a journalist, are you ever off-duty? A doctor isn't. Doctors take an oath to treat the sick. If you witness something at a friend's house or at a party, do you tell your news director about it?

One reporter was fired when his boss discovered that he attended a post-concert party of a rock band where lines of cocaine were openly available. The reporter did not include this information in his coverage of the band. His defense was that if he reported the drug abuse, he would never get interviews or get close to other rock groups, and he would be finished as a music critic. His defense didn't work.

If you learn that a political candidate is "sleeping around," would you withhold that information? Would you do so even if you knew that if the public had that information, the candidate would not be elected? Suppose after the election it became clear that you had had the information before the election but did not publish it? *The (Portland) Oregonian* apologized to its readers for not publishing reports about former Sen. Bob Packwood's alleged sexual harassment charges until after he was re-elected. Suppose the story mentioned earlier in this chapter were true—that Sen. McCain had had an affair with a lobbyist? The

editors of *The New York Times* certainly knew they would be charged
with political bias for running the story. Should they have refrained
from running it? Did they have an obligation to their readers to inform
them of what they thought they knew?

When should you withhold information because the police ask
you to or because it may jeopardize a case? When a suspect in the BTK
serial murder case in Wichita, Kan., was finally arrested, *Seattle Times*
reporter Cathy Henkel recalled the copy of a two-page memo she had
that BTK sent to the police in the 1970s when Henkel was working for
the weekly *Wichita Sun*. The letter, filled with graphic content and bad
grammar, discussed four types of knots the murderer used to strangle
his victims. Because the police felt the release of the information
would hurt their case, the paper thought it best to do nothing with the
information, despite the public's right to know.

The Wichita Eagle and ABC affiliate television station KAKE had
even more information about BTK the year before his arrest, but both
said nothing.

Poynter Institute columnist Kelly McBride says, "Cutting deals to
withhold information is dangerous. It should be done with great caution, much forethought and only in rare circumstances." She also warns
that "we too readily agree with police and keep information from the
public."

PLAGIARISM

No one wants you to use his or her work as your own. No one con-
dones plagiarism. The problem is defining exactly what constitutes plagiarism. Most of the time you know when you plagiarize even if no one
else does.

If you read Jim Romenesko's blog (and you should) on the Poynter
Web site (**www.poynter.org/medianews**), it seems that nearly every other
day there is a story about some reporter admitting to plagiarism. Perhaps
it's even more of a temptation to plagiarize material published online.
But you also might be tempted to lift words from your own newspaper's stories in the library, or to take words out of a wire story. Some
reporters have felt justified taking quotes and verbatim sentences from
news releases and inserting them into their stories. You always serve
your readers better when you get your own quotations. Don't even use
your own material or stories or columns again without letting your
readers know what you are doing.

Though many believe it is impossible, others believe that writers
sometimes plagiarize and have absolutely no idea they are doing so. It's

Three final guidelines

- Be free of obligations
  to anyone or to any
  interest except the
  truth. The primary
  obligation of the jour-
  nalist is to be free.
- Be fair. Even children
  know when you treat
  them unfairly or when
  they are being unfair.
  So do you.
- Remember good taste.
  Some actions and sto-
  ries may be ethical, but
  they may be in bad
  taste.

possible that something one has read becomes so familiar that one later considers it one's own. At times plagiarism is a matter of sloppy note taking. See the box below, "Beware of Plagiarism!" by Roy Peter Clark of the Poynter Institute.

Of course, many reporters say that nothing whatsoever excuses plagiarism. Columnist Lizette Rabe wrote, "Of all our journalistic sins, plagiarism might be the most unforgivable."

You must fight every impulse, question and check any doubts, and avoid any hint of plagiarism. And just as certainly you must resist the temptation to make up people, to fabricate events and to invent quotations from fictional people. A reporter on *The Sacramento Bee* did that, and he was fired. An AP Washington reporter did that, and he was fired.

It's hard to say what's worse — making up material or stealing it. Don't do either. Ever.

Beware of Plagiarism!

Taking material verbatim from the newspaper library. Even when the material is from your own newspaper, it is still someone else's work. Put it in your own words or attribute it.

Using material verbatim from the wire services. Sometimes writers take Associated Press material, add a few paragraphs to give some local flavor, and publish it as their own work. Even though it is a common practice, it is not right.

Using material from other publications. Some blame electronic databases for a whole new explosion of plagiarism. Sometimes writers steal the research of others without attribution. And sometimes they use others' work without realizing it.

Using news releases verbatim. The publicists are delighted, but you should be ashamed — especially if you put your name on an article. Rewrite it, except perhaps for the direct quotations, and use them sparingly. If you use a whole release, cite its source.

Using the work of fellow reporters. If more than one reporter works on a story, if you use a byline on top, put the other names at the end of the story.

Using old stories over again. Columnists, beware! Your readers have a right to know when you are recycling your material. Some of them might catch you at it, and there goes your credibility.

—Roy Peter Clark, Poynter Institute

Suggested Readings

Christians, Clifford G., Mark Fackler, Kim B. Rotzoll, and Kathy Brittain McKee. *Media Ethics: Cases and Moral Reasoning*, 8th ed. Boston: Allyn & Bacon, 2008. Applies the Potter Box method of principled reasoning to dozens of journalism, advertising and public-relations cases.

Christians, Clifford G., and Lee Wilkins. *Handbook of Media Ethics*. New York: Lawrence Erlbaum, 2008. Various scholars look at the intellectual history of mass media ethics over the past 25 years and summarize past and possible future research.

Day, Louis Alvin. *Ethics in Media Communications*, 5th ed. Belmont, Calif.: Wadsworth, 2005. Begins with a superb discussion of ethics and moral development, ethics and society, and ethics and moral rea-soning, and goes on to discuss nearly every problem facing journalists. Includes actual cases.

Fletcher, Joseph. *Situation Ethics: The New Morality*. Louisville, Ky.: Westminster John Knox Press, 1997. A classic work on Christian situation ethics. For some, it's a breath of fresh air, for others pure heresy.

Lambeth, Edmund B. *Committed Journalism*, 2nd ed. Bloomington: Indiana University Press, 1992. Creates an ethics framework specific to the practice of journalism.

Wilkins, Lee, and Philip Patterson. *Media Ethics, Issues and Cases*, 6th ed. Burr Ridge, Ill.: McGraw-Hill Humanities, Social Sciences & World Languages, 2007. An excellent discussion of journalism ethics with up-to-date cases.

Suggested Web Sites

www.ijnet.org   Site of the International Journalists' Network. Here you can find the codes of ethics of nearly every country or press association that has one. It also reports on the state of media around the world and contains media directories.

http://journalism.indiana.edu/resources/ethics
This site of the School of Journalism of Indiana University–Bloomington contains a large set of cases to help you explore ethical issues in journalism. The initial cases were published in "FineLine," a newsletter of Barry Bingham Jr.

www.ojr.org   A Web-based journal produced at the Annenberg School for Communication at the University of Southern California. It contains a worthwhile section on ethics as well as links to other articles about journalism ethics.

www.spj.org/ethics.asp   The ethics site of the Society of Professional Journalists. It provides the SPJ code of ethics, ethics news, an ethics hotline, an SPJ ethics listserv and other ethics sources. It also provides ethics case studies.

Exercises

1. You learn that the daughter of a local bank president has been kidnapped. The kidnappers have not contacted the family, and police officials ask you to keep the matter secret for fear the abductors might panic and injure the child. Describe how a deontologist, a teleologist and a situation ethicist would make their decisions about how to handle the situation.

2. You're assigned to write a piece on a new bus service from your town to Chicago. Your editor tells you to ask the bus company for a free round-trip ticket. What would you do?

3. For at least a year, on four or five occasions, reporters on your paper have heard rumors that a retirement home is negligent in its care of the elderly. Your editor asks you to get a job there as a janitor and report what you find. What would be your response?

4. Do a computer search of articles written in the past three years on whether journalists should publish the names of juvenile delinquents. Then write a brief summary of your findings.

APPENDIX 1
Copy Editing and Proofreading Symbols

Writing and editing for today's media are done almost exclusively on computers. Only in the book industry are most manuscripts still prepared on paper. Nevertheless, at some small newspapers and magazines, some editors prefer to edit on paper. For that reason, failure to learn the copy editing symbols used in manuscript preparation is a mistake. There is a good chance you will need to use these symbols at some point in your career, if only to satisfy the occasional editor who prefers doing things the old-fashioned way.

You are even more likely to use proofreading symbols, which are used on page proofs, to correct typeset copy. There are some similarities in the two sets of symbols, but there also are differences. The following chart illustrates the most common proofreading symbols (used to correct typeset copy), and the chart on page 346 shows the most common copy editing symbols (used in manuscript preparation).

⋀	Insert at this point.	ⱴⱴ	Space evenly.
⊥	Push down space.	◌	Close up entirely.
ⱷ	Take out letter, letters or words.	⊏	Move to left.
℈	Turn inverted letter.	⊐	Move to right.
ⓛⓒ	Set lowercase.	⊔	Lower letter or word.
ⓦⓕ	Wrong font letter.	⊓	Raise letter or word.
ⓘⓣⓐⓛ	Reset in italic type.	*out, see copy*	Words are left out.
ⓡⓞⓜ	Reset in roman (regular) type.	∥≡	Straighten lines.
ⓑⓕ	Reset in boldface type.	⑨	Start new paragraph.
○	Insert period.	*no* ⑨	No paragraph. Run together.
ⱱ	Insert comma.	*tr*	Transpose letters or words.
⋀	Insert semicolon.	②	Query; is copy right?
ⱨ	Insert hyphen.	⊢	Insert dash.
ⱱ	Insert apostrophe.	▢	Indent 1 em.
ⱴ ⱴ	Enclose in quotation marks.	⊔⊔	Indent 2 ems.
≡	Replace with a capital letter.	▢▢▢	Indent 3 ems.
#	Insert space.	*stet*	Let it stand.

Proofreading symbols.

Indent for new paragraph

no ¶   No paragraph (in margin)

Run in or bring

copy together

Join words: week end

Insert a *single* word or phrase

Insert a missing letter

Take out any extra letter

Transpose tow letters

Transpose words two

Make letter lower case

Capitalize columbia

Indicate *bf* boldface type

Abbreviate January 30

Spell out abbrev.

Spell out number 9

Make figures of thirteen

Separate run together words

Join letters in a w ord

Insert period.

Insert comma,

Insert quotation marks

Take out some word

Don't make this correction *stet*

Mark]centering[like this

]Indent copy from both sides[
by using these marks

Spell name Smyth as written

or

Spell name Smyth as written *fc*

There's more story: *More*

This ends story: # 30

Do not obliterate copy;
mark it out with a thin
line so it can be compared
with editing.

Mark in hyphen:

Mark in dash:

a and u

o and n

Copy editing symbols.

APPENDIX 2
Wire Service Style Summary

Most publications adhere to rules of style to avoid annoying inconsistencies. Without a stylebook to provide guidance in such matters, writers would not know whether *president* should be capitalized when preceding or following a name, whether the correct spelling is *employee* or *employe* (dictionaries list both), or whether a street name should appear as *Twelfth* or *12th*.

Newspapers use *The Associated Press Stylebook* to provide such guidance. Most newspapers, many magazines and their Web sites follow Associated Press style, although a few large newspapers and many magazines produce stylebooks of their own. Even if they use AP style, many publications make local exceptions to the AP rules, usually with some rationale for doing so. So, when you go to work at a publication or Web site, find out quickly what style manual governs.

This appendix is a brief summary of the primary rules of wire service style. We include the rules used most frequently, arranged by topic to make them easy to learn. About 10 percent of the rules in a stylebook account for 90 percent of the style you will use regularly; the rest of the rules you will use about 10 percent of the time. Thus, learning the rules you will use most often makes sense. This summary should be helpful even if you do not have a stylebook, but we assume that most users of this book do have one.

For online practice with AP style, please go to Exercise Central for AP Style, available with this text (bedfordstmartins.com/newscentral).

ABBREVIATIONS AND ACRONYMS
Punctuation of Abbreviations

- Generally speaking, abbreviations of two letters or fewer have periods:

  600 B.C., A.D. 1066
  8 a.m., 7 p.m.
  U.N., U.S., R.I., N.Y.
  8151 Yosemite St.
  EXCEPTIONS: AM radio, FM radio, 35 mm camera, AP, LA, D-Mass., R-Kan., IQ, TV, EU

- Generally speaking, abbreviations of three letters or more do not have periods:

  CIA, FBI, NATO
  mpg, mph
  EXCEPTION: c.o.d.

Symbols

- Always write out % as *percent* in a story, but you may use the symbol in a headline.
- Always write out & as *and* unless it is part of a company's formal name.
- Always write out ¢ as *cent* or *cents*: *7 cents*.
- Always use the symbol $ rather than the word *dollar* with any actual figure, and put the symbol before the figure: *$5*. Write out *dollar* only if you are speaking of, say, the value of the dollar on the world market.

Dates

- Never abbreviate days of the week.
- Don't abbreviate a month unless used with a specific date: *December 2008*; *Dec. 17*; *Dec. 17, 2008*.
- Never abbreviate the five months spelled with five letters or fewer: *March*; *April 20*; *May 13, 2009*; *June 1956*; *July of that year*.
- Never abbreviate *Christmas* as *Xmas*, even in a headline.
- Always write out *Fourth of July*.
- *Sept. 11* is preferred over *9/11*.

People and Titles

- Some publications still use courtesy titles (*Mr., Mrs., Ms., Miss*) on second reference in stories, although most seem to have moved away from them because they are considered sexist by many. Many publications use them only in quotations from sources. Others use them only in obituaries and editorials or on second reference in stories mentioning a husband and wife. In the last case, some newspapers prefer to repeat the person's whole name or, especially in features, use the person's first name. The Associated Press suggests using a courtesy title when someone requests it, but most journalists don't bother to ask.
- Use the abbreviations *Gov., Lt. Gov., Rep., Sen.* and *the Rev.*, as well as abbreviations of military titles, on first reference; then drop the title on subsequent references. Some titles you might expect to see abbreviated before a name are not abbreviated in AP style: *Attorney General, District Attorney, President, Professor, Superintendent*.
- Use the abbreviations *Jr.* and *Sr.* after a name on first reference if appropriate, but do not set them off by commas as you learned to do in English class.

Organizations

- Write out the first reference to most organizations in full rather than using an acronym: *National Organization for Women*. For *CIA, FBI* and *GOP*, however, the acronym may be used on the first reference.
- You may use well-known abbreviations such as *FCC* and *NOW* in a headline even though they would not be acceptable on first reference in the story.

- Do not put the abbreviation of an organization's name in parentheses after the full name on first reference. If an abbreviation seems likely to be confusing, don't use it at all; instead, refer to the organization as, for example, "the gay rights group" or "the bureau" on second reference.
- Use the abbreviations *Co., Cos., Corp., Inc.* and *Ltd.* at the end of a company's name even if the company spells out the word; do not abbreviate these words if followed by words like "of America." The abbreviations *Co., Cos.* and *Corp.* are used, however, if followed by *Inc.* or *Ltd.*, and *Inc.* and *Ltd.* are not set off by commas even if the company uses them.
- Abbreviate political affiliations after a name in the following way:

    Sen. Christopher Bond, R-Mo., said . . .

    Note the use of a single letter without a period for the party and the use of commas around the party and state.
- Never abbreviate the word *association*, even as part of a name.

Places

- Don't abbreviate a state name unless it follows the name of a city in that state:

    Nevada; Brown City, Mich.
- Never abbreviate the six states spelled with five or fewer letters or the two noncontiguous states:

    Alaska, Hawaii, Idaho, Iowa, Maine, Ohio, Texas, Utah
- Use the two-letter postal abbreviations only when a full address is given that includes a ZIP code.
- Use the traditional state abbreviations in normal copy:

Ala.	Md.	N.D.
Ariz.	Mass.	Okla.
Ark.	Mich.	Ore.
Calif.	Minn.	Pa.
Colo.	Miss.	R.I.
Conn.	Mo.	S.C.
Del.	Mont.	S.D.
Fla.	Neb.	Tenn.
Ga.	Nev.	Vt.
Ill.	N.H.	Va.
Ind.	N.J.	Wash.
Kan.	N.M.	W.Va.
Ky.	N.Y.	Wis.
La.	N.C.	Wyo.

- Use state abbreviations with domestic towns and cities unless they appear in the wire service dateline list of cities that stand alone. Many publications add to the wire service list their own list of towns well-known in the state or region.
- Use nations' full names with foreign towns and cities unless the towns and cities appear in the wire service dateline list of cities that stand alone. Once a state or nation has been identified in a story, it is unnecessary to repeat the name unless clarity demands it.

- The list of cities in the U.S. and the rest of the world that the AP says may stand alone without a state abbreviation or nation is too lengthy to include here. Consult the stylebook. A handy rule of thumb is that if it's an American city and has a major sports franchise, it probably stands alone. Likewise, if it's a foreign city that most people have heard of, it probably stands alone.
- Don't abbreviate the names of thoroughfares if there is no street address with them:

Main Street, Century Boulevard West

- If a thoroughfare's name includes the word *avenue, boulevard, street* or any of the directions on a map, such as *north* or *southeast*, abbreviate those words in a street address:

1044 W. Maple St.; 1424 Lee Blvd. S.; 999 Jackson Ave.

- In a highway's name, always abbreviate *U.S.* but never abbreviate a state's name. In the case of an interstate highway, the name is written in full on first reference, abbreviated afterward:

U.S. 63 or U.S. Highway 63; Massachusetts 2
Interstate 70 (first reference); I-70 (second reference)

- Never abbreviate *Fort* or *Mount*.
- Use the abbreviation *St.* for *Saint* in place-names.
EXCEPTIONS: *Saint John* in New Brunswick, *Ste. Genevieve* in Missouri, *Sault Ste. Marie* in Michigan and Ontario.
- Abbreviate *United States* and *United Nations* as *U.S.* and *U.N.* in all usages.

Miscellaneous

- Use the abbreviation *IQ* (no periods) in all references to *intelligence quotient*.
- Abbreviate and capitalize the word *number* when followed by a numeral: *No. 1*.
- Use the abbreviation *TV* (no periods) as a noun or adjective and in constructions like *cable TV*.
- Use the abbreviation *UFO* in all references to an *unidentified flying object*.
- Use the abbreviation *vs.*, not *v.*, for *versus* in short expressions: *guns vs. butter*. Use *v.* for court cases.

CAPITALIZATION

- Proper nouns are capitalized; common nouns are not. Unfortunately, this rule is not always easy to apply when the noun is the name of an animal, food or plant or when it is a trademark that has become so well-known that people mistakenly use it generically.
- Regions are capitalized; directions are not:

We drove east two miles to catch the interstate out West.

  – Adjectives and nouns pertaining to a region are capitalized: *Southern accent, Western movie, a Southerner, the Midwestern drought*.

- A region combined with a country's name is not capitalized unless the region is part of the name of a politically divided country: *eastern United States, North Korea*.
- A region combined with a state name is capitalized only if it is famous: *Southern California, southern Colorado*.

• When two or more proper nouns share a plural common noun, the shared plural is lowercased:

Missouri and Mississippi rivers
Chrisman and Truman high schools

• Government and college terms are not always as consistent as you might think:

- College departments follow the animal, food and plant rule. Capitalize only words that are already proper nouns: *Spanish department, sociology department*.
- Always capitalize a specific government department, even without the city, state or federal designator, and even if the department's name is turned around with *of* deleted: *Police Department, Fire Department, State Department, Department of Commerce*.
- Capitalize college and government committees if the formal name is given; lowercase any shorter, descriptive designation: *Special Senate Select Committee to Investigate Improper Labor-Management Practices*; *rackets committee*.
- Spell out and lowercase the names of academic degrees: *bachelor of arts degree, master's degree*. Avoid the abbreviations *Ph.D., M.A., B.A.*, etc., except in lists.
- Always capitalize (unless plural or generic) *City Council* and *County Commission* (but alone, *council* and *commission* are lowercased). Capitalize *Cabinet* when referring to advisers. Capitalize *Legislature* if the state's legislative body is formally named that. *Capitol*, meaning the building, is capitalized; *capital*, meaning the city, is not.
- Never capitalize *board of directors* or *board of trustees* (but capitalize *Board of Curators* and *Board of Education*). Do not capitalize *federal, government* and *administration*.
- Capitalize *president* and *vice president* before a name; otherwise, lowercase.
- Capitalize military titles *(Sgt., Maj., Gen.*, etc.) before a name. Note that the older form of military titles is preferred to the ones currently used in the military *(SGT, MAJ, BG)*. Capitalize *Air Force, Army, Marines* and *Navy* if referring to U.S. forces.
- Capitalize political parties, including the word *party*: *Democratic Party, Socialist Party*. Capitalize words such as *communist, democratic, fascist* and *socialist* only if they refer to a formal party rather than to a philosophy.

• Some Internet terms are capitalized; some are not.

- *Internet* and *Net* (acceptable in later references) are capitalized.
- *World Wide Web* and *Web* (as in *the Web, Web site* and *Web page*) are capitalized. But *webcam, webcast* and *webmaster* are lowercased.
- *E-mail* and similar terms (*e-book, e-commerce, e-business*) are lowercased.

- Religious terms are variously capitalized and lowercased:

  - *Pope* is lowercased except before a name: *the pope, Pope Gregory.*
  - *Mass* is always capitalized.
  - Names of religious figures are capitalized: *Prophet Muhammad, Buddha.*
  - Pronouns for God and Jesus are lowercased.
  - Names of holy books are capitalized: *Talmud, Quran* (preferred to *Koran*).
  - *Bible* is capitalized when meaning the Holy Scriptures and lowercased when referring to another book: *a hunter's bible.*
  - Sacraments are capitalized if they commemorate events in the life of Jesus or signify his presence: *The Lord's Supper, Holy Communion*, but *baptism, confirmation.*
  - Most other religious terms (except holidays) are lowercased: *bar mitzvah, nirvana, Hanukkah.*

- Proper names of races and nationalities are capitalized, but color descriptions are not: *Arab, Asian* (preferred to *Oriental* for people), *Caucasian, Cherokee, Chinese* (singular and plural), *French Canadian, Negro* (used only in names of organizations and quotations), *white, black.*

- Formal titles of people are capitalized before a name, but occupational titles are not:

  President John F. Kennedy, Mayor Dennis Archer, Coach Bill Self, Dean Fred Wilson

  astronaut Mary Gardner, journalist Anita Black, plumber Phil Sanders, pharmacist Roger Wheaton

  When in doubt about whether a title is formal or occupational, put the title after the name, set off with commas, and use lowercase.

- Formal titles that are capitalized before a name are lowercased after a name:

  Richard M. Nixon, former president of the United States
  Michael Bloomberg, mayor of New York City
  Roy Williams, coach of the North Carolina Tar Heels
  Fred Wilson, dean of students

- Formal titles that are abbreviated before a name are written out and lowercased if they follow a name:

  Gov. Arnold Schwarzenegger; Arnold Schwarzenegger, governor of California
  Sen. Lindsey Graham of South Carolina; Lindsey Graham, senator from South Carolina

- The first word in a direct quotation is capitalized only if the quote meets these three criteria:

  - It is a complete sentence. Don't capitalize a partial quote.
  - It stands alone as a separate sentence or paragraph, or it is set off from its source by a comma or colon.
  - It is a direct quotation (it appears in quotation marks).

- A question within a sentence is capitalized: *My only question is, When do we start?*

NUMBERS

- Cardinal numbers (numerals) are used in:
  - Addresses: Use numerals for street addresses: *1322 N. 10th St.*
  - Ages: Use numerals, even for days or months: *3 days old; John Burnside, 56.*
  - Aircraft and spacecraft: *F-4, DC-10, Apollo 11.* EXCEPTION: *Air Force One.*
  - Clothes sizes: *size 6.*
  - Dates: Use the numeral alone—no *nd, rd, st* or *th* after it: *March 20.*
  - Decades: *the '80s.*
  - Dimensions: *5 foot-6-inch guard* (but no hyphen when the word modified is associated with size: *3 feet tall, 10 feet long*).
  - Highways: *U.S. 63.*
  - Millions, billions, trillions: *6 million, 1.2 billion, 4 trillion.*
  - Money: Use numerals: *18 pesos, 10 francs.* Write millions, billions and trillions like this: *$1.4 million, £10.7 billion.*
  - Numbers: *No. 1, No. 2.*
  - Percentages: Use numerals except at the beginning of a sentence: *4 percent.*
  - Recipes: Use numerals for ingredient amounts: *2 teaspoons, 3 cups.*
  - Speeds: *55 mph, 4 knots.*
  - Sports: Use numerals for just about everything: *8-6 score, 2 yards, 3-under-par, 2 strokes.*
  - Temperatures: Use numerals for all except *zero.* Below zero, spell out *minus: minus 6,* not *-6* (except in tabular data).
  - Times: *4 a.m., 6:32 p.m., noon, midnight, five minutes, three hours.*
  - Weights: *7 pounds, 11 ounces.*
  - Years: Use numerals without commas. A year is the only numeral that can start a sentence: *2007 was a good year.*
- Ordinal numbers (ending with *nd, rd, st* and *th*) are used for:
  - Amendments to the Constitution after the *Ninth.* For *First* through *Ninth,* use words: *First Amendment, 16th Amendment.*
  - Courts: *2nd District Court, 10th Circuit Court of Appeals.*
  - Military units: *1st Battalion, 2nd Division, 7th Fleet.*
  - Political divisions (precincts, wards, districts): *3rd Congressional District.*
  - Streets after *Ninth.* For *First* through *Ninth,* use words: *Fifth Avenue, 13th Street.*
- Words are used for:
  - Any number at the start of a sentence except for a year: *Sixteen years ago . . .*
  - Casual numbers: *about a hundred or so.*
  - Fractions less than one: *one-half.*
  - Numbers less than 10, with the exceptions noted above: *five people, four rules.*
- Numerals are used for fractions greater than one: *1 1/2.*
- Roman numerals are used for a man who is the third or later in his family to bear a name and for a king, queen, pope or world war: *John D. Rockefeller III, Queen Elizabeth II, Pope Benedict XVI, World War I.*

APPENDIX 3
Twenty Common Errors of Grammar and Punctuation

Grammar provides a language's rules of the road. When you see a green light, you proceed on faith that the other driver will not go through the red light. Drivers have a shared understanding of the rules of the road. Writers and readers have a shared understanding of the grammar rules that ensure we understand what we are reading. Occasionally, as on the road, there is a wreck. We dangle participles, misplace modifiers and omit commas. If we write "Running down the street, his pants fell off," we are saying a pair of pants ran down a street. If we write "He hit Harry and John stopped him," the missing comma causes us, at least momentarily, to misread the meaning as "He hit Harry and John."

To say what you mean—to avoid syntactical wrecks—you must know the rules of grammar. We have compiled a list of 20 common errors that we find in our students' stories and in the stories of many professionals. Avoid them, and you'll write safely.

For online practice with grammar, please go to Exercise Central for AP Style, available with this text (bedfordstmartins.com/newscentral). There you will find advice and activities that go beyond grammar; the updated Exercise Central offers much more on Associated Press style—the style that makes newswriting distinctly journalistic.

1. Incorrect Comma in a Series in Associated Press Style

Use commas to separate the items in a series, but do not put a comma before *and* or *or* at the end of the series unless the meaning would be unclear without a comma.

INCORRECT
COMMA BEFORE
"AND"

The film was fast-paced, sophisticated, and funny.

CLEAR
WITHOUT COMMA

The film was fast-paced, sophisticated and funny.

The comma is sometimes needed to prevent misreading.

UNCLEAR
WITHOUT COMMA

He demanded cheese, salsa with jalapeños and onions on his taco.

A comma before *and* would prevent readers from wondering if he demanded salsa containing both jalapeños and onions or if he wanted the salsa and the onions as two separate toppings.

| COMMA NEEDED BEFORE "AND" | He demanded cheese, salsa with jalapeños, and onions on his taco. |

One way to indicate salsa with both jalapeños and onions is to add *and* before *salsa* and remove all commas.

| NO COMMAS | He demanded cheese and salsa with jalapeños and onions on his taco. |

2. Comma Splice

An independent clause contains a subject and a predicate and makes sense by itself. A run-on sentence—also known as a *comma splice*—occurs when two or more independent clauses are joined incorrectly with a comma.

| RUN-ON | John Rogers left the family law practice, he decided to become a teacher. |

You can correct a run-on sentence in several ways. Join the clauses with a comma and one of the coordinating conjunctions—*and, but, for, nor, or, yet* or *so*—or join the clauses with a semicolon if they are closely related. Use a subordinating conjunction such as *after, because, if* or *when* to turn one of the clauses into a dependent clause. Or rewrite the run-on as two separate sentences.

CORRECTING A RUN-ON WITH A COMMA AND A COORDINATING CONJUNCTION

John Rogers left the family law practice, <u>for</u> he decided to become a teacher.

CORRECTING A RUN-ON WITH A SEMICOLON

John Rogers left the family law practice; he decided to become a teacher.

CORRECTING A RUN-ON BY MAKING ONE INDEPENDENT
CLAUSE A DEPENDENT CLAUSE

John Rogers left the family law practice <u>when</u> he decided to become a teacher.

CORRECTING A RUN-ON BY WRITING TWO SEPARATE SENTENCES

John Rogers left the family law practice. He decided to become a teacher.

3. Sentence Fragment

A sentence fragment is a word group that lacks a subject, a verb or both yet is punctuated as though it were a complete sentence. Another type of fragment is a word group that begins with a subordinating conjunction such as *because* or *when*, yet is punctuated as though it were a complete sentence.

| FRAGMENTS | After she had placed her watch and an extra pencil on the table. |
| | Without feeling especially sorry about it. |

Correct a fragment by joining it to the sentence before or after it or by adding the missing elements so that the fragment contains a subject and a verb and can stand alone.

CORRECTING A FRAGMENT BY JOINING IT TO ANOTHER SENTENCE

After she had placed her watch and an extra pencil on the table, the student opened the exam booklet.

CORRECTING A FRAGMENT BY TURNING IT INTO A SENTENCE

She apologized to her boss for the outburst without feeling especially sorry about it.

4. Missing Comma(s) with a Nonrestrictive Element

A nonrestrictive element is a word, phrase or clause that gives information about the preceding part of the sentence but does not restrict or limit the meaning of that part. A nonrestrictive element is not essential to the meaning of the sentence; you can delete it and still understand clearly what the sentence is saying. Place commas before and (if necessary) after a nonrestrictive element.

UNCLEAR	The mayor asked to meet Alva Johnson a highly decorated police officer.
CLEAR	The mayor asked to meet Alva Johnson, a highly decorated police officer.
UNCLEAR	His wife Mary was there.
CLEAR	His wife, Mary, was there.

5. Confusion of *That* and *Which*

The pronoun *that* always introduces restrictive information, which is essential to the meaning of the sentence; do not set off a *that* clause with commas. The pronoun *which* introduces nonrestrictive, or nonessential, information; set off a nonrestrictive *which* clause with commas.

INCORRECT	The oldest store in town, Miller and Company, that has been on Main Street for almost a century, will close this summer.
CORRECT	The oldest store in town, Miller and Company, which has been on Main Street for almost a century, will close this summer.
INCORRECT	The creature, which has been frightening residents of North First Street for the past week, has turned out to be a screech owl.
CORRECT	The creature that has been frightening residents of North First Street for the past week has turned out to be a screech owl.

6. Missing Comma After an Introductory Element

A sentence may begin with a dependent clause (a word group that contains a subject and a verb and begins with a subordinating conjunction such as *because* or *when*), a prepositional phrase (a word group that begins with a preposition like *in* or *on* and ends with a noun or pronoun), an adverb such as *next* that modifies the whole sentence, or a participial phrase (a word group that contains a past or present participle, such as *determined* or *hoping*, that acts as an adjective). Use a comma to separate these introductory elements from the main clause of the sentence.

DEPENDENT CLAUSE	<u>After the applause had died down,</u> the conductor raised his baton again.
PREPOSITIONAL PHRASE	<u>Without a second thought,</u> the chicken crossed the road.
ADVERB	<u>Furthermore,</u> the unemployment rate continues to rise.
PARTICIPIAL PHRASE	<u>Waiting in the bar,</u> Jose grew restless. <u>Saddened by the news from home,</u> she stopped reading the letter.

Although it is always correct to use a comma after an introductory element, the comma may be omitted after some adverbs and short prepositional phrases if the meaning is clear:

Suddenly it's spring.

In Chicago it rained yesterday.

Always place a comma after two or more introductory prepositional phrases.

In May of last year in Toronto, Tom attended three conventions.

Here are more examples:

INCORRECT	Shaking her head at the latest budget information the library administrator wondered where to find the money for new books.
CORRECT	Shaking her head at the latest budget information, the library administrator wondered where to find the money for new books.
INCORRECT	After a week of foggy, rainy mornings had passed he left Seattle.
CORRECT	After a week of foggy, rainy mornings had passed, he left Seattle.

7. Missing Comma(s) Between Coordinate Adjectives

Adjectives are coordinate if they make sense when you insert *and* between them or place them in reverse order.

The frightened, angry citizens protested the new policy.
The frightened and angry citizens protested the new policy.

The adjectives make sense with *and* between them, so they are coordinate.

The angry, frightened citizens protested the new policy.

The adjectives make sense in reverse order, so they are coordinate. Separate coordinate adjectives with commas.

INCORRECT	**The gaunt lonely creature was also afraid.**
CORRECT	**The gaunt, lonely creature was also afraid.**

8. Missing Comma in a Compound Sentence

Two or more independent clauses—word groups containing a subject and a verb and expressing a complete thought—joined with a coordinating conjunction (*and, but, for, nor, or, yet* or *so*) form a compound sentence. Place a comma before the conjunction in a compound sentence to avoid confusion.

UNCLEAR	**She works as a pharmacist now and later she plans to go to medical school.**
CLEAR	**She works as a pharmacist now, and later she plans to go to medical school.**

9. Missing Semicolons Between Items in a Series with Internal Commas

When commas appear within the items in a series, separate the items in the series with semicolons for clarity.

UNCLEAR	**The injured include Barney Corrigan, 31, of 445 Main St., Sheila Okafur, 28, of 333 Elm St., and Shawna Taylor, 35, of 71 Edgewood Ave.**
CLEAR	**The injured include Barney Corrigan, 31, of 445 Main St.; Sheila Okafur, 28, of 333 Elm St.; and Shawna Taylor, 35, of 71 Edgewood Ave.**

10. Misplaced or Dangling Modifier

Modifiers are words or phrases that change or clarify the meaning of another word or word group in a sentence. Place modifiers immediately before or directly after the word or words they modify. A *misplaced modifier* appears too far from the word or words it is supposed to modify in the sentence. A *dangling modifier* appears in a sentence that does not contain the word or words it is supposed to modify. A modifier at the beginning of a sentence should refer to the grammatical subject of the sentence.

MISPLACED MODIFIER	*subject* **Having predicted a sunny morning, the downpour surprised the meteorologist.**
CORRECT	*subject* **Having predicted a sunny morning, the meteorologist did not expect the downpour.**

DANGLING MODIFIER	*subject* <u>Working in the yard,</u> the sun burned her badly.
CORRECT	*subject* Working in the yard, she became badly sunburned.

11. Missing or Misused Hyphen(s) in a Compound Modifier

A compound modifier consists of two or more adjectives or an adjective-adverb combination used to modify a single noun. When a compound modifier precedes a noun, you should hyphenate the parts of the compound unless the compound consists of an adverb ending in -*ly* followed by an adjective.

INCORRECT	His <u>over the top</u> performance made the whole film unbelievable.
	The <u>freshly-printed</u> counterfeit bills felt like genuine dollars.
	The local chapter of Parents without Partners will sponsor an <u>open-toga</u> party on Saturday.
CORRECT	His over-the-top performance made the whole film unbelievable.
	The freshly printed counterfeit bills felt like genuine dollars.
	The local chapter of Parents without Partners will sponsor an open toga party on Saturday.

12. Missing or Misused Apostrophe

Do not confuse the pronoun *its*, meaning "belonging to it," with the contraction *it's*, meaning "it is" or "it has." The possessive form of a noun uses an apostrophe; possessive pronouns never take apostrophes.

INCORRECT	The car is lying on it's side in the ditch.
	Its a blue 2007 Ford Taurus.
	That new car of her's rides very smoothly.
CORRECT	The car is lying on its side in the ditch.
	It's a blue 2007 Ford Taurus.
	That new car of hers rides very smoothly.

For clarity, avoid using the contraction ending in -*'s* to mean "has" instead of "is."

UNCLEAR	She's held many offices in student government.
CLEAR	She has held many offices in student government.

13. Incorrect Pronoun Case

A pronoun that is the subject of a sentence or clause must be in the subjective case (*I, he, she, we, they*). A pronoun that is the direct object of a verb, the indirect object of a verb, or the object of a preposition must be in the objective case (*me, him, her, us, them*). To decide whether a pronoun in a compound construction—two or more nouns or pronouns joined with *and* or *or*—should be subjective or objective, omit everything in the compound except the pronoun, and see whether the subjective or objective case sounds correct.

INCORRECT   **He took my wife and I to dinner.**

(Try that sentence without the first part of the compound, *my wife and.*)

CORRECT   **He took my wife and me to dinner.**

INCORRECT   **Her and her family donated the prize money.**

(Try that sentence without the second part of the compound, *and her family.*)

CORRECT   **She and her family donated the prize money.**

The pronouns *who* and *whom* often cause confusion. *Who* (or *whoever*) is subjective; *whom* (or *whomever*) is objective. If the pronoun appears in a question, answer the question using a pronoun (such as *I* or *me*) to determine whether to use the subjective or objective form.

INCORRECT   **Who does Howard want to see?**

Answering the question—*Howard wants to see me*—reveals that the pronoun should be objective.

CORRECT   **Whom does Howard want to see?**

When *who* or *whom* is not part of a question, it introduces a dependent clause. Determine the case of the pronoun in the clause by removing the clause from the sentence and replacing *who* or *whom* with *I* and *me* to see which form is correct.

INCORRECT   **She welcomed whomever knocked on her door.**

The dependent clause is *whomever knocked on her door.* Replacing *whomever* with *I* and *me*—*I knocked on her door; me knocked on her door*—reveals that the subjective form *whoever* is correct.

CORRECT   **She welcomed whoever knocked on her door.**

14. Lack of Agreement Between Pronoun and Antecedent

Pronouns must agree in number (singular or plural) and person (first, second or third) with their *antecedents*—the nouns or pronouns to which they refer. Do not shift, for example, from a singular antecedent to a plural pronoun, or from a third-person antecedent to a first- or second-person pronoun.

INCORRECT   **The class must check their work.**

CORRECT   **The class must check its work.**

                   Class members must check their work.

15. Biased Language

Avoid stereotypes and biased language. Take special care to avoid gender-specific pronouns.

BIASED	A reporter must always check his work.
ACCEPTABLE	Reporters must always check their work.
	If you are a reporter, you must always check your work.
BIASED	Local politicians and their wives attended a dinner in honor of the visiting diplomat.
ACCEPTABLE	Local politicians and their spouses attended a dinner in honor of the visiting diplomat.

16. Lack of Agreement Between Subject and Verb

Subject and verb must agree in number. Use the form of the verb that agrees with a singular or plural subject. Be especially careful to identify the subject correctly when words separate subject from verb.

INCORRECT	The bag with the green stripes <u>belong</u> to her.
CORRECT	The bag with the green stripes <u>belongs</u> to her.

A compound subject with parts joined by *and* is always plural. When parts of a compound subject are joined by *or*, make the verb agree with the part of the compound closest to the verb.

INCORRECT	A mystery writer and her daughter <u>lives</u> in the house by the river.
CORRECT	A mystery writer and her daughter <u>live</u> in the house by the river.
INCORRECT	Either Mike or his sisters <u>has</u> the spare key.
CORRECT	Either Mike or his sisters <u>have</u> the spare key.

17. Incorrect Complement with Linking Verb

A linking verb such as *be, appear, feel* or *become* links a subject with a word or words that identify or describe the subject. When the identifying word—called a *subject complement*—is a pronoun, use the subjective case for the pronoun.

INCORRECT	That was <u>him</u> on the telephone five minutes ago.
CORRECT	That was <u>he</u> on the telephone five minutes ago.

When a word or words describing the subject follow a linking verb, the word or words must be adjectives.

INCORRECT	She feels <u>terribly</u> about the things she said.
CORRECT	She feels <u>terrible</u> about the things she said.

18. Incorrect Use of Subjunctive Mood

Conditions contrary to fact require a verb to be in the subjunctive mood. Apply this rule in stories about all pending legislation at all levels of government. Use the subjunctive mood in "that" clauses after verbs of wishing, suggesting and requiring; in other words, use the subjunctive in clauses, dependent or independent, that do not state a fact.

INCORRECT	The bylaws require that he <u>declares</u> his candidacy by April 10.
CORRECT	The bylaws require that he <u>declare</u> his candidacy by April 10.
INCORRECT	The bill <u>will</u> require everyone to register for the draft at age 18.
CORRECT	The bill <u>would</u> require everyone to register for the draft at age 18.

19. Wrong Word

Wrong-word errors include using a word that sounds similar to, or the same as, the word you need but means something different (such as writing *affect* when you mean *effect*) and using a word that has a shade of meaning that is not what you intend (such as writing *slender* when you want to suggest *scrawny*). Check the dictionary if you are not sure whether you are using a word correctly.

INCORRECT	Merchants who appear <u>disinterested</u> in their customers may lose business.
CORRECT	Merchants who appear <u>uninterested</u> in their customers may lose business.
INCORRECT	The guests gasped and applauded when they saw the <u>excessive</u> display of food.
CORRECT	The guests gasped and applauded when they saw the <u>lavish</u> display of food.

20. Incorrect Verb Form

Every verb has five forms: a base form, a present-tense form, a past-tense form, a present-participle form used for forming the progressive tenses, and a past-participle form used for forming the passive voice or one of the perfect tenses.

Dropping the ending from present-tense forms and regular past-tense forms is a common error.

INCORRECT	The police are <u>suppose</u> to protect the public.
CORRECT	The police are <u>supposed</u> to protect the public.

Regular verbs end in *-ed* in the past tense and past participle, but irregular verbs do not follow a set pattern for forming the past tense and past participle, so these forms of irregular verbs are frequently used incorrectly. Look up irregular verbs if you are uncertain of the correct form.

INCORRECT	The manager was not in the restaurant when it was robbed because he had <u>went</u> home early.
CORRECT	The manager was not in the restaurant when it was robbed because he had <u>gone</u> home early.
INCORRECT	The thieves <u>taked</u> everything in the safe.
CORRECT	The thieves <u>took</u> everything in the safe.

APPENDIX 4
Crisis Coverage: An Interactive CD-ROM Journalism Simulation

As mentioned in Chapter 9, crime, accidents and fires, and disasters are staples of news reporting. Almost every journalist working on a newspaper will write these types of stories, and many cover such stories frequently. Unfortunately, gaining real-world experience with this reporting is nearly impossible in an introductory newswriting class. Robberies, house fires and car accidents do not fit neatly into a syllabus, nor do listening to a police scanner and driving to such events fit neatly into a student schedule.

The exercises in Chapter 9 of the *Workbook for TELLING THE STORY* provide a good starting point for learning the fundamentals of crime, accident and fire, and disaster reporting, but they can't simulate the news-gathering process. To help prepare you for these genres, we provide a CD-ROM simulation of an actual tragedy, the shooting of a police officer and four bystanders in St. Joseph, Mo.

TIPS FOR USING THE PROGRAM

The simulation program puts you in the news room the night of the shooting. After a brief introduction and opening segment, you begin your news gathering at your desk in the news room. Your job is to get information from paper, human and electronic sources as the night progresses and then to write up a story as more information becomes available (see the section "Types of Articles and Assignments" for possible stories and assignments). The simulation progresses from approximately 5 p.m. until deadline at 11 p.m.

The main interface is the news room cubicle. On and around your desk are items to click on to get information, as the accompanying screen capture illustrates.

Clicking on the Desk Items

Just as in real-world reporting, sources develop over the course of the story, and some will not be immediately available to you. For example, when the scenario first begins, the reporters dispatched to the scene (under Map of Area) will not be ready to talk to you, nor will a phone call to the police station or hospital give you any information. Be sure to check back on these sources frequently as the night progresses and as more bits of news become available. The sources include the following:

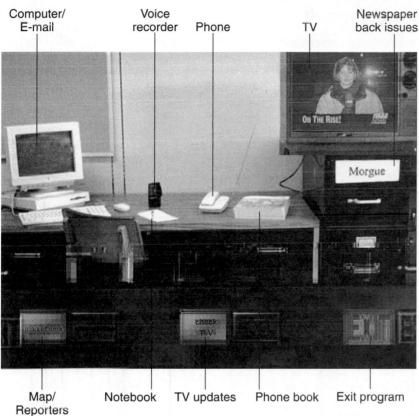

Computer/E-mail • Voice recorder • Phone • TV • Newspaper back issues • Morgue • Map/Reporters on scene • Notebook • TV updates • Phone book • Exit program

- *Television.* You will watch actual news broadcasts from the night of the shooting.
- *Phone book.* Good reporters use the phone extensively. You will call some of your sources, and they will give you quotes and information.
- *Phone.* Sources will call you with updated information throughout the night.
- *Morgue.* Background research is crucial to quality reporting. You will want to check to see if there are any related articles from back issues of the newspaper.
- *Map/reporters.* Three reporters will be on the scene. They will give you updates and quotes from eyewitnesses.
- *Notebook.* Reporters will bring back their notebooks with interview notes for you to use in your story.
- *Voice recorder.* One reporter will bring back a recorded interview from the scene.
- *Computer/e-mail.* There will be e-mail and Web sources for you to use. In addition to the information provided on the CD-ROM, you may wish to do additional Web research.

Because these sources will be available at different times, be sure to click on all of the buttons in the time periods between the TV clips.

Pacing Yourself

The simulation covers a period of approximately six hours, but it will likely take you only between 30 and 60 minutes to run through the scenario. If you are running the program during a 75-minute or longer class, you should not have difficulty finishing the simulation during a full class period. If you are trying to complete the program within a 50-minute class period, be sure to be in class on time or early, take notes quickly and make good decisions about what information you will likely not need to copy down. Remember the principles of newsworthiness and definitions of "news" outlined in Chapter 1, and consider what information your readers will be interested in knowing.

Taking Notes

We pointed out in Chapter 1 that accuracy is a cornerstone of good journalism. Accuracy is especially important—and difficult—in breaking news stories about tragedies, stories that often are at the top of Page One and are read by nearly all of your audience. So be sure to take careful notes. This is not like a book exercise for which you can easily copy down notes and double-check them at a later time. Just as in real-world reporting, for many of these sources you will have only one opportunity to get the information right and to decide what information and quotes to include in your notes. If you're using the TV sources, you won't be able to replay these segments, so take good shorthand and reconstruct your notes after each segment, as we suggested in Chapter 3.

For your notes, you may wish to use a legal pad or a reporter's notebook. Depending on your writing and typing skills, you may prefer to take notes on the computer because you can later copy and paste segments from your computer notes into your final draft. To take the computer notes, you'll want to open up a word-processing program before starting the simulation and move the program's window to the side of the screen so you can click back and forth between the simulation program and the word-processing window when taking notes. Be sure to save your computer notes often, in case your computer crashes.

Using the TV

Good news reporters watch their broadcast colleagues—and competitors—all the time, especially during tragedies. You'll be watching several clips from the local TV station, which include selections from the local 6 p.m. and 10 p.m. newscasts and cut-ins with breaking news before and after those newscasts. In all, there are 10 video clips, some of which play automatically and some that play when you click on the Check TV button. *Be sure to try all of your other sources before you click on the Check TV button*, because the TV segment will jump you to a later part in the scenario.

Typically, a print journalist will not use quotes from radio or TV broadcasts. Before you begin the simulation, be sure to check with your instructor about using quotes from the television in your story. Your instructor may forbid you from using any TV quotes or allow you to cite such quotes sparingly (example: "In an interview with KQ2 TV last night, witness James Smith said, . . ."). He or she may allow you to quote the sources (not the reporters or anchors) as if you were interviewing them yourself. You need to know your instructor's wishes *before* you start the simulation so you'll know how carefully to take notes during the TV segments. You won't have a chance to hear and see these segments again.

Adjusting Sound and Using Headphones

Before you begin the scenario, you'll want to test the sound levels of your computer and make sure the sound is working, because you'll need to hear all the audio and video clips in order to write up your story. In addition, you may want to bring headphones that fit your computer port, to keep sound levels in the room down and to muffle the sound coming from nearby computers. Then again, the wide array of sounds and voices coming from a dozen or more computers might mimic the bedlam found in a news room near deadline.

Quitting and Restarting the Program

Because the program replicates the timing and flow of information in a tragedy, you will not be able to jump around in the program or quit and later restart the program where you left off. If you have to restart the program, you will be placed back at the very beginning of the scenario. So be absolutely sure you want to quit before you click on the red EXIT button. Likewise, to prevent the program from crashing and thus prevent you from needing to start over, make sure you are working on a reliable computer with sufficient RAM available.

For this assignment, your instructor may want you to run through the program only once, because you would get only one shot at gathering information under deadline in any crime or accident, fire, or disaster story. Or your instructor may allow you to run through the program multiple times to make sure you find all of the sources.

TIPS FOR WRITING YOUR ARTICLE

Keep in mind one key tip in newswriting: Listen carefully to your editor — in this case, your instructor — about what type of article he or she wants you to write. For a spot news story like this, neither you nor your editor would have time to do a rewrite.

In addition, make sure you understand the nature of the publication and your audience. If you want to replicate the actual situation, assume you are writing for the *St. Joseph News-Press*, an independently owned daily that has a circulation of approximately 10,000 and serves the 70,000 residents of St. Joseph, as well as people in the surrounding counties in northwest Missouri. Your instructor may prefer that you write the story for a larger paper, such as *The Kansas City Star*, or for a small, nearby weekly or for the Associated Press or another wire service. Which publication you write for will help determine how you write your story and what information you include.

Because most people will be writing an inverted-pyramid account of the main story, the majority of the tips in this section are geared toward this type of story. If you are writing a different type of story, you may want to refer to the sections of the book that address that type of story in more detail.

Rank Your Information in Order of Importance

You will have a lot of information to deal with and to try to fit into your story. To write an inverted-pyramid story, you may want to rank or mark each fact or quote to help you decide what material will go near the beginning, the middle and the end of the story and what information you probably won't need to use.

Prepare Information for a Summary Lead

You may not end up using a summary lead in your final draft, but drafting up such a lead will help you write the rest of the story. Using the ranking mentioned above, write down the key answers to these questions:

Who?
What?
Where?
When?
Why?
How?

Decide which of these items need to be in the lead (the "why," for example, might not be necessary or might be unknown). Put the most important of the 5 Ws and H at the beginning of the lead. Try to keep the lead to 25 or 30 words and preferably to one sentence.

Write Several Alternate Leads

Even if you think you are going to use a straight summary lead, you should try other types of leads as well because you may discover that one of these works better. Given the complexity of the situation, you may decide to use a multiple-element lead. Maybe the best choice will be a delayed-identification lead. If you are writing for the St. Joseph community, you may decide an immediate-identification lead is most appropriate. After trying several lead types, you may find that a flair lead that contains elements of description or narration would work best.

Draw a Map

Drawing a map of the scene or the area on a piece of paper can help you organize your thoughts and understand what happened, especially if you are a visually oriented person.

Make a Chronology

Even if you don't use a chronological format for your article, a timeline of the events will help you understand the events and write your article.

TYPES OF ARTICLES AND ASSIGNMENTS

In a situation like this tragedy, the entire reporting and editing staff is mobilized. Those who were off for the day or who had already put in their hours are called back, and the whole staff works together to produce the in-depth coverage that readers want and expect. Some reporters go to the scene and collect information. Others are stationed at the police department, city hall or hospital; still other staffers may research information in the news room morgue or online. Using all of these resources, the staff produces not only one main article but also three, four or more sidebars to accompany it.

The simulation program lends itself well to writing a variety of different stories and sidebars. Before you begin the simulation, you'll need to be clear about exactly what type of article or articles your instructor wants you to write, because the article's focus will affect what notes to take and what sources to pay especially close attention to.

The most typical assignment is covering the main story and using the inverted pyramid, the organizational format most often used for hard news stories like crime and accidents, fires, and disasters. Before you write such a story, be sure to reread Chapter 6 to review the principles for writing inverted-pyramid stories. Carefully consider what information is most important, and put that information early in the story. Don't bury key information that may end up getting cut or not getting read.

Using the inverted pyramid is not the only way to tell the story. In Chapter 9 the example of the Kansas man who was killed by a police marksman illustrated how a chronological approach sometimes works better. Your instructor may choose to have you write a chronological story instead of—or in addition to—an inverted-pyramid account. To do this, you probably will want to reconstruct a timeline and reorganize your notes to represent the order in which events happened, rather than the order in which the information became available to you. Your instructor may also assign you or give you the freedom to use one of the other alternatives to the inverted pyramid outlined in Chapter 7.

Regardless of which story type you are assigned, remember to include the key information and sources for crime and accident, fire, and disaster stories:

- Eyewitnesses.
- Police or other officials in charge of handling the situation.
- Victims and friends and relatives of the victims (when possible and appropriate).

Chapter 9 also stresses the importance of obtaining official documents for these types of stories, such as an accident report, a fire marshal's casualty report or a police report. For this simulation, however, an official document is not available before your deadline.

Your instructor may give you a word limit for your article, in the same way a managing editor, news editor or copy editor might tell a reporter in this situation, "Make it x inches, no more, no less," because the number of column inches allotted to the story might already have been set by the time the writer finishes the story. The editors and layout personnel would likely have been scrambling to assemble all of the new shooting-related articles, photos and informational graphics. The main story might have been held until the very last minute so that the most current information would appear in the next day's paper. Consequently, there might be little leeway given for the length of the article.

A word or inches limit is a restriction for print newspapers only, of course. The space limitations of the physical newspaper don't apply in an online environment. The print newspaper might have space for only a 700-word article and two photos, but the online edition could have 1,000-plus words and nearly unlimited photos and graphics.

Your instructor may choose one of the following articles or exercises or may give you some other assignment.

Main Story

Inverted Pyramid

Write a main news story that contains all of the important facets of the story. This is the story that would run under the headline at the top of Page One if you were writing for the local newspaper (see notes in the previous section about what publication you are writing for).

Alternative Organization

Consulting Chapter 7, use a different organizational method for writing the story, such as narration (chronological), vivid scenes, a focus structure or anecdotes.

Early Online Edition

Readers in the community and across the state or country who have heard about the shooting are not going to be content to wait until the next morning to find out more. As suggested on the first page of Chapter 1, the reporter will need to create text—and perhaps prepare multimedia—for the newspaper's Web site so that readers can access that information very soon after the incident. They may return several times in the next 24 hours, expecting updates.

There are two places in the CD-ROM simulation where you will be able to stop and write a story and an update for the online edition.

Wire Story

Assume that you are responsible for writing a story that will go out on the Associated Press wire and will likely be picked up by many of the daily newspapers across the state. Write a 750-word story.

Sidebar Stories

Shooting injuries.   Write a sidebar about the people injured. As detailed in Chapter 9, be sure to include the names, ages, addresses and conditions of the victims.

Neighbor/witness accounts.   Write a sidebar that focuses on the eyewitnesses and includes quotes and anecdotes about the shooting and the shooter.

Killing the shooter.   Write a sidebar about the killing of the shooter, making sure to include details about the event, eyewitness quotes and information about police procedures and policy during and after a shooting.

Historical/contextual piece.   This type of sidebar could take one of several different paths. It could look at the history of officers killed in the line of duty in the area. It could look at other mass shootings in the area. Or it could look at police officer deaths from a national perspective, requiring you to go online and research statistics.

Practice and Follow-Up

Writing leads.   Write a variety of leads for a main story, following the advice in Chapter 6 when composing an immediate-identification lead, a delayed-identification lead, a multiple-element lead and one or more flair leads.

Interviewing.   Pick two sources mentioned in the simulation that you would like to be able to interview in greater depth, and write up 10 questions for each person. As you learned in Chapter 3, you'll want to phrase and order these questions carefully because this situation is so sensitive. Because you will be wanting detailed quotes, make sure that at least seven of the questions are open-ended.

Ethics

After reading Chapter 15 and the section in Chapter 9 about victims and witnesses in the accidents and fires section, write a pro or con essay about calling to interview the spouse of the slain police officer. If you would call her, explain why and describe the approach you would take. If you would not call her, explain why and cite examples from the ethical codes to support your decision.

Glossary

absolute privilege   The right of legislators, judges and government executives to speak without threat of libel when acting in their official capacities.

absolutism   The ethical philosophy that there is a fixed set of principles or laws from which there is no deviation. To the absolutist journalist, the end never justifies the means.

actual malice   Reckless disregard for the truth. It is a condition in libel cases.

actual malice test   Protection for reporters to write anything about an office-holder or candidate unless they know that the material is false or they recklessly disregard the truth.

add   A printed page of copy following the first page. "First add" would be the second page of printed copy.

advance   A report dealing with the subjects and issues to be dealt with in an upcoming meeting or event.

advertising department   The newspaper department responsible for advertisements. Most advertising departments have classified and display ad sections.

anchor   A person in a television studio who ties together a newscast by reading the news and providing transitions from one story to the next.

anecdote   An informative and entertaining story within a story.

angle   The focus of, or approach to, a story. The latest development in a continuing controversy, the key play in a football game or the tragedy of a particular death in a mass disaster may serve as an angle.

annual percentage rate (APR)   The annual cost of a loan expressed as a percentage. The basic method for computing this figure is set forth in the Truth in Lending Act of 1968.

antinomianism   The ethical philosophy that recognizes no rules. An antinomian journalist judges each ethical situation on its own merits. Unlike the situation ethicist, the antinomian does not use love of neighbor as an absolute.

AP   The Associated Press, a worldwide news-gathering cooperative owned by its subscribers.

APME   Associated Press Managing Editors, an organization of managing editors and editors whose papers are members of the Associated Press.

arithmetic mean   See *average*.

assessed value   The amount that a government appraiser determines a property is worth.

assistant news director   The second in command in a television station news room.

average   A term used to describe typical or representative members of a group. In mathematics, it refers to the result obtained when a set of numbers is added together, then divided by the number of items in the set.

background   Information that may be attributed to a source by title but not by name; for example, "a White House aide said."

backgrounder   A story that explains and updates the news.

beat   A reporter's assigned area of responsibility. A beat may be an institution, such as a courthouse; a geographical area, such as a small town; or a subject, such as science. The term also refers to an exclusive story.

blog   Short for *Web log*. A Web-based publication in which articles, issued periodically, appear in reverse chronological order.

blotter   An old-fashioned term for the arrest sheet that summarizes the bare facts of an arrest. Today this information is almost always stored on computer.

book   Assembled sheets of paper, usually newsprint, and carbon paper on which reporters prepare stories. Books are not used with modern computerized processes.

Boolean search   A system used to search computer databases in which the search is narrowed through the use of operators such as AND, OR or NOT.

bureau   A news-gathering office maintained by a newspaper somewhere other than its central location. Papers may have bureaus in the next county; in the state capital; in Washington, D.C.; or in foreign countries.

byline   A line identifying the author of a story.

calendar year   The 12-month period from January through December.

change of venue   An order moving a court proceeding to another jurisdiction for prosecution. This transfer often occurs when a party in a case claims that local media coverage has prejudiced prospective jurors.

circulation department   The department responsible for distribution of the newspaper.

citizen journalism (participatory journalism)   A new form of media in which citizens actively participate in gathering and writing information, often in the form of news.

city editor   The individual (also known as the *metropolitan*, or *metro*, *editor*) in charge of the city desk, which coordinates local news-gathering operations. At some papers the desk also handles regional and state news done by its own reporters.

clip   A story clipped from a newspaper.

closed-ended question   A direct question designed to draw a specific response; for example, "Will you be a candidate?"

community portal   A Web site designed as a general entry point for Internet users in a city and its nearby suburbs.

compound interest   Interest paid on the total of the principal (the amount borrowed) and the interest that has already accrued.

conditional privilege   See *qualified privilege*.

constant dollars   Money numbers adjusted for inflation.

Consumer Price Index   A tool used by the government to measure the rate of inflation. CPI figures, reported monthly by the Bureau of Labor Statistics of the U.S. Department of Labor, compare the net change in prices between the current period and a specified base period. Reporters should use these data to accurately reflect the actual costs of goods and services.

contextual advertising   Advertising on a Web site directed to likely users of that site based on demographic profiles.

contributing editor   A magazine columnist who works under contract and not as an employee of the magazine.

convergence   A term defined in different ways by different people in the media industry but generally used to describe the coordination of print, broadcast and online reporting in a news operation.

copy   What reporters write. A story is a piece of copy.

copy desk   The desk at which final editing of stories is done, headlines are written and pages are designed.

copy editor   A person who checks, polishes and corrects stories written by reporters. Usually copy editors write headlines for these stories; sometimes they decide how to arrange stories and pictures on a page.

cover   To keep abreast of significant developments on a beat or to report on a specific event. The reporter covering the police beat may be assigned to cover a murder.

cutline   The caption that accompanies a newspaper or magazine photograph. The term dates from the days when photos were reproduced with etched zinc plates called *cuts*.

deadline   The time by which a reporter, editor or desk must have completed scheduled work.

deep background   Information that may be used but that cannot be attributed to either a person or a position.

delayed-identification lead   The opening paragraph of a story in which the "who" is identified by occupation, city, office or any means other than by name.

deontelics   Ethical thinking that considers both duties and ends.

deontological ethics   The ethics of duty.

desk   A term used by reporters to refer to the city editor's or copy editor's position, as in "The desk wants this story by noon."

desk assistant   An entry-level position in television news rooms. Desk assistants handle routine news assignments, such as monitoring wire services and listening to police scanners.

developing story   A story in which newsworthy events occur over several days or weeks.

dialogue   A conversation between two or more people, neither of whom normally is the reporter.

documentary   In-depth coverage of an issue or event, especially in broadcasting.

editor   The top-ranking individual in the news department of a newspaper, also known as the *editor in chief*. The term may refer as well to those at any level who edit copy.

editorial department The news department of a newspaper, responsible for all content of the newspaper except advertising. At some papers this term refers to the department responsible for the editorial page only.

editorialize To inject the reporter's or the newspaper's opinion into a news story or headline. Most newspapers restrict opinion to analysis stories, columns and editorials.

editorial page editor The individual in charge of the editorial page and, at larger newspapers, the op-ed page. See also *op-ed page*.

executive producer The television executive with overall responsibility for the look of the television newscast.

fair comment and criticism Opinion delivered on the performance of anyone in the public eye. Such opinion is legally protected if reporters do not misstate any of the facts on which they base their comments or criticism, and it is not malicious.

field producer A behind-the-scenes television reporter who often does much of the field work for a network's on-camera correspondents.

fiscal year Any 12-month period used to calculate annual revenues and expenditures.

flat-file database A simple database program that allows users to keep track of data of almost any type. A simple address book is an example.

focus structure A story organization that begins with the story of an individual person, broadens out to include a trend or issue, and then brings the issue back to the person featured at the beginning of the story.

follow A story supplying further information about an item that has already been published; *folo* is an alternate spelling.

foreshadowing A technique of teasing readers with material coming later in the story as a way of encouraging them to keep reading.

Freedom of Information Act A law passed in 1966 to make it easier to obtain information from federal agencies. The law was amended in 1974 to improve access to government records.

free-form database A database that is not limited in structure and allows almost any type of content to be included.

free press/fair trial controversy The conflict between a defendant's right to an impartial jury and a reporter's responsibility to inform the public.

full-text database A database that permits searches of any text in an article.

futures file A collection — filed according to date — of newspaper stories, letters, notes and other information to remind editors of stories to assign. See also *tickler*.

gatekeepers Editors who determine what readers or viewers read, hear and see.

Golden Mean A moral position, derived from Aristotle, that avoids extremes.

graf A shortened form of *paragraph*, as in "Give me two grafs on that fire."

graphics editor Usually, the editor responsible for all nonphotographic illustrations in a newspaper, including information graphics, maps and illustrations.

handout See *news release*.

hard lead A lead that reports a new development or newly discovered fact. See also *soft lead*.

hard news   Coverage of the actions of government or business; or the reporting of an event, such as a crime, an accident or a speech. The time element often is important. See also *soft news*.

HTML   Hypertext markup language, the coding language used to create texts on the Web.

hyperlink   A connection among two places on the Web.

hyperlocal   Information that is intensely local in its emphasis.

hypermedia   Web links among audio, video and pictures.

hypertext   A Web document coded in HTML.

immediate-identification lead   The opening paragraph of a story in which the "who" is reported by name.

income tax   An annual tax on an individual's income or a business's profit. It is levied by the federal government and in some cases by state and local governments. It is calculated as a percentage.

inflation   A term that describes the rising cost of living as time goes by. See also *Consumer Price Index*.

infomedium   Short for *information medium*, a term coined to represent the merger of the Internet, television, wireless and other technologies as the medium of the future.

information graphic   A visual representation of data.

interest   A measure of the cumulative effect of all the news values. The more elements of each of the six news values that appear in the story, the more interesting that story will be to readers.

Internet   The vast network that links computers around the world.

interviewing   Having conversations with sources.

invasion of privacy   Violation of a person's right to be left alone.

inverted pyramid   The organization of a news story in which information is arranged in descending order of importance.

investigative piece   A story intended to reveal material not generally known.

investigative reporting   The pursuit of information that has been concealed, such as evidence of wrongdoing.

IRE   Investigative Reporters and Editors, a group created to exchange information and investigative reporting techniques. IRE has its headquarters at the University of Missouri School of Journalism.

lay out (v.)   To prepare page drawings to indicate where stories and pictures are to be placed in the newspaper.

layout (n.)   The completed page drawing, or page dummy.

lead   (1) The first paragraph or first several paragraphs of a newspaper story (sometimes spelled *lede*); (2) the story given the best display on Page One; (3) a tip.

lead-in   An introduction to a filmed or recorded excerpt from a news source or from another reporter.

libel   Damage to a person's reputation caused by a false written statement that brings the person into hatred, contempt or ridicule or injures his or her business or occupational pursuit.

line-item budget   A budget showing each expenditure on a separate line.

maestro   The leader of a news-gathering team. Reporters, copy editors, editors and graphic designers work with a maestro to create special reports.

managing editor   The individual with primary responsibility for day-to-day operation of the news department.

margin of error   The difference between results from the entire population (all registered voters in your county) and taking a random sample of the population. It is usually expressed as plus or minus x points. The x depends on the size of the sample. The larger the sample, the smaller the margin of error.

median   The middle number in a series arranged in order of magnitude; it is often used when an average would be misleading. (If the series has an even number of items, the median is the average of the two "middle" numbers.) See also *average*.

millage rate   The tax rate on property, determined by the government.

moblog   A form of Internet blogging in which the user publishes blog entries directly to the Web from a mobile phone or other mobile device.

more   A designation used at the end of a page of copy to indicate that one or more pages follow.

morgue   The news room library, where published stories, photographs and resource material are stored for reference.

multimedia assignment desk   The news desk in a converged news room where the efforts of print, broadcast and online reporters are coordinated. See also *convergence*.

multimedia editor   An editor responsible for coordinating or producing news content for various media.

multimedia journalist   A journalist capable of producing content in more than one medium, such as radio and newspapers.

multiple-element lead   The opening paragraph of a story that reports two or more newsworthy elements.

narration   The telling of a story, usually in chronological order.

negligence test   The legal standard that requires reporters gathering facts and writing a story to use the same degree of care that any reasonable individual would use in similar circumstances.

network correspondent   A television reporter who delivers the news on-camera. Network correspondents do not necessarily do the actual news gathering for their stories.

new media   Emerging forms of computer-delivered news.

news conference   An interview session, also called a *press conference*, in which someone submits to questions from reporters.

news director   The top news executive of a local television station.

news editor   The supervisor of the copy desk. At some newspapers, this title is used for the person in charge of local news-gathering operations.

news release   An item, also called a *handout* or *press release*, that is sent out by a group or individual seeking publicity.

news story   A story, often written in inverted-pyramid style, that emphasizes the facts.

news value   How important or interesting a story is.

nominal dollars   Money numbers not adjusted for inflation.

not for attribution   An expression indicating that information may not be ascribed to its source.

nut paragraph   A paragraph that summarizes the key element or elements of a story. Usually found in a story not written in inverted-pyramid form. Also called a *nut graf*.

off-camera reporter   A reporter who gathers news for television but does not report on the air.

off the record   An expression that usually means "Don't quote me." Some sources and reporters use it to mean "Don't print this." Phrases with similar, and equally ambiguous, meanings are "not for attribution" and "for background only."

online editor   The editor of a Web site for a newspaper or television station.

online media   See *new media*.

op-ed page   The page opposite the editorial page, frequently reserved for columns, letters to the editor and personality profiles.

open-ended question   A question that permits the respondent some latitude in the answer; for example, "How did you get involved in politics?"

open-meetings law   A state or federal law, often called a *sunshine law*, guaranteeing public access to meetings of public officials.

open-records law   A state or federal law guaranteeing public access to many—but not all—kinds of government records.

payola   Money or gifts given in the expectation of favors from journalists.

per capita   A Latin term meaning "by heads." It is determined by dividing a total figure—such as a budget—by the number of people to which it applies.

percentage   A mathematical way to express the portion of a whole; literally, a given part of every hundred. A percentage is determined by taking the number of the portion, dividing by the number of the whole and moving the decimal point right two places.

percentage change   A number that explains by how much something goes up or down.

percentage point   A unit of measure used to express the difference between two percentages. For example, the difference between 25 percent and 40 percent is 15 percentage points.

personal digital assistant (PDA)   A hand-carried device that allows the user to keep track of contacts, appointments, electronic mail and the like.

photo editor   The individual who advises editors on the use of photographs in the newspaper. The photo editor also may supervise the photography department.

piece   See *story*.

plagiarism   Using any part of another person's writing and passing it off as your own.

play   A shortened form of *display*. A good story may be played at the top of Page One; a weak one may be played inside.

podcasting   A method of distributing multimedia files, usually audio or video, to mobile devices or personal computers so that consumers can listen or watch on demand. The term derived from Apple Computer's iPod, but podcasts may be received by almost any music player or computer.

population   In scientific language, the whole group being studied. Depending on the study, the population may be, for example, voters in St. Louis, physicians in California or all residents of the U.S.

press   The machine that prints the newspaper. Also a synonym for *journalism*, as in the phrase "freedom of the press." Sometimes used to denote print journalism, as distinguished from broadcast journalism.

press box   The section of a stadium or arena set aside for reporters.

press conference   See *news conference*.

press release   See *news release*.

principal   The amount of money borrowed.

principled reasoning   Reasoning that reflects ethical principles.

Privacy Protection Act   A law passed in 1980 that requires federal, state and local enforcement officers to get a subpoena to obtain documents from reporters and news rooms, rather than a search warrant—unless the reporter is involved in a crime or immediate action is needed to prevent bodily harm, loss of life or destruction of the material.

privilege   A defense against libel that claims the right to repeat what government officials say or do in their official capacities.

production department   The department of the newspaper that transforms the work of the news and advertising departments into the finished product. The composing room and pressroom are key sections of this department.

profile   A story intended to reveal the personality or character of an institution or person.

program budget   A budget that clearly shows what each agency's activities cost.

property tax   An annual tax, figured as a percentage, on the value of houses, buildings and land, that is usually levied by a local or state government.

proportion   An explanation that relates one specific number to another or to the quantity or magnitude of a whole; for example, "The Tigers finished fifth out of 20 teams."

public figure   A person who has assumed a role of prominence in the affairs of society and who has persuasive power and influence in a community or who has thrust himself or herself to the forefront of a public controversy. Courts have given journalists more latitude in reporting on public figures than on private citizens.

public information utility   A commercial online service such as CompuServe.

public journalism   The new (or rediscovered) approach to journalism that emphasizes connections with the community rather than separation from it. Among the newspapers best known for practicing public journalism are *The Wichita (Kan.) Eagle* and *The Charlotte (N.C.) Observer*.

publisher   The top-ranking executive of a newspaper. This title often is assumed by the owner, although chains sometimes designate as publisher the top local executive.

Pulitzer Prize   The most prestigious of journalism awards. It was established by Joseph Pulitzer and is administered by Columbia University.

qualified privilege   The right to report what government officials say or do in their official capacities if the report is full, fair and accurate. Also called *conditional privilege*.

quote   As a noun, the term refers to a source's exact words, as in "I have a great quote here." As a verb, it means to report those words inside quotation marks.

rate   The amount or degree of something measured in relation to a unit of something else or to a specified scale. In statistics, rate often expresses the incidence of a condition per 100,000 people, such as a murder or suicide rate. Rate also can reflect the speed at which something is changing, such as inflation or the percentage increase in a budget each year.

records column   The part of the newspaper featured regularly that contains such information as routine police and fire news, births, obituaries, marriages and divorces.

relational database program   A database program that permits users to determine relationships between two or more dissimilar databases. For example, a relational database program would enable a reporter to compare one database of people convicted of drunken driving with another database of school-bus drivers. The result would show how many bus drivers had drunken-driving convictions.

relevance   The impact of a story as measured by the number of readers it affects and how seriously it affects them.

reporter   A person whose job is to gather and write the news for a publication or a broadcast outlet.

roundup   A story including a number of related events. After a storm, for example, a reporter might do a roundup of accidents, power outages and other consequences of the storm.

RSS   Short for *really simple syndication*, a form of content distribution over the Internet that relies on a common markup language, XML (extensible markup language).

sales tax   A tax, figured as a percentage, on the price of goods. It is usually levied by a local or state government and is paid by the consumer to the retailer at the time of purchase.

sample   A portion of a group, or population, chosen for study as representative of the entire group.

second-cycle story   A second version of a story already published, also called a *second-day story*. It usually has new information or a new angle.

senior editor   A person who edits a section of a major magazine.

senior writer   A title reserved for a magazine's best and most experienced reporters.

series   Two or more stories on the same or related subjects, published on a predetermined schedule.

service journalism   An aspect or type of journalism that recognizes usefulness as one of the criteria of news. Taking into consideration content and presentation, service journalism presents useful information in a usable way—for instance, by placing key information in a list or graphic box.

setup In broadcasting, an introductory statement to pique the interest of listeners or viewers. In written accounts, the material between the opening of a narrative story and the body. It generally consists of the transition to the theme paragraph, the nut paragraph, and, when appropriate, the "so what" and "to be sure" statements and foreshadowing.

shield law Legislation giving journalists the right to protect the identity of sources.

shovelware Stories posted on the Web exactly as they appeared in print.

show producer A television news specialist who produces individual newscasts and who reports to the executive producer.

sidebar A secondary story intended to be run with a major story on the same topic. A story about a disaster, for example, may have a sidebar that tells what happened to a single victim.

simple interest Interest paid on the principal (the amount borrowed).

situation ethics The philosophy that recognizes that a set of rules can be broken if circumstances indicate that the community would be served better by breaking them. For example, a journalist who generally believes that deceiving a news source is unethical may be willing to conceal his or her identity to infiltrate a group operating illegally.

slug A word that identifies a story as it is processed through the newspaper plant or on broadcast news. A slug is usually placed in the upper left-hand corner of each take of a newspaper story. See also *take*.

sniff The preliminary phase of an investigation.

social networking The practice of connecting with others for business or social purposes. Social-networking sites make it easy for individuals to connect with others who have similar interests or goals.

soft lead A lead that uses a quote, anecdote or other literary device to attract the reader. See also *hard lead*.

soft news Stories about trends, personalities or lifestyles. The time element usually is not important. See also *hard news*.

sources People or records from which a reporter gets information. The term often is used to describe people, as opposed to documents.

spot news A timely report of an event that is unfolding at the moment.

spreadsheet A computer program adept at analyzing numbers. It is often used in tracking changes in budgets and expenditures.

story The term most journalists use for a newspaper article. Another synonym is *piece*, as in "I saw your piece on the mayor." A long story may be called a *takeout* or a *blockbuster*.

strategic communication A "new" name for public relations (sometimes including advertising) that emphasizes the stronger role of professionals in these fields in conducting research, problem solving and decision making.

stylebook A book of rules on grammar, punctuation, capitalization and abbreviation in newspaper text. The AP and UPI publish similar stylebooks that are used by most papers.

substantial truth   The correctness of the essential elements of a story.

summary lead   The first paragraph of a news story in which the writer presents a synopsis of two or more actions rather than focusing on any one of them.

sunshine law   See *open-meetings law*.

take   A page of printed copy for newspaper use.

teleological ethics   The ethics of final ends.

30   A designation used to mark the end of a newspaper story. The symbol # is an alternate designation.

tickler   A file of upcoming events kept on paper or stored electronically at the assignment desks of most news organizations. See also *futures file*.

tie-back   The sentence or sentences relating a story to events covered in a previous story. Used in follow-up or continuing stories or in parts of a series of stories. Also, the technique of referring to the opening in the ending of the story.

truth   Actuality or reality. Truth is the best defense against libel.

universal desk   A copy desk that edits material for all editorial departments of a newspaper.

update   A type of follow that reports on a development related to an earlier story. See also *follow*.

UPI   United Press International, a worldwide news-gathering organization that is privately owned.

URL   Uniform Resource Locator, the address of an Internet site.

usefulness   A quality of news that increases the impact of the story. The story has information that readers can use to act on, such as notification of a meeting before it occurs.

videographer   A television camera operator.

videoprompter   A mechanical or electronic device that projects broadcast copy next to the television camera lens so that a newscaster can read it while appearing to look straight into the lens.

Web site   A location on the World Wide Web, the Internet service that connects hypertext data.

wiki   A type of Web site that allows users to add or alter content. Wikipedia, for example, is a user-written and user-updated encyclopedia.

wikinews   Wikinews is a wiki (a form of Web site) at which users can post or update information in news format.

wrap-up   The completion of commentary that comes at the end of a taped segment in broadcasting; a strong ending to a report.

"you" lead   The first paragraph of a story, written using the informal, second-person pronoun "you."

Acknowledgments

AP Leads. "Fort Worth, Texas (AP)—Dallas Cowboys Cornerback Adam 'Pacman' Jones was suspended" (10/14/08); "Narragansett, R.I. (AP)—The wedding guests included drug suspects, the social coordinator" (6/9/06); "Spring Lake (AP)—Aubrey Cox keeps giving the police the slip"; "Jefferson City, Mo. (AP)—Missouri is tapping into its prison system budget" (9/15/08); "EPA Grants Ill. Incinerator Key Permit" (9/15/08); "Absentee Ranch Owner Accused in Deaths of 32 Bison"; "Buchanan County Sheriff's deputies find stolen monkeys" (9/20/08). Copyright © The Associated Press. Reprinted with permission. All rights reserved.

Matthew Benjamin. "The global financial crisis . . ." (10/10/08). Source: Bloomberg LP.

Sonja Bjelland. "On the Job" Interview. Reprinted by permission of Sonja Bjelland.

Chicago Tribune. "Illinois governor arrested in 'corruption crime spree'." From *Chicago Tribune*, 12/10/08. Copyright © 2008 Chicago Tribune. All rights reserved. Used by permission and protected by the Copyright Laws of the United States. The printing, copying, redistribution, or retransmission of the Material without express written permission is prohibited.

Bernard Choi. "On the Job" Interview. Reprinted by permission of Bernard Choi.

Chris Cillizza. "Obama Widens Lead in Four Key States." From Washingtonpost.com, October 14, 2008. Copyright © 2008. Reprinted by permission of Washington Post Newsweek Interactive (WPNI). All rights reserved.

Roy Peter Clark. "Beware of Plagiarism!" Reprinted by permission of Roy Peter Clark, The Poynter Institute.

CNN. "Ike Wears Itself Out Beating Up on Texas." CNN's Jeanne Meserve, Rusty Dornin, Sean Callebs, Rob Marciano, Gary Tuchman, Arthur Brice, Deb Krajnak and Elise Miller contributed to this report. September 14, 2008. From http://edition.cnn.com/2008/US/weather/09/13/hurricane.ike.texas/index.html. Copyright © 2008 CNN Image Source. Reprinted by permission.

Kevin Colby. "Feds Helping Out Cities with Tax Subsidies for New Stadiums." From http://kevincolby.com/2008/11/02/feds-helping-out-cities-with-tax-subsidies-for-new-stadiums/. Reprinted by permission of the author.

Norman Draper. "U Earns C Average in Student-Access Report." Minneapolis Star Tribune. November 21, 2006. Copyright © 2006 Minneapolis Star Tribune. Reprinted with permission, Star Tribune (Minneapolis, Minn.).

April Eaton. "On the Job" Interview. Reprinted by permission of April Eaton.

Steve Fainaru. "Cutting Costs, Bending Rules, and a Trail of Broken Lives." From *The Washington Post*, Sunday, July 29, 2007; p. A01. Copyright © 2007 The Washington Post. All rights reserved. Used by permission and protected by the Copyright Laws of the United States. The printing, copying, redistribution, or retransmission of the Material without express written permission is prohibited.

Ken Fuson. "On the Job" Interview. Reprinted by permission of Ken Fuson.

Major Garrett. "On the Job" Interview. Reprinted by permission of Major Garrett.

Derrick Goold. "Interview." Reprinted by permission of Derrick Goold.

James Grimaldi. "On the Job" Interview. Reprinted by permission of James Grimaldi.

Valerie Schremp Hahn. "Ex-prosecutor's husband charged. He is accused of producing marijuana plants in his home." From the *St. Louis Post-Dispatch*. November 15, 2006. Copyright © 2006 by The Associated Press. Reprinted with permission. All rights reserved.

Charles Hammer. "On the Job" Interview. Reprinted by permission of Charles Hammer.

Stan Ketterer. "Guidelines for Evaluating Information on the Web." Reprinted by permission of the author.

Jennifer LaFleur. "On the Job" Interview. Reprinted by permission of Jennifer LaFleur.

Mark Landler and Eric Dash. "Drama Behind a $250 Billion Banking Deal." From *The New York Times*, Business Section, October 15, 2008. p. 1. Copyright © 2008 The New York Times. All rights reserved. Used by permission and protected by the Copyright Laws of the United States. The printing, copying, redistribution, or retransmission of the Material without express written permission is prohibited. www.nytimes.com.

J.D. Lasica. "Six Types of Citizen Journalism." From "What Is Participatory Journalism?" in *Online Journalism*

Review, August 7, 2003. Reprinted by permission of the author.

Jeré Longman. "Waiting for Power in the Cajun Prairie." From *The New York Times*, BLOG section. September 3, 2008. Copyright © 2008 The New York Times. All rights reserved. Used by permission and protected by the Copyright Laws of the United States. The printing, copying, redistribution, or retransmission of the Material without express written permission is prohibited. www.nytimes.com.

Tina Macias. "On the Job" Interview. Reprinted by permission of Tina Macias.

Sophia Maines. "On the Job" Interview. Reprinted by permission of Sophia Maines.

Jean McHale. "On the Job" Interview. Reprinted by permission of Jean McHale.

Larry McShane. AP Lead, "In an unprecedented show of terrorist horror, the 110 story World Trade Center . . ." From The Associated Press, September 11, 2001. Copyright © 2001 The Associated Press. Reprinted with permission. All rights reserved.

Jane Meinhardt. "Mother Accused of Being Criminal Ringleader." From *The St. Petersburg Times*, October 21, 1994. Copyright © 1994. Reprinted by permission of the St. Petersburg Times.

Lori Montgomery and Paul Kane. "Bush Calls Bailout Vital to Economy, Will Meet with McCain and Obama: Proposal Takes Shape in Congress, but Broad Support Is Lacking." From *The Washington Post*, September 25, 2008. p. A1. Copyright © 2008 The Washington Post. All rights reserved. Used by permission and protected by the Copyright Laws of the United States. The printing, copying, redistribution, or retransmission of the Material without express written permission is prohibited. www.washingtonpost.com.

MSNBC.com. "MSNBC is looking for your help . . ." Used with permission of MSNBC from www.msnbc.msn .com/id/6639760/; permission conveyed through Copyright Clearance Center, Inc.

Barry Murov. "On the Job" Interview. Reprinted by permission of Barry Murov.

New Directions for News. From *Undercovered: Reaching the New USA*. Copyright © 2001 New Directions for News. Funded by the Freedom Foundation. Reprinted by permission of the American Press Institute.

Scott Norvell. "On the Job" Interview. Reprinted by permission of Scott Norvell.

Helen O'Neill. "Kidnapping Grandma Brown." From The Associated Press, March 21, 2004. Copyright © 2004 by The Associated Press. Reprinted with permission. All rights reserved.

Elizabeth Phillips. "Man Arrested in Attack, Charged with Child Endangerment." From the *Columbia Missourian*, Nov. 17, 2006. Copyright © 2006 Columbia Missourian. Reprinted by permission.

Sarah Rupp. "On the Job" Interview. Reprinted by permission of Sarah Rupp.

Wright Thompson. "On the Job" Interview. Reprinted by permission of Wright Thompson.

Loretta Waldman. "Small Towns Need $ for Websites, but From Where?" (Lead only). From the *Hartford Courant*, October 30, 2008. http://blogs.courant.com/ itowns_fv/2008/10/website-back-within-few-weeks .html. Reprinted by permission of TMS Reprints on behalf of the Hartford Courant.

Brad Whitworth. "On the Job" Interview. Reprinted by permission of Brad Whitworth.

Troy Wolverton. "On the Job" Interview. Reprinted by permission of Troy Wolverton.

Photo credits

1 Marty Heitner/The Image Works; **16** AP Photo; **20** Courtesy of MSNBC; **23** Courtesy of BlufftonToday .com; **25** Courtesy of KenRadio.com; **27** Courtesy of Bakotopia; **28** Courtesy of *Lawrence (Kans.) Journal World*; **31** Web page image courtesy of TBO.com/Media General; **43** Bob Daemmrich/The Image Works; **52** Robert Kalman/The Image Works; **57** AP Photo; **66** Mark Richards/PhotoEdit; **70** Fancy/Veer/Corbis; **81** Courtesy of Mercury News; **89** Wil Yas/Masterfile; **91** Courtesy of The Dallas Morning News; **110** Joe Skipper/Reuters/Corbis; **122** Allen Tannenbaum; **135** Rogelio Solis/AP Photo; **157** Tannen Maury/epa/Corbis; **161** Odd Anderson/AFP/Getty; **163** Samantha Appleton/ Aurora Photos; **173** Peter Morgan/Reuters/Landov; **190** Mark Foley/AP Photos; **193** AP Wide World Photos; **201** James Leynse; **203** Jeff Greenberg/PhotoEdit; **210** Peter Morgan/Corbis; **215** Jeff Greenberg/The Image Works; **228** Michael Halle/Getty Images; **237** Francis M. Roberts; **241** John Berry/Syracuse Newspaper/The Image Works; **258** Courtesy of Red Cross; **276** Missouri Department of Conservation; **280** (1) Courtesy of The Sacramento Bee; (2) Reprinted with permission of The Wall Street Journal. Copyright © 2009 Dow Jones and Company, Inc. All Rights Reserved World Wide; (3) Courtesy of The Boston Herald; **281** Courtesy of Donald W. Reynolds Journalism Institute; **283** Courtesy of NOLA.com; **287** Courtesy of Seattle Times Resale and Permissions; **289** (1) Todd Heisler/The New York Times/Redux; (2) Ciao Cortes/Reuters; **291** Courtesy of SunSentinel.com; **294** Courtesy of YGS Group; **297** Courtesy of Mercury News; **299** Copyright 2009 TPM Media LLC. All Rights Reserved; **305** Alan Schien/ Corbis; **323** AP Photo.

Index